AI's Transformative Impact on Finance, Auditing, and Investment

Fadi Ghosn
Lebanese International University, Lebanon

Ghina Awad
ICN Business School, France

Karim Darwich
ICN Business School, France

IGI Global
Scientific Publishing
Publishing Tomorrow's Research Today

Published in the United States of America by
IGI Global Scientific Publishing
701 East Chocolate Avenue
Hershey, PA, 17033, USA
Tel: 717-533-8845
Fax: 717-533-7115
Website: https://www.igi-global.com E-mail: cust@igi-global.com

Library of Congress Cataloging-in-Publication Data

Names: Ghosn, Fadi, 1981- editor. | Awad, Ghina, 1989- editor. | Darwich, Karim, 1993- editor.
Title: AI's transformative impact on finance, auditing, and investment / edited by Fadi Ghosn, Ghina Awad, and Karim Darwich.
Other titles: Artificial intelligence's transformative impact on finance, auditing, and investment
Description: Hershey, PA : IGI Global Scientific Publishing, [2025] | Includes bibliographical references and index. | Summary: "This book examines how AI not only enhances human expertise but also fundamentally reshapes the way financial and banking processes are conceptualized and executed"-- Provided by publisher.
Identifiers: LCCN 2024058234 (print) | LCCN 2024058235 (ebook) | ISBN 9798337301297 (hardcover) | ISBN 9798337301303 (paperback) | ISBN 9798337301310 (ebook)
Subjects: LCSH: Artificial intelligence--Financial applications. | Auditing--Technological innovations. | Fintech. | Investments--Technological innovations.
Classification: LCC HG4515.5 .A39 2025 (print) | LCC HG4515.5 (ebook) | DDC 657/.45--dc23/eng/20240515
LC record available at https://lccn.loc.gov/2024058234
LC ebook record available at https://lccn.loc.gov/2024058235
British Cataloguing in Publication Data
A Cataloguing in Publication record for this book is available from the British Library.

We dedicate this book to all the pioneers and practitioners who are shaping the future of finance through innovation and integrity.

To our families—whose unwavering support, patience, and encouragement made this work possible.

And to the academic and professional communities that continue to inspire our pursuit of knowledge and impact.

Table of Contents

Detailed Table of Contents

increased efficiency, minimize costs, and provide more options in reaction to changes in financial markets. This study aims to point out the latest patterns being observed regarding ML and AI applications within finance.

The rise of artificial intelligence (AI) has significantly transformed the internal auditing profession, introducing new challenges and opportunities that demand a blend of technical expertise and interpersonal skills. As AI reshapes auditing processes, internal auditors are required to adapt to an era of rapid technological advancements, leveraging AI-driven tools for enhanced efficiency and accuracy. Simultaneously, they must ensure that these technologies are used ethically, transparently, and in compliance with regulatory standards. This book explores the dual competencies—technical and soft skills—necessary for auditors to excel in this evolving landscape. By examining critical areas such as data analytics, cybersecurity, emotional intelligence, and adaptability, it provides a comprehensive roadmap for auditors to navigate the complexities of AI-enhanced auditing. Through actionable insights and strategies, this book aims to equip internal auditors with the tools to uphold the integrity of their profession while embracing the transformative potential of AI.

The integration of artificial intelligence (AI) in Islamic finance offers great opportunities to improve risk management, operational efficiency, auditing, and compliance with sharia principles. This chapter explores how AI can identify risks in real-time, speed up the sharia audit process, and ensure compliance with principles such as the prohibition of usury, gharar, and maysir. In addition, AI supports the development of innovative financial products that are in line with Islamic values. The adoption of artificial intelligence (AI) in Islamic finance has major implications for financial institutions, regulators, fintech, academics, and society. For Islamic financial institutions, AI improves operational efficiency, accelerates the sharia audit process, and supports product innovation in accordance with Islamic principles. Regulators need to develop a regulatory framework that governs the use of AI to remain sharia-compliant, ensure transparency and reduce the risk of algorithmic bias.

In the fast changing landscape of financial markets, artificial intelligence is making inroads into it. Artificial intelligence is a concept or technological advancement which aims to mirror intelligence exhibited by the human beings and executes all the jobs to the perfection. Financial or investment domain is not an exception to this. Before making any investment decision one has to look at various aspects and pay attention to various reports and constantly monitor the changes in stock prices, which is a very difficult job every person can't claim to master this art, in this artificial intelligence comes to the rescue of such persons who can't perform such tasks carefully. Data was collected with the help of questionnaire and analyzed by employing multiple regression method to ascertain the effect of perceived utility and subjective norms on the usage of robo-advisory in investment and personal finance management which was another factor studied with artificial intelligence.

Artificial intelligence (AI) is poised to significantly transform the fields of finance, auditing, and investment over the coming decade. In financial services, AI is anticipated to enhance decision-making processes, improve risk management practices, and facilitate the delivery of personalized financial solutions. The auditing profession will be reshaped by AI and automation, enabling continuous auditing, real-time reporting, and more effective fraud detection mechanisms. In the investment domain, AI is expected to revolutionize portfolio management and asset allocation through advanced predictive analytics and data-driven market strategies. Despite these advancements, the rapid proliferation of AI presents considerable challenges, including ethical considerations, regulatory compliance, and the necessity of re-skilling financial professionals. This strategic overview examines both the opportunities and risks associated with AI integration and provides guidance for organizations seeking to maintain competitiveness in an increasingly AI-driven financial landscape.

Preface

INTRODUCTION

The convergence of artificial intelligence (AI) and financial sciences marks a defining shift in the architecture of global markets, corporate governance, and investment decision-making. This book, AI's Transformative Impact on Finance, Auditing, and Investment, explores how intelligent algorithms and machine learning tools are reshaping the way financial data is analyzed, risks are assessed, and capital is allocated. It reflects the rapid diffusion of AI technologies across critical sectors of financial systems, underscoring the need to assess their implications, applications, and limitations.

AI has moved beyond experimentation to become an integral part of financial operations—from automated trading systems and robo-advisors to fraud detection algorithms and AI-driven audit procedures. These technologies are not merely enhancing efficiency; they are fundamentally altering the roles of financial professionals, regulators, and investors alike. In parallel, the adoption of AI in Islamic finance is opening new possibilities for real-time risk assessment, enhanced shariah compliance, and the development of innovative products aligned with Islamic ethical principles. As AI becomes increasingly embedded in decision-making infrastructure, it is vital to explore how finance, auditing, investment, and Islamic finance domains are evolving in response.

Moreover, AI is playing an increasingly influential role in advancing ESG (Environmental, Social, and Governance) objectives within financial decision-making. By leveraging natural language processing, image recognition, and sentiment analysis, AI enables institutions to process vast quantities of ESG-related data from diverse sources, including sustainability reports, social media, and regulatory disclosures. This allows for more transparent ESG evaluations, real-time risk identification, and alignment of investment portfolios with sustainability goals. As responsible investing gains momentum globally, AI-driven ESG analytics are becoming essential tools for both institutional investors and policymakers.

This book presents a comprehensive and interdisciplinary approach to understanding the interplay between AI technologies and the financial ecosystem. Drawing upon both theoretical frameworks and empirical analyses, the chapters within offer academic insights, practical solutions, and critical reflections on the emerging AI-driven landscape. Several chapters include case studies that illustrate real-world applications of AI in finance, auditing, investment, and Islamic finance, providing tangible examples of both the opportunities and challenges encountered in practice. This body of work highlights the transformative capacity of AI, particularly in enhancing forecasting, decision accuracy, compliance monitoring, and the overall robustness of financial systems.

Where the Topic Fits in the World Today?

In today's data-centric economy, AI serves as a powerful tool for unlocking insights from vast, complex data sets, allowing financial professionals to make faster, smarter, and more informed decisions. In this context, AI has become a pivotal element of innovation and competition, redefining business models and operational paradigms. This transformation holds relevance not only for financial institutions but also for policymakers, regulators, technologists, educators, and other stakeholders seeking to navigate and govern AI's disruptive potential.

The integration of AI into finance aligns with broader technological developments in big data analytics, blockchain, and cloud computing. As these forces converge, financial institutions are increasingly investing in intelligent systems that can automate processes, improve client engagement, identify anomalies, and generate adaptive investment strategies. Yet, these gains are tempered by emerging challenges—including algorithmic transparency, data governance, and cybersecurity threats—which must be addressed to ensure responsible innovation.

An increasingly significant dimension of AI in finance involves the use of alternative data sources, particularly social media. Platforms like Twitter, Reddit, and LinkedIn provide real-time sentiment indicators that AI systems can analyze to forecast market behavior, detect emerging trends, or flag reputational risks. By mining social media data, financial institutions can capture consumer sentiment, monitor brand perception, and even anticipate market volatility, thereby gaining a competitive edge in dynamic financial environments.

AI's application across commercial banking activities is equally transformative. From credit scoring and loan underwriting to customer relationship management and fraud prevention, AI-driven tools enhance operational efficiency and decision quality. Natural language processing and chatbots are widely used for 24/7 customer service, while machine learning models support dynamic credit assessments and risk profiling. Banks also utilize AI to personalize financial products, optimize asset-liability management, and ensure compliance through automated reporting and anomaly detection.

In the domain of auditing, AI is redefining traditional practices by introducing real-time, continuous auditing processes that significantly improve accuracy and timeliness. Automated systems powered by AI can analyze entire data sets—rather than samples—making audits more comprehensive and reliable. Additionally, AI tools are used to detect fraud patterns, assess internal controls, and flag irregularities with minimal human intervention. The ability to process unstructured data, such as emails and contracts, further enhances the auditor's capability to provide value-added insights beyond conventional financial statements.

In investment management, AI plays a pivotal role in portfolio optimization, risk assessment, and predictive market analysis. Algorithmic trading platforms leverage high-frequency data and real-time analytics to execute trades with precision and speed. Robo-advisory services use AI to offer tailored investment strategies based on individual risk profiles and financial goals. Moreover, sentiment analysis from news and social media sources supports macroeconomic forecasting and asset pricing models, enabling more adaptive and forward-looking investment decisions. As AI tools become more sophisticated, they are not only reshaping investment strategies but also expanding access to financial advisory services, democratizing investment opportunities for broader segments of the population.

Target Audience

This book is intended for a diverse audience, including scholars, finance professionals, policy analysts, technologists, students, and industry leaders. It seeks to serve as a reference for academic researchers examining the nexus of AI and financial studies, while also offering practical insights for practitioners implementing AI-driven systems. Additionally, educators and learners in the fields of finance, auditing, economics, data science, and business administration will find value in its evidence-based analyses, real-world case studies, and critical discussion of ethical and regulatory dimensions.

For policymakers and regulators, the chapters provide a useful foundation for assessing policy frameworks governing the use of AI in financial markets. For industry leaders and consultants, the book acts as a roadmap for designing resilient, ethical, and efficient AI-infused strategies. Finally, for students and early-career professionals, it delivers a comprehensive primer on the interdisciplinary competencies necessary to thrive in AI-augmented financial environments.

CHAPTER OVERVIEWS

Artificial Intelligence in Investment and Wealth Management

This chapter delves into AI's applications in investment strategies, wealth management, and financial personalization. It contrasts traditional investment techniques with emerging technologies such as algorithmic trading, robo-advisors, and predictive analytics. The discussion extends to AI's role in portfolio diversification, risk mitigation, and tailored investment services. Ethical and regulatory challenges, including algorithmic bias and data privacy—are analyzed, and the chapter concludes with foresight into quantum computing and blockchain integration.

Machine Learning in Finance: The Revolutionary Fusion

Focusing on machine learning (ML), this chapter explores how AI technologies are reshaping financial services through predictive modeling, automated decision-making, and personalized customer experiences. Case studies highlight the use of ML in fraud detection, risk analysis, sentiment assessment, and credit scoring. The chapter further illustrates how AI enhances market responsiveness and efficiency while identifying patterns that guide investment and lending strategies.

Internal Auditor Soft Skills and Hard Skills in the Era of Artificial Intelligence

This chapter addresses the evolving competencies required of internal auditors in an AI-enhanced environment. It emphasizes the importance of technical proficiency in data analytics and cybersecurity, alongside soft skills such as adaptability, critical thinking, and ethical reasoning. Through comprehensive analysis, the chapter provides a roadmap for upskilling auditors and aligning audit processes with technological advancements.

Artificial Intelligence in Islamic Finance

This chapter presents a unique perspective on AI's role in Islamic finance. It examines how AI facilitates Shariah compliance, enhances auditing processes, and enables innovative financial product design. The discussion also includes the development of regulatory frameworks needed to ensure that AI usage aligns with Islamic principles such as the prohibition of riba, gharar, and maysir.

Bridging the Gap: Essential Soft and Hard Skills for the AI-Driven Banking Workforce

The chapter highlights the dual competencies necessary in AI-integrated banking systems. It explores the intersection of technical skills—like machine learning and data security—and interpersonal skills, such as communication, adaptability, and ethical judgment. The chapter advocates for workforce development strategies that align human capabilities with AI functionalities.

Fintech Implications on ESG Practices: Evidence from the Indian Banking Industry

This evidence-based study analyzes how fintech tools support Environmental, Social, and Governance (ESG) objectives in India's banking sector. Using case studies and secondary data, the chapter investigates fintech's impact on green finance, risk governance, agri-financing, and financial inclusion. It also proposes a conceptual model to strengthen fintech's contribution to sustainable finance.

Influence of Robo-Advisory on Investment Decisions of Young Investors

Based on empirical data from Delhi-NCR, this chapter explores how young investors perceive and utilize robo-advisory tools in personal finance. Through quantitative analysis, it investigates how perceived utility and social norms influence the adoption of AI in investment management. The findings offer practical insights into enhancing robo-advisory services for tech-savvy investor demographics.

AI's Impact on Financial Services, Auditing, and Investment Strategies: The Future Ahead

This chapter provides a strategic overview of AI's anticipated impact across finance, auditing, and investment sectors. It explores how predictive analytics and automation are redefining risk management, fraud detection, and asset allocation. It also addresses regulatory, ethical, and human capital challenges, emphasizing the need for adaptive leadership and institutional reform.

The Future of Financial Decision-Making

The final chapter offers a forward-looking analysis of AI's long-term effects on financial decision-making. It covers technological developments in blockchain, natural language processing, and cognitive computing. While outlining emerging opportunities, it also critiques the risks and ethical concerns associated with increasingly autonomous financial systems.

CONCLUSION: A TRANSFORMATIVE CONTRIBUTION

The convergence of artificial intelligence (AI) and financial sciences marks a defining shift in the architecture of global markets, corporate governance, and investment decision-making. This book, AI's Transformative Impact on Finance, Auditing, and Investment, delves into how intelligent algorithms and machine learning tools are revolutionizing the ways financial data is analyzed, risks are managed, and capital is allocated. It reflects the rapid integration of AI technologies across various facets of financial systems and underscores the urgency of understanding their implications, applications, and limitations in a globally interconnected economy.

AI has evolved from a peripheral innovation to a core component of modern financial operations—from high-frequency trading and robo-advisory platforms to AI-empowered fraud detection systems and real-time, automated audit processes. These technologies not only enhance speed and accuracy but are fundamentally redefining the roles and responsibilities of financial professionals, auditors, regulators, and investors. In auditing, AI tools facilitate continuous auditing, anomaly detection, and compliance monitoring, allowing auditors to transition from reactive to proactive assurance strategies. In investment management, AI is driving predictive analytics, personalized asset allocation, and sentiment-based market forecasting, ushering in a new era of data-driven strategy and efficiency.

The adoption of AI in Islamic finance is particularly noteworthy, as it offers a path to more efficient, transparent, and shariah-compliant financial systems. AI enables real-time screening of contracts and transactions for compliance with Islamic principles such as the prohibition of interest (riba), excessive uncertainty (gharar), and gambling (maysir). Moreover, it supports the creation of ethically aligned financial products tailored to a growing global Muslim population. AI is also streamlining shariah audits and contributing to more dynamic risk profiling and zakat calculation systems, thereby fostering innovation within the ethical boundaries of Islamic finance.

Equally transformative is AI's growing impact on Environmental, Social, and Governance (ESG) practices. As financial institutions and investors face rising pressure to integrate sustainability into their decision-making frameworks, AI-powered tools are proving indispensable. By analyzing vast volumes of structured and unstructured data—including sustainability reports, climate disclosures, regulatory filings, and social media sentiment—AI can uncover ESG risks and opportunities with unprecedented speed and precision. This facilitates more transparent ESG scoring, green investment strategies, and responsible lending policies. AI also assists in tracking progress toward carbon neutrality, assessing social impact, and identifying governance failures, thus becoming a cornerstone of future-proof financial ecosystems committed to sustainable development.

This book offers a comprehensive, interdisciplinary, and forward-looking exploration of these themes. Drawing upon both theoretical frameworks and empirical research, it provides academic insights, practical methodologies, and real-world case studies that demonstrate the dynamic interplay between AI and financial practice. Chapters examine AI applications in traditional finance, Islamic finance, ESG analytics, auditing processes, and investment strategy formulation. Several contributions also critically assess the ethical, regulatory, and professional challenges posed by AI, emphasizing the need for responsible innovation, transparency, and the re-skilling of the financial workforce.

Looking ahead, the future of finance, auditing, and investment will be inseparable from the evolution of AI. As technologies such as generative AI, quantum computing, and decentralized finance (DeFi) continue to emerge, financial institutions will need to adapt rapidly to remain competitive and compliant. The rise of autonomous decision-making systems, explainable AI, and hybrid human-machine collaboration will define new paradigms of value creation, risk governance, and ethical accountability. By capturing this transformative moment, this book aims to serve as a foundational resource for scholars, practitioners, regulators, and students navigating the complex and exciting future of AI-driven finance.

Acknowledgment

The completion of this book would not have been possible without the support, insights, and encouragement of many individuals and institutions.

First and foremost, I extend my deepest gratitude to the contributors, researchers, and practitioners whose expertise and thoughtful analyses enriched the content and scope of this work. Their commitment to advancing understanding in the fields of artificial intelligence and finance has been invaluable.

I am especially thankful to my editorial team and colleagues, whose critical feedback, editorial guidance, and tireless effort helped shape this manuscript into its final form. Your professionalism and attention to detail ensured both clarity and depth throughout the writing process.

I also wish to acknowledge the academic institutions, research centers, and industry professionals who provided resources, data, and case studies that grounded this work in real-world relevance. Your collaboration was essential in bridging theory with practice.

To my family and close friends, thank you for your patience, encouragement, and unwavering belief in this project. Your support sustained me through the long hours and intellectual demands of this endeavor.

Finally, I express my appreciation to all readers and scholars who continue to explore the evolving intersection of AI and financial innovation. It is my hope that this book serves as both a resource and an inspiration for future research and responsible progress in the field.

Introduction

The advent of artificial intelligence (AI) has ushered in a paradigm shift across the domains of finance, auditing, and investment. As financial systems become increasingly data-driven, AI technologies such as machine learning, natural language processing, and automation are reshaping the foundations of decision-making, risk assessment, and operational management. These developments have significantly altered traditional financial practices by enhancing predictive capabilities, streamlining complex processes, and improving the precision and speed of financial analysis.

In the realm of finance, AI is revolutionizing how institutions manage risk, optimize portfolios, and respond to market dynamics. Real-time analytics, algorithmic trading, and adaptive financial modeling are enabling more informed and timely decisions. In auditing, intelligent systems automate routine procedures, facilitating continuous monitoring, and improving the detection of anomalies and irregularities. These innovations are not only enhancing audit quality but also redefining the role of auditors in a digital environment. Within the investment sector, AI empowers analysts and fund managers to process large volumes of structured and unstructured data, identify hidden patterns, and generate forward-looking insights that enhance strategic planning and asset allocation.

The impact of AI extends beyond these core areas to include significant transformations within commercial banking, insurance, and Islamic finance. Commercial banks are integrating AI to refine credit assessment, detect fraudulent activities, personalize services, and enhance customer engagement through intelligent interfaces. In the insurance industry, AI applications are improving the efficiency of underwriting, claims management, and risk-based pricing models, contributing to more dynamic and responsive service delivery. Islamic banking, while embracing digital transformation, must navigate the incorporation of AI within the constraints of Shariah principles. This involves ensuring that AI-driven financial solutions adhere to ethical norms, transparency, and religious compliance, presenting both opportunities and regulatory challenges unique to the sector.

Concurrently, the financial sector is experiencing growing pressure to align operations with sustainability goals, giving rise to the prominence of green finance and environmental, social, and governance (ESG) considerations. AI is playing an increasingly important role in this transition by enabling the evaluation of ESG performance, enhancing climate risk modeling, and supporting investment strategies that prioritize long-term environmental and social outcomes. Through advanced data analytics and real-time monitoring, AI is facilitating greater transparency and accountability in sustainability reporting, helping financial institutions integrate ethical and environmental criteria into their core decision-making frameworks.

This book explores the transformative role of AI across these interrelated financial fields, offering a critical analysis of its applications, benefits, and limitations. By examining current technological developments and institutional responses, the discussion highlights how AI is not only reshaping operational practices but also redefining the strategic direction of the global financial services industry in the era of digitalization and sustainable development.

Chapter 1
Artificial Intelligence in Investment and Wealth Management

Fadi Ghosn
https://orcid.org/0000-0002-2450-0478
Lebanese International University, Lebanon

ABSTRACT

This chapter examines the transformative role of artificial intelligence (AI) in investment and wealth management, emphasizing its impact on decision-making, portfolio management, financial service personalization, and sustainable finance. It contrasts traditional investment methods with AI-driven strategies such as algorithmic trading, robo-advisors, and predictive analytics. The chapter explores AI's role in portfolio diversification, risk management, and tailored investment solutions, highlighting advancements in machine learning and natural language processing. AI-powered sentiment analysis in market forecasting is also analyzed, along with ethical and regulatory challenges like algorithmic bias, data privacy, and compliance. The systematic discussion concludes with future trends, including quantum computing and blockchain, and the challenges of integrating AI into legacy financial systems.

1- INTRODUCTION

Investors are continuously striving to maximize returns on their portfolios. Studies and researchers seek to approach this objective through implementing different investment strategies. The modern portfolio theory leaded by (Markowitz, 1952) aims at distributing investment funds into a diversified portfolio by selecting instruments that maximize portfolio returns and minimizes risks using the mean-

DOI: 10.4018/979-8-3373-0129-7.ch001

variance analysis. The theory focuses on the risk of the entire portfolio, rather than studying the risk of individual assets, thus a less risky portfolio could be built from high-risk individual assets. For each level of return, an optimal portfolio could be created, thus forming an efficient frontier for different return levels.

The availability of big data in the financial sector, and the need to analyze it and transmit it into models that assist in making decisions, made it crucial to use machines due to its importance in recording, saving, reading, and transmitting (Flood, Jagadish, and Raschid, 2016). Projected assets under management for the Robo-Advisors segment are around US$2.76 trillion by 2023 and estimated to reach $2,062.00bn in 2025, and to experience a steady annual growth rate 3.66% resulting in a projected total amount of US$2,381.00bn by 2029. Furthermore, the number of users in the Robo-Advisors is expected to amount to 34.050m users by 2029 ("Statista Robo-Advisors", n.d.).

Different industries use Artificial intelligence in optimizing different portfolios, from solar energy forecasts (Lima et al., 2020), Bioenergy investments in sugarcane mills by combining portfolio theory with neural networks (Mutran et al., 2018), commercial banks in creating their loan portfolio (Babaei and Bamdad, 2020), ship building projects in the military sector (Diaz et al., 2020), investment banking and others. Analysts in the financial industry analyze financial information in its different forms, whether fundamental, technical, or behavioral, in addition to information outside the borders of the company trying to accomplish an optimized portfolio.

Integration of Artificial Intelligence (AI) in Finance

The usage of artificial intelligence and machine learning is spreading to different aspects of the financial industry, from commercial banks, insurance companies, investment banks, and other Fintech providers. Challenges in forecasting markets and generating profits, have opened the appetite and exerted pressures on the use of artificial intelligence (AI) and machine learning (ML) in an attempt to beat the markets and expand returns (Rather, Sastry, and Agarwal, 2017).

An important motive for using AI is due to its role in eliminating human behavioral biases. AI gives more accurate results when used in behavioral finance, since psychological biases can be minimized (Singh, Garg, and Tiwari, 2020). Robo advisors exert a role in diluting the behavioral biases of investors, even though it is not totally able to solely perform risk analysis for retail investors (Bhatia, Chandani, and Chhateja, 2020). AI has a great impact on the financial advisory sector, it plays a role in building a reliable portfolio, taking into consideration the behavioral financial decisions (Shanmuganathan, 2020).

AI is used to predict trends in different instruments. Support Vector Machine predicts five steps ahead bitcoin price levels over different time horizons (Aggarwal, Chandrasekaran, and Annamalai, 2020). A specialized artificial neural network modeling framework has been developed specifically for utilization as an active data-driven robo-advisor to accurately predict future changes in copper prices up to five days in advance, utilizing input data that can be automatically collected and fed into the model (Méndez-Suárez, García-Fernández, and Gallardo, 2019).

Artificial neural network and logistic regression techniques are used to estimate the return and the probability of default (PD) for loans in P2P lending, on an individual loan basis, where the return variable is represented by the internal rate of return (IRR), and the investment decision-making process is framed as a multi-objective portfolio optimization problem using the mean-variance theory. The optimization is accomplished through the utilization of the non-dominated sorting genetic algorithm (Babaei and Bamdad, 2020).

AI helps investors and traders making their decisions and managing risk, not only based on traditional criterions like fundamental and economic indicators, it also integrates alternative data like published articles, social media interactions, environmental and governance aspects, smartphones and satellite data (In, Rook, and Monk 2019, #). Deep probabilistic convolutional neural networks can be utilized to make accurate and confident predictions of the volatility index, enabling informed decisions on ethical investing, sustainable investment strategies, and performance analysis. (Daniali et al., 2021). The availability of big data propels investors to incorporate such data in their analysis, which is hard to accomplish using traditional methods. The use of machine learning helps investors in processing such data and solving complex equations to obtain reliable and verifiable models that predict future trends and optimize portfolios. Investment in AI is increasing from both private or public institutions, in addition to its integration in universities curricula (Holzinger et al., 2018).

The Role of Artificial Intelligence in Investment and Wealth Management

The increasing complexity of financial markets and the exponential growth of big data have driven institutional and individual investors to seek advanced technologies for more confident investment decision-making. Traditional financial models have become insufficient in explaining and predicting market behaviors due to their static nature and the dynamic, complex environment of global capital markets (Golghar, Roitman, & Neginsky, 2018). Even seasoned professionals struggle to adapt to technological innovations and the continuous influx of market-moving information, as evidenced by the declining alpha generation of hedge funds over the past 15 years.

This evolving landscape necessitates the adoption of self-learning systems capable of modeling the ever-changing financial markets.

AI and Deep Learning: Adaptable and Self-Learning Capital Markets

Artificial intelligence (AI) and deep learning have emerged as critical tools for modeling and forecasting in capital markets. Systems like multilayered neural networks enable market modeling without human-derived assumptions, enhancing adaptability and flexibility (Golghar et al., 2018). These AI models detect patterns in historical stock market data, generating ranked forecasts that evolve with updated information. They adapt to new conditions and maintain predictive accuracy even in unprecedented circumstances.

The algorithms model financial markets as non-stationary chaotic systems with fractal properties, employing multi-representation and data munging to expose significant data features. Regularization techniques and fitness factors optimize the learning process, allowing the model to make predictions based on previously unseen data. Principal Component Analysis (PCA) further refines data inputs, enhancing exploratory analysis and visualization (Golghar et al., 2018).

Genetic algorithms constantly refine the predictor pool by selecting optimal predictors and discarding underperformers. This natural selection-based optimization ensures adaptability to shifting market conditions, reinforcing the system's forecasting capabilities.

Partially Versus Purely AI-Driven Investing

AI applications in investment management fall into two categories. The first involves AI analyzing market data—such as price patterns, trading volumes, and sentiment analysis through natural language processing—to produce insights that inform human decision-making. These machine-generated observations are then filtered by human managers or predetermined rules (Golghar et al., 2018). This hybrid approach effectively condenses big data into actionable insights.

Alternatively, purely AI-driven models operate autonomously, executing investment decisions without human intervention. Firms first utilize AI to generate daily stock forecasts, providing investors with positive or negative signals indicating investment opportunities. Predictability indicators measure signal confidence, allowing for risk-adjusted performance optimization. Financial institutions can integrate these forecasts into research and advisory services or offer them as trading tools to clients (Golghar et al., 2018).

Real-Time Decision-Making in Wealth Management

Real-time decision-making has become essential for maximizing returns and managing risk in wealth management. AI-powered systems process vast datasets almost instantaneously, enabling wealth managers to respond promptly to market changes. Predictive analytics continuously assess market conditions, identify emerging trends, and facilitate proactive risk management (Rai, Padyana, & Patil, 2023).

Robo-advisors have democratized wealth management by offering data-driven investment solutions with lower fees, appealing to mass-affluent clients underserved by traditional advisors. Empirical studies reveal that robo-advisors can match or outperform human advisors. However, limitations such as the lack of emotional intelligence, transparency issues, and regulatory challenges persist (Rai et al., 2023).

The Impact of Wealth Tech on Wealth Management

Wealth Tech, driven by AI, big data, and blockchain, has become a transformative force in wealth management, attracting younger and less affluent clients (Dziawgo, 2021). The COVID-19 pandemic accelerated this digital transformation, prompting significant investments in Wealth Tech solutions.

Robo-advisory services offer clients accessible, cost-effective, and unbiased investment advice. These services automate wealth development, protection, and tax minimization strategies, ensuring comprehensive financial planning (Singh & Kaur, 2017).

2- AI-DRIVEN INVESTMENT STRATEGIES:

Algorithmic Trading:

The advent of algorithmic trading (AT) and artificial intelligence (AI) has significantly transformed investment and wealth management. These technological advancements have redefined market dynamics, trading efficiency, and decision-making processes in financial markets. While AI and algorithmic trading offer considerable benefits in terms of speed, efficiency, and data processing, they also introduce complex challenges related to information acquisition, market efficiency, and regulatory frameworks. This part examines the multifaceted role of AI and algorithmic trading in shaping modern financial markets, exploring their impact on price discovery, market quality, and investor behavior.

Algorithmic trading, which automates the execution of trades through pre-programmed instructions, has been significantly enhanced by AI technologies. Machine learning algorithms can rapidly process large volumes of market data, uncover intricate patterns, and execute trades with high accuracy. High-frequency trading (HFT), a specialized form of algorithmic trading characterized by rapid order placements and cancellations, leverages AI to exploit short-lived market inefficiencies. AI models analyze order book dynamics, trade execution times, and microstructure data at microsecond speeds, thereby enabling firms to gain competitive advantages (Kondapaka, 2019).

Algorithmic Trading and Information Acquisition

Algorithmic trading has reshaped the landscape of information acquisition and price discovery. Weller (2018) highlights that while algorithmic trading enhances price efficiency concerning acquired information, it simultaneously reduces the volume of new information integrated into market prices. This dual effect creates a tension between improved market responsiveness and diminished informational richness. The reduction in information acquisition stems from two main channels: first, order anticipation by algorithmic traders diminishes the returns for those who actively seek new information (Yang & Zhu, 2017; Stiglitz, 2014); second, advanced signal processing by algorithmic liquidity providers lowers adverse selection costs but erodes profits linked to informational advantages (Baldauf & Mollner, 2017). This trade-off raises concerns about the long-term implications for market quality and social welfare.

Human and Algorithmic Interaction in Markets

The interplay between human traders and algorithmic systems introduces further complexity. Bao et al. (2022) review experimental markets where algorithmic and human traders interact, revealing that the profitability of algorithmic traders depends heavily on market conditions and asset characteristics. The study underscores how algorithmic traders, ranging from simple zero-intelligent agents to sophisticated adaptive algorithms, influence human decision-making and market psychology. These interactions can amplify market volatility and affect the strategic behavior of human traders, raising questions about market fairness and stability.

Algorithmic Trading and Market Efficiency

Yadav (2015) argues that algorithmic trading undermines capital market efficiency by distorting price signals that are essential for effective capital allocation. The inherent model risks associated with algorithmic systems, driven by the reliance on pre-set programming and predictive modeling, introduce inefficiencies. Informed traders, critical of enriching market information, face diminished incentives to participate due to competition with high-speed algorithms, resulting in less informative prices. This deterioration in market quality has profound implications for regulatory frameworks that depend on accurate price signals to ensure efficient capital distribution.

Evolutionary Computation in Algorithmic Trading

Evolutionary computation (EC) techniques have gained traction in developing trading algorithms, particularly in rule discovery for stock markets. Hu et al. (2015) observe a strong preference for genetic algorithms (GA) and genetic programming (GP) in crafting technical trading strategies. However, these models tend to perform better in declining markets and struggle in rising markets, partly due to uniform factor selection and inadequate transaction cost considerations. The study emphasizes the need for more adaptive and context-sensitive algorithmic models to improve trading outcomes across diverse market conditions.

Addressing Model Uncertainty in Algorithmic Strategies

Cartea et al. (2017) explore how market makers address model uncertainty in algorithmic trading by incorporating ambiguity aversion into their strategies. By adjusting quotes to manage inventory risk and adverse selection costs, market makers can enhance the robustness of their trading models. This approach improves the Sharpe ratio and allows for a balanced trade-off between profit expectations and risk exposure. Their findings suggest that robust market-making strategies can lead to higher profitability without proportionally increasing risk, offering a pathway for more resilient trading practices.

The Role of Simplicity in Machine Learning Models

As machine learning models become more prevalent in algorithmic trading, managing their complexity becomes paramount. Hansen (2020) highlights how quants apply Ockham's razor—a preference for simplicity—to prevent excessive complexity in machine learning models. This principle ensures that models remain interpretable and controllable, thereby safeguarding against overfitting and enhancing accountability. The balance between model sophistication and human oversight is crucial, as even the most advanced algorithms require human judgment to ensure reliability and explainability in decision-making processes.

Advanced Machine Learning Models

Deep learning models, particularly recurrent neural networks (RNNs), have demonstrated effectiveness in predicting short-term price movements by capturing complex temporal dependencies in market data. These insights are critical for developing adaptive HFT strategies. Additionally, reinforcement learning offers a dynamic framework for optimizing trading strategies by enabling systems to learn from market feedback and adapt to changing conditions (Kondapaka, 2019).

Challenges and Ethical Considerations

Despite the advantages, integrating AI into algorithmic and high-frequency trading poses challenges. The development of explainable and robust models is crucial for risk mitigation and regulatory compliance. Furthermore, ethical concerns such as market manipulation and systemic risks necessitate careful oversight to ensure that AI-driven trading strategies do not compromise market integrity (Kondapaka, 2019).

AI-Driven Risk Assessment in Stock Trading

AI models have revolutionized risk assessment and management in stock trading by improving prediction accuracy and aligning investment strategies with individual risk tolerances. Hybrid models incorporating Support Vector Machines (SVM), Principal Component Analysis (PCA), and Neural Networks (NN) demonstrate high accuracy in stock recommendations, balancing potential returns with associated risks (Bhardwaj et al., 2024). This technological advancement underscores AI's capacity to refine trading strategies and optimize portfolio performance.

Robo-Advisors in Investment and Wealth Management

The financial landscape has undergone significant transformation due to technological advancements, notably with the emergence of Robo-Advisors (RAs). These automated platforms have disrupted the traditional wealth management industry by offering cost-effective, transparent, and technologically advanced investment solutions (Phoon & Koh, 2018). By leveraging quantitative finance and algorithmic models, RAs deliver scalable wealth management services that appeal to a broad spectrum of investors. This section explores the evolution, advantages, limitations, and prospects of robo-advisors, supported by empirical research and theoretical frameworks.

The Rise and Evolution of Robo-Advisors

Robo-advisors emerged as a response to the global financial crisis in 2008, offering alternative wealth management solutions designed to mitigate irrational investment behavior and improve financial decision-making (Nguyen et al., 2023). Initially launched in the United States, these platforms gained traction globally due to their affordability, ease of access, and integration of advanced algorithms. In Malaysia, for instance, the Securities Commission began licensing Robo-Advisors in 2017, with the industry witnessing a 763% surge in registrations during the COVID-19 pandemic (Nguyen et al., 2023). This growth highlights the increasing demand for accessible and technology-driven investment solutions.

Technological Frameworks and Methodologies

Robo-Advisors primarily employ Modern Portfolio Theory (MPT) as the foundational framework for asset allocation and portfolio optimization (Beketov et al., 2018). MPT emphasizes diversification to maximize returns for a given level of risk. However, there is a growing trend toward integrating more sophisticated quantitative methods, such as factor investing and machine learning algorithms, to enhance investment strategies. Beketov et al. (2018) note that platforms utilizing advanced methodologies tend to attract higher assets under management (AUM), suggesting a market preference for innovation-driven advisory services.

Behavioral Finance and Investment Decision-Making

Behavioral biases, such as overconfidence and loss aversion, significantly influence investor decision-making, often leading to suboptimal financial outcomes (Bhatia et al., 2022). Robo-advisors, by design, aim to mitigate these biases through algorithmic decision-making and standardized investment processes. However, empirical evidence indicates that RAs alone are insufficient in fully addressing these biases. Bhatia et al. (2022) found that while RAs offer structured investment strategies, they do not entirely eliminate the psychological factors that drive irrational investor behavior. This underscores the need for hybrid models that combine automated services with human financial advisors to offer personalized behavioral coaching.

Accessibility and Market Penetration

One of the most notable impacts of Robo-Advisors is their role in democratizing access to wealth management services. Traditionally, comprehensive wealth management was a luxury reserved for affluent clients. However, innovations in fintech have enabled middle-class investors to access sophisticated investment tools through RAs (Reher & Sokolinski, 2024). A significant reduction in account minimums by leading RAs led to increased participation among middle-income investors, though the poorest segments remain underserved. This shift underscores the potential of RAs to bridge socioeconomic gaps in financial advisory services.

Advantages of Robo-Advisors

Robo-advisors offer numerous advantages over traditional financial advisory services:

Cost Efficiency: Lower management fees due to automation and reduced operational costs (Phoon & Koh, 2018).

Accessibility: 24/7 access to investment platforms, enabling users to monitor and adjust portfolios in real time (Nguyen et al., 2023).

Transparency: Clear fee structures and algorithm-driven decisions enhance transparency in investment processes (Phoon & Koh, 2018).

Customization Opportunities: Although limited, advancements in data analytics enable some level of personalization in portfolio recommendations (Nguyen et al., 2023).

Limitations and Challenges

Despite their advantages, Robo-Advisors face several limitations:

Lack of Personalization: Standardized onboarding processes often result in generic asset allocation strategies that fail to capture individual client needs (Phoon & Koh, 2018).

Emotional and Complex Decision-Making: RAs struggle to address complex financial situations requiring human empathy and judgment (Singh & Kaur, 2017).

Technological Risks: System failures, algorithmic errors, and cybersecurity threats pose significant risks to users (Nguyen et al., 2023).

Regulatory Uncertainty: The rapid evolution of fintech services has outpaced regulatory frameworks, raising concerns over investor protection (Singh & Kaur, 2017).

To overcome inherent limitations, hybrid models that integrate human advisors with algorithmic platforms are emerging as a viable solution. These models, referred to as "bionic advisory," leverage human expertise alongside computational efficiency to provide tailored financial advice (Phoon & Koh, 2018). Additionally, the ongoing development of artificial intelligence and machine learning is expected to enhance the predictive accuracy and adaptability of RAs. As these technologies mature, Robo-Advisors are poised to offer more dynamic asset allocation models and incorporate real-time market data for superior portfolio management (Beketov et al., 2018).

3- AI-DRIVEN PREDICTIVE ANALYTICS IN FINANCE

Artificial intelligence (AI)-driven predictive analytics has emerged as a transformative force in the financial sector, particularly in enhancing risk assessment and decision-making processes. By leveraging advanced machine learning (ML) algorithms and vast datasets, financial institutions can predict market trends, customer behavior, and potential risks with unprecedented precision (Javaid, 2024). This capability facilitates proactive risk management by identifying threats before they materialize and supports more informed investment strategies. Automated analyses combined with real-time data streams empower professionals to make swift, data-driven decisions, thereby enhancing profitability and operational agility. AI-driven predictive analytics represents a paradigm shift in financial services, fostering resilience and competitiveness in an increasingly dynamic environment.

AI-driven predictive analytics is redefining the financial industry by revolutionizing risk assessment and decision-making processes. Through advanced algorithms and real-time data, firms can anticipate trends, optimize strategies, and mitigate risks more effectively. This integration not only drives efficiency and profitability but also fosters a more adaptive financial ecosystem. As AI technology evolves, its role in financial systems will become even more foundational, ensuring institutions remain agile and competitive in a rapidly changing market landscape (Javaid, 2024).

Market Trend Forecasting Through Predictive Analytics

Predictive analytics, powered by AI, is revolutionizing the ability to understand and forecast market trends, particularly in consumer behavior analysis. AI algorithms analyze extensive datasets to detect patterns and predict future trends with remarkable accuracy. This capability is critical in today's dynamic markets, where consumer behavior is influenced by economic conditions, social media trends, and other external factors (Okeleke et al., 2024). AI techniques such as machine learning, natural language processing (NLP), and deep learning have significantly enhanced predictive accuracy. Machine learning algorithms uncover hidden correlations within large-scale data, NLP provides insights from textual sources like social media, and deep learning refines predictions by identifying intricate data patterns.

Businesses increasingly use AI-driven predictive analytics to improve operational efficiency and customer satisfaction. However, challenges such as data quality, privacy concerns, and the demand for specialized expertise remain significant hurdles. Addressing these challenges is essential to fully leverage AI's potential.

Advancing Annuity Products Through AI

Annuity products, essential for providing individuals with a guaranteed income during retirement, rely on accurate risk assessment and pricing strategies. Traditional actuarial methods often struggle to account for evolving market dynamics and nuanced individual risk profiles. AI and ML techniques offer significant advancements in this domain by improving the granularity of risk assessments and enhancing pricing accuracy (Perumalsamy et al., 2022). Supervised learning algorithms like Gradient Boosting Machines and Random Forests, along with unsupervised approaches such as k-means clustering, are employed to analyze complex data. Additionally, deep learning architectures, including Recurrent Neural Networks (RNNs) and Convolutional Neural Networks (CNNs), process intricate datasets like medical records and financial histories, uncovering hidden patterns for more precise risk predictions.

Feature engineering is pivotal in this process, as it involves selecting, transforming, and creating data points relevant to annuity pricing. Factors such as socioeconomic indicators, lifestyle habits, and healthcare utilization data enhance the models' accuracy. Ethical considerations are also critical, with issues like algorithmic bias and fairness requiring the adoption of explainable AI (XAI) techniques to ensure transparency and accountability. Cross-validation methods and tools like the Kaplan-Meier estimator are essential for robust model evaluation.

AI-Driven Financial Forecasting and Data Warehousing

The integration of data warehousing with AI-driven predictive models represents a groundbreaking development in financial forecasting. Data warehousing consolidates vast amounts of historical and real-time financial data from disparate sources into a unified repository, forming the backbone of effective predictive modeling (Machireddy et al., 2021). This integration enables the application of machine learning algorithms, deep learning architectures, and advanced statistical techniques to generate precise and actionable insights.

Supervised learning methods like regression analysis and classification, alongside unsupervised approaches such as clustering, are employed to process and interpret these extensive datasets. The scalability of AI-enhanced forecasting models is particularly notable, as they can accommodate growing data volumes and computational demands. Despite their potential, challenges such as data quality, integration complexities, and the need for robust computational infrastructure must be addressed to ensure successful implementation.

Challenges and Opportunities in Predictive Analytics

The implementation of AI-driven predictive analytics in finance is not without challenges. Data quality and integration issues can undermine the reliability of predictions, while privacy concerns necessitate stringent data protection measures. The rapid pace of technological advancements also requires ongoing investment in specialized skills and training. Furthermore, ethical considerations such as algorithmic bias and transparency must be addressed to ensure fair and equitable outcomes (Javaid, 2024; Okeleke et al., 2024).

Despite these challenges, the benefits of predictive analytics are substantial. Businesses can achieve enhanced accuracy in forecasting, personalized consumer experiences, and improved decision-making capabilities. By anticipating market shifts, optimizing resource allocation, and tailoring offerings to consumer demands, organizations can gain a competitive edge. For example, predictive analytics enables retailers to manage inventory more effectively, e-commerce platforms to enhance user engagement, and marketing firms to design campaigns with higher ROI.

The integration of AI with emerging technologies offers exciting opportunities for the future of predictive analytics. Advances in edge computing and quantum computing promise to enhance real-time data processing and predictive accuracy. Organizations must address challenges related to data quality, privacy, and skill development to fully capitalize on these advancements. (Javaid, 2024; Okeleke et al., 2024).

4- MACHINE LEARNING IN RISK MANAGEMENT: ENHANCING FINANCIAL STABILITY

The financial industry has witnessed a significant transformation with the integration of machine learning (ML) techniques, particularly in the domain of risk management. The 2008 global financial crisis underscored the need for robust risk management frameworks in banking institutions. Since then, there has been an increased focus on identifying, measuring, reporting, and managing various types of financial risks. Despite the advancements in machine learning and the growing emphasis on risk management, the adoption of ML in addressing key banking risks—credit risk, market risk, operational risk, and liquidity risk—remains insufficient (Leo, Sharma, & Maddulety, 2019).

Machine learning has been successfully applied to several core risk management functions, including volatility forecasting, credit rating, bankruptcy prediction, and fraud detection (Mashrur et al., 2020). Advanced models, particularly deep learning algorithms, have been instrumental in enhancing predictive accuracy and uncovering complex patterns within financial data. For instance, neural networks and ensemble methods have demonstrated superior performance in detecting fraudulent transactions and predicting market volatility.

Methodological Approaches in Machine Learning for Risk Management

Machine learning models can be broadly classified into supervised and unsupervised learning methods, each offering unique advantages for financial risk management (Aziz & Dowling, 2018). Supervised learning involves training models on labeled data to predict specific outcomes. Regression techniques, such as LASSO and Ridge regression, allow for the management of multicollinearity and feature selection by penalizing irrelevant variables, thereby refining risk prediction models (Aziz & Dowling, 2018). For example, Hu et al. (2015) demonstrated improved trading performance by using LASSO regression in automated trading systems.

Principal Component Analysis (PCA), a dimensionality reduction technique, is widely used to simplify complex datasets by identifying common factors. Zhong and Enke (2017) applied PCA to reduce 60 economic indicators into core components, subsequently using neural networks to forecast the S&P 500 index. This methodology exemplifies how PCA can enhance predictive accuracy in financial markets by eliminating noise and focusing on key risk factors.

In contrast, classification methods such as decision trees and support vector machines (SVM) classify data into distinct categories based on input features. Decision trees offer intuitive, interpretable models, although they risk overfitting, while SVMs create optimal hyperplanes for classification tasks, proving effective in predicting bondholder losses post-default (Nazemi et al., 2018).

Unsupervised Learning and Deep Learning in Risk Management

Unsupervised learning models, including clustering algorithms like K-means, are instrumental in grouping data without predefined categories. This approach is effective in anomaly detection and fraud prevention, as seen in email spam detection systems. Clustering can similarly be employed in financial risk management to identify abnormal transaction patterns indicative of fraud or financial distress (Aziz & Dowling, 2018).

Deep learning models, particularly neural networks, represent the frontier of machine learning applications in finance. These models utilize multiple hidden layers to capture complex, non-linear relationships between input variables, offering superior predictive capabilities. Heaton et al. (2017) highlighted the potential of deep learning in financial forecasting, though the "black box" nature of these models raises concerns regarding interpretability and regulatory compliance. This opacity poses a unique challenge in risk management, where transparency in decision-making is crucial.

Machine Learning Applications in Banking Risk Management

Machine learning has the potential to revolutionize risk management in banking by enabling more accurate risk models through the detection of complex, non-linear patterns in large datasets. Credit risk, a critical concern for banking institutions, has primarily seen the application of ML in credit scoring models. However, ML can be further explored to predict probabilities of default and loss given default, offering a more comprehensive assessment of credit exposure (Leo et al., 2019). Similarly, market risk management has benefited from ML models that forecast volatility, interest rate curves, and market regime changes.

The Role of Machine Learning in Financial Risk Management

Financial risk management (FRM) is fundamental to mitigating losses and maximizing profits across various business sectors. Given its reliance on data-driven decision-making, machine learning (ML) has emerged as a promising tool for developing innovative methods and technologies in this field (Mashrur et al., 2020). The growing complexity of financial markets and the exponential increase in data availability have further accelerated the integration of ML techniques in risk management. However, the vast and intricate nature of financial domain knowledge presents challenges for ML researchers attempting to navigate this evolving landscape (Mashrur et al., 2020).

Application for Credit Risk Management

Credit risk represents the economic loss stemming from a counterparty's failure to meet contractual obligations, such as timely payment of interest or principal, or from increased default risk over the duration of a transaction (Aziz & Dowling, 2019). Historically, financial firms utilized classical linear, logit, and probit regressions to model credit risk (Altman, 1968). However, these traditional methods have shown limitations in fully capturing complex risk dynamics. Consequently, financial institutions are increasingly adopting artificial intelligence (AI) and machine learning (ML) techniques to enhance credit risk management, leveraging their capability to semantically analyze unstructured data (Aziz & Dowling, 2019).

Early comparative studies, such as Altman et al. (1994), demonstrated that integrating neural network algorithms with traditional statistical methods significantly improved distress and bankruptcy prediction accuracy. The complexity inherent in credit risk assessment, particularly within the growing credit default swap (CDS) market, has further underscored the need for ML applications. Son et al. (2016) empirically showed that nonparametric deep learning models outperformed traditional benchmarks in predicting default events and devising effective hedging strategies.

In consumer and small-medium enterprise (SME) lending, ML models have yielded substantial improvements. Khandani et al. (2010) employed decision trees and support vector machines (SVM), achieving up to 25% cost savings in lending decisions. Similarly, Figini et al. (2017) demonstrated that multivariate outlier detection techniques enhanced credit risk estimation for SME lending at UniCredit Bank. These findings underscore the transformative impact of ML models in refining credit risk management strategies.

Application for Market Risk Management

Market risk arises from exposure to financial markets through investing and trading activities. Machine learning techniques offer comprehensive support in market risk management, spanning data preparation, modeling, stress testing, and model validation (Kumar, 2018; Financial Stability Board, 2017). ML's adaptability makes it particularly suitable for stress testing market models and detecting emerging risks in trading behavior.

For instance, the French investment firm Natixis utilizes unsupervised learning algorithms to conduct over three million nightly simulations, identifying anomalous asset connections and investigating irregular patterns (Woodall, 2017). Similarly, Nomura employs ML models to monitor internal trading, ensuring compliance with asset usage guidelines. Real-time model monitoring and validation, as exemplified by firms like Yields.io, showcase the efficacy of AI-driven solutions in managing model risk.

Large trading firms also harness clustering techniques to mitigate market impact costs when managing large positions in illiquid markets (Day, 2017). Capital Fund Management reports that up to two-thirds of trading profits can erode due to market impact. By leveraging ML-driven cluster analysis (Calvalcante et al., 2016) and deep learning models (Heaton et al., 2017), firms can discreetly enter positions through interconnected assets, reducing transaction costs. Reinforcement learning presents a promising future direction, enabling trading algorithms to adapt to market reactions dynamically (Hendricks & Wilcox, 2014). Additionally, combining neural networks and decision trees offers real-time trading pattern warnings, enhancing market risk mitigation (Chandrinos et al., 2018).

Application for Operational Risk Management

Operational risk encompasses financial losses stemming from internal failures (e.g., process inefficiencies, human error) or external events (e.g., cyberattacks, fraud) (Moosa, 2007). The increasing complexity and scale of operational risks necessitate AI and ML-driven solutions (Choi et al., 2017). AI facilitates risk identification, measurement, assessment, and the selection of mitigation strategies (Sanford & Moosa, 2015).

Financial fraud detection remains a significant operational risk management area where AI excels. By automating routine tasks and processing unstructured data, AI minimizes human error and enhances fraud detection capabilities. Banks utilize clustering and classification techniques to profile trader behavior, predict latent risks, and prioritize alerts based on suspicious activities (Ngai et al., 2011). Collaborative initiatives, such as the Nordic KYC Utility and HSBC's partnership with Quantexa, exemplify AI-driven anti-money laundering (AML) solutions. Moreover, the Royal Bank of Scotland and Vocalink's joint venture employs ML to detect fraudulent invoices (Colladon & Remondi, 2017).

Application to Regulatory Technology (RegTech)

Regulatory compliance is integral to risk management, especially post-financial crisis. RegTech, a subset of FinTech, leverages AI and ML to streamline compliance processes by processing vast and unconventional datasets (Arner et al., 2016). Continuous real-time monitoring reduces compliance breaches and regulatory capital requirements, contributing to significant cost savings (Arner et al., 2016).

IBM's acquisition of Promontory underscores the industry's interest in AI-driven RegTech solutions. Their systems utilize natural language processing (NLP) to analyze voice conversations for compliance breaches. Furthermore, firms like Waymark automate regulatory document interpretation, aiding financial institutions in maintaining compliance.

Emerging Trends: Federated Learning and Model Explainability

Key machine learning advancements, including federated learning, offer promising solutions for the financial industry. Federated learning enables decentralized model training across multiple data sources while preserving data privacy, addressing concerns related to handling sensitive financial information (Mashrur et al., 2020). This approach allows financial institutions to collaborate on model development without compromising data security.

Moreover, explainability and fairness have become critical considerations in the deployment of ML models for risk management. Given the regulatory and ethical implications, developing interpretable models that provide transparent decision-making processes is vital. (Mashrur et al., 2020).

5- AI'S ROLE IN PORTFOLIO MANAGEMENT: PORTFOLIO DIVERSIFICATION USING AI

The intersection of artificial intelligence (AI) and finance has catalyzed a transformative era in portfolio management and optimization. Advanced AI models have significantly improved financial decision-making processes, leveraging deep learning, reinforcement learning, and generative adversarial networks (GANs) to enhance portfolio construction, risk management, and investment strategies (Kondapaka, 2019). Financial institutions now harness vast and complex datasets to uncover hidden correlations, enabling data-driven decisions with unprecedented speed and precision. This evolution marks a paradigm shift in the investment landscape, introducing more sophisticated tools for asset allocation and risk mitigation.

AI-Enhanced Portfolio Optimization

The integration of artificial intelligence (AI) and machine learning (ML) into portfolio management represents a transformative shift in investment strategies, offering advanced methodologies for balancing risk and return (Kasaraneni, 2021).

Traditional portfolio optimization models, such as the mean-variance optimization introduced by Markowitz, often struggle with processing large and complex datasets, limiting their effectiveness in dynamic markets. In contrast, AI and ML models possess superior capabilities to handle vast amounts of financial data, detect hidden patterns, and adapt swiftly to market fluctuations, thus offering a more responsive approach to asset allocation (Kasaraneni, 2021).

Supervised learning methods, including linear regression, decision trees, and support vector machines, have been extensively applied to forecast asset returns and market trends. Unsupervised learning techniques like clustering and dimensionality reduction facilitate the identification of asset groupings and market regimes. Furthermore, neural networks, deep learning models, and reinforcement learning algorithms have demonstrated significant potential in enhancing portfolio optimization strategies by enabling adaptive decision-making processes (Kasaraneni, 2021). These models simultaneously optimize multiple objectives, balancing return maximization and risk minimization, thus offering a comprehensive solution to investor needs.

Despite these advantages, the adoption of AI-enhanced models introduces challenges, such as the necessity for high-quality, extensive datasets, risks of overfitting, and complexities in model interpretability. Nevertheless, these challenges can be mitigated through the use of robust data preprocessing techniques, cross-validation methods, and explainable AI models. A notable case study involving a deep learning model for asset diversification highlighted substantial improvements in risk-adjusted returns and portfolio stability compared to traditional models (Kasaraneni, 2021). Future research should focus on enhancing model interpretability, integrating alternative data sources, and exploring AI-driven optimization in sustainable investing.

Diversification in the Age of the 4th Industrial Revolution

The advent of the 4th industrial revolution has profoundly impacted portfolio diversification strategies, with AI, green bonds, and cryptocurrencies playing pivotal roles (Huynh, Hille, & Nasir, 2020). Analyzing daily data from 2017 to 2020, Huynh et al. (2020) employed tail dependence and Generalized Forecast Error Variance Decomposition (GFEVD) to examine volatility connectedness among diverse asset classes. Findings revealed that portfolios including AI and robotics stocks, green bonds, and cryptocurrencies exhibit heavy-tail dependence, implying heightened joint loss probabilities during economic downturns. Volatility transmission was more pronounced in the short term, necessitating cautious short-term investment strategies, while long-term holdings mitigated this risk.

Bitcoin and gold emerged as effective hedging assets, albeit Bitcoin's past volatility influenced its risk profile. In contrast, gold demonstrated consistent safe-haven properties, particularly during market downturns, with minimal shock transmission to AI stocks (Huynh et al., 2020). The study highlighted the critical need for meticulous diversification, given the substantial self-transmitting risks inherent in portfolios blending traditional and innovative asset classes. Policymakers are urged to address information asymmetries and establish regulatory frameworks to mitigate risks associated with fintech and AI-driven assets.

Investors are advised to adopt long-term strategies to manage volatility spillovers and avoid combining highly correlated assets, such as NASDAQ AI indices with general equity markets.

Performance of AI-Related Stocks versus Traditional Indices

Karoui, Sayari, Dammak, and Jeribi (2024) conducted an empirical analysis comparing AI and robotics-related stocks with traditional IT indices and specialized ETFs. The study assessed different risk management strategies, from "buy and hold" to daily rebalancing, using data from 2021 to 2023. Findings indicated that AI-related stocks consistently outperformed traditional indices like the Nasdaq, driven by increasing market interest and speculative investments in AI technologies.

Metrics such as the Sharpe and Treynor ratios demonstrated the superior performance of AI stocks, particularly when incorporated into actively managed portfolios with frequent rebalancing (Karoui et al., 2024). However, the study cautioned about the potential "AI bubble" and stressed the importance of balancing high returns with the sector's inherent volatility. Limitations included the focus on specific markets and the evolving nature of AI technology, suggesting the need for broader comparative analyses across global markets.

Interpretable Machine Learning in Portfolio Diversification

Advanced AI models enable more efficient decision-making by analyzing vast datasets, identifying complex patterns, and executing trades with unparalleled precision (Kondapaka, 2019). Jaeger et al. (2021) explored the application of interpretable machine learning in diversified portfolio construction, comparing Hierarchical Risk Parity (HRP) with Equal Risk Contribution (ERC) strategies. Using a dataset of 17 equity index, government bond, and commodity futures markets over two decades, the study employed XGBoost to analyze the Calmar ratio spread between HRP and ERC strategies. Results indicated that HRP consistently outperformed ERC, aligning more effectively with volatility targets and demonstrating improved resilience during drawdowns (Jaeger et al., 2021).

The study leveraged explainable AI techniques, such as Shapley values, to uncover implicit decision-making rules within the models. This approach provided transparency in understanding how portfolio allocation strategies respond to varying market conditions. HRP's superior performance was attributed to its ability to better account for hierarchical correlations in financial markets compared to ERC's reliance on covariance matrix inversion.

AI-Smart Beta Exchange Traded Funds (ETFs)

AI-driven smart-beta ETFs adjust traditional market capitalization weightings based on opportunities identified by predictive algorithms. These funds maintain exposure to existing index constituents but dynamically rebalance allocations according to AI-generated forecasts. Predictability levels, signal directions, and strengths guide asset weighting adjustments, enhancing risk-adjusted returns while maintaining passive investment structures (Golghar et al., 2018).

AI in Alternative Asset Classes

AI's application extends beyond traditional asset classes to alternative investments such as real estate and private equity. By analyzing complex datasets and identifying lucrative investment opportunities, AI enables investors to diversify portfolios and discover new sources of alpha (Kondapaka, 2019). This capability is particularly valuable in managing illiquid and opaque markets where traditional analysis falls short.

The convergence of AI with emerging technologies like blockchain, natural language processing (NLP), quantum computing, and the Internet of Things (IoT) holds immense potential for financial innovation. These synergies can lead to the creation of novel financial products and services, enhancing transparency, efficiency, and the overall investor experience (Kondapaka, 2019). For example, combining AI and blockchain can improve transaction security, while quantum computing could exponentially accelerate data processing capabilities.

6- PERSONALIZATION OF WEALTH MANAGEMENT THROUGH ARTIFICIAL INTELLIGENCE

Adapting to a New Generation of Investors

AI has fundamentally reshaped wealth management by enabling personalized financial services. Machine learning models analyze clients' spending habits, investment preferences, and risk profiles, delivering tailored recommendations that align with individual financial goals (Challoumis, 2024). This personalization enhances client engagement and fosters trust, positioning wealth managers as partners in clients' financial journeys.

The wealth management industry is undergoing a significant transformation, driven by the generational shift of wealth from Baby Boomers to Millennials and Generation Z. This transition necessitates the adoption of digital technologies to meet the evolving expectations of younger, tech-savvy clients (Boston Consulting Group, 2020). The COVID-19 pandemic has further accelerated this digital transformation, compelling wealth managers to prioritize technological innovations and digital channels for client interaction and portfolio management. As a result, WealthTech has emerged as a dominant force within the wealth management sector, bolstered by substantial investments in artificial intelligence (AI), robo-advisory services, big data analytics, and blockchain technologies. These innovations not only streamline operations but also attract younger and less affluent clients, expanding the industry's demographic reach.

AI-Driven Robo-Advisors: Transforming Wealth Management Services

AI-driven robo-advisors have revolutionized wealth management by automating portfolio management, improving risk assessment, and providing personalized investment strategies (Kumar et al., 2024). These platforms offer cost-efficient, accessible, and continuously monitored investment solutions, making sophisticated financial services more inclusive. However, robo-advisors face limitations, including the absence of personalized human interaction and reliance on algorithms driven by historical data. The future of wealth management is expected to embrace a hybrid model that combines the efficiency of AI-driven automation with the empathetic and nuanced guidance of human financial advisors. This integrated approach aims to balance cost-effectiveness with emotional intelligence, enhancing the overall client experience (Belanche, Casaló, & Flavián, 2019; Fisch, Labouré, & Turner, 2019).

Enhanced Personalization through Advanced AI Technologies

Advancements in AI and machine learning are poised to deliver unprecedented levels of personalization in wealth management. Technologies such as natural language processing (NLP), blockchain, and enhanced cybersecurity measures are reshaping client engagement and service delivery. NLP facilitates more intuitive and user-friendly communication between clients and robo-advisors, improving client support and satisfaction. Blockchain technology enhances transaction transparency and data security, addressing concerns about privacy and data integrity (Fisch, Labouré, & Turner, 2019). Despite these technological advantages, challenges persist, including algorithmic biases, lack of human judgment, regulatory compliance, and ethical considerations. Addressing these issues is critical to ensuring that AI-driven wealth management solutions are ethical, reliable, and effective.

Real-Time Personalized Financial Recommendations

Integrating real-time AI and machine learning analytics into wealth management enables the delivery of highly personalized financial recommendations (Devan, Tillu, & Shanmugam, 2023). By employing clustering techniques and predictive algorithms, wealth management systems can segment clients based on their risk profiles and tailor investment strategies accordingly. Continuous refinement of these machine learning models improves predictive accuracy and adaptability to market dynamics. Real-time data feeds and advanced predictive analytics enhance the system's responsiveness, ensuring timely and relevant investment recommendations. Furthermore, expanding the system's capabilities to include diverse financial products and integrating emerging technologies like blockchain and decentralized finance (DeFi) can broaden service offerings and drive innovation. These advancements empower individuals to manage their financial goals more effectively, signifying a paradigm shift in wealth management towards data-driven, client-centric solutions.

Intelligent Budgeting and Tax Optimization

AI-powered budgeting applications and tax optimization tools offer practical solutions for everyday financial management. Intelligent budgeting applications analyze income and spending patterns to create adaptive financial plans, while AI-assisted tax tools identify deductions and optimize tax strategies, improving overall financial efficiency (Challoumis, 2024). These innovations democratize access to sophisticated financial management tools.

Safeguarding Consumer Protections

The rapid integration of AI in finance necessitates vigilant consumer protection measures. Transparency in algorithmic decision-making and robust ethical frameworks are essential to safeguard consumer interests and prevent discriminatory practices (Challoumis, 2024). Regulators and financial institutions must prioritize fairness, inclusivity, and accountability in deploying AI-driven financial services.

7- ETHICAL AND REGULATORY CONSIDERATIONS IN AI-DRIVEN WEALTH MANAGEMENT

As artificial intelligence (AI) continues to reshape wealth management, regulatory frameworks must evolve to address emerging challenges and uphold ethical standards. Key regulatory concerns include algorithmic transparency, data privacy, and the prevention of biases in AI systems. Transparent algorithms are critical for ensuring that AI-driven decisions are both explainable and accountable. Additionally, robust data protection measures are necessary to safeguard individual privacy, particularly as AI systems require extensive data for training and operation. Ethical considerations, such as fairness and inclusiveness, are equally vital to foster trust and reliability in financial services (Kumar et al., 2024).

The establishment of industry-wide ethical guidelines and best practices will play a pivotal role in navigating this complex landscape. Regulatory frameworks must enforce compliance with these standards, ensuring AI systems do not perpetuate discrimination or inequity. Stakeholder collaboration, including policymakers, developers, and financial institutions, is crucial for creating a consensus around these ethical principles (Agu et al., 2024). By addressing these issues, the wealth management industry can strike a balance between innovation and ethical responsibility.

AI and Sustainable Finance

Addressing global challenges such as climate change and social inequality necessitates the integration of AI with sustainable finance and impact investment. AI-driven tools can assess environmental, social, and governance (ESG) risks, identify impact investment opportunities, and measure social returns, supporting financial institutions in aligning profitability with sustainability goals (Kondapaka, 2019). This alignment fosters a dual objective of achieving financial returns while contributing to societal well-being

Future wealth management platforms will likely emphasize financial literacy and education to empower clients. By offering educational resources and personalized advice, AI-driven platforms can help bridge the gap between automated services and the need for personal financial understanding. Such initiatives not only enhance user confidence but also enable investors to make informed decisions about their financial futures (Fein, 2019).

In addition to education, AI-powered wealth management solutions have the potential to promote financial inclusion. The accessibility and scalability of robo-advisors position them to serve underserved markets, democratizing access to financial services globally. Tailored solutions that adapt to diverse regulatory environments and cultural contexts will be essential for reaching broader populations, particularly in developing economies (Fisch et al., 2019). This democratization aligns with the overarching goal of reducing economic disparities and fostering financial empowerment on a global scale.

Ethical Challenges in AI-Driven Financial Services

The integration of AI into financial decision-making brings significant ethical challenges, including biases in algorithms, lack of transparency, and accountability issues. Biases inherent in training data can lead to discriminatory outcomes, disproportionately affecting certain demographic groups. Moreover, the opacity of AI decision-making processes poses challenges to understanding and trusting AI-driven outcomes (Agu et al., 2024). Transparency and accountability are critical for addressing these concerns and fostering public trust.

Privacy concerns are another major issue, as AI systems rely on extensive data collection. Strong data protection measures and ethical AI design principles are necessary to ensure equitable outcomes. Achieving algorithmic fairness is a complex task that requires continuous efforts to mitigate biases and enhance inclusivity. Algorithmic audits and inclusive data practices are effective solutions to promote fairness and transparency in AI systems (Ridzuan et al., 2024).

Advancing AI Governance Frameworks

AI governance frameworks are integral to addressing the ethical challenges posed by AI in the financial sector. These frameworks should incorporate rules and guidelines that address data privacy, accountability, and transparency. Regulatory initiatives, such as those implemented in Hong Kong SAR, the United States, China, and the European Union, offer examples of how governance can be tailored to address these challenges (Ridzuan et al., 2024).

The adoption of ethical AI frameworks requires collaboration between regulators, industry stakeholders, and developers. Key recommendations include algorithmic audits, robust impact assessments, and consumer education initiatives. By enhancing transparency and accountability, these measures can build public confidence in AI technologies and promote responsible integration in financial services (Owolabi et al., 2024).

Applications and Benefits of AI in Wealth Management

AI technologies have revolutionized wealth management by enabling fraud detection, credit risk assessment, customer service automation, and investment management. These applications enhance operational efficiency and decision-making while reducing costs. Trading algorithms and forecasting models, powered by machine learning, improve portfolio optimization and risk management, contributing to better outcomes for investors (Ridzuan et al., 2024).

The benefits of these technologies extend beyond efficiency. Enhanced personalization allows wealth management platforms to offer tailored investment strategies based on individual risk profiles and preferences. This level of customization fosters stronger client relationships and improves the overall customer experience. However, these advancements also highlight the need for ethical and regulatory oversight to ensure responsible use (Kumar et al., 2024).

Ethical Implications and Future Directions

Despite the transformative potential of AI, its adoption in finance raises significant ethical concerns. Bias, discrimination, and risks to market stability underscore the need for ethical frameworks that prioritize fairness and transparency. These frameworks should guide every stage of AI implementation, from design and development to deployment (Owolabi et al., 2024).

Future research should focus on developing advanced techniques for bias detection and mitigation, explainable AI (XAI) for enhanced transparency, and comprehensive ethical guidelines tailored to financial services. Additionally, impact assessments and interdisciplinary collaboration will be crucial for understanding the societal implications of AI adoption. By prioritizing these efforts, stakeholders can build an equitable and trustworthy AI ecosystem that benefits both financial institutions and consumers.

8- FUTURE TRENDS AND CHALLENGES IN AI-DRIVEN WEALTH MANAGEMENT

The Evolving Role of AI in Active vs. Passive Investment Management

Artificial intelligence (AI) is progressively reshaping both active and passive investment management strategies. In active investment management, AI algorithms are utilized to generate predictive insights and trading strategies, allowing fund managers to identify new alpha sources and mitigate risk through real-time data analysis (Golgher, Roitman, & Neginsky, 2018). Conversely, in passive investment management, AI enhances the construction of data-driven allocation schemes, optimizing portfolio diversification while reducing costs. The integration of machine learning models allows for the automation of routine portfolio management tasks, contributing to cost savings and operational efficiency. As AI becomes integral to these strategies, firms unable to adapt risk losing competitiveness in an evolving financial landscape (Golgher et al., 2018).

Emerging Technologies and Their Impact on Wealth Management

The intersection of emerging technologies such as quantum computing and blockchain with AI is set to transform wealth management further. Quantum computing promises unparalleled computational power, enabling complex risk modeling and optimization algorithms beyond the capabilities of classical computing systems (Rai, Padyana, & Patil, 2023). Blockchain technology, with its decentralized and transparent nature, can enhance data security and integrity in AI-driven systems, fostering trust among investors. The convergence of these technologies with AI will facilitate more secure, efficient, and adaptive wealth management solutions. However, leveraging these technologies requires significant investment in infrastructure and expertise, posing challenges for traditional financial institutions (Rai et al., 2023).

Challenges in Integrating AI into Traditional Financial Institutions

Integrating AI into traditional financial institutions presents several challenges, including legacy systems, workforce transformation, and regulatory compliance. Many established firms operate on outdated infrastructure that is incompatible with AI technologies, necessitating costly system upgrades and data integration efforts (Kumar et al., 2024). Additionally, workforce transformation is required to balance AI-driven automation with human advisory roles. A hybrid model, combining robo-advisors for data processing with human advisors for personalized guidance, offers a solution to this challenge. This approach demands collaboration between technology providers, traditional firms, and regulators to develop standardized practices that prioritize innovation while safeguarding consumer interests. Effective implementation will also require continuous performance monitoring and responsiveness to client feedback (Kumar et al., 2024).

Future Outlook and Growth Potential of AI in Wealth Management

Looking forward, the role of AI in wealth management is expected to expand significantly, driven by continuous technological advancements and the growing demand for personalized financial services. Next-generation robo-advisors will incorporate more sophisticated AI models, leveraging deep learning and reinforcement learning to refine investment recommendations further (Kumar et al., 2024). Additionally, the integration of quantum computing and blockchain technology will enhance data processing capabilities and strengthen security measures, ensuring greater transparency in financial transactions (Hu et al., 2015).

A crucial trend shaping the future of AI in wealth management is the emergence of hybrid advisory models that combine AI-driven automation with human expertise. These models offer a balance between efficiency and personalization, preserving the critical human element necessary for trust-building and nuanced financial planning (Rai, Padyana, & Patil, 2023). As AI technologies become more sophisticated, firms will need to address challenges related to system integration, workforce adaptation, and regulatory compliance to unlock AI's full potential in wealth management.

Moreover, AI-driven financial services present a unique opportunity for promoting financial inclusion. By offering scalable, cost-effective solutions, AI can extend wealth management services to underserved populations, democratizing access to financial planning and investment opportunities (Fisch, Labouré, & Turner, 2019). This shift will help bridge economic disparities and provide broader segments of society with the tools necessary for wealth accumulation and financial security.

Future Research Directions and Emerging Technologies in AI-Driven Wealth Management

AI's application in wealth management is an evolving field with substantial opportunities for future research and innovation. Several areas warrant further exploration, including the integration of alternative data sources, advanced clustering methods, and adaptive forecasting models. The incorporation of social media sentiment analysis and real-time market dynamics into AI-driven investment strategies could significantly enhance predictive capabilities.

Quantum computing represents another frontier in AI-driven financial analysis. With its ability to process complex calculations exponentially faster than classical computers, quantum computing holds the potential to revolutionize risk assessment, portfolio optimization, and high-frequency trading strategies (Machireddy et al., 2021). As these technologies mature, financial institutions must invest in research and development to harness their full capabilities while ensuring robust ethical and regulatory safeguards.

Additionally, the financial industry must prioritize the ethical implications of AI deployment, particularly in areas such as credit scoring, loan approvals, and automated wealth management decisions. Algorithmic fairness, bias detection techniques, and responsible AI frameworks should be at the forefront of AI research to promote equitable financial outcomes. Collaborative efforts between financial institutions, technology developers, and regulatory bodies will be essential in shaping the future of AI-driven wealth management.

9- CONCLUSION

The integration of artificial intelligence (AI) into investment and wealth management has significantly reshaped the industry, enhancing decision-making, optimizing portfolio management, and personalizing client services. AI-driven robo-advisors, powered by sophisticated machine learning algorithms, have revolutionized traditional investment strategies by leveraging predictive analytics to tailor financial solutions to individual client needs (Kumar et al., 2024). These advancements enable more effective investment decisions by continuously adapting to market fluctuations and investor preferences, thereby improving overall portfolio performance and risk mitigation (Fein, 2019; Lam, 2016).

Advancements in AI methodologies, such as federated learning and generative adversarial networks (GANs), hold immense potential for further refining predictive analytics in finance. Federated learning offers a decentralized approach to AI model training, ensuring data privacy while fostering collaboration across financial institutions. Similarly, GANs can be employed for stress-testing portfolio strategies under extreme market conditions, improving resilience in volatile economic environments (Machireddy et al., 2021). Future research should continue exploring these advanced techniques to enhance the accuracy and reliability of AI-driven financial forecasting.

Furthermore, AI has transformed risk assessment and asset allocation by utilizing natural language processing (NLP) and machine learning models to analyze vast amounts of financial data. These tools enhance wealth managers' ability to detect hidden market patterns, forecast economic trends, and provide real-time insights, thus fostering a more data-driven and responsive investment landscape (Hu et al., 2015). AI-powered financial models have also demonstrated increased precision in identifying risks and opportunities, helping investment firms gain a competitive edge in an increasingly complex financial ecosystem.

AI and algorithmic trading have undeniably revolutionized investment and wealth management, offering enhanced efficiency and data-driven insights. However, these advancements also introduce significant challenges concerning information acquisition, market efficiency, and regulatory oversight. Striking a balance between technological innovation and market integrity is essential for sustaining fair, efficient, and resilient financial markets. Ongoing research and thoughtful regulation are critical in navigating the complex trade-offs inherent in the integration of AI and algorithmic trading in financial markets.

Robo-Advisors have fundamentally reshaped the wealth management industry by offering scalable, cost-effective, and technology-driven investment solutions. While they excel in delivering standardized financial services to a broad client base, their limitations in personalization and emotional intelligence underscore the continued relevance of human financial advisors. Hybrid advisory models and advancements in AI are likely to define the future of wealth management, balancing efficiency with personalized client engagement. Traditional wealth managers must innovate and adapt to remain competitive in this evolving landscape.

The personalization of wealth management through AI represents a significant evolution in the industry, addressing the needs of a new generation of investors. The integration of AI-driven robo-advisors, advanced machine learning models, and emerging technologies offers scalable, efficient, and personalized financial services. However, achieving a balance between technological innovation and human insight is crucial for delivering holistic wealth management solutions. Ongoing research and development in AI technologies will further enhance personalization, enabling wealth managers to offer tailored strategies that align with individual client goals and risk profiles.

The Role of AI in Risk Management and Regulatory Compliance

AI and machine learning have emerged as powerful tools for enhancing financial risk management. AI-driven models can assess credit risk, market volatility, and liquidity concerns with unparalleled precision, enabling financial institutions to implement proactive risk mitigation strategies (Mashrur et al., 2020). However, the opaque nature of deep learning models presents challenges in regulatory compliance, as financial regulators emphasize transparency and explainability in risk assessment frameworks (Leo et al., 2019).

One of the most pressing challenges in AI-driven risk management is liquidity risk prediction. Despite its critical role in financial stability, liquidity risk remains underexplored in AI research. Developing predictive models capable of identifying liquidity crises in real time will be crucial for enhancing financial institutions' resilience (Leo et al., 2019). Additionally, AI can play a significant role in operational risk management by analyzing large-scale operational data to detect fraud, cybersecurity threats, and compliance violations.

Future research should focus on integrating explainable AI (XAI) techniques into risk management models to improve regulatory transparency. Hybrid AI models that combine deep learning with rule-based systems can offer both predictive accuracy and interpretability, bridging the gap between innovation and compliance. As financial institutions continue adopting AI, establishing standardized frameworks for ethical AI deployment will be essential in ensuring long-term sustainability.

Challenges and Ethical Considerations in AI Integration

Despite its transformative potential, AI integration into investment and wealth management presents several challenges. The rapid adoption of AI-driven financial solutions raises concerns regarding algorithmic bias, data privacy, and regulatory compliance (Kondapaka, 2019). Machine learning models, if not properly trained, can inadvertently reinforce biases present in financial data, leading to unfair or discriminatory investment decisions. Addressing these issues requires robust data governance frameworks, algorithmic transparency, and ethical AI development practices.

Regulatory complexities further complicate AI adoption in financial services. Compliance with evolving regulations regarding data protection, financial transparency, and consumer rights necessitates continuous oversight and adaptation. Financial institutions must work closely with regulatory bodies to establish ethical standards that balance innovation with consumer protection (Agu et al., 2024). Algorithmic audits, inclusive data practices, and transparency measures will play a critical role in ensuring responsible AI implementation in wealth management.

Future of AI in Investment and Wealth Management

The future of wealth management lies in the strategic integration of AI with emerging technologies and human expertise. As AI continues to revolutionize investment strategies, firms must navigate the challenges of technological integration, regulatory compliance, and workforce adaptation. By embracing hybrid advisory models and leveraging innovations like quantum computing and blockchain, wealth management can become more efficient, secure, and inclusive. Addressing these challenges within ethical and regulatory frameworks will be essential to realizing AI's full potential in transforming the industry.

In conclusion, AI is poised to redefine investment and wealth management, offering enhanced efficiency, personalized financial services, and data-driven decision-making capabilities. However, fully realizing AI's transformative potential requires continuous advancements in technology, adherence to evolving regulatory standards, and a balanced integration of human expertise with AI capabilities.

While AI-driven solutions hold promise for improving financial inclusion and democratizing access to wealth management services, financial institutions must remain vigilant in addressing ethical and regulatory challenges. Algorithmic transparency, data governance, and ethical AI practices will be critical in fostering trust and ensuring responsible AI adoption in the financial sector.

As AI continues to evolve, its role in investment and wealth management will become increasingly integral, shaping a more adaptive, resilient, and inclusive financial ecosystem. Financial institutions that strategically embrace AI while prioritizing regulatory compliance and ethical considerations will be well-positioned to lead the next wave of innovation in the wealth management industry.

REFERENCES

Abdelazim, H. Y., & Wahba, K. (2006). An artificial intelligence approach to portfolio selection and management. *International Journal of Financial Services Management, 1*(2-3), 243–254. DOI: 10.1504/IJFSM.2006.009629

Aggarwal, D., Chandrasekaran, S., & Annamalai, B. (2020). A complete empirical ensemble mode decomposition and support vector machine-based approach to predict Bitcoin prices. *Journal of Behavioral and Experimental Finance*, *27*, 27. DOI: 10.1016/j.jbef.2020.100335

Agu, E. E., Abhulimen, A. O., Obiki-Osafiele, A. N., Osundare, O. S., Adeniran, I. A., & Efunniyi, C. P. (2024). Discussing ethical considerations and solutions for ensuring fairness in AI-driven financial services. International Journal of Frontier Research in Science, 3(2), 001-009.

Altman, E. I. (1968). Financial ratios, discriminant analysis and the prediction of corporate bankruptcy. *The Journal of Finance*, *23*(4), 589–609. DOI: 10.1111/j.1540-6261.1968.tb00843.x

Altman, E. I., Marco, G., & Varetto, F. (1994). Corporate distress diagnosis: Comparisons using linear discriminant analysis and neural networks (the Italian experience). *Journal of Banking & Finance*, *18*(3), 505–529. DOI: 10.1016/0378-4266(94)90007-8

Arner, D. W., Barberis, J., & Buckley, R. P. (2015). The evolution of Fintech: A new post-crisis paradigm. *SSRN*, *47*, 1271. DOI: 10.2139/ssrn.2676553

Aziz, S., & Dowling, M. (2019). Machine learning and AI for risk management. In Disrupting finance: FinTech and strategy in the 21st century (pp. 33-50). DOI: 10.1007/978-3-030-02330-0_3

Aziz, S., & Dowling, M. M. (2018). AI and machine learning for risk management. In Lynn, T., Mooney, G., Rosati, P., & Cummins, M. (Eds.), *Disrupting Finance: FinTech and Strategy in the 21st Century* (pp. 33–50). Palgrave Macmillan.

Babaei, G., & Bamdad, S. (2020). A multi-objective instance-based decision support system for investment recommendation in peer-to-peer lending. *Expert Systems with Applications*, *150*, 113278. DOI: 10.1016/j.eswa.2020.113278

Baker, H., Kumar, S., Goyal, K., & Sharma, A. (2021). International review of financial analysis: A retrospective evaluation between 1992 and 2020. *International Review of Financial Analysis*, *78*, 78. DOI: 10.1016/j.irfa.2021.101946

Baldauf, M., & Mollner, J. (2015). *High-frequency trading and market performance*. Stanford Inst. for Economic Policy Research.

Ballings, M., Poel, D., Hespeels, N., & Gryp, R. (2015). Evaluating multiple classifiers for stock price direction prediction. *Expert Systems with Applications, 42*(20), 7046–7056. DOI: 10.1016/j.eswa.2015.05.013

Bao, T., Nekrasova, E., Neugebauer, T., & Riyanto, Y. E. (2022). Algorithmic trading in experimental markets with human traders: A literature survey. In Handbook of Experimental Finance (pp. 302–322). DOI: 10.4337/9781800372337.00030

Beccalli, E., Elliot, V., & Virili, F. (2020). *Artificial Intelligence and Ethics in Portfolio Management. Digital Business Transformation, 38*. Springer.

Beketov, M., Lehmann, K., & Wittke, M. (2018). Robo Advisors: Quantitative methods inside the robots. *Journal of Asset Management, 19*(6), 363–370. DOI: 10.1057/s41260-018-0092-9

Belanche, D., Casaló, L. V., & Flavián, C. (2019). Artificial Intelligence in FinTech: Understanding robo-advisors adoption among customers. *Industrial Management & Data Systems, 119*(7), 1411–1430. DOI: 10.1108/IMDS-08-2018-0368

Benhamou, E., Saltiel, D., Ohana, J., Atif, J., & Laraki, R. (2020). Deep Reinforcement Learning (DRL) for portfolio allocation. The European Conference on Machine Learning and Principles and Practice of Knowledge Discovery in Database - ECML PKKDD. *Proceedings, 12461*, 527–531.

Bhardwaj, A., Ranjan, O., Biswas, S., Gupta, L., Chanti, Y., & Sharma, M. (2024, March). Risk Assessment and Management in Stock Trading using Artificial Intelligence. In 2024 3rd International Conference on Sentiment Analysis and Deep Learning (ICSADL) (pp. 138-145). IEEE. DOI: 10.1109/ICSADL61749.2024.00029

Bhatia, A., Chandani, A., & Chhateja, J. (2020). Robo advisory and its potential in addressing the behavioral biases of investors — A qualitative study in Indian context. *Journal of Behavioral and Experimental Finance, 25*, 25. DOI: 10.1016/j.jbef.2020.100281

Bhatia, A., Chandani, A., Divekar, R., Mehta, M., & Vijay, N. (2022). Digital innovation in wealth management landscape: The moderating role of robo advisors in behavioural biases and investment decision-making. *International Journal of Innovation Science, 14*(3/4), 693–712. DOI: 10.1108/IJIS-10-2020-0245

Cartea, Á., Donnelly, R., & Jaimungal, S. (2017). Algorithmic trading with model uncertainty. *SIAM Journal on Financial Mathematics, 8*(1), 635–671. DOI: 10.1137/16M106282X

Challoumis, C. (2024, October). AI IN WEALTH MANAGEMENT-TRANSFORMING PERSONAL FINANCE FOR THE BETTER. In *XVI International Scientific Conference* (pp. 30-61).

Chan Kok, T., & Seah, E. (2010). Optimizing portfolio construction using artificial intelligence. 5th International Conference on Computer Sciences and Convergence Information Technology, Seoul, Korea (South), 338-343.

Chandrinos, S. K., Sakkas, G., & Lagaros, N. D. (2018). AIRMS: A risk management tool using machine learning. *Expert Systems with Applications*, *105*, 34–48. DOI: 10.1016/j.eswa.2018.03.044

Chen, W., Zhang, H., Mehlawat, M., & Jia, L. (2021). Mean–variance portfolio optimization using machine learning-based stock price prediction. *Applied Soft Computing*, *100*(106943), 106943. DOI: 10.1016/j.asoc.2020.106943

Costa, D., Carvalho, F., Moreira, B., & Prado, J. (2017). Bibliometric analysis on the association between behavioral finance and decision making with cognitive biases such as overconfidence, anchoring effect and confirmation bias. *Scientometrics*, *111*(3), 1775–1799. DOI: 10.1007/s11192-017-2371-5

Daniali, S. M., Barykin, S. E., Kapustina, I. V., Khortabi, F. M., Sergeev, S. M., Kalinina, O. V., & Senjyu, T. (2021). Predicting Volatility Index According to Technical Index and Economic Indicators on the Basis of Deep Learning Algorithm. *Sustainability (Basel)*, *13*(24), 14011. DOI: 10.3390/su132414011

Devan, M., Tillu, R., & Shanmugam, L. (2023). Personalized Financial Recommendations: Real-Time AI-ML Analytics in Wealth Management. Journal of Knowledge Learning and Science Technology ISSN: 2959-6386 (online), 2(3), 547-559.

Diaz, R., Smith, K., Landaeta, R., & Padovano, A. (2020). Shipbuilding Supply Chain Framework and Digital Transformation: A Project Portfolios Risk Evaluation. *Procedia Manufacturing*, *42*, 173–180. DOI: 10.1016/j.promfg.2020.02.067

Du, J. (2022). Mean–variance portfolio optimization with deep learning based-forecasts for cointegrated stocks. Expert Systems with Applications: An International Journal, 201(C).

Dziawgo, T. (2021). Wealth Tech impact on wealth management sector.

Fein, M. L. (2019). Robo-Advisors: A Portfolio Management Perspective. *Journal of Financial Planning*, *32*(1), 48–55.

Fisch, J. E., Laboure, M., & Turner, J. A. (2019). The Emergence of the Robo-advisor. The disruptive impact of FinTech on retirement systems, 13, 13-37.

Fisch, J. E., Labouré, M., & Turner, J. A. (2019). The Emergence of the Robo-Adviser. *University of Pennsylvania Law Review, 168*(4), 1269–1305.

Flood, M., Jagadish, H., & Raschid, L. (2016). Big data challenges and opportunities in financial stability monitoring. *Financial Stability Review*, (20), 129–142.

Ghandar, A., Michalewicz, Z., Schmidt, M., To, T.-D., & Zurbrugg, R. (2009). Computational Intelligence for Evolving Trading Rules. *IEEE Transactions on Evolutionary Computation, 13*(1), 71–86. DOI: 10.1109/TEVC.2008.915992

Golghar, Y., Roitman, L., & Neginsky, D. (2018). AI-powered wealth management products and investment vehicles. The WealthTech Book: The FinTech Handbook for Investors, Entrepreneurs and Finance Visionaries, 138-141.

Goodell, J., Kumar, S., Marc Lim, W., & Pattnaik, D. (2021). Artificial intelligence and machine learning in finance: Identifying foundations, themes, and research clusters from bibliometric analysis. *Journal of Behavioral and Experimental Finance, 32*, 32. DOI: 10.1016/j.jbef.2021.100577

Hansen, K. B. (2020). The virtue of simplicity: On machine learning models in algorithmic trading. *Big Data & Society, 7*(1), 2053951720926558. DOI: 10.1177/2053951720926558

Heaton, J., Polson, N., & Witte, J. (2016). Deep Portfolio Theory. arXiv:1605.07230.

Heaton, J. B., Polson, N. G., & Witte, J. H. (2017). Deep learning for finance: Deep portfolios. *Applied Stochastic Models in Business and Industry, 33*(1), 3–12. DOI: 10.1002/asmb.2209

Holzinger, A., Kieseberg, P., Weippl, E., & Tjoa, A. (2018). *Current Advances, Trends and Challenges of Machine Learning and Knowledge Extraction: From Machine Learning to Explainable AI. Machine Learning and Knowledge Extraction, 11015*. Springer.

Hu, Y., Liu, K., Zhang, X., Su, L., Ngai, E. W. T., & Liu, M. (2015). Application of evolutionary computation for rule discovery in stock algorithmic trading: A literature review. *Applied Soft Computing, 36*, 534–551. DOI: 10.1016/j.asoc.2015.07.008

Hu, Y., Zhang, X., Feng, B., Xie, K., & Liu, M. (2015). itrade: A mobile data-driven stock trading system with concept drift adaptation. [IJDWM]. *International Journal of Data Warehousing and Mining, 11*(1), 66–83. DOI: 10.4018/ijdwm.2015010104

Hung, S.-Y., Liang, T.-P., & Liu, V.-C.Victor Wei-Chi Liu. (1996). Integrating arbitrage pricing theory and artificial neural networks to support portfolio management. *Decision Support Systems, 18*(3-4), 301–316. DOI: 10.1016/S0167-9236(96)80006-6

Huynh, T. L. D., Hille, E., & Nasir, M. A. (2020). Diversification in the age of the 4th industrial revolution: The role of artificial intelligence, green bonds and cryptocurrencies. *Technological Forecasting and Social Change*, *159*, 120188. DOI: 10.1016/j.techfore.2020.120188

In, 0., Rook, D., & Monk, A. (2019). Integrating Alternative Data (Also Known as ESG Data) in Investment Decision Making. Global Economic Review, 48(3), 237-260.

Jaeger, M., Krügel, S., Marinelli, D., Papenbrock, J., & Schwendner, P. (2021). Interpretable machine learning for diversified portfolio construction. *The Journal of Financial Data Science*, *3*(3), 31–51. DOI: 10.3905/jfds.2021.1.066

Jang, J., & Seong, N. (2023). Deep reinforcement learning for stock portfolio optimization by connecting with modern portfolio theory. *Expert Systems with Applications*, *218*, 218. DOI: 10.1016/j.eswa.2023.119556

Javaid, H. A. (2024). AI-driven predictive analytics in finance: Transforming risk assessment and decision-making. Advances in Computer Sciences, 7(1).

Karoui, A. T., Sayari, S., Dammak, W., & Jeribi, A. (2024). Unveiling outperformance: A portfolio analysis of top AI-related stocks against IT indices and robotics ETFs. *Risks*, *12*(3), 52. DOI: 10.3390/risks12030052

Kasaraneni, R. K. (2021). AI-Enhanced Portfolio Optimization: Balancing Risk and Return with Machine Learning Models. *African Journal of Artificial Intelligence and Sustainable Development*, *1*(1), 219–265.

Khandani, A. E., Kim, A. J., & Lo, A. W. (2010). Consumer credit-risk models via machine-learning algorithms. *Journal of Banking & Finance*, *34*(11), 2767–2787. DOI: 10.1016/j.jbankfin.2010.06.001

Kondapaka, K. K. (2019). Advanced AI Models for Portfolio Management and Optimization in Finance: Techniques, Applications, and Real-World Case Studies. *Distributed Learning and Broad Applications in Scientific Research*, *5*, 560–597.

Kumar, K. R.. (2024). AI-Driven Robo-Advisors in Wealth Management. *Educational Administration: Theory and Practice*, *30*(5), 13478–13486.

Kumar, K. R., Balaji, C., Suresh, M., Nagaraju, E., Natarajan, S., & Kumar, R. (2024). Study The Impact Of Ai Driven Rob Advisors On Wealth Management Services. Evaluate Their Effectiveness In Portfolio Management, Risk Assessment, And Personalized Investment Strategies. *Educational Administration: Theory and Practice*, *30*(5), 13478–13486.

Kumar, S., Lim, W., Sivarajah, U., & Kaur, J. (2023). Artificial Intelligence and Blockchain Integration in Business: Trends from a Bibliometric-Content Analysis. *Information Systems Frontiers*, *25*, 871–896. PMID: 35431617

Kumar, S., Rao, S., Goyal, K., & Goyal, N. (2022). Journal of Behavioral and Experimental Finance: A bibliometric overview. *Journal of Behavioral and Experimental Finance*, •••, 34.

Lam, J. (2016). *Implementing Enterprise Risk Management: From Methods to Applications*. Wiley.

Le Trung, H. (2020). Deep Reinforcement Learning for Stock Portfolio Optimization. *International Journal of Modeling and Optimization*, *10*(5), 139–144. DOI: 10.7763/IJMO.2020.V10.761

Leo, M., Sharma, S., & Maddulety, K. (2019). Machine learning in banking risk management: A literature review. *Risks*, *7*(1), 29. DOI: 10.3390/risks7010029

Lima, M. A., Carvalho, P. C., Fernández-Ramírez, L. M., & Braga, A. P. (2020). Improving solar forecasting using Deep Learning and Portfolio Theory integration. *Energy*, *195*, 117016. DOI: 10.1016/j.energy.2020.117016

Machireddy, J. R., Rachakatla, S. K., & Ravichandran, P. (2021). AI-Driven Business Analytics for Financial Forecasting: Integrating Data Warehousing with Predictive Models. *Journal of Machine Learning in Pharmaceutical Research*, *1*(2), 1–24.

Maia, S., de Benedicto, G., do Prado, J., Robb, D., Bispo, O., & de Brito, M. (2019). Mapping the literature on credit unions: A bibliometric investigation grounded in Scopus and Web of Science. *Scientometrics*, *120*(3), 929–960. DOI: 10.1007/s11192-019-03165-1

Markowitz, H. (1952). Portfolio Selection. *The Journal of Finance*, *7*(1), 77–91.

Mashrur, A., Luo, W., Zaidi, N. A., & Robles-Kelly, A. (2020). Machine learning for financial risk management: A survey. *IEEE Access : Practical Innovations, Open Solutions*, *8*, 203203–203223. DOI: 10.1109/ACCESS.2020.3036322

Mazraeh, N., Daneshvar, A., zaj, M., & Roodposhti, F. (2022). Stock Portfolio Optimization Using a Combined Approach of Multi Objective Grey Wolf Optimizer and Machine Learning Preselection Methods. Computational Intelligence and Neuroscience- Hindawi.

Méndez-Suárez, M., García-Fernández, F., & Gallardo, F. (2019). Artificial Intelligence Modelling Framework for Financial Automated Advising in the Copper Market. *Journal of Open Innovation*, *5*(81), 81. DOI: 10.3390/joitmc5040081

Mohammadi, S., & Nazemi, A. (2020). On portfolio management with value at risk and uncertain returns via an artificial neural network scheme. *Cognitive Systems Research, 59*, 247–263. DOI: 10.1016/j.cogsys.2019.09.024

Mutran, V. M., Ribeiro, C. O., Nascimento, C. A., & Rêgo, E. E. (2018). Bioenergy investments in sugarcane mills: An approach combining portfolio theory with neural networks. *Computer-Aided Chemical Engineering, 44*, 967–972. DOI: 10.1016/B978-0-444-64241-7.50156-7

Nazemi, A., Heidenreich, K., & Fabozzi, F. J. (2018). Improving corporate bond recovery rate prediction using multi-factor support vector regressions. *European Journal of Operational Research, 271*(2), 664–675. DOI: 10.1016/j.ejor.2018.05.024

Ngai, E. W., Hu, Y., Wong, Y. H., Chen, Y., & Sun, X. (2011). The application of data mining techniques in financial fraud detection: A classification framework and an academic review. *Decision Support Systems, 50*(3), 559–569. DOI: 10.1016/j.dss.2010.08.006

Nguyen, T. P. L., Chew, L. W., Muthaiyah, S., Teh, B. H., & Ong, T. S. (2023). Factors influencing acceptance of Robo-Advisors for wealth management in Malaysia. *Cogent Engineering, 10*(1), 2188992. DOI: 10.1080/23311916.2023.2188992

Okeleke, P. A., Ajiga, D., Folorunsho, S. O., & Ezeigweneme, C. (2024). Predictive analytics for market trends using AI: A study in consumer behavior. *International Journal of Engineering Research Updates, 7*(1), 36–49. DOI: 10.53430/ijeru.2024.7.1.0032

Owolabi, O. S., Uche, P. C., Adeniken, N. T., Ihejirika, C., Islam, R. B., & Chhetri, B. J. T. (2024). Ethical implications of artificial intelligence (AI) adoption in financial decision-making. *Computer and Information Science, 17*(1), 1–49. DOI: 10.5539/cis.v17n1p49

Pai, N., & Ilango, V. (2020). Neural Network Model for Efficient portfolio Management and Time Series Forecasting. IEEE, *4th International Conference on Intelligent Computing and Control Systems (ICICCS)*, Madurai, India, 150-155. DOI: 10.1109/ICICCS48265.2020.9121049

Pandl, K., Thiebes, S., Schmidt-Kraepelin, M., & Sunyaev, A. (2020). On the Convergence of Artificial Intelligence and Distributed Ledger Technology: A Scoping Review and Future Research Agenda. *IEEE Access : Practical Innovations, Open Solutions, 8*, 57075–57095. DOI: 10.1109/ACCESS.2020.2981447

Perumalsamy, J., Althati, C., & Shanmugam, L. (2022). Advanced AI and Machine Learning Techniques for Predictive Analytics in Annuity Products: Enhancing Risk Assessment and Pricing Accuracy. *Journal of Artificial Intelligence Research*, *2*(2), 51–82.

Phoon, K. F., & Koh, C. C. F. (2018). Robo-advisors and wealth management. *Journal of Alternative Investments*, *20*(3), 79–94. DOI: 10.3905/jai.2018.20.3.079

Prado, J., Alcântara, V., Carvalho, F., Vieira, K., Machado, L., & Tonelli, D. (2016). Multivariate analysis of credit risk and bankruptcy research data: A bibliometric study involving different knowledge fields (1968---2014). *Scientometrics*, *106*(3), 1007–1029. DOI: 10.1007/s11192-015-1829-6

Rai, H. P., Padyana, U., & Patil, G. (2023). Real-time decision making in wealth management: The role of AI and predictive analytics. *ESP JETA*, *3*(2), 110–119.

Rather, A., Sastry, V., & Agarwal, A. (2017). Stock market prediction and Portfolio selection models: A survey. *OPSEARCH*, *54*(3), 558–579. DOI: 10.1007/s12597-016-0289-y

Reher, M., & Sokolinski, S. (2024). Robo advisors and access to wealth management. *Journal of Financial Economics*, *155*, 103829. DOI: 10.1016/j.jfineco.2024.103829

Ridzuan, N. N., Masri, M., Anshari, M., Fitriyani, N. L., & Syafrudin, M. (2024). AI in the financial sector: The line between innovation, regulation and ethical responsibility. *Information (Basel)*, *15*(8), 432. DOI: 10.3390/info15080432

Samo, Y.-L., & Vervuurt, A. (2016). Stochastic Portfolio Theory: A Machine Learning Perspective. arXiv:1605.02654 [q-fin.PM].

Shanmuganathan, M. (2020). Behavioural finance in an era of artificial intelligence: Longitudinal case study of robo-advisors in investment decisions. *Journal of Behavioral and Experimental Finance*, *27*, 27. DOI: 10.1016/j.jbef.2020.100297

Singh, G., Garg, V., & Tiwari, P. (2020). *Application of Artificial Intelligence on Behavioral Finance*. Springer. DOI: 10.1007/978-3-030-34152-7_26

Singh, I., & Kaur, N. (2017). Wealth management through robo advisory. *International Journal of Research-Granthaalayah*, *5*(6), 33–43. DOI: 10.29121/granthaalayah.v5.i6.2017.1991

Statista Robo-Advisors. (n.d.). Retrieved May 7, 2023, from https://www.statista.com/outlook/dmo/fintech/digital-investment/robo-advisors/worldwide

Stiglitz, J. E. (2014). Tapping the brakes: Are less active markets safer and better for the economy?.

Tang, W., & Wang, Y. (2004). Intelligent method for dynamic portfolio selection with probability criterion. IEEE International Conference on Systems, Man and Cybernetics (IEEE Cat. No.04CH37583).The Hague, Netherlands, 4, 3323-3327.

Weller, B. M. (2018). Does algorithmic trading reduce information acquisition? *Review of Financial Studies*, *31*(6), 2184–2226. DOI: 10.1093/rfs/hhx137

Wilson, H. J., Daugherty, P., & Bianzino, N. (2017). The jobs that artificial intelligence will create. *MIT Sloan Management Review*, *58*(4), 14–16.

Yadav, Y. (2015). How algorithmic trading undermines efficiency in capital markets. *Vanderbilt Law Review*, *68*, 1607.

Yang, L., & Zhu, H. (2020). Back-running: Seeking and hiding fundamental information in order flows. *Review of Financial Studies*, *33*(4), 1484–1533. DOI: 10.1093/rfs/hhz070

Zhong, X., & Enke, D. (2017). Forecasting daily stock market return using dimensionality reduction. *Expert Systems with Applications*, *67*, 126–139. DOI: 10.1016/j.eswa.2016.09.027

Chapter 2
Machine Learning in Finance:
The Revolutionized Fusion

Saifullahi Adam Bayero
SR University, India

Geetha Manoharan
https://orcid.org/0000-0002-8644-8871
SR University, India

Sanjeev Kumar
https://orcid.org/0000-0002-7375-7341
Lovely Professional University, India

ABSTRACT

The implementation of Machine Learning (ML) and Artificial Intelligence (AI) in the financial sector has led to a transformative shift in the industry which redefines traditional practices. These modern technologies have enabled financial institutions to make use of large amounts of data for accurate predictive modeling, personalized customer experiences, and automated decision-making processes. Among the dramatic changes we witnessed were the adoption of AI-driven robot advisors for personalized investment strategies, ML algorithms for real-time fraud detection, and AI-based credit scoring systems that improve lending accuracy. Naturally, advancements in sentiment analysis and risk measurement through natural language processing do enhance predictive market abilities. When these technologies progress, they promote increased efficiency, minimize costs, and provide more options in reaction to changes in financial markets. This study aims to point out the latest patterns being observed regarding ML and AI applications within finance.

DOI: 10.4018/979-8-3373-0129-7.ch002

INTRODUCTION TO ARTIFICIAL INTELLIGENCE AND MACHINE LEARNING IN THE FINANCIAL SECTOR

What AI and ML are doing is all about transforming the financial sector that was dominated by humans as well as traditional models and methods (Zheng et al., 2019). Until then, those technologies were just happening in academic research circles or Computer Science fields alone, but they have gone ahead to revolutionize the operations of financial institutions and competition among them (Paramesha et al., 2024). The coming together of finance with AI and ML goes beyond a mere technological innovation to represent a total transformation of its operational environment (Kirilyuk, 2022).Financial institutions can process huge amounts of data at speeds unimaginable to any human being using AI (Praveen Borra, 2024). These technologies are good at identifying trends, predicting scenarios, or even performing sophisticated tasks automatically—in an industry where there is so much information to analyze (Saini, 2024). For instance, in risk management, AI models can analyze both current market conditions and historical data in real-time thereby increasing their precision and enhancing forecasting accuracy (Paramesha et al., 2024). Therefore, this accuracy and insight were not possible before using conventional techniques.

There is so much work that has been done to show the revolutionary impact of AI and ML in trading, analytical models as well as in financial inclusion. AI tools that analyze real-time data mean traders are now in a position through microsecond intervals that enable them to make trades at a high frequency (Nguyen et al., 2023). The machine learning models trained on the market data history can make trading decisions on their own this indicates that they could self-adapt to new input directions leading to enhanced predictive capability (Rahmani et al., 2023).

And realizing accuracy in financial forecasts, artificial intelligence and machine learning work with vast and heterogeneous datasets that contain unstructured data from various sources, yielding maximum levels of accuracy in their respective field. By doing so they have leverage in predicting trends within markets helping in making sound financial decisions (N Rane et al., 2023). Among other AI-driven innovations that have contributed to the democratization of financial services through delivering personalized investment advice and credit access, are robo-advisors (Allen et al., 2021; G. Manoharan, et al., 2024). In any case, however, controversy around algorithmic bigotry or data leakage emerging from an AI integration is warranted (Maple et al., 2023).

Thankfully, it is very difficult to avoid the use of AI and ML in such an ever-evolving industry as finance. These technologies are altering how various types of banks work and provide better opportunities than what was obtainable before in risk management and fraud In the same way, it provide customer-centric services that were not possible before (Simhadri & Polireddi, 2024; Selvaraj et al., 2024). In the current market conditions as well as with ever-growing amounts of data, the application of AI and ML helps these institutions decisions faster and more accurately. Conventional financial models are not well-suited to this environment's fluidity, which means they can't operate without the assistance of these AI and ML systems (Sharbek, 2022).

As an example, one way AI (artificial intelligence) together with Machine learning (ML) has made a significant contribution towards finance is its application in credit-risk assessment and customer service based on alternative sources of data for better analysis and decision-making(Mhlanga, 2021). If these technologies are not adopted by financial institutions they will be left behind compared to flexible Fintech firms that utilize AI to change processes such as service delivery (Chowdhury et al., 2023).

Because of the complicated nature of global markets, a surge in data generation, and demand for quicker as well as better informed decisions this is why there is a growing interest in Artificial Intelligence (AI) and Machine Learning (ML). There has been a shift towards more complex models that can work on their own rather than depend on human intuition and historical trends. In addition, it has become necessary for such institutions to adopt artificial intelligence solutions that will reduce costs while at the same time improving customer satisfaction levels (Mhlanga, 2021). Such automation would include algorithmic trading, fraud detection systems, and risk management tools all of which are areas where AI can greatly assist (Bogojevic Arsic, 2021). Thus, if they want to remain competitive in the global finance market space, these banks should consider using advanced technologies based on AI principles (Padmaavathy, P. A., et al., 2024).

Jain et al., (2023), financial decision-making is being transformed by Machine Learning and Artificial Intelligence. This is mainly because these institutions can execute comprehensive data analysis quickly which enhances accuracy and efficiency in real time (G. Manoharan, et al., 2024). Besides that, fraud detection risk management and personalization have been very advanced through the use of these technologies thus revolutionizing service delivery in finance (El Hajj & Hammoud, 2023) (El Hajj & Hammoud, 2023). Though there are so many advancements taking place in AI systems today, some still grapple with transparency issues or even how they can be aligned with existing regulations on finance as stated by (Osterrieder, 2023) Osterrieder et al., (2023). In an attempt to solve these problems, financial managers have started making use of explainable Artificial Intelligence tools like SHAP that would enable them to understand AI-based anomaly detection hence making it easier for their organizations to adopt such technologies. It marks a new dawn for innovation in this sector as it shows the increasing importance of AI and ML in reshaping financial institutions and their services (Sabharwal et al., 2024).

That means any financial institution that does not englobe AI and ML will fall behind in the modern economies, amidst the obvious competition from the Fintech companies that embraced this technology to innovate and streamline services (Sinha & Lee, 2024). These technologies have now become right at the heart of modern finance, in a world where AI has been integrated into literally every aspect: handling the mass load of data, generating real-time insights, and so on (El Hajj & Hammoud, 2023). While many of those advantages are quite obvious, an array of challenges that are related to transparency, compliance with regulatory requirements, and ethics in the use of AI remain open, which means further research is needed in this direction (Osterrieder, 2023).

For the future of finance, it is crucial to comprehend the potentialities that AI and ML possess in transforming financial decision-making processes, increasing operating efficiencies, as well as minimizing risks assigned thereto (Sabharwal et al., 2024). The financial sector in this study uses AI and ML (Artificial Intelligence and Machine Learning). For example, data mining, pattern detection, classification text mining, and signal processing are some important attributes that AI and ML possess which help in unfolding how these technologies are changing finances. This paper will also take a look at the pros and cons associated with using AI and ML in finance.In an elaborate discourse, the paper intends to enlighten industry participants, policymakers, and scholars about the future implications of AI and ML on financial activities.

AI in Finance

The finance sector has significantly transformed due to artificial intelligence, which is applicable in many finance sectors such as fraud detection, portfolio management, market segmentation, stock price forecasting, and even detecting security anomalies (El Hajj & Hammoud, 2023). These changes have made it easier for companies in this sector to evaluate and control their risks, improve decision-making, and reduce transaction costs by optimizing quantitative trading strategies (Das et al., 2024)). The journey of the use of AI in credit scoring is impressive. Because it has helped to make better analyses and predictions about default risk and it has enhanced the safety of the financial institutions (Buchanan & Wright, 2021). In the future when it is fully developed one can expect even greater developments as far as finance is concerned leading to increased safety measures and fresh ideas.

The transformative nature of AI affects all aspects of the finance industry including trading, fraud prevention, customer service, portfolio optimization as well as total risk management (Paramesha et al., 2024; Yi et al., 2023). In particular, it has been successful at improving market and credit risk management model validation, stress testing, and data preparation processes (Bogojevic Arsic, 2021; Lim,

2024). This led the banking sector to witness a significant transformation owing to various AI technologies including, but not limited to, deposit applications, lending services, insurance systems, payment methods as well as investment management and capital markets (Cao, 2018; Ozbayoglu et al., 2020).

Yet it turns out that there are major considerations in ethics attached to using AI for financial decision making this is why we have them here. Some of these factors include the need for high-quality data; bias in algorithms owned by AI; and the use of AI to make investment decisions (Kurshan et al., 2021). Data privacy, regulatory compliance, and ethical issues must be taken into account so that AI can be adopted in the right way by finance companies (Kurshan et al., 2021).

Integration of Artificial Intelligence (AI) and machine learning with financial markets is growing rapidly especially in areas like algorithmic trading risk management fraud detection credit scoring while at the same time serving customers (Sarin et al., 2024). The potential exists for these technologies to enhance investment decisions through market movement prediction and will consider how investors behave. Nevertheless, some serious challenges remain including the urgent need for top-notch data and instances when AI algorithms may be biased (Zheng et al., 2023).

So too does the finance industry face significant obstacles in validating AI models especially when it comes to developing validation norms and frameworks for sophisticated AI algorithms that go beyond credit risk into other sectors (Osterrieder, 2023). Often financial institutions experience such challenges as a lack of understanding of technological infrastructure, insufficient capital inflow, minimal staff awareness, and poor partnerships with IT (Al-Baity, 2023).

Integrating AI into financial institutions starts with overcoming these challenges, which include regulatory compliance, data privacy, and ethical considerations. As a result, professionals and organizations must adjust their skills and methods to the changing demands (Maple et al., 2023). Moving forward, the financial services industry is anticipated to be redefined by artificial intelligence in a significant way through its impacts on processes, products, services, and customer involvement. It is estimated that AI could yield an important monetary profit that may amount up to nearly $1 trillion by 2030 for the banking sector (Rane et al., 2024).

Machine Learning in Finance

The finance area is revolutionizing the financial sector with extensive research showing that it gets integrated in standard financial models such as econometrics and forecasting. For instance, Karachun et al., (2021) show that neural networks can help facilitate the analysis and decision-making processes. The utilization of statistical surrogates like neural networks combined with Gaussian processes to achieve better option pricing accuracy while improving model calibration in quantitative finance is further substantiated by their achievements (Ludkovski, 2023). Fraud detection, risk management, and portfolio optimization have received important applications suggested by (Pistoia et al., 2021) while Mironowicz et al., (2024) see QML as a promising horizon. Case studies presented by Mathur, (2018) show that machine learning (ML) can be applied in many ways across various financial settings and to assist business expansion.

Probably when writing out financial applications regarding algorithmic trading machine learning (ML) should be considered at all times for its vast capacity to utilize big data efficiently. The areas include; predicting stock market trends, assessing credit risks, detecting fraud, and optimizing portfolios every one of them relying on big data so that they run smoothly and effectively (Lin et al., 2023; Sen & Das, 2023; D. Song, 2022). ML has also reached into behavioral economics and finance with some focus on investor sentiment, decision making and consumer behavior although there are still gaps in research (Hojaji et al., 2022; Motwani et al., 2024; Manoharan, G., Jyothi, B. S., et al., 2024). By ML's ability to find out rational relations from large populations, it becomes very useful in determining default probabilities on bonds predicting appropriate loan amounts as well as suggesting best investment strategies. However, for computational finance to take full advantage of machine learning's potential/machines have to be trained using robust models whose predictions can be understood (Hoang & Wiegratz, 2023; Hojaji et al., 2022).

The Machine Learning (ML) discipline also enhances risk management through accurate stock market forecasting, credit risk assessment, and fraud detection by analyzing large datasets (Kour, 2023). These algorithms have proved their usefulness in analyzing and predicting various risk factors thereby contributing to the stability of financial institutions (Almoubayyed et al., 2023). On the contrary, ML is more flexible than traditional statistical techniques in managing diverse complex patterns of risk across various financial domains (Abdulla & Al-Alawi, 2024; Garg et al., 2024). On the other hand, whenever ML is used in financial decision-making it brings about some ethical issues such as algorithmic explain ability, data quality, and privacies; therefore, utmost care has to be taken so that maximum benefits can be realized without necessarily incurring so much harm as estimated (Bejjar & Siala, 2024; El Hajj & Hammoud 2023). More so, for this to happen financial institutions must adopt increased openness and develop requisite capabilities within themselves (Kumar et al., 2024).

Furthermore, some issues have been identified to be associated with the application of ML in finance agencies such as; model robustness, model interpretability, quality of data, and lastly, issues of regulation. This is a result of the conflict between the two major schools of thought in ML and the research philosophy of finance economics (Ahmad et al., 2024). Frequently in conventional applications of ML, adjustment is required primarily in terms of addressing characteristics of financial markets (Kour, 2023; Tripathi, 2019). Notwithstanding all these limitations that exist; ML still has great potential for future investigation and development offering significant benefits compared with traditional approaches (Lommers et al., 2021; Natarajan et al., 2024). Furthermore, algorithmic trading continues to be influenced by machine learning showing its capacity to handle intricate financial systems and address global economic (Shukla, et al., 2024) challenges inter alia aggravated by the COVID-19 pandemic -(Milojević & Redzepagic, 2021; Sen & Das, 2023).

Evolution of Finance

The financial journey is quite complicated, as shown by some of the keys to understanding from Bonis and Pozzolo, (2016). Hence, one must constantly keep pace with the recent financial innovations and development of analytical instruments that are crucial to comprehending the ever-changing nature of finance (Song & Thakor, 2010). The architecture of financial systems is not constant but rather evolves through competition, complementarily, and co-evolution between banks and markets. It can be seen from this that securitization and bank equity capital have played vital roles in this evolution as indicated by Nesvetailova, (2014).

The structural strength of finance has been enhanced by financial innovation-a central theme in this evolution of a complex ecological system. This system exhibits a notable degree of autonomy and an amazing ability to adapt and develop as economic theory incorporates finance. Models that explain this integration show how financial instruments and companies have evolved together. However, often the public's attention on financial power oscillates with political clout changes and associated income levels (Epstein & Jayadev, 2019). Moreover, finance constantly stretches its reach into diverse institutions, and technical infrastructures including both public and private sectors thereby frequently disrupting existing orders (Sassen, 2000).

Lo, (2021) highlights how finance has changed dramatically throughout the ages as a result of a complex interaction between technological innovations, the demands of the economy and government regulations. The Adaptive Markets Hypothesis gives us a good lens in understanding this evolution by applying principles from evolutionary biology and ecology to our monetary system. Historical analysis shows that finance has gone through eight distinct "ages" with each characterized by different combinations of economic needs and technological advancements leading to the development of new financial products, services, and institutions (Ferguson, 2009). Analyzing financial history from an evolutionary perspective unveiled a rich "biodiversity" in this arena marked by a drive for financial innovation which significantly influenced areas like trading operations, credit-risk modeling, and corporate strategy among others (Brabazon, 2018).

The consequence of market and institution financial change has been severe resulting in a " hypermarket" hatched by consumer-targeted factors and technological progress and computerization (Ülgen, 2014). Nonetheless, this evolution carries certain dangers. At times, even though they are the engines of development, financial innovations can also incite irresponsible behaviors that undermine long-term economic stability (Nesvetailova, 2014). The structural power of finance is depicted in its capacity to adapt, alter, and develop which makes it independent from politics, society, and economy (Raj et al., 2024). This function is more important for emerging economies since there is a close relationship between the quality of their institutions and the progress of their financial markets (Aman et al., 2023).

New studies show that technology is responsible for all developments in finances because it creates FinTech which enhances new financial inventions and makes them more vibrant (Nithya, G., Manoharan, G., & Ashtikar, S. P., 2024). Changes in how we engage, process operations, and run finance services are what constitute transformative shifts caused by this technological revolution (Erić, 2022). Furthering this point, Ahmed et al., (2015) note that the moment the digital revolution took over it changed significantly how finance-related activities are carried out with emphasis on what FinTech means to various actors in such industry. The fact that creative individuals rely increasingly on technology to modify the way we think about money underscores its growing importance as a driving force behind continuous reform within the sector.

In the future, there might be a growing need for ongoing and reasonable rules to direct capitalist finance toward more proper ways of making a profit that is stable and lead to general improvement, especially after periods of financial chaos (Ülgen, 2014). Modern finance has entered a new phase of development similar to Industrial Revolution 4.0 with irreversible processes that promise further changes and innovations (Erić, 2022). The integration of technology advancements, financial innovation, and adequate regulation has contributed significantly to the birth of a transformed and progressive financial system by amalgamating all these elements together in one place forever at once in time and space. This transformation is still ongoing due to several forces that show how mobile finance is today on the world stage (Ashtikar, S. P., & Manoharan, G., 2024).

Feature of AI in Finance

We observe great changes happening in the financial sector thanks to AI which has made it possible for different tasks to be automated within this industry, and improved decision-making abilities. It has also improved control over risks as well as enhanced customer experience in banking (Manoharan, G., Nithya, G., et al., 2024). The reason behind this is that AI can assess abundant information which allows banks and other financial institutions to manage their diverse business aspects (Sangeetha, et al., 2024). For instance, AI employs different data including social media activity to evaluate whether a person should receive loans or not (Maple et al., 2023). AI also takes part in algorithmic trading where it takes trades at an unimaginable speed while coming up with strategies on how to go about it (Cao, 2018). The trends prediction as well as the risk anticipation, for example, defaulting on loans can be done more easily by financial institutions using AI-driven predictive analytics which assists an institution in making strategic decisions (Rane et al., 2024). Additionally through automation of repetitive processes such as data entering or payment processing machine learning helps not only cut down on costs but also eliminates human error enabling an organization to concentrate more on focusing its resources on development and customer care excellence (Andriosopoulos et al., 2019).

AI is crucial for managing risks, especially in terms of fraud detection. Machine learning algorithms can learn continuously by processing historical datasets and honing their ability to identify as well as preempt fraudulent acts (Maree et al., 2020). To illustrate this point one way through which AI does it is flagging atypical transactions like a huge withdrawal and thus encouraging further examination by the bank (Tsaih et al., 2014). On top of that, there are AI-enabled customer assistive technologies such as chatbots and online assistance services that offer round-the-clock individualized help. They do many tasks such that they may give explanations or economic advice thereby improving overall user experience (Zhou & Jiang, 2023). You could visualize a situation whereby a chatbot aids a client in knowing their account balance or asks for loan products anytime at all hence making the provision of financial services simpler and more user-friendly (Maree & Omlin, 2021). In line with this, it can be said that as AI advances its contribution towards finance will inter alia increase and consequently it becomes part and parcel of modern-day banking sectors. And with sophisticated analytics plus improved decision-making skills is ushering in new standards of efficiency, accuracy as well and client satisfaction within different areas of finance.

Pros and Cons of AI in Finance

Through time, artificial intelligence (AI) has completely transformed industries like finance bringing both good and bad things to it. This is because there has been an improvement in efficiency of financial institutions than before (Sharma & Manhas, 2023). These scientists are quite knowledgeable about this subject and they have based their explanation on what it does for them. The main advantage of AI is increased performance since complex jobs can now be automated and sound recommendations made with lower prices also involved in this process. Consequently, enhanced operational efficiency allows firms to utilize their resources optimally which leads to increased revenue generation while at the same time reducing expenditure (Shakdwipeeetal.,2023).

Shakdwipee et al. (2023) also observe that customer experience has been vastly improved because of AI. Interaction with customers through machine learning technologies and analysis of big data allows computers to act more personally towards them, predict their future wants before even being voiced or provide accurate insights about their personal choices. This not only fulfills clients' wishes but also helps in cementing cords between banks and the people who use them. In addition, Balavenu et al., (2022) indicated that there are other advantages resulting from financial industry transformation due to artificial intelligence such as enhanced risk management. There is an increasing application of AI strategies in fraud detection, portfolio optimization, and general risk assessment. By looking at large amounts of data in real time, it can identify possible threats and irregularities that would otherwise slip through the hands of human analysts enabling the protection of monetary properties as well as securing compliance with regulations (Shakdwipee et al., 2023; Sharma & Manhas, 2023).

By the predictive characteristics of the technology, all components in fiscal administration were removed. AI models get enhanced accuracy, such as changing using the algorithmic trading approach or establishing assets based on prior statistics and existing trends in the financial markets (Balavenu et al., 2022). Therefore, this leads to the ability of finance specialists to point their decisions and not make random decisions hence minimizing chances of losses while at the same time maximizing returns on investment (Lahmini & Zine, 2024). However, the application of AI has its difficulties when applied to the field of finance. One of the important considerations is the data quality upon which these artificial intelligence systems rely. Said or prejudiced data entails wrong conclusions that in effect, produce wrong decision-making processes. Also, due to the interpretability issue, stakeholders cannot understand or rely on what these algorithms bring about generating ethical and regulatory issues (Shakdwipee et al., 2023).Further, Shakdwipee et al., (2023) highlighted that while the phenomenon is not yet fully adopted there are certain significant disadvantages; more especially as it relates to the implementation and integration cost factor. Many organizations are struggling with this issue because they need to integrate these technologies into their systems that predate them but maintain the financial company's relevance in a technologically driven world. Still, a much harder test is presented especially when third-party vendors take it since it entails scaling complexities among other things like preserving confidential business information. Furthermore, the factor of labor transition should be of utmost importance as it may lead to job elimination/unemployment when shifting to AI-based operations thus, additional costs such as retraining costs which otherwise would not have been incurred when dealing with a human workforce only. As much as this device is very useful in serving risk management purposes in a dynamic environment, there are risks inherent in it. Financial institutions must confront the very complexity involved in dealing with AI systems and their propensity for increasing market volatility headlong (Li, 2020). Although AI has got various benefits within the financial sector, including: enhanced efficiency and improved customer experience it also faces some challenges.

Features of Machine Learning in Finance

Financial technology has been transformed by machine learning (ML) which has effectively increased efficiency, accuracy, and decision-making in fields such as pattern recognition, financial econometrics, and statistical computing (Karachun et al., 2021). Banks and fintech firms are using ML algorithms more easily than other financial institutions for forecasting financial risks, automating processes, or giving real-time investment advice (Zakaria et al., 2023). With the immense size and complexity of the resulting data sets involved in the finance sector, including stock market prediction, credit risk evaluation, fraud detection or portfolio optimization (Sivakumar, P., et al., 2024). Thus it is suitable for the application of ML techniques (Liao, 2024).

Because it implies enhancement in decision-making processes, decrease of risks, more satisfying customer experience among others, the influence of ML on financial indicators is great. For instance Predictive Analytics makes use of ML Algorithms that analyze past data from big databases in order to predict trends in stock prices and other economic indicators which would therefore help both investors and institutions make informed decisions (Owolabi et al., 2024; Bhavya, K. R., et al., 2024). Furthermore, it is also used to improve credit scoring through ML models which determine how much an individual or a company could repay on their loans depending on their transaction history including what they buy and their social behavior resulting into fairer evaluation (Nazemi & Fabozzi, n.d.).

ML models are how unusual behaviors in transactions are identified for purposes of anti-fraud detection (Ali et al., 2022; Gandhar et al., 2024). This is because these models are capable of learning new data continuously; for that matter, they become more adept at identifying and preventing fraud as strategies evolve (Zakaria et al., 2023). One example is in risk management where ML helps out by making sure an investor gets value for his money in terms of investing optimally taking into consideration historical data plus the current situation as it pertains to the marketplace as well (Liao, 2024). Also, to conduct a stress test on portfolios and thereby stand guard against the newly emerging players and potential threats, financial firms employ ML (Liao, 2024).

In the realm of algorithmic trading, this technology excels because high-frequency trading models include the execution of trades in a very short period and at high volumes using tiny price differences among different markets to eliminate human error so as to enhance profits (Addy et al., 2024; Karachun et al., 2021). Furthermore, ML allows market analysis by utilizing sentiment analysis where programs analyze investors' perceptions using news articles, social media updates (Senjith, A et al., 2024) and other texts that can be studied alongside stock prices (Koelbl et al., 2024).

Another way to explain this is by making sure that businesses do not end up on penalties or other administrative measures by regulating them at a lower cost of enforcement while providing timely preventive actions (Xin et al., 2021). Using their machine learning algorithms they collect and process relevant data from various sources like social media or news articles trying to find out warnings about possible disruptions in its area of operation by comparing this information with that contained in an organization's database (Mullankandy, 2024). Thus, these models are used by the top regulation bodies for decision-making so as not to be left behind with changes taking place within the sector (Gursky, 2025). Some of the preventive mechanisms embraced by RegTech solutions are risk profiling and alerting authorities when people receive big sums of money through abnormal channels, among others where prior identification of potential money laundering cases is possible (Tillu et al., 2023). For several years now, financial companies have been including machine learning models in their operations as they often offer higher quality service compared to traditional transaction analysis (Zheng et al., 2024).

Machine learning makes it easier to analyze transaction data, social media activity and other behavioral signals for predicting customers' needs to enable proactive engagement through personalized service offerings based on sentiment and behavior analysis (Koelbl et al., 2024). In addition, as investor sentiments help them make informed decisions, ML models examine how public perceives different companies or industries (Fakhouri et al., 2023) hence the incorporation of machine learning (ML) in biometric identification has improved security when using for example voice or face recognition systems for online banking authentication or account logins.

Data management and analysis are also transformed by machine learning, which includes algorithms that analyze and process big data in finance to extract results that might be impossible using old-fashioned methods (Sarker, 2021). With machine learning (ML), it is possible to make data analysis in real-time; hence institutions will quickly adjust themselves when there are changes in the market or new risks. Even with difficulties surrounding model robustness, interpretability, data quality and compliance with regulation (ML) aid research in finance such as estimation, discovery empirical, testing causal inference and prediction (Karachun et al., 2021). In the future as technology continues advancing, more integration of ML into financial systems will take place leading to further changes in the deliverance of financial services and consumption patterns. Nevertheless, due to the particular characteristics of financial markets and the social science's empirical framework, traditional ML methods have to be adjusted for these sophisticated tools to address specific challenges facing the finance industry (Sarker, 2021).

Pros and Cons of Machine Learning in Finance

In a transformative way, the banking sector can be disrupted by machine learning (ML). Some areas where ML is making strides include decision-making, risk management, fraud detection, and client services among others. One major benefit of this technology is that it can analyze huge volumes of financial data within minutes and present them precisely leading to good investments decisions, improved market prophecy as well as adequate risk evaluation (Al-Baity, 2023). The ML models are known to be superior in identifying complex trends that may have gone unnoticed before thus decreasing risks associated with credit scoring and portfolio management than any other method (Zheng et al., 2024). Apart from that, ML has been contributing to more developments in counter-fraud systems by illustrating abnormal characteristics in the transactions or preventing unauthorized trade within real-time (Saini, 2024). For instance, automated trading systems employ the use of machine learning algorithms for order execution in the process which makes it possible for one to gain competitiveness from small changes in the prices which may differ by minutes in financial markets (Paramesha et al., 2024). It has also favored customers by giving them what they want in terms of financial products and services thus improving their quality and effectiveness while satisfying customers (Ridzuan et al., 2024).

Despite its numerous advantages finance has big challenges when it comes to using ML in this sector. One of the major issues is that ML models are sensitive to data quality; in other words, if there are any contaminated or trusted values, prediction accuracy will drop, which also affects monetary decisions that depend on it (Maple et al., 2023). Another challenge facing ML models is over fitting because they may perform very well with historical data but not with changing market conditions. Most ML algorithms have 'black box' nature therefore it is difficult to understand how they arrive at their decisions making them controversial particularly in finance industry where deep learning is applied (Sarker et al., 2024). Furthermore, they are quite expensive to implement or maintain since setting up infrastructure and hiring professionals comes with high cost (Barta & Görcsi, 2019). Also there are ethical and regulatory issues related to the use of this technology for credit scoring and lending (VY, 2023). Finally, it has been noted that there are cybersecurity treats associated with ML systems that must be continuously updated along with the requirement of human supervision due to market fluctuations thereby turning into an expensive business endeavor (Sarker et al., 2024).

In sum, there is a great opportunity for machine learning to transform finance by better decision making and automation of processes although this technology has some limitations that need solving. One important aspect of keeping accuracy in banks and other related financial institutions may include having a proper management of data quality and checking whether any sign of change in model exists (Sinha & Lee, 2024). In areas such as banking and finance which are heavily regulated, it is important for transparency especially to adhere to some compliance regulations. The advantage of machine learning can only be exploited by ensuring regulatory compliance and upholding ethical standards (Ratzan & Rahman, 2023).

Discussion

The combination of Artificial Intelligence (AI), and Machine Learning (ML) specifically into finance is one of the most important revolutions which changes in core values of that sector (Jain, S., et al., 2024). This transformation is a move away from traditional financial practices to tech-driven methods which further enhance operational efficiencies, improve risk management strategies, and overall decision-making processes. Financial institutions can, for instance, analyze a lot of information with AI and ML thus getting revelations previously never seen which increases dependability of forecasts hence enhancing decision-making processes leading to knowledge-based actions. Through predictive algorithms, the key to risk assessment and management revolution comes as firms use past and real time data to identify possible threats or irregularities in markets. It facilitates better credit risk management, fraud detection, and thus banks are able to make proactive decisions instead of reactive ones, by driving market volatility in various sectors (Manoharan, G., Ashtikar, S. P., & Kumar, S., 2024).

Technological advancement has also extended into the management of investment where the use of robo-advisors has also played a great role in the management of investment portfolios for everyone. Self-directed investors can now control their own portfolios employing their own algorithms, which not only helps to reduce the effect of mistakes and bias, but also to increase efficiency and profitability at the same time. Such a level of performance and accuracy of these trades cannot be matched even by human traders taking into consideration the sophisticated market patterns the trades work upon. Algorithmic trading approach in the use of ML models achieving time-efficient trade through high-frequency trading systems for instant profit-making implementation has also transformed the speed of the trades and their efficiency.

At your own wishes, I won't prevent you from using this service. This means that when encountering the information given above, there is much one is yet to discover, in terms of potential approaches to take. In summary, modern finance has received a massive boost with chat bots and virtual assistant that has enhanced customers' experience through real time response and 24/7 support thus enabling the provision of first hand individualized touch at scale. Because of this, they are able to offer individualized financial advice hence increasing their client satisfaction and loyalty by effectively and accurately responding to their demands.

However, AI and machine learning have come along with their own problems in finance. The first question mark is if organizations can adopt such systems safely because they possess huge amounts of individual or financial data which raises doubts on privacy; compliance with rules; or even abuse by third parties. Furthermore, there is minimal clarity on many AI applications where decisions are reached without any rational basis thus raising queries about that bear responsibility or whether such decisions are fair? Essentially this means that those financial systems which utilize black box algorithms will find it hard to earn people's trust. Additionally, high implementation costs coupled with job losses due to job automation complicate matters further making it hard for these technologies become common practice.

Also, as long as AI and ML continue to grow, they are going to reshape the future of finance very fundamentally. In the future, the landscape will be formed by a continuously sophisticated and automated financial service at the heart of data-driven insight and real-time analytics. Financial institutions have to navigate this revolution with ethical considerations, regulatory compliance, and transparency. Policymakers will need to develop robust frameworks that balance the scales on data privacy and algorithmic accountability-a Goldilocks balance in which advances in technology could culminate in the erosion of consumer trust. The financial practitioners will need to be tuned into such emerging technologies in order to exploit their efficiencies and manage the risks in deploying them.

The integration of AI and ML is not only increasing the scope of existing practices in finance but also laying the ground for a new era in finance. This requires cooperation, from a policymaker to a financial expert, on how to handle the challenges and ethical issues that come about with each new innovation. This way, they can be guaranteed that the benefits of AI and ML will be equitably and sustainably realized to chart a path toward a more efficient, transparent, and inclusive financial future.

In conclusion, AI and ML in finance is a good area which should be conducted with caution during its implementation to balance between the principles, responsibility and control by government regulators. These novelties will define how finance is going to develop in the future, as well as the ethical, operational and social aspects associated with this field (Ananthan, M., et al., 2024). However, with the rate of advancement of AI and machine learning technology in finance as this, they have a sustainable base on how well companies understand how to integrate innovation into existing practices while maintaining a genuine sense of honesty and the human factor (Durai, S., Manoharan, G., & Ashtikar, S. P., 2024).

CONCLUSION

The integration of Artificial Intelligence and Machine Learning disrupts completely the finance industry and the way the companies in that particular sector operate and make decisions as well as provide services to their customers. The scope and precise accuracy that these technologies can deliver alongside the efficiency and personalization should allow finance to be more responsive to changes in demand from all over the world. AI and ML's use in the financial industry is already showing worth in service delivery in areas such as risk management, fraud detection, and even when providing clients with personal services in investment. Such integration however comes with several obstacles that require solutions in the effort to encourage sustainable and ethical use. The first crucial condition that needs to be maintained is to allow regulation to progress in line with the technological revolution; the second important condition that needs to be observed is the absolute clarity and sensitivity of the handling of data by banks. This transition to an advanced stage of AI is mainly possible due to the proper usage of AI that should follow the fundamental principle of finance. The application of AI and ML will discontinue finance amid growth impulses that foster innovation; however, there will be a revolution in the operations of financial institutions. Thus, it is possible to conclude that to leverage these technologies is to achieve the right balance between opportunities for tomorrow's world of economics on the one hand and the risks on the other.

REFERENCES

Abdulla, Y. Y., & Al-Alawi, A. I. (2024). Advances in Machine Learning for Financial Risk Management: A Systematic Literature Review. *2024 ASU International Conference in Emerging Technologies for Sustainability and Intelligent Systems, ICETSIS 2024*, 531–535. https://doi.org/DOI: 10.1109/ICETSIS61505.2024.10459536

Addy, W. A., Ajayi-nifise, A. O., Bello, B. G., & Tula, S. T. (2024). Machine learning in financial markets : A critical review of algorithmic trading and risk management. *International Journal of Science and Research Archive*, *11*(01), 1853–1862. DOI: 10.30574/ijsra.2024.11.1.0292

Ahmad, A. Y. B., Gupta, P., Thimmiaraja, J., Goswami, B., Arun, M., Manoharan, G., & Younis, D. (2024). A Comparison of the Effects of Robotics and Artificial Intelligence on Business Management and Economics. In *Recent Advances in Management and Engineering* (pp. 132–137). CRC Press. DOI: 10.1201/9781003532026-22

Ahmed, I., Forde, B., Laplanche, R., Mitra, A., Prida Bay, N., & Scandurra, A. (2015). The Fintech Revolution. *London Business School Review*, *3*, 50–53.

Al-Baity, H. H. (2023). The Artificial Intelligence Revolution in Digital Finance in Saudi Arabia: A Comprehensive Review and Proposed Framework. *Sustainability (Basel)*, *15*(18), 13725. Advance online publication. DOI: 10.3390/su151813725

Ali, A., Razak, S. A., Othman, S. H., Abdalla, T., Eisa, E., Al-dhaqm, A., Nasser, M., Elhassan, T., Elshafie, H., & Saif, A. (2022). applied sciences Financial Fraud Detection Based on Machine Learning : A Systematic Literature Review. Applied Sciences Review, 12(9637.). https://doi.org/DOI: 10.3390/app12199637

Allen, F., Gu, X., & Jagtiani, J. (2021). A Survey of Fintech Research and Policy Discussion. *Review of Corporate Finance*, *1*(3–4), 259–339. DOI: 10.1561/114.00000007

Almoubayyed, H., Bastoni, R., Berman, S. R., Galasso, S., Jensen, M., Lester, L., & Murphy, A. Swartz1, M., Weldon, K., Fancsali, S. E., Gropen, J., & Ritter, S. (2023). Rewriting Math Word Problems to Improve Learning Outcomes for Emerging Readers: A Randomized Field Trial in Carnegie Learning's MATHia. In Artificial Intelligence in Education (pp. 200–205). https://doi.org/DOI: 10.1007/978-3-031-36336-8_34

Aman, A., Khan, M. A., Khan, M. A., Haider, A., Oláh, J., & Fenyves, V. (2023). Role of institutions in promoting finance in emerging markets: A panel data analysis. PLoS ONE, 18(3 March), 1–26. https://doi.org/DOI: 10.1371/journal.pone.0280849

Ananthan, M., Shanmugam, V., Udayanan, M., Selvaraj, F., & Manoharan, G. (2024, June). Corporate social responsibility is used as a marketing strategy during Covid-19 pandemic. In AIP Conference Proceedings (Vol. 2971, No. 1). AIP Publishing. DOI: 10.1063/5.0195948

Andriosopoulos, D., Doumpos, M., Pardalos, P. M., & Zopounidis, C. (2019). Computational approaches and data analytics in financial services : A literature review. *The Journal of the Operational Research Society*, *70*(10), 1–19. DOI: 10.1080/01605682.2019.1595193

Ashtikar, S. P., & Manoharan, G. (2024, June). Digital Transformation in Higher Education: A Pedagogical Perspective. In 2024 3rd International Conference on Computational Modelling, Simulation and Optimization (ICCMSO) (pp. 210-215). IEEE. DOI: 10.1109/ICCMSO61761.2024.00051

Ashtikar, S. P., & Manoharan, G. (2024, June). Work-Load Management and Job Gratification: A Study on the Work-life Equilibrium of Higher Education Instructors. In 2024 3rd International Conference on Computational Modelling, Simulation and Optimization (ICCMSO) (pp. 193-197). IEEE. DOI: 10.1109/ICCMSO61761.2024.00048

Balavenu, R., Khan, A. K., Faisal, S. M., Sriprasadh, K., & Sisodia, D. R. (2022). An Empirical Investigation in Analysing the Proactive Approach of Artificial Intelligence in Regulating the Financial Sector. In Balas, V. E., Sinha, G. R., Agarwal, B., Sharma, T. K., Dadheech, P., & Mahrishi, M. (Eds.), *Emerging Technologies in Computer Engineering Cognitive Computing and Intelligent IoT* (Vol. 1591, pp. 90–98). Springer Nature Switzerland., DOI: 10.1007/978-3-031-07012-9_8

Bejjar, M. A., & Siala, Y. (2024). Machine learning: A revolution in accounting. In *Artificial Intelligence Approaches to Sustainable Accounting* (pp. 110–134). IGI Global., DOI: 10.4018/979-8-3693-0847-9.ch007

Bhavya, K. R., Dharmaraj, A., Pareek, P., Sathe, M. A., Tiwari, M., & Manoharan, G. (2023, September). Application of Soft Computing Techniques for Predictive Analytics in Financial Markets. In 2023 6th International Conference on Contemporary Computing and Informatics (IC3I) (Vol. 6, pp. 1756-1760). IEEE.

Bogojevic Arsic, V. (2021). Challenges of Financial Risk Management: AI Applications. Management:Journal of Sustainable Business and Management Solutions in Emerging Economies, 1–7. https://doi.org/DOI: 10.7595/management.fon.2021.0015

Borra, P. (2024). The Evolution and Impact of Google Cloud Platform in Machine Learning and AI. International Journal of Advanced Research in Science. *Tongxin Jishu*, *4*(3), 72–77. Advance online publication. DOI: 10.48175/IJARSCT-18908

Brabazon, A. (2018). Grammatical Evolution in Finance and Economics: A Survey. In Ryan, C., O'Neill, M., & Collins, J. J. (Eds.), *Handbook of Grammatical Evolution* (pp. 1–497). Springer International Publishing AG., DOI: 10.1007/978-3-319-78717-6_11

Buchanan, B. G., & Wright, D. (2021). The impact of machine learning on UK financial services. *Oxford Review of Economic Policy*, *37*(3), 537–563. DOI: 10.1093/oxrep/grab016 PMID: 34642572

Cao, L. (2018). AI in Finance: A Review. *SSRN*, *9*(39). Advance online publication. DOI: 10.2139/ssrn.3647625

Chowdhury, M. A., Sahabuddin, D. M., Miyan, M. U., Sozon, M., & Miah, M. T. (2023). Assessing The Evolution of Fintech Adoption In Traditional Banking : A Bibliometric Analysis Using R. *Journal of Management and Economic Studies*, *5*(3), 153–164. DOI: 10.26677/TR1010.2023.1349

Das, S. K., Anwar, D. S., Tulsyan, U., Gupta, Y., Vudatha, R., & Gardezi, D. S. H. I.Sunil Kumar Das. (2024). The Role of AI in Financial Markets: Impacts on Trading, Portfolio Management, and Price Prediction. *Journal of Electrical Systems*, *20*(6s), 1000–1006. DOI: 10.52783/jes.2804

De Bonis, R., & Pozzolo, A. F. (2016). Financial Systems: Introduction and Summary. In De Bonis, R., & Pozzolo, A. F. (Eds.), *The Financial Systems of Industrial Countries Evidence from Financial Accounts* (pp. 1–23). Springer-Verlag Berlin., DOI: 10.1007/978-3-642-23111-7_1

Durai, S., Manoharan, G., & Ashtikar, S. P. (2024). Harnessing Artificial Intelligence: Pioneering Sustainable Solutions for a Greener Future. In Social and Ethical Implications of AI in Finance for Sustainability (pp. 89-117). IGI Global.

El Hajj, M., & Hammoud, J. (2023). Unveiling the Influence of Artificial Intelligence and Machine Learning on Financial Markets: A Comprehensive Analysis of AI Applications in Trading, Risk Management, and Financial Operations. *Journal of Risk and Financial Management*, *16*(10), 434. Advance online publication. DOI: 10.3390/jrfm16100434

Epstein, G. A., & Jayadev, A. (2019). *The Rise of Rentier Incomes in OECD Countries*. Financialization, Central Bank Policy and Labor Solidarity. In The Political Economy of Central Banking., DOI: 10.4337/9781788978415.00022

Erić, D. (2022). Innovation and Fintech. In Vukovic, D. B., Maiti, M., & Grigorieva, E. M. (Eds.), *Digitalization and the future of financial services : innovation and impact of digital finance* (pp. 19–39). Springer Nature., DOI: 10.1007/978-3-031-11545-5_2

Fakhouri, H. N., Alawadi, S., Awaysheh, F. M., Hani, I. B., Alkhalaileh, M., & Hamad, F. (2023). A Comprehensive Study on the Role of Machine Learning in 5G Security : Challenges, Technologies, and Solutions. *Electronics (Basel)*, *12*(4604), 1–44. DOI: 10.3390/electronics12224604

Ferguson, N. (2009). An evolutionary approach to financial history. Cold Spring Harbor Symposia on Quantitative Biology, 74(Economist 2008), 449–454. https://doi.org/DOI: 10.1101/sqb.2009.74.050

Gandhar, A., Gupta, K., Kumar, A., & Dharm, P. (2024). Fraud Detection Using Machine Learning and Deep Learning. *SN Computer Science*, *5*(453), 453. Advance online publication. DOI: 10.1007/s42979-024-02772-x

Garg, D., Shelke, N. A., Kitukale, G., & Mehlawat, N. (2024). Leveraging Financial Data and Risk Management in Banking sector using Machine Learning. 9th International Conference for Convergence in Technology, I2CT 2024, 10544336. https://doi.org/DOI: 10.1109/I2CT61223.2024.10544336

Hoang, D., & Wiegratz, K. (2023). Machine learning methods in finance: Recent applications and prospects. *European Financial Management*, *29*(5), 1657–1701. DOI: 10.1111/eufm.12408

Hojaji, S. N., Yahyazadehfar, M., & Abedin, B. (2022). Machine learning in behavioral finance: A systematic literature review. *The Journal of Financial Data Science*, *4*(3), 129–151. DOI: 10.3905/jfds.2022.1.100

Jain, R., Jain, S., & Jain, D. (2023). CRITICAL REVIEW ON APPLICATIONS OF AI & ML IN FINANCE. SSRN Electronic Journal. https://doi.org/DOI: 10.2139/ssrn.4399885

Jain, S., Satyala, H., Ranjit, P. S., Tatsiana, V., Patil, D. T., Manoharan, G., & Chakravarthi, D. S. (2024). Artificial Intelligence's Implications on Project Management. In Recent Technological Advances in Engineering and Management (pp. 105-109). CRC Press. DOI: 10.1201/9781003531395-22

Karachun, I., Vinnichek, L., & Tuskov, A. (2021). Machine learning methods in finance. SHS Web of Conferences, 110, 05012. https://doi.org/DOI: 10.1051/shsconf/202111005012

Kirilyuk, I. L. (2022). model risKs in the financial sphere under the conditions of the use of artificial intelligence and machine learning. *Russian Journal of Economics and Law*, *16*(1), 54–76. DOI: 10.21202/2782-2923.2022.1.40-50

Koelbl, M., Laschinger, R., Steininger, B. I., Schaefers, W., Koelbl, M., Laschinger, R., Steininger, B. I., & Schaefers, W. (2024). Revealing the risk perception of investors using machine learning. *European Journal of Finance*, *30*(17), 2032–2058. Advance online publication. DOI: 10.1080/1351847X.2024.2364831

Kour, M. (2023). Challenges and opportunities of machine learning in the financial sector. In *Algorithmic Approaches to Financial Technology* (pp. 61–73). Forecasting, Trading, and Optimization., DOI: 10.4018/979-8-3693-1746-4.ch004

Kumar, A., Kumar, A., Kumari, S., Kumar, S., Kumari, N., & Behura, A. K. (2024). Artificial Intelligence: The Strategy of Financial Risk Management. Finance. *Theory into Practice*, *28*(3), 174–182. DOI: 10.26794/2587-5671-2024-28-3-174-182

Kurshan, E., Chen, J., Storchan, V., & Shen, H. (2021). On the current and emerging challenges of developing fair and ethical AI solutions in financial services. In ICAIF 2021 - 2nd ACM International Conference on AI in Finance. Association for Computing Machinery. https://doi.org/DOI: 10.1145/3490354.3494408

Lahmini, H. M., & Zine, D. (2024). The Role of Artificial Intelligence in Optimizing Portfolio Management : A Literature Review. International Conference on Business and Technology, ICBT, 122–131. https://doi.org/DOI: 10.1007/978-3-031-67444-0_12

Li, P. (2020). Research on the application and security of artificial intelligence in financial industry. *IOP Conference Series: Materials Science and Engineering*. https://doi.org/DOI: 10.1088/1757-899X/750/1/012102

Liao, X. (2024). Machine Learning Algorithm Applications in Empirical Finance: A Review of the Empirical Literature. *3rd International Conference on Economic Development and Business Culture (ICEDBC 2023)*, 311–316. https://doi.org/DOI: 10.2991/978-94-6463-246-0_38

Lim, T. (2024). Environmental, social, and governance (ESG) and artificial intelligence in finance: State-of-the-art and research takeaways. In Artificial Intelligence Review (Vol. 57, Issue 4). Springer Netherlands. https://doi.org/DOI: 10.1007/s10462-024-10708-3

Lin, C. C., Tseng, C. H., & Ho, S. L. (2023). Applying Random Forest Algorithm and Mean-Variance Model in Portfolio Optimization in the China Stock Market. Eurasia Conference on IOT, Communication and Engineering, ECICE 2023, 361–364. https://doi.org/DOI: 10.1109/ECICE59523.2023.10382968

Lo, A. W. (2021). The Financial System Red in Tooth and Claw: 75 Years of Co-Evolving Markets and Technology. *Financial Analysts Journal, 77*(3), 5–33. DOI: 10.1080/0015198X.2021.1929030

Lommers, K., El Harzli, O., & Kim, J. (2021). Confronting Machine Learning with Financial Research. *The Journal of Financial Data Science, 3*(3), 67–96. DOI: 10.3905/jfds.2021.1.068

Ludkovski, M. (2023). Statistical Machine Learning for Quantitative Finance. *Annual Review of Statistics and Its Application, 15*(19), 271–295. DOI: 10.1146/annurev-statistics-032921-042409

Manoharan, G., Ali, S. D. N. H., Sathe, D. M., Karthik, A., Nagpal, A., & Sidana, A. "Fraud Detection in E-commerce Transactions: A Machine Learning Perspective," *2024 International Conference on Advances in Computing, Communication and Applied Informatics (ACCAI)*, Chennai, India, 2024, pp. 1-5, DOI: 10.1109/ACCAI61061.2024.10601813

Manoharan, G., Ashtikar, S. P., & Kumar, S. (2024). Extenuating Digital Transformation: Revolutionizing Hotel Operations Through AI Technology. In Talukder, M., Kumar, S., & Tyagi, P. (Eds.), *Hotel and Travel Management in the AI Era* (pp. 257–274). IGI Global., DOI: 10.4018/979-8-3693-7898-4.ch012

Manoharan, G., Ashtikkar, S. P., & Nivedha, M. (2024). Artificial Intelligence in Decision-Making: Reinventing Business Strategies. In Generative AI for Transformational Management (pp. 25-50). IGI Global.

Manoharan, G., Jyothi, B. S., Bhat, R., Acharjee, P. B., Sharma, A., & Rawal, P. (2023, December). Utilizing Machine Learning for Advanced Natural Language Processing and Sentiment Analysis in Social Media Platforms. In International Conference on Mechanical and Energy Technologies (pp. 111-125). Singapore: Springer Nature Singapore.

Manoharan, G., Mishra, A. B., Adusumilli, S. B. K., Chavva, M., Damancharla, H., & Sahaya Lenin, D. "Supervised Learning for Personalized Marketing Strategies," *2024 International Conference on Advances in Computing, Communication and Applied Informatics (ACCAI)*, Chennai, India, 2024, pp. 1-6, DOI: 10.1109/ACCAI61061.2024.10602307

Manoharan, G., Nithya, G., Rajchandar, K., Razak, A., Gupta, S., Durai, S., & Ashtikar, S. P. (2024). AI in Finance and Banking: The Act of Gyration. In Revolutionizing Customer-Centric Banking Through ICT (pp. 1-28). IGI Global.

Manoharan, G., Nithya, G., Razak, A., Durai, S., Sharma, S., & Ashtikar, S. P. (2024). Enhancing Financial Literacy: Strategies, Challenges, and Global Initiatives. In Singh, D., Bansal, R., Gupta, S., & Ansari, Y. (Eds.), *Emerging Perspectives on Financial Well-Being* (pp. 111–128). IGI Global., DOI: 10.4018/979-8-3693-1750-1.ch006

Manoharan, G., Nithya, G., Razak, A., Sharma, S., & Ashtikkar, S. P. (2024). Challenges and Opportunities in Green Finance: Overcoming Barriers and Scaling up Sustainable Investments. In Misra, S., Jadeja, R., & Mittal, M. (Eds.), *Practical Approaches to Agile Project Management* (pp. 398–413). IGI Global., DOI: 10.4018/979-8-3693-3318-1.ch022

Manoharan, G., & Rajoli, S. B. (2024). Leveraging Technology for Enhancing Performance Appraisal. In Employee Performance Management for Improved Workplace Motivation (pp. 289-310). IGI Global. DOI: 10.4018/979-8-3693-4387-6.ch012

Maple, C., Szpruch, L., Epiphaniou, G., Staykova, K., Singh, S., Penwarden, W., Wen, Y., Wang, Z., Hariharan, J., & Avramovic, P. (2023). The AI Revolution: Opportunities and Challenges for the Finance Sector. http://arxiv.org/abs/2308.16538

Maree, C., Modal, J. E., & Omlin, C. W. (2020). Towards Responsible AI for Financial Transactions. *2020 IEEE Symposium Series on Computational Intelligence (SSCI)*. https://doi.org/DOI: 10.1109/SSCI47803.2020.9308456

Maree, C., & Omlin, C. W. (2021). Understanding Spending Behavior : Recurrent Neural Network Explanation and Interpretation. https://doi.org//arxiv.2109.11871DOI: 10.48550

Mathur, P. (2018). Machine learning applications using python: Cases studies from healthcare, retail, and finance. *Apress Media, LLC*. Advance online publication. DOI: 10.1007/978-1-4842-3787-8

Mhlanga, D. (2021). Financial Inclusion in Emerging Economies : The Application of Machine Learning and Artificial Intelligence in Credit Risk Assessment. *International Journal of Financial Studies*, *9*(39), 39. DOI: 10.3390/ijfs9030039

Milojević, N., & Redzepagic, S. (2021). Prospects of Artificial Intelligence and Machine Learning Application in Banking Risk Management. *Journal of Central Banking Theory and Practice*, *10*(3), 41–57. DOI: 10.2478/jcbtp-2021-0023

Mironowicz, P., Mandarino, A., Yilmaz, A., & Ankenbrand, T. (2024). Applications of quantum machine learning for quantitative finance. arXiv preprint arXiv:2405.10119.

Motwani, B., Haryani, S., Manoharan, G., & Razak, A. (2024). Impact of Workforce Emotional Intelligence on Patient Satisfaction: A Sentiment Analysis Approach Using Supervised Machine Algorithms. In Rajapakshe, W. (Ed.), *Employee Performance Management for Improved Workplace Motivation* (pp. 263–288). IGI Global., DOI: 10.4018/979-8-3693-4387-6.ch011

Mullankandy, S. (2024). Transforming Data into Compliance : Harnessing AI / ML to Enhance Regulatory Reporting Processes Introduction : Objectives : Method : Journal of Artificial Intelligence General Science (JAIGS), 24(1). https://ojs.boulibrary.com/index.php/JAIGS%0ATransforming

Natarajan, S., Salgotra, P., Krishna, M. H., Revathi, V., Sobti, R., & Adhav, S. (2024). Risk Management in Financial Institutions with Applied Machine Learning. International Conference on Communication, Computer Sciences and Engineering, IC3SE 2024, 1514–1519. https://doi.org/DOI: 10.1109/IC3SE62002.2024.10593631

Nazemi, A., & Fabozzi, F. J. (n.d.). Interpretable Machine Learning for Creditor Recovery Rates. 1–32.

Nesvetailova, A. (2014). Innovations, fragility and complexity: Understanding the power of finance. In Government and Opposition (Vol. 49, Issue 3, pp. 542–568). Cambridge University Press. https://doi.org/DOI: 10.1017/gov.2014.12

Nguyen, D. K., Sermpinis, G., & Stasinakis, C. (2023). Big data, artificial intelligence and machine learning: A transformative symbiosis in favour of financial technology. *European Financial Management*, *29*(2), 517–548. DOI: 10.1111/eufm.12365

Nithya, G., Manoharan, G., & Ashtikar, S. P. (2024). India's Fintech and AI-Related Regulation Framework. In The Adoption of Fintech (pp. 51-72). Productivity Press.

Osterrieder, J. (2023). Machine Learning for Asset Management:Revolutionizing Financial Analysis and Decision-Making with Data Science Techniques. SSRN Electronic Journal. https://doi.org/DOI: 10.2139/ssrn.4638186

Owolabi, O. S., Uche, P. C., Adeniken, N. T., Efijemue, O., Attakorah, S., Emi-johnson, O. G., & Hinneh, E. (2024). Comparative Analysis of Machine Learning Models for Customer Churn Prediction in the U. S. Banking and Financial Services : Economic Impact and Industry-Specific Insights. *Journal of Data Analysis and Information Processing*, *12*(3), 388–418. DOI: 10.4236/jdaip.2024.123021

Ozbayoglu, A. M., Gudelek, M. U., & Sezer, O. B. (2020). Deep learning for financial applications: A survey. *Applied Soft Computing*, *93*, 106384. DOI: 10.1016/j.asoc.2020.106384

Padmaavathy, P. A., Manoharan, G., Billa, P., Purushottamashtikar, S., Selvaraj, F., & Razak, A. (2024, June). Retail customers' utilization of bank kiosk among selected private sector banks in coimbatore. In AIP Conference Proceedings (Vol. 2971, No. 1). AIP Publishing.

Paramesha, M., Rane, N., & Rane, J. (2024). Artificial intelligence, machine learning, deep learning, and blockchain in financial and banking services: A comprehensive review. [PUMRJ]. *SSRN*, *01*(02), 68–83. DOI: 10.2139/ssrn.4855893

Pistoia, M., Ahmad, S. F., Ajagekar, A., Buts, A., Chakrabarti, S., Herman, D., Hu, S., Jena, A., Minssen, P., Niroula, P., Rattew, A., Sun, Y., & Yalovetzky, R. (2021). Quantum Machine Learning for Finance. https://doi.org/DOI: 10.1109/ICCAD51958.2021.9643469

Rahmani, A. M., Rezazadeh, B., Haghparast, M., Chang, W. C., & Ting, S. G. (2023). Applications of Artificial Intelligence in the Economy, Including Applications in Stock Trading, Market Analysis, and Risk Management. *IEEE Access : Practical Innovations, Open Solutions*, *11*(July), 80769–80793. DOI: 10.1109/ACCESS.2023.3300036

Raj, R., Dimitrov, B. G., Acharya, B., Lourens, M., Ashtikar, S. P., & Manoharan, G. (2024). The Influence of Power and Politics on Human Resource Management. In *Recent Advances in Management and Engineering* (pp. 286–290). CRC Press. DOI: 10.1201/9781003532026-51

Rane, N., Choudhary, S., & Rane, J. (2023). Education 4.0 and 5.0: Integrating Artificial Intelligence (AI) for Personalized and Adaptive Learning. SSRN Electronic Journal, 1(1), 29–43. https://doi.org/DOI: 10.2139/ssrn.4638365

Rane, N. L., Choudhary, S. P., & Rane, J. (2024). Artificial Intelligence-driven corporate finance: Enhancing efficiency and decision-making through machine learning, natural language processing, and robotic process automation in corporate governance and sustainability. *Studies in Economics and Business Relations*, *5*(2), 1–22. DOI: 10.48185/sebr.v5i2.1050

Ratzan, J., & Rahman, N. (2023). Measuring responsible artificial intelligence (RAI) in banking : A valid and reliable instrument. *AI and Ethics*, *0123456789*. Advance online publication. DOI: 10.1007/s43681-023-00321-5

Ridzuan, N. N., Masri, M., Anshari, M., Fitriyani, N. L., & Syafrudin, M. (2024). AI in the Financial Sector : The Line between Innovation, Regulation and Ethical Responsibility. *Information (Basel)*, *15*(432), 1–30. DOI: 10.3390/info15080432

Sabharwal, R., Miah, S. J., Wamba, S. F., & Cook, P. (2024). Extending application of explainable artificial intelligence for managers in financial organizations. *Annals of Operations Research*. Advance online publication. DOI: 10.1007/s10479-024-05825-9

Saini, A. (2024). The Impact of Business Analytics in the Finance Industry. SSRN Electronic Journal. https://doi.org/DOI: 10.2139/ssrn.4843086

Sangeetha, M., Gupta, R., Reddy, K. S., Nanda, C. S. K., Mannar, B. R., Manoharan, G., & Liudmyla, I. (2024). Detailed Investigation of Digital Transformational Strategies to Enhance Business Productivity. In Recent Advances in Management and Engineering (pp. 45-51). CRC Press. DOI: 10.1201/9781003532026-8

Sarin, S., Singh, S. K., Kumar, S., Goyal, S., Gupta, B. B., Alhalabi, W., & Arya, V. (2024). Unleashing the Power of Multi-Agent Reinforcement Learning for Algorithmic Trading in the Digital Financial Frontier and Enterprise Information Systems. *Computers, Materials & Continua*, *80*(2), 3123–3138. DOI: 10.32604/cmc.2024.051599

Sarker, I. H. (2021). Machine Learning : Algorithms, Real - World Applications and Research Directions. *SN Computer Science*, *2*(3), 1–21. DOI: 10.1007/s42979-021-00592-x PMID: 33778771

Sarker, I. H., Janicke, H., Amine, M., & Abuadbba, A. (2024). Internet of Things Multi-aspect rule-based AI : Methods, taxonomy, challenges and directions towards automation, intelligence and transparent cybersecurity modeling for critical infrastructures. Internet of Things, 25(September 2023), 101110. https://doi.org/DOI: 10.1016/j.iot.2024.101110

Sassen, S. (2000). Is High-Finance an Extractive Sector? *Indiana Journal of Global Legal Studies*, *25*(2), 583–593. DOI: 10.2979/indjglolegstu.25.2.0583

Selvaraj, F. J., Sheeja, R., Manoharan, G., Razak, A., Kukreja, J., & Ashtikar, S. P. (2024, June). Evaluation of Customer Loyalty and Customer Relationship Management in Mobile Communication Lesson from New Normal. In 2024 3rd International Conference on Computational Modelling, Simulation and Optimization (ICCMSO) (pp. 216-221). IEEE. DOI: 10.1109/ICCMSO61761.2024.00052

Sen, R., & Das, S. (2023). Supervised Learning. In Computational Finance with R (pp. 1–351). Springer Nature Singapore. https://doi.org/DOI: 10.1007/978-981-19-2008-0_20

Senjith, A., Manoharan, G., Razak, A., Rao, C. B., Kukreja, J., & Ashtikar, S. P. (2024, June). Social Media Marketing: Does it Create Impact on Women Entrepreneurs. In 2024 3rd International Conference on Computational Modelling, Simulation and Optimization (ICCMSO) (pp. 222-227). IEEE.

Shakdwipee, P., Agarwal, K., Kunwar, H., & Singh, S. (2023). Artificial Intelligence in Finance and Accounting: Opportunities and Challenges. In Tuba, M., Akashe, S., & Joshi, A. (Eds.), *ICT Systems and Sustainability* (Vol. 765, pp. 165–177). Springer Nature Singapore Pte Ltd., DOI: 10.1007/978-981-99-5652-4_17

Sharbek, N. (2022). How Traditional Financial Institutions have adapted to Artificial Intelligence, Machine Learning and FinTech? *Proceedings of the International Conference on Business Excellence*, 16(1), 837–848. DOI: 10.2478/picbe-2022-0078

Sharma, P., & Manhas, S. (2023). The future of finance: Revolutionizing the industry with artificial intelligence. Leveraging AI and Emotional Intelligence in Contemporary Business Organizations, 187–210. https://doi.org/DOI: 10.4018/979-8-3693-1902-4.ch011

Shukla, S. S., Rajput, K., Tripathi, S., Gambhir, V., Manoharan, G., Bukhari, S. N. H., & Younis, D. (2024). Artificial Intelligence as a Contributing Factor for Economic Growth and Sustainable Development among Emerging Economies. In *Recent Advances in Management and Engineering* (pp. 39–44). CRC Press. DOI: 10.1201/9781003532026-7

Simhadri, N., & Polireddi, A. (2024). Measurement : Sensors An effective role of artificial intelligence and machine learning in banking sector. Measurement: Sensors, 33(November 2023), 101135. https://doi.org/DOI: 10.1016/j.measen.2024.101135

Sinha, S., & Lee, Y. M. (2024). Challenges with developing and deploying AI models and applications in industrial systems. *Discover Artificial Intelligence*, *4*(55), 55. Advance online publication. DOI: 10.1007/s44163-024-00151-2

Sivakumar, P., Pillai, A. D., Manoharan, G., Rajesh, G. A., Razak, A., & Ashtikar, S. P. (2024, June). Blockchain technology moving beyond cryptocurrencies in finance sector. In AIP Conference Proceedings (Vol. 2971, No. 1). AIP Publishing. DOI: 10.1063/5.0195724

Song, D. (2022). Application of Machine Learning in Finance. In B. J. Jansen, H. Liang, & J. Ye (Eds.), International Conference on Cognitive based Information Processing and Applications (CIPA 2021) (Vol. 85, pp. 543–549). Springer Nature. https://doi.org/DOI: 10.1007/978-981-16-5854-9_69

Song, F., & Thakor, A. V. (2010). Financial system architecture and the co-evolution of banks and capital markets. *Economic Journal (London), 120*(547), 1021–1055. DOI: 10.1111/j.1468-0297.2009.02345.x

Tillu, R., Muthusubramanian, M., & Periyasamy, V. (2023). From Data to Compliance : The Role of AI / ML in Optimizing Regulatory Reporting Processes RBC Capital Markets, USA Discover Financial Services, USA Hexaware Technologies, USA. *Journal of Knowledge Learning and Science Technology, 2*(3). Advance online publication. DOI: 10.60087/jklst.vol2.n3.p391

Tripathi, V. (2019). On present use of machine learning based automation in finance. 11th International Joint Conference on Knowledge Discovery, Knowledge Engineering and Knowledge Management, 3(k), 412–418. https://doi.org/DOI: 10.5220/0008480504120418

Tsaih, R.-H., Lin, H.-W. W., & Ke, W. (2014). An Abductive-Reasoning Guide for Finance Practitioners. *Computational Economics, 43*(4), 411–431. DOI: 10.1007/s10614-013-9390-y

Ülgen, F. (2014). Schumpeterian economic development and financial innovations: A conflicting evolution. *Journal of Institutional Economics, 10*(2), 257–277. DOI: 10.1017/S1744137414000022

Vy, N. N. T.VY. (2023). Ai implementation in odr: A game-changer or a troublemaker of data protection. *Vietnamese Journal of Legal Sciences, 08*(01), 1–24. DOI: 10.2478/vjls-2023-0001

Xin, D., Wu, E. Y., Lee, D. J.-L., Salehi, N., & Parameswaran, A. (2021). Whither AutoML? Understanding the Role of Automation in Machine Learning Workflows. *CHI Conference on Human Factors in Computing Systems (CHI '21)*. https://doi.org/DOI: 10.1145/3411764.3445306

Yi, Z., Cao, X., Chen, Z., & Li, S. (2023). Artificial Intelligence in Accounting and Finance: Challenges and Opportunities. *IEEE Access : Practical Innovations, Open Solutions, 11*(November), 129100–129123. DOI: 10.1109/ACCESS.2023.3333389

Zakaria, N., Sulaiman, A., Min, F. S., Feizollah, A., Zakaria, N., Sulaiman, A., Min, F. S., & Feizollah, A. (2023). Machine learning In the financial industry : A bibliometric approach to evidencing applications MEDIA & COMMUNICATION STUDIES | REVIEW ARTICLE Machine learning In the financial industry : A bibliometric approach to evidencing applications. *Cogent Social Sciences, 9*(2), 2276609. Advance online publication. DOI: 10.1080/23311886.2023.2276609

Zheng, L., Wang, C., Chen, X., Song, Y., Meng, Z., & Zhang, R. (2023). Evolutionary machine learning builds smart education big data platform: Data-driven higher education. *Applied Soft Computing*, *136*, 110114. DOI: 10.1016/j.asoc.2023.110114

Zheng, X., Gildea, E., Chai, S., Zhang, T., & Wang, S. (2024). Data Science in Finance: Challenges and Opportunities. *AI*, *5*(1), 55–71. DOI: 10.3390/ai5010004

Zheng, X., Zhu, M., Li, Q., Chen, C., & Tan, Y. (2019). FinBrain: When finance meets AI 2.0. *Frontiers of Information Technology & Electronic Engineering*, *20*(7), 914–924. DOI: 10.1631/FITEE.1700822

Zhou, Y., & Jiang, R. (2023). Advancing Explainable AI Toward Human-Like Intelligence : Forging the Path to Artificial Brain. https://doi.org//arxiv.2402.06673DOI: 10.48550

Chapter 3
Internal Auditor:
Soft Skills and Hard Skills in the Era of Artificial Intelligence

Ghina Awad
https://orcid.org/0009-0002-4636-7134
ICN Business School, France

ABSTRACT

The rise of artificial intelligence (AI) has significantly transformed the internal auditing profession, introducing new challenges and opportunities that demand a blend of technical expertise and interpersonal skills. As AI reshapes auditing processes, internal auditors are required to adapt to an era of rapid technological advancements, leveraging AI-driven tools for enhanced efficiency and accuracy. Simultaneously, they must ensure that these technologies are used ethically, transparently, and in compliance with regulatory standards. This book explores the dual competencies—technical and soft skills—necessary for auditors to excel in this evolving landscape. By examining critical areas such as data analytics, cybersecurity, emotional intelligence, and adaptability, it provides a comprehensive roadmap for auditors to navigate the complexities of AI-enhanced auditing. Through actionable insights and strategies, this book aims to equip internal auditors with the tools to uphold the integrity of their profession while embracing the transformative potential of AI.

INTRODUCTION

The advent of artificial intelligence (AI) has profoundly reshaped the internal auditing profession, ushering in a new era filled with both unprecedented challenges and significant opportunities. This transformative technology has introduced a dynamic landscape where internal auditors must go beyond traditional practices

DOI: 10.4018/979-8-3373-0129-7.ch003

and adapt to innovative methods. To thrive in this environment, auditors need a unique blend of technical expertise and interpersonal skills that enable them to leverage AI-driven tools while maintaining the ethical and regulatory standards that are the backbone of their profession. AI is revolutionizing how audits are conducted, offering tools that enhance efficiency, improve accuracy, and provide deeper insights into data. Internal auditors are now tasked with mastering these advanced technologies, such as machine learning algorithms, predictive analytics, and real-time monitoring systems, to streamline processes and uncover risks that would have been challenging to detect using conventional methods. However, with these advancements comes the responsibility of ensuring that AI tools are implemented in a manner that is ethical, transparent, and compliant with ever-evolving regulatory frameworks.This book delves into the essential dual competencies required for success in this rapidly changing field: technical skills and soft skills. On the technical front, internal auditors must develop expertise in areas such as data analytics, machine learning, cybersecurity, and automation. These hard skills are fundamental for navigating the technical intricacies of AI systems and for enhancing the overall effectiveness of the auditing process. At the same time, the book emphasizes the indispensable role of soft skills, including communication, collaboration, adaptability, and emotional intelligence. These skills ensure that auditors can bridge the gap between complex technologies and the human elements of their roles, such as stakeholder engagement and ethical oversight. Each chapter of this book is designed to provide a comprehensive exploration of the key areas that are shaping the future of internal auditing. Topics such as advanced data analytics and cybersecurity will equip auditors with the technical knowledge needed to harness the power of AI responsibly. Meanwhile, discussions on emotional intelligence and adaptability will highlight how interpersonal skills are critical for navigating the nuanced challenges of human-AI collaboration. Through these insights, readers will gain a clear understanding of how to balance technological acumen with the human-centered aspects of auditing.In addition to exploring the required competencies, this book offers practical strategies and actionable guidance for internal auditors aiming to excel in an AI-driven environment. It addresses critical questions, such as how to stay updated with emerging technologies, foster a culture of ethical AI use, and build resilience in the face of rapid industry changes. By integrating these strategies into their professional practice, auditors can not only maintain the integrity of their work but also position themselves as valuable contributors to their organizations. Ultimately, this book aims to serve as both a guide and a resource for internal auditors navigating the complexities of AI-enhanced auditing. By providing a roadmap that bridges the technical and interpersonal dimensions of the profession, it empowers auditors to adapt to technological advancements while safeguarding the principles of transparency, accountability, and ethical governance. Through this balanced approach, internal auditors can embrace the transformative potential of AI while ensuring they remain indispensable in a rapidly evolving industry.

1- THE ROLE OF INTERNAL AUDITORS IN THE AGE OF AI

The role of internal auditors in the age of Artificial Intelligence (AI) is becoming increasingly significant as financial institutions navigate the complexities of integrating advanced technologies into their operations. Internal auditors are tasked with ensuring that AI systems are implemented effectively, ethically, and in compliance with regulatory standards. This literature review synthesizes various studies that explore the evolving responsibilities of internal auditors in the context of AI, highlighting the opportunities and challenges they face. One of the primary roles of internal auditors in an AI-driven environment is to enhance the effectiveness of auditing practices. Thottoli discusses how leveraging information communication technology (ICT) and AI can significantly improve auditing processes by automating routine tasks and enhancing data analysis capabilities Thottoli (2024). This automation allows internal auditors to focus on more complex and value-added activities, such as risk assessment and strategic decision-making. By embracing AI technologies, internal auditors can improve the efficiency and effectiveness of their audits, ultimately contributing to better organizational governance. Moreover, the study by Ríkharðsson et al. emphasizes the expectations and applications of AI in auditing, particularly for small- and medium-sized enterprises (SMEs) (Ríkharðsson et al., 2022). As AI technologies become more accessible, internal auditors in these organizations can leverage AI to enhance their auditing capabilities, thereby increasing trust in the audit process. This shift towards AI-augmented auditing is expected to create a competitive advantage for firms that adopt these technologies, as clients increasingly seek assurance that their financial statements are accurate and reliable. However, the integration of AI in auditing also presents challenges that internal auditors must address. Karmila's research highlights the determinants of fraud prevention and the critical role of internal audit quality in mitigating risks (Karmila, 2024). As AI systems are implemented, internal auditors must ensure that these technologies are used responsibly and ethically to prevent potential abuses and fraud. This responsibility requires auditors to possess a deep understanding of AI technologies and their implications for risk management and compliance. The ethical considerations surrounding AI adoption in auditing are further explored by Ayling and Chapman, who examine the importance of ethical governance in the context of AI (Ayling & Chapman, 2021). The study underscores the necessity for internal auditors to navigate the complexities of algorithmic decision-making and ensure that AI systems operate transparently and fairly. By fostering an ethical culture within organizations, internal auditors can help mitigate the risks associated with AI adoption. Additionally, Zhao's research on voluntary internal audit practices emphasizes the need for internal auditors to adapt to the changing landscape brought about by AI technologies (Zhao, 2023). As AI continues to evolve, auditors must stay informed about the latest developments and best practices in AI auditing to maintain their effectiveness. This commitment to continuous learning and professional development is essential for internal auditors to remain relevant and effective in their roles.

2- MASTERING AI TOOLS FOR INTERNAL AUDITING

In the age of Artificial Intelligence (AI), the role of internal auditors is evolving significantly as they adapt to new technologies that enhance their auditing capabilities. Mastering AI tools is essential for internal auditors to improve efficiency, accuracy, and effectiveness in their audits. This literature review synthesizes various studies that explore the integration of AI in internal auditing, the skills required for auditors, and the implications of these advancements for the auditing profession. AI technologies offer substantial opportunities for enhancing the internal audit function. Wassie discusses how AI can provide actionable predictions that assist internal auditors in making informed insights Wassie (2024). By automating routine tasks and analyzing large datasets, AI tools can help auditors identify anomalies, assess risks, and enhance the overall quality of audits. This shift allows internal auditors to focus on more strategic activities, such as risk management and compliance monitoring, thereby adding greater value to their organizations. Moreover, the study by Thottoli emphasizes the importance of leveraging information communication technology (ICT) and AI to enhance auditing practices (Thottoli, 2024). The integration of these technologies enables auditors to conduct more comprehensive analyses and improve the accuracy of their findings. As AI continues to evolve, internal auditors must develop the skills necessary to effectively utilize these tools, including data analytics, machine learning, and automation techniques. The ethical implications of AI adoption in auditing are also critical to consider. Tabbassum highlights the need for regular ethical audits of AI systems to ensure compliance with ethical standards and to identify potential biases (Tabbassum, 2024). Internal auditors play a vital role in conducting these audits, ensuring that AI technologies are used responsibly and transparently. By fostering an ethical culture within organizations, internal auditors can help mitigate the risks associated with AI adoption and build trust with stakeholders. Furthermore, the research by Rawashdeh indicates that AI-based audit services can significantly impact client trust (Rawashdeh, 2023). As organizations increasingly rely on AI for auditing processes, internal auditors must ensure that these technologies deliver value and maintain high standards of quality. The ability to demonstrate the effectiveness of AI-driven audits is essential for building and maintaining client trust in the auditing profession. The challenges associated with AI adoption in internal auditing are also noteworthy. Monteiro discusses how the intensity of AI adoption positively contributes to the quality of internal control systems (Monteiro, 2023). However, the implementation of AI technologies requires significant investment in training and infrastructure to ensure that auditors are equipped with the necessary skills to leverage these tools effectively. This investment is crucial for maintaining the quality and reliability of audits in an increasingly digital environment. Moreover, the study by Odeyemi highlights the transformative role of AI in auditing practices (Odeyemi, 2023). Traditional auditing methods, often constrained by manual processes, are being supplanted by AI-driven approaches that offer comprehensive analysis and real-time insights. This shift enables auditors to identify anomalies, fraud, and operational inefficiencies more effectively, thereby improving the overall accuracy and reliability of audit outcomes.

3- DATA ANALYTICS FOR AUDITORS: TURNING DATA INTO INSIGHTS

Data analytics has emerged as a transformative force in the auditing profession, enabling auditors to derive deeper insights from vast datasets, enhance audit quality, and improve decision-making processes. The integration of data analytics into auditing practices addresses the complexities of modern financial environments and helps auditors meet the increasing demands for transparency and accountability. This paper synthesizes various studies to elucidate the role of data analytics in auditing, focusing on its impact on audit quality, efficiency, and the overall effectiveness of audit engagements. The incorporation of data analytics into auditing practices has been shown to significantly enhance audit quality. For instance, the use of advanced data analytics tools allows auditors to identify anomalies and patterns that may indicate potential fraud or misstatements in financial statements. This capability is particularly crucial in today's data-rich environment, where traditional audit methods may fall short in detecting irregularities. Studies indicate that auditors who leverage data analytics are better equipped to provide high-quality audits, as they can analyze large volumes of data more efficiently and effectively than through manual processes (Sari, 2024;, Hezam et al., 2023). Furthermore, the application of data analytics facilitates a more thorough understanding of the client's business and risk environment, thereby improving the auditor's ability to assess risk and allocate resources appropriately (Odeyemi, 2023;, Sari, 2024). Moreover, the effectiveness of data analytics in auditing is underscored by its ability to enhance the efficiency of audit processes. By automating routine tasks and employing predictive analytics, auditors can focus their efforts on higher-risk areas that require more scrutiny. This shift not only streamlines the audit process but also allows auditors to allocate their time and resources more strategically, ultimately leading to a more effective audit outcome (Alotaibi & Alnesafi, 2023;, Sari, 2024). For example, the use of data analytics can reduce the time spent on substantive testing by identifying areas of higher risk, allowing auditors to concentrate their efforts where they are most needed (Odeyemi, 2023;, Sari, 2024). Additionally, the integration of data analytics into audit methodologies has been shown to improve the accuracy of audit findings, as auditors can rely on data-driven insights rather than solely on historical knowledge or intuition (Sari, 2024;, Hezam et al., 2023). The role of technology in enhancing audit quality is further emphasized by the findings of studies that highlight the positive perceptions of auditors regarding the impact of audit software on audit quality. Research indicates that auditors believe that the use of specialized audit software improves the efficiency of the audit process and enhances the overall quality of the audit (Alotaibi & Alnesafi, 2023;, Esther, 2023). This sentiment is echoed in the literature, which suggests that the adoption of technology in auditing not only facilitates better data management but also supports the auditor's judgment and decision-making processes (Odeyemi, 2023;, Sari, 2024). As auditors increasingly embrace technology, the expectation is that audit quality will continue to improve, leading to greater stakeholder confidence in financial reporting. In addition to improving audit quality and efficiency, data analytics also plays a critical role in addressing the challenges posed by the evolving regulatory landscape. As regulatory bodies demand greater transparency and accountability from organizations, auditors are required to adapt their methodologies to meet these expectations. The integration of data analytics into audit practices allows auditors to comply with regulatory requirements more effectively, as they can provide more comprehensive and detailed audit reports that demonstrate due diligence and thoroughness (Odeyemi, 2023;, Sari, 2024). Furthermore, the use of data analytics can help auditors identify potential compliance issues before they escalate, thereby mitigating risks associated with non-compliance and enhancing the overall governance framework of the organization (Esther, 2023;, Odeyemi, 2023). The application of data analytics in auditing also fosters a culture of continuous improvement within audit firms. By analyzing past audit engagements and outcomes, auditors can identify trends and areas for improvement, leading to the development of best practices and enhanced audit methodologies (Sari, 2024;, Hezam et al., 2023). This iterative process not only contributes to the professional development of auditors but also ensures that audit firms remain competitive in an increasingly complex and dynamic environment. As auditors become more proficient in utilizing data analytics, they are better positioned to provide valuable insights to their clients, thereby enhancing the perceived value of the audit function (Esther, 2023;, Sari, 2024). Furthermore, the integration of data analytics into auditing practices has implications for auditor training and education. As the demand for data-driven insights increases, it is essential for auditors to possess the necessary skills and knowledge to effectively leverage data analytics tools and techniques. This shift necessitates a reevaluation of audit education programs to ensure that future auditors are equipped with the competencies required to thrive in a data-centric environment (Odeyemi, 2023;, Sari, 2024). By fostering a culture of continuous learning and adaptation, audit firms can enhance their capabilities and ensure that their auditors remain at the forefront of industry developments (Esther, 2023;, Sari, 2024). The impact of data analytics on audit quality is also reflected in the evolving expectations of stakeholders. Investors, regulators, and other stakeholders increasingly demand greater transparency and accountability from organizations, placing pressure on auditors to deliver high-quality audits that meet these expectations (Esther, 2023;, Sari, 2024). As a result, auditors are compelled to adopt innovative approaches and methodologies that leverage data analytics to provide more meaningful insights and enhance the overall quality of their work (Odeyemi, 2023;, Sari, 2024). This shift not only benefits auditors but also contributes to the overall integrity of the financial reporting process, ultimately fostering greater trust and confidence among stakeholders (Esther, 2023;, Sari, 2024).

4- CYBERSECURITY FUNDAMENTALS FOR INTERNAL AUDITORS

Cybersecurity has become an essential area of focus for internal auditors, as the increasing prevalence of cyber threats poses significant risks to organizational integrity and operational continuity. Internal auditors are uniquely positioned to assess and enhance cybersecurity measures, ensuring that organizations not only comply with regulatory requirements but also protect their information assets effectively. This synthesis explores the fundamentals of cybersecurity for internal auditors, emphasizing their roles, responsibilities, and the strategic importance of integrating cybersecurity into the audit process. The role of internal auditors in cybersecurity is multifaceted, encompassing risk assessment, compliance monitoring, and the evaluation of internal controls. Internal auditors must possess a comprehensive understanding of the cybersecurity landscape, including the various threats and vulnerabilities that organizations face. A study by Islam et al. highlights that internal audit functions must incorporate detailed knowledge of cybersecurity concerns into their risk management frameworks, suggesting that sophisticated enterprise risk management (ERM) practices implicitly cover cybersecurity risks without necessitating separate focus (Islam et al., 2018). This integration is crucial, as it allows auditors to address cybersecurity as a core component of their audit processes rather than as an ancillary concern. Moreover, the effectiveness of internal auditors in managing cybersecurity risks is contingent upon their ability to adapt to the evolving threat landscape. As Calderon and Gao note, the disclosure of cybersecurity risks can influence audit fees, indicating that auditors are increasingly required to assess the implications of cybersecurity on financial reporting and risk management (Calderon & Gao, 2020). This underscores the need for internal auditors to be proactive in identifying potential cybersecurity issues and communicating these risks to management and stakeholders. By doing so, auditors can help organizations mitigate risks before they escalate into significant threats. Training and continuous professional development are vital for internal auditors to remain effective in their cybersecurity roles. Karjalainen and Ojala emphasize the importance of authentic learning environments for in-service training in cybersecurity, suggesting that auditors should engage in ongoing education to stay abreast of the latest developments in cybersecurity practices and technologies (Karjalainen & Ojala, 2023). This commitment to professional development not only enhances auditors' technical skills but also fosters a culture of cybersecurity awareness within organizations. The relationship between internal auditors and management is critical in fostering an effective cybersecurity posture. Internal auditors must navigate the complexities of organizational dynamics while advocating for robust cybersecurity measures. As highlighted by Kamariotou and Kitsios, the alignment of information systems strategy with security policy is essential for ensuring that cyber security initiatives are integrated into the broader organizational framework (Kamariotou & Kitsios, 2023). This alignment facilitates collaboration between internal auditors and management, enabling a more cohesive approach to risk management and compliance. Furthermore, the implementation of comprehensive cybersecurity audits is essential for organizations to assess their current security posture and identify areas for improvement. Sabillon proposes a practical model for conducting cybersecurity audits that emphasizes the need for a systematic approach to evaluating an organization's cybersecurity framework (Sabillon, 2018). This model serves as a guide for internal auditors to assess the effectiveness of existing controls, identify vulnerabilities, and recommend enhancements to mitigate risks. The increasing reliance on technology in auditing processes also presents challenges and opportunities for internal auditors. As organizations adopt advanced technologies, including artificial intelligence and machine learning, auditors must develop the skills necessary to leverage these tools effectively. As noted by Teoh and Mahmood, the development of a cybersecurity workforce is critical for addressing the skills gap in the cybersecurity domain, emphasizing the need for auditors to enhance their competencies in this area (Teoh & Mahmood, 2018). By investing in both technical and soft skills, internal auditors can position themselves as valuable partners in the organization's cybersecurity efforts. The evolving regulatory landscape surrounding cybersecurity also impacts the responsibilities of internal auditors. As organizations face increasing scrutiny from regulators and stakeholders regarding their cybersecurity practices, auditors must ensure that their audit processes align with regulatory requirements. This alignment not only enhances compliance but also strengthens the organization's overall cybersecurity posture. Research indicates that auditors are responding to cybersecurity incidents by increasing their audit efforts and adjusting audit fees accordingly, reflecting the heightened importance of cybersecurity in the audit process (Rosati et al., 2020). Moreover, the implications of cybersecurity incidents extend beyond compliance; they can significantly affect an organization's reputation and financial performance. Internal auditors play a critical role in safeguarding the organization's reputation by ensuring that robust cybersecurity measures are in place and effectively communicated to stakeholders. As highlighted by Epp, the willingness of investors to engage with organizations is influenced by their perceptions of management's credibility in managing cybersecurity risks (Epp, 2024). Thus, internal auditors must prioritize cybersecurity as a strategic imperative that impacts the organization's overall success.

5- CRITICAL THINKING AND PROBLEM-SOLVING IN AI AUDITING

The integration of artificial intelligence (AI) into auditing practices has introduced a paradigm shift in the way auditors approach their work, particularly in the realms of critical thinking and problem-solving. As AI technologies evolve, they offer auditors enhanced capabilities for data analysis, anomaly detection, and risk assessment, which are essential for maintaining audit quality and integrity. This paper synthesizes various studies to explore the implications of AI in auditing, focusing on the critical thinking and problem-solving skills required for auditors to effectively leverage these technologies. One of the primary benefits of AI in auditing is its ability to process vast amounts of data quickly and accurately, enabling auditors to identify patterns and anomalies that may indicate potential fraud or misstatements. According to Antwi, AI-driven auditing tools utilize machine learning algorithms and advanced data analytics to scrutinize financial records with a high level of detail, surpassing traditional methods that often rely on sampling and manual checks Antwi (2024). This capability not only enhances the efficiency of audits but also improves the overall accuracy of audit findings, allowing auditors to focus their critical thinking on interpreting the results and making informed decisions based on data-driven insights. Moreover, the application of AI in auditing necessitates a shift in the skill set required for auditors. As noted by Ríkharðsson et al., the expectations for auditors are evolving, with a growing emphasis on their ability to understand and apply AI technologies effectively (Ríkharðsson et al., 2022). This shift highlights the importance of continuous professional development and training for auditors, ensuring they are equipped with the necessary skills to navigate the complexities of AI-augmented auditing. The integration of AI into auditing processes also requires auditors to engage in higher-order thinking, as they must critically evaluate the outputs generated by AI systems and assess their implications for audit quality and risk management. The ethical considerations surrounding AI in auditing further complicate the role of auditors in this new landscape. As highlighted by Odeyemi, the integration of AI-driven tools raises important ethical questions regarding transparency, accountability, and the potential for algorithmic bias (Odeyemi, 2023). Auditors must exercise critical thinking to navigate these ethical dilemmas, ensuring that their use of AI aligns with professional standards and ethical guidelines. This includes being vigilant about the data used to train AI models, as biased or incomplete data can lead to skewed results and undermine the integrity of the audit process. In addition to ethical considerations, auditors must also address the challenges posed by the "black box" nature of some AI models, which can obscure the decision-making processes behind AI-generated outputs. Onwubuariri emphasizes the need for auditors to develop strategies for interpreting and explaining AI-driven risk assessments, as transparency is crucial for maintaining stakeholder trust (Onwubuariri, 2024). This requirement underscores the importance of critical thinking in auditing, as auditors must not only understand the technology but also communicate its implications effectively to clients and stakeholders. Furthermore, the collaboration between auditors and AI systems can enhance problem-solving capabilities within the audit process. As noted by Kend and Nguyen, AI can assist auditors in identifying high-risk areas and prioritizing audit procedures, thereby enabling a more focused and efficient audit approach (Kend & Nguyen, 2020). This collaborative dynamic allows auditors to leverage AI as a tool for enhancing their problem-solving strategies, enabling them to address complex audit challenges more effectively. The evolving landscape of auditing also necessitates a reexamination of traditional audit methodologies. As AI technologies become more prevalent, auditors must adapt their approaches to incorporate data analytics and AI-driven insights into their audit planning and execution. As highlighted by Fedyk et al., the introduction of AI in auditing is expected to improve prediction in audit and fraud detection processes, necessitating a shift in how auditors conceptualize and conduct audits (Fedyk et al., 2022). This evolution requires auditors to engage in critical thinking to assess the relevance and reliability of AI-generated insights within the context of their audit objectives. Moreover, the integration of AI into auditing practices raises questions about the future of the audit profession. As AI continues to advance, auditors must be prepared to embrace new technologies and adapt their skill sets accordingly. As noted by Wassie, internal auditors need to remain flexible and current with the changing technological environment to effectively leverage AI in their work (Wassie, 2024). This adaptability is crucial for auditors to maintain their relevance in an increasingly automated and data-driven audit landscape.

6- EFFECTIVE COMMUNICATION IN AI-DRIVEN AUDITING

Effective communication is a cornerstone of successful auditing, particularly in the context of AI-driven auditing practices. As artificial intelligence technologies increasingly permeate the auditing landscape, auditors must adapt their communication strategies to ensure clarity, transparency, and collaboration with stakeholders. This synthesis explores the critical role of effective communication in AI-driven auditing, emphasizing its impact on audit quality, auditor performance, and stakeholder relationships. One of the primary reasons effective communication is vital in AI-driven auditing is its influence on audit quality. Research by Indrastuti highlights that communication is not merely a tool for conveying information but a key factor in enhancing audit quality and improving auditor performance Indrastuti (2024). In an environment where AI tools generate complex data analyses and insights, auditors must effectively communicate these findings to clients and stakeholders. This requires not only technical proficiency in understanding AI outputs but also the ability to articulate these insights in a manner that is comprehensible and actionable for non-technical audiences. Moreover, the integration of AI into auditing processes necessitates a shift in the communication dynamics between auditors and clients. As noted by Carlisle and Hamilton, the mode of communication—whether face-to-face, email, or other digital platforms—can significantly impact auditor-client interactions (Carlisle & Hamilton, 2020). Given that AI can automate routine tasks and generate data-driven insights, auditors must ensure that their communication effectively conveys the implications of these insights while fostering trust and collaboration with clients. This is particularly important in maintaining strong auditor-client relationships, which are essential for successful audit engagements. The competencies required for effective communication in AI-driven auditing extend beyond technical skills. As highlighted by Rumasukun, continuous training and education are crucial for auditors to develop the necessary communication skills to navigate the complexities of AI technologies (Rumasukun, 2024). This training should encompass not only the technical aspects of AI but also the interpersonal skills needed to engage with clients and stakeholders effectively. Emotional intelligence, for instance, plays a significant role in enhancing auditor-client relationships, as it enables auditors to understand and respond to clients' concerns and expectations (Rumasukun, 2024). Furthermore, auditors must be adept at managing the communication of risks associated with AI technologies. As AI systems can introduce new risks and uncertainties, auditors must effectively communicate these risks to stakeholders. This includes not only articulating the potential implications of AI-driven insights but also addressing any ethical considerations related to the use of AI in auditing. Odeyemi emphasizes the importance of transparency in communicating the limitations and potential biases of AI systems, which is crucial for maintaining stakeholder trust (Odeyemi, 2023). By fostering open and honest communication about the capabilities and limitations of AI, auditors can enhance the credibility of their findings and recommendations. In addition to enhancing audit quality, effective communication also plays a critical role in facilitating collaboration among audit teams. As AI technologies enable auditors to analyze large datasets and generate insights, effective communication becomes essential for ensuring that team members can collaborate effectively and leverage each other's expertise. Research indicates that auditors who engage in clear and open communication are better positioned to identify and address complex audit challenges (Djogo, 2023). This collaborative approach not only enhances the overall effectiveness of the audit process but also fosters a culture of continuous improvement within audit teams. Moreover, the role of communication in AI-driven auditing extends to the training and development of future auditors. As the demand for auditors with strong communication skills increases, educational institutions must prioritize the development of these competencies in their curricula. As noted by Setyaningrum et al., the importance of soft skills, including communication, is increasingly recognized in the context of auditing education (Setyaningrum et al., 2022). By equipping future auditors with the necessary communication skills, educational institutions can help ensure that they are prepared to navigate the complexities of AI-driven auditing environments. The impact of effective communication in AI-driven auditing is also reflected in the increasing emphasis on stakeholder engagement. As auditors are required to communicate their findings and recommendations to a diverse range of stakeholders, including management, boards of directors, and regulators, the ability to convey complex information clearly and concisely is essential. Research by Nadiah et al. underscores the importance of communication as a core competency for auditors, emphasizing that effective communication is critical for achieving successful audit outcomes (Nadiah et al., 2018). By prioritizing stakeholder engagement and communication, auditors can enhance their credibility and foster trust among stakeholders.

7- COLLABORATIVE AUDITING: WORKING WITH AI AND CROSS-FUNCTIONAL TEAMS

Collaborative auditing, particularly in the context of artificial intelligence (AI) and cross-functional teams, represents a significant evolution in the auditing profession. As organizations increasingly adopt AI technologies, auditors must work collaboratively with various stakeholders, including IT specialists, data scientists, and business leaders, to enhance audit quality and effectiveness. This synthesis explores the importance of collaboration in AI-driven auditing, highlighting the roles of interdisciplinary teamwork, communication, and ethical considerations. The integration of AI into auditing processes necessitates a collaborative approach that leverages the expertise of various functional areas. Ghobakhloo emphasizes that achieving transparency and fairness in AI systems requires interdisciplinary collaboration among internal experts, technology providers, and external stakeholders Ghobakhloo (2024). This collaboration is essential for developing AI tools that are not only effective but also accountable and transparent. By fostering a collaborative environment, auditors can ensure that AI technologies are implemented in a manner that aligns with organizational goals and ethical standards. Moreover, the governance of AI applications in auditing is enhanced through collaborative efforts. Hu discusses the importance of a fusion fuzzy multiple rule-based decision-making model that facilitates collaboration between AI service providers and auditors (Hu, 2023). This model underscores the need for a comprehensive approach to AI governance, where auditors play a critical role in overseeing the development and maintenance of AI-driven audit tools. By working closely with AI developers, auditors can ensure that the tools used in auditing are reliable, effective, and aligned with regulatory requirements. The ethical implications of AI in auditing also highlight the necessity for collaboration among various stakeholders. Tabbassum suggests that regular ethical audits of AI systems, conducted by independent bodies, can help identify and mitigate emerging ethical issues (Tabbassum, 2024). This proactive approach requires collaboration between auditors, ethicists, and technology developers to ensure that AI applications adhere to ethical standards and do not inadvertently introduce biases or other ethical dilemmas. By engaging in ongoing dialogue about ethical considerations, auditors can foster a culture of accountability and responsibility within their organizations. The relationship between AI adoption intensity and the quality of internal control systems further illustrates the importance of collaboration in auditing. Monteiro's research indicates that a higher intensity of AI adoption positively contributes to the quality of internal control systems (Monteiro, 2023). This relationship emphasizes the need for auditors to collaborate with IT and data management teams to ensure that AI tools are effectively integrated into existing control frameworks. By working together, auditors and technology specialists can enhance the overall effectiveness of internal controls and improve audit outcomes. In addition to technical collaboration, effective communication is crucial in cross-functional teams involved in AI-driven auditing. Wassie highlights that the utilization of AI can lead to actionable predictions that assist internal auditors in making informed decisions (Wassie, 2024). However, for these predictions to be effectively utilized, auditors must communicate their insights clearly to stakeholders. This requires not only technical proficiency in understanding AI outputs but also strong interpersonal skills to engage with clients and team members effectively. Furthermore, the application of AI in auditing raises questions about the future of the audit profession and the skills required for auditors. As AI technologies continue to evolve, auditors must adapt their skill sets to remain relevant. Research by Hasan emphasizes the need for interdisciplinary collaboration in the auditing profession, as it enables auditors to harness the full potential of AI-driven technologies (Hasan, 2022). By collaborating with professionals from diverse backgrounds, auditors can enhance their understanding of AI and its implications for auditing practices. The role of AI in enhancing audit efficiency and effectiveness is also contingent upon the collaborative efforts of cross-functional teams. Fares et al. note that AI can simplify internal audit reports and evaluate strategic initiatives, thereby improving the overall quality of audits (Fares et al., 2022). This capability underscores the importance of collaboration between auditors and business leaders to ensure that AI tools are aligned with organizational objectives and can effectively address the unique challenges faced by the organization. Moreover, the ethical implications of AI in auditing necessitate a collaborative approach to ensure that AI systems are designed and implemented responsibly. As highlighted by Fedyk et al., the ethical considerations surrounding AI in auditing require auditors to engage in discussions about the potential risks and benefits of AI technologies (Fedyk et al., 2022). By collaborating with ethicists and regulatory bodies, auditors can develop frameworks that promote ethical AI use while ensuring compliance with relevant regulations.

8- ADAPTABILITY IN A RAPIDLY EVOLVING AUDIT LANDSCAPE

In the rapidly evolving landscape of auditing, adaptability has become a critical competency for auditors. The convergence of technological advancements, regulatory changes, and shifting business environments necessitates that auditors not only embrace new tools and methodologies but also develop the agility to respond to emerging challenges. This synthesis explores the various dimensions of adaptability in auditing, particularly in light of recent developments such as the COVID-19 pandemic, the integration of artificial intelligence (AI), and the increasing complexity of digital environments. The COVID-19 pandemic has significantly impacted auditing practices, forcing auditors to adapt their methodologies to ensure continuity and effectiveness. As highlighted by Kusuma, the pandemic has necessitated innovative solutions to enhance audit effectiveness and efficiency, prompting the accelerated adoption of technology-driven tools Kusuma (2024). Auditors have had to navigate remote working conditions while maintaining audit quality and integrity. This shift has underscored the importance of flexibility in audit processes, as auditors must now rely on virtual communication and digital tools to conduct audits effectively. Moreover, the integration of AI into auditing practices has further emphasized the need for adaptability. AI technologies enable auditors to analyze vast amounts of data quickly and accurately, enhancing their ability to detect anomalies and assess risks. As noted by Azizi, the role of IT audits has evolved in response to digital transformation, requiring auditors to evaluate the adequacy of controls in increasingly complex IT environments (Azizi, 2024). This evolution necessitates that auditors continuously update their skills and knowledge to effectively leverage AI tools and methodologies, ensuring they remain relevant in a rapidly changing landscape. The adaptability of auditors is also crucial in the context of regulatory changes. As the regulatory environment becomes more dynamic, auditors must be prepared to adjust their practices to comply with new requirements. Harjoto and Laksmana found that the COVID-19 lockdown led to increased audit fees and delays due to heightened perceived audit risks, necessitating additional training and the implementation of new procedures (Harjoto & Laksmana, 2022). This highlights the importance of proactive adaptation in response to external pressures, ensuring that auditors can meet compliance demands while maintaining audit quality. In addition to external factors, the internal dynamics of audit teams play a significant role in fostering adaptability. Lorentzon's research indicates that remote auditing has implications for auditors' work-life balance and overall job satisfaction (Lorentzon, 2023). By promoting a culture of collaboration and open communication, audit firms can enhance their teams' adaptability, allowing them to respond more effectively to the challenges posed by remote work and digital auditing practices. This collaborative approach not only improves team dynamics but also fosters innovation and creativity in problem-solving. The concept of dynamic auditing capabilities is particularly relevant in the context of small and medium-sized audit practices. Kaawaase emphasizes the necessity for these firms to develop spontaneous reactions and reconfigure resources to navigate turbulent business environments effectively (Kaawaase, 2022). By cultivating dynamic capabilities, auditors can enhance their resilience and adaptability, enabling them to thrive amidst uncertainty and change. Furthermore, the rise of digital technologies, including blockchain and quantum computing, presents both opportunities and challenges for auditors. As noted by Fakeyede, the evolving threat landscape necessitates that auditors adapt their methodologies to ensure robust IT security and audit practices (Fakeyede, 2023). This requires a proactive approach to understanding emerging technologies and their implications for auditing, ensuring that auditors are equipped to address new risks and challenges. The adaptability of auditors is also influenced by their self-efficacy in utilizing technology. Muterera's study highlights the importance of confidence in technical skills and technological adaptation for auditors to navigate the complexities of modern auditing environments (Muterera, 2024). By fostering a culture of continuous learning and professional development, audit firms can enhance their auditors' self-efficacy, empowering them to embrace new technologies and methodologies with confidence. Moreover, the integration of agile methodologies into auditing practices can significantly enhance adaptability. As discussed by Ilori, agile approaches allow auditors to respond more flexibly to changing circumstances and client needs, improving the overall effectiveness of audit engagements (Ilori, 2024). By adopting agile principles, auditors can enhance their ability to collaborate with cross-functional teams and leverage technology to streamline audit processes.

9- LIFELONG LEARNING FOR INTERNAL AUDITORS: STAYING RELEVANT IN THE AI ERA

In the rapidly evolving landscape of auditing, particularly with the advent of artificial intelligence (AI) and other technological advancements, the concept of lifelong learning has become increasingly critical for internal auditors. As organizations adapt to new technologies and methodologies, internal auditors must continuously update their skills and knowledge to remain relevant and effective in their roles. This synthesis explores the importance of lifelong learning for internal auditors, focusing on the skills required to navigate the AI era, the role of emotional intelligence, and the necessity of adapting to changing regulatory environments. The integration of AI into auditing practices presents both opportunities and challenges for internal auditors. As noted by Wassie, the successful utilization of AI within the internal audit function is highly dependent on the continuous training and development of auditors Wassie (2024). This training is essential not only for understanding AI technologies but also for effectively applying them in audit processes. Internal auditors must develop competencies in data analytics, machine learning, and AI-driven risk assessment to leverage these tools effectively. Continuous professional development programs that focus on these areas are crucial for ensuring that auditors can adapt to the technological landscape and enhance their audit quality. Moreover, emotional intelligence is a vital component of effective auditing, particularly in the context of AI. Mulyandini emphasizes that internal auditors must possess a high level of emotional intelligence to navigate complex organizational dynamics and build strong relationships with stakeholders (Mulyandini, 2023). As AI tools automate routine tasks, auditors will increasingly need to engage with clients and stakeholders to interpret AI-generated insights and provide strategic recommendations. Therefore, developing emotional intelligence through lifelong learning initiatives can enhance auditors' ability to communicate effectively and foster collaboration within cross-functional teams. In addition to technical skills and emotional intelligence, internal auditors must also be adaptable to changing regulatory environments. The regulatory landscape surrounding auditing is continuously evolving, with new standards and requirements emerging in response to technological advancements and societal expectations. Harijani et al. highlight the importance of internal auditors in systematically helping organizations improve risk management and controls, which requires them to stay informed about regulatory changes and best practices (Haryani, 2023). Lifelong learning enables auditors to remain current with these developments, ensuring compliance and enhancing the effectiveness of their audit engagements. The role of internal auditors in fraud prevention and detection is another area where lifelong learning is essential. Nurlaela et al. assert that the professionalism of internal auditors is key to successfully preventing fraud within organizations (Nurlaela et al., 2021). By engaging in continuous education and training, auditors can develop the necessary skills to identify potential fraud risks and implement effective controls. This proactive approach not only enhances the auditors' capabilities but also contributes to the overall integrity of the organization's financial reporting processes. Furthermore, the adoption of AI technologies in auditing necessitates a shift in the skill set required for auditors. While Khelil et al. discuss moral courage in the context of auditing, the integration of AI into auditing practices indeed requires auditors to develop new competencies, including an understanding of AI algorithms, data privacy, and cybersecurity risks (Khelil et al., 2018). Lifelong learning initiatives that focus on these emerging areas are crucial for preparing auditors to navigate the complexities of AI-driven audits and ensure the reliability of audit outcomes. The importance of adaptability in the face of technological advancements is further underscored by the findings of Setyaningrum et al., which emphasize the need for auditors to possess skills such as critical thinking, communication, and teamwork (Setyaningrum et al., 2022). These competencies are essential for effectively collaborating with IT specialists and data scientists in cross-functional teams. Lifelong learning programs that foster these skills can enhance auditors' ability to work collaboratively and leverage the expertise of diverse team members, ultimately improving audit quality. In addition to technical and interpersonal skills, auditors must also cultivate a mindset of continuous improvement. As the auditing profession evolves, auditors should embrace a culture of learning and innovation. This mindset encourages auditors to seek out new knowledge, share best practices, and explore innovative approaches to auditing.

By fostering a culture of continuous improvement, organizations can empower their internal audit teams to adapt to changing circumstances and enhance their overall effectiveness. The role of technology in facilitating lifelong learning for internal auditors cannot be overlooked. Online training platforms, webinars, and virtual workshops provide auditors with flexible learning opportunities that can be tailored to their specific needs and schedules. Haryani discusses the importance of internal auditors in enhancing the effectiveness and efficiency of their roles, which can be supported by leveraging technology for training and development (Haryani, 2023). This accessibility is particularly important in the context of the ongoing digital transformation of the auditing profession.

10- ETHICAL AUDITING IN THE AGE OF ARTIFICIAL INTELLIGENCE

In the age of artificial intelligence (AI), ethical auditing has emerged as a crucial component of ensuring that AI systems operate in alignment with societal values and ethical standards. As organizations increasingly integrate AI technologies into their operations, the need for robust ethical frameworks and auditing practices becomes paramount. This synthesis explores the significance of ethical auditing in the context of AI, highlighting the challenges, methodologies, and best practices for ensuring ethical compliance in AI systems. One of the primary challenges in ethical auditing of AI systems is the inherent complexity and opacity of these technologies. Akbar et al. emphasize that ethical audits systematically review AI systems to identify potential ethical concerns, ensuring that organizations address issues before they escalate into significant problems Akbar et al. (2023). This proactive approach is essential for maintaining trust and accountability in AI applications, particularly in high-stakes environments such as finance, healthcare, and public services. Furthermore, the auditing process must encompass the entire lifecycle of AI systems, from development to deployment. Bubinger and Dinneen suggest that auditing should evaluate the systems, development processes, and data used throughout the software lifecycle (Bubinger & Dinneen, 2021). This comprehensive approach allows auditors to systematically consider the myriad potential unintended consequences of AI implementations, ensuring that ethical considerations are integrated into every stage of the AI lifecycle. Regular ethical audits are crucial for maintaining compliance with evolving ethical standards and regulations. Tabbassum advocates for conducting periodic audits by independent bodies to ensure ongoing adherence to ethical principles (Tabbassum, 2024). These audits can help organizations identify and mitigate emerging ethical issues, fostering a culture of accountability and transparency. By establishing a routine of ethical auditing, organizations can demonstrate their commitment to ethical AI practices and build trust with stakeholders. The development of practical tools and frameworks for operationalizing AI ethics is also essential for effective auditing. Ayling and Chapman highlight the importance of reviewing existing AI guidelines and frameworks to identify best practices for assessing the ethical implications of AI technologies (Ayling & Chapman, 2021). By leveraging these tools, auditors can systematically evaluate AI systems and ensure that they align with ethical standards and societal expectations. Moreover, the ethical implications of AI extend beyond technical considerations; they encompass broader societal impacts. Moral agency and responsibility in AI systems are critical areas that require careful consideration. As noted by Saraiva, achieving transparency and accountability in AI necessitates robust mechanisms for auditing and monitoring AI behavior, as well as frameworks for assigning responsibility in cases of misconduct or error (Saraiva, 2024). This focus on accountability is essential for addressing public concerns about the ethical use of AI technologies. The integration of AI into auditing practices also raises questions about algorithmic bias and fairness. As highlighted by Mökander et al., auditing AI systems for fairness and bias is crucial for ensuring that these technologies do not perpetuate existing inequalities or create new forms of discrimination (Mökander et al., 2023). Ethical audits should include assessments of how AI algorithms are trained, the data used, and the potential biases that may arise from these processes. By addressing these issues, auditors can help organizations develop fair and equitable AI systems. In addition to addressing bias, ethical auditing must also consider the implications of AI on privacy and data security. As AI systems often rely on vast amounts of personal data, ensuring the ethical handling of this information is paramount. González emphasizes the need for ethical frameworks that address cybersecurity concerns in AI applications, ensuring that organizations protect sensitive data while leveraging AI technologies (González, 2024). This focus on data ethics is essential for maintaining public trust and compliance with data protection regulations. The role of stakeholders in ethical auditing is another critical aspect. As noted by Mökander and Floridi, effective ethical auditing should involve collaboration among various stakeholders, including developers, auditors, and regulatory bodies (Mökander & Floridi, 2021). This collaborative approach ensures that diverse perspectives are considered in the auditing process, enhancing the overall effectiveness of ethical assessments. By fostering stakeholder engagement, organizations can create a more inclusive and comprehensive approach to ethical auditing. Moreover, the evolving regulatory landscape surrounding AI necessitates that auditors stay informed about new laws and guidelines. Dixon highlights the importance of understanding the legal implications of AI technologies and ensuring compliance with relevant regulations (Dixon, 2022). As governments and regulatory bodies develop frameworks for AI governance, auditors must adapt their practices to align with these changes, ensuring that organizations remain compliant and accountable.

11- EMOTIONAL INTELLIGENCE: MANAGING STAKEHOLDER RELATIONSHIPS

Emotional intelligence (EI) plays a pivotal role in managing stakeholder relationships within the auditing profession, particularly in the context of internal audits. As auditors navigate complex organizational dynamics and diverse stakeholder expectations, the ability to understand and manage emotions—both their own and those of others—becomes increasingly important. This synthesis explores the significance of emotional intelligence in auditing, focusing on its impact on stakeholder engagement, communication strategies, and overall audit effectiveness. One of the primary ways emotional intelligence enhances stakeholder relationships is through improved communication. Effective communication is essential for auditors to convey their findings and recommendations clearly and persuasively. Oladeinde emphasizes that tailoring communication strategies to diverse stakeholders is crucial for effective engagement Oladeinde (2023). By leveraging emotional intelligence, auditors can better understand the perspectives and concerns of various stakeholders, allowing them to adapt their communication styles accordingly. This adaptability fosters trust and collaboration, which are essential for successful audit outcomes. Moreover, emotional intelligence enables auditors to navigate challenging conversations and manage conflicts that may arise during the audit process. Ren et al. highlight that effective internal audit work attracts higher management adoption of audit conclusions, underscoring the importance of building positive relationships with stakeholders (Ren et al., 2022). Auditors equipped with strong emotional intelligence skills can approach difficult discussions with empathy and understanding, facilitating constructive dialogue and minimizing resistance from stakeholders. This proactive approach not only enhances the audit process but also contributes to a more positive organizational culture. The ability to recognize and respond to the emotional states of stakeholders is another critical aspect of emotional intelligence in auditing. Groenewald and Odendaal's research on the experiences of female audit managers reveals that understanding the emotional dynamics within teams can significantly impact decision-making and stakeholder engagement (Groenewald & Odendaal, 2021). By being attuned to the emotions of others, auditors can foster a supportive environment that encourages open communication and collaboration. This emotional awareness is particularly important in high-stress situations, where stakeholders may feel anxious or defensive about the audit findings. In addition to enhancing communication and conflict resolution, emotional intelligence also plays a vital role in building stakeholder trust. Hennein et al. discuss the importance of stakeholder engagement in complex environments, emphasizing that trust is essential for the successful implementation of initiatives (Hennein et al., 2022). Auditors who demonstrate emotional intelligence can cultivate trust by being transparent, approachable, and responsive to stakeholder concerns. This trust is critical for ensuring that stakeholders view the audit process as a valuable and constructive endeavor rather than a punitive measure. Furthermore, emotional intelligence contributes to the overall effectiveness of the audit process by enabling auditors to engage in active listening. Effective listening is a key component of emotional intelligence, allowing auditors to fully understand stakeholder concerns and perspectives. Indriyanto notes that the quality of audit opinions can significantly influence stakeholder perceptions of management (Indriyanto, 2023). By actively listening to stakeholders, auditors can gather valuable insights that inform their assessments and recommendations, ultimately enhancing the quality of the audit. The integration of emotional intelligence into auditing practices also aligns with the growing emphasis on corporate social responsibility (CSR) and ethical governance. Ehsan et al. discuss the relationship between earnings management and stakeholder activism, highlighting the importance of transparency and accountability in fostering stakeholder trust (Ehsan et al., 2020). Auditors who prioritize emotional intelligence are better equipped to navigate the ethical complexities of their work, ensuring that they uphold the highest standards of integrity and professionalism. Moreover, emotional intelligence can enhance the effectiveness of audit committees and governance structures. Garad et al. emphasize that strong corporate governance attributes, including effective communication and stakeholder engagement, are essential for achieving organizational objectives (Garad et al., 2021). By fostering emotional intelligence within audit committees, organizations can improve their decision-making processes and enhance their ability to address stakeholder concerns effectively.

CONCLUSION

As artificial intelligence (AI) continues to reshape the landscape of internal auditing, achieving a balance between technical proficiency and interpersonal skills has become more critical than ever. Internal auditors are no longer just tasked with mastering traditional auditing practices; they must now become adept in the use of advanced AI tools, such as machine learning algorithms, predictive analytics, and robotic process automation, which are revolutionizing how audits are conducted. These technologies enable auditors to analyze vast datasets with unprecedented speed and accuracy, uncover hidden patterns, and mitigate risks more effectively. However, technical expertise alone is not enough to navigate the broader implications of AI adoption. Auditors must also cultivate essential interpersonal skills such as emotional intelligence, adaptability, ethical awareness, and communication proficiency to address the complex challenges posed by this technological evolution. Emotional intelligence allows auditors to understand and respond to the concerns of diverse stakeholders, fostering trust and collaboration, while adaptability ensures they can remain resilient in the face of rapid advancements and shifting regulatory landscapes. Furthermore, ethical awareness is vital to maintaining transparency, accountability, and fairness in the application of AI systems, ensuring that these tools are implemented responsibly and align with organizational and societal values. This book underscores the importance of continuous learning and professional development as a cornerstone for success, highlighting how auditors can remain relevant by staying ahead of emerging trends, fostering innovation, and collaborating effectively with cross-functional teams. By embracing this dual competency approach, internal auditors can not only enhance the quality and efficiency of their audits but also contribute significantly to the development of robust governance frameworks that uphold organizational integrity. Ultimately, this convergence of cutting-edge technology and human expertise positions internal auditors as indispensable guardians of ethical practices, risk management, and accountability in an era of transformative change. Through this multidimensional skill set, they can navigate the complexities of the AI-driven auditing environment while ensuring they add value to their organizations and the profession at large.

REFERENCES

Akbar, M. A., Khan, A. A., Mahmood, S., Rafi, S., & Demi, S. (2024). Trustworthy artificial intelligence: A decision-making taxonomy of potential challenges. *Software, Practice & Experience*, *54*(9), 1621–1650. DOI: 10.1002/spe.3216

Alotaibi, E. M., & Alnesafi, A. (2023). Assessing the impact of audit software on audit quality: Auditors' perceptions. International Journal of Applied Economics. *Finance and Accounting*, *17*(1), 97–108.

Antwi, B. O., Adelakun, B. O., Fatogun, D. T., & Olaiya, O. P. (2024). Enhancing audit accuracy: The role of AI in detecting financial anomalies and fraud. *Finance & Accounting Research Journal*, *6*(6), 1049–1068. DOI: 10.51594/farj.v6i6.1235

Ayling, J., & Chapman, A. (2022). Putting AI ethics to work: Are the tools fit for purpose? *AI and Ethics*, *2*(3), 405–429. DOI: 10.1007/s43681-021-00084-x

Azizi, M., Hakimi, M., Amiri, F., & Shahidzay, A. K. (2024). The Role of IT (Information Technology) Audit in Digital Transformation: Opportunities and Challenges. *Open Access Indonesia Journal of Social Sciences*, *7*(2), 1473–1482. DOI: 10.37275/oaijss.v7i2.230

Bubinger, H., & Dinneen, J. D. (2021). Actionable approaches to promote ethical AI in libraries. *Proceedings of the Association for Information Science and Technology*, *58*(1), 682–684. DOI: 10.1002/pra2.528

Calderon, T. G., & Gao, L. (2021). Cybersecurity risks disclosure and implied audit risks: Evidence from audit fees. *International Journal of Auditing*, *25*(1), 24–39. DOI: 10.1111/ijau.12209

Carlisle, M., & Hamilton, E. L. (2021). The role of communication mode in auditor-client interactions: Insights from staff auditors. *Current Issues in Auditing*, *15*(1), A19–A37. DOI: 10.2308/CIIA-2020-007

Dixon, R. B. L. (2023). A principled governance for emerging AI regimes: Lessons from China, the European Union, and the United States. *AI and Ethics*, *3*(3), 793–810. DOI: 10.1007/s43681-022-00205-0

Djogo, Y. O. (2023). Internal Auditor Human Resources Development Strategy in the Era of Disruption. Atestasi. *Jurnal Ilmiah Akuntansi*, *6*(2), 627–639.

Ehsan, S., Nurunnabi, M., Tahir, S., & Hashmi, M. H. (2020). Earnings management: A new paradigm of corporate social responsibility. *Business and Society Review*, *125*(3), 349–369. DOI: 10.1111/basr.12198

Epp, N., Pentikis, J., & Roohani, S. (2024). The Sunk Costs of Cybersecurity Testing: Who Bears Responsibility? *Journal of Applied Business & Economics*, *26*(2). Advance online publication. DOI: 10.33423/jabe.v26i2.7042

Fakeyede, O. G., Okeleke, E. C., Okeleke, P. A., & Adaramodu, O. R. (2023). A Comprehensive Review of IT Audit Methodologies in The Age of Quantum Computing. *Journal of Technology & Innovation*, *3*(2), 85–92. DOI: 10.26480/jtin.02.2023.85.92

Fedyk, A., Hodson, J., Khimich, N., & Fedyk, T. (2022). Is artificial intelligence improving the audit process? *Review of Accounting Studies*, *27*(3), 938–985. DOI: 10.1007/s11142-022-09697-x

Garad, A., Rahmawati, A., & Pratolo, S. (2021). The impact of board directors, audit committee and ownership on financial performance and firms value. evaluation, 17, 18-19.

Ghobakhloo, M., Fathi, M., Iranmanesh, M., Vilkas, M., Grybauskas, A., & Amran, A. (2024). Generative artificial intelligence in manufacturing: Opportunities for actualizing Industry 5.0 sustainability goals. *Journal of Manufacturing Technology Management*, *35*(9), 94–121. DOI: 10.1108/JMTM-12-2023-0530

González, A. L., Moreno, M., Román, A. C. M., Fernández, Y. H., & Pérez, N. C. (2024). Ethics in Artificial Intelligence: An Approach to Cybersecurity. *Inteligencia Artificial*, *27*(73), 38–54. DOI: 10.4114/intartif.vol27iss73pp38-54

Groenewald, J., & Odendaal, E. (2021). The experiences leading to resignation of female audit managers: An interpretative phenomenological analysis. *Gender in Management*, *36*(8), 912–929. DOI: 10.1108/GM-11-2020-0352

Harjoto, M. A., & Laksmana, I. (2022). The impact of COVID-19 lockdown on audit fees and audit delay: International evidence. *International Journal of Accounting & Information Management*, *30*(4), 526–545. DOI: 10.1108/IJAIM-02-2022-0030

Haryani, F., Nasta'in, F., Novitasari, I., Putri, W., & Manurung, H. (2023). Internal Auditor's Responsibilities for Quality Control of Financial Reporting at PT Asabri (Persero): A Qualitative Analysis. *Jurnal Ilmiah Manajemen Kesatuan*, *11*(2), 593–598. DOI: 10.37641/jimkes.v11i2.2152

Hasan, A. R. (2021). Artificial Intelligence (AI) in accounting & auditing: A Literature review. *Open Journal of Business and Management*, *10*(1), 440–465. DOI: 10.4236/ojbm.2022.101026

Hennein, R., Goddard, E., & Sherman, J. D. (2022). Stakeholder perspectives on scaling up medical device reprocessing: A qualitative study. *PLoS One*, *17*(12), e0279808. DOI: 10.1371/journal.pone.0279808 PMID: 36584081

Hezam, Y. A., Anthonysamy, L., & Suppiah, S. D. K. (2023). Big data analytics and auditing: A review and synthesis of literature. *Emerging Science Journal*, *7*(2), 629–642. DOI: 10.28991/ESJ-2023-07-02-023

Hu, K. H., Chen, F. H., Hsu, M. F., & Tzeng, G. H. (2023). Governance of artificial intelligence applications in a business audit via a fusion fuzzy multiple rule-based decision-making model. *Financial Innovation*, *9*(1), 117. DOI: 10.1186/s40854-022-00436-4

Ilori, O., Nwosu, N. T., & Naiho, H. N. N. (2024). Enhancing IT audit effectiveness with agile methodologies: A conceptual exploration. *Engineering Science & Technology Journal*, *5*(6), 1969–1994. DOI: 10.51594/estj.v5i6.1217

Indrastuti, S., Mardianty, D., Hasan, H., & Nugroho, G. (2024). Optimizing Auditor Performance: Examining the Mediating Role of Communication in the Work Environment. Atestasi. *Jurnal Ilmiah Akuntansi*, *7*(1), 248–259.

Indriyanto, E., Molina, M., Nur, M., & Digdowiseiso, K. (2023). The Quality of Company Audit in Indonesia during COVID-19 Pandemic: A Review of Literature. Global Journal of Business, Economics &. *Social Development*, *1*(2), 108–115.

Islam, M. S., Farah, N., & Stafford, T. F. (2018). Factors associated with security/cybersecurity audit by internal audit function: An international study. *Managerial Auditing Journal*, *33*(4), 377–409. DOI: 10.1108/MAJ-07-2017-1595

Kaawaase, T. K. (2022). Anchoring on dynamic auditing capabilities to manage small and medium audit practices in a Covid-19-induced turbulent business environment. *Management Matters*, *19*(1), 73–90. DOI: 10.1108/MANM-01-2022-0003

Kai, R., Yusheng, K., Ntarmah, A. H., & Ti, C. (2022). Constructing internal audit quality evaluation index: Evidence from listed companies in Jiangsu province, China. *Heliyon*, *8*(9), e10598. DOI: 10.1016/j.heliyon.2022.e10598 PMID: 36164523

Kamariotou, M., & Kitsios, F. (2023). Information systems strategy and security policy: A conceptual framework. *Electronics (Basel)*, *12*(2), 382. DOI: 10.3390/electronics12020382

Karjalainen, M., & Ojala, A. L. (2023). Authentic learning environments for in-service training in cybersecurity: A qualitative study. *International Journal of Continuing Engineering Education and Lifelong Learning*, *33*(1), 128–147. DOI: 10.1504/IJCEELL.2023.127853

Karmila, Y., & Wahad, A. (2024). Determinants of Fraud Prevention PT Perkebunan Nusantara XIV Takalar. *Formosa Journal of Applied Sciences*, *3*(2), 759–774. DOI: 10.55927/fjas.v3i2.7981

Kend, M., & Nguyen, L. A. (2020). Big data analytics and other emerging technologies: The impact on the Australian audit and assurance profession. *Australian Accounting Review*, *30*(4), 269–282. DOI: 10.1111/auar.12305

Khelil, I., Hussainey, K., & Noubbigh, H. (2018). Chief audit executives' perceptions of drivers of moral courage: Tunisian evidence. International Journal of Accounting. *Auditing and Performance Evaluation*, *14*(4), 315–337. DOI: 10.1504/IJAAPE.2018.095107

Kusuma, B. W. (2024). The Impact of the COVID-19 Pandemic on Auditing Practices: A Qualitative Analysis. *Golden Ratio of Auditing Research*, *4*(1), 24–32. DOI: 10.52970/grar.v4i1.385

Lorentzon, J. I., Fotoh, L. E., & Mugwira, T. (2024). Remote auditing and its impacts on auditors' work and work-life balance: Auditors' perceptions and implications. *Accounting Research Journal*, *37*(1), 1–18. DOI: 10.1108/ARJ-06-2023-0158

Mökander, J., & Floridi, L. (2021). Ethics-based auditing to develop trustworthy AI. *Minds and Machines*, *31*(2), 323–327. DOI: 10.1007/s11023-021-09557-8

Mökander, J., Schuett, J., Kirk, H. R., & Floridi, L. (2023). Auditing large language models: A three-layered approach. *AI and Ethics*, •••, 1–31.

Monteiro, A., Cepêda, C., Da Silva, A. C. F., & Vale, J. (2023). The relationship between ai adoption intensity and internal control system and accounting information quality. *Systems*, *11*(11), 536. DOI: 10.3390/systems11110536

Mulyandini, V. C. (2023). The Relationship between Emotional Intelligence and Audit Judgment: A Study on Internal Auditors in Indonesian Financial Institutions. Asian Journal of Economics. *Business and Accounting*, *23*(9), 34–38.

Muterera, J. (2024). THE AUDITOR SELF-EFFICACY SCALE: MEASURING CONFIDENCE IN TECHNICAL SKILLS, TECHNOLOGICAL ADAPTATION, AND INTERPERSONAL COMMUNICATION. *Finance & Accounting Research Journal*, *6*(3), 331–346. DOI: 10.51594/farj.v6i3.873

Nadiah, A. H., Hajar, A. S., & Zarinah, A. R. (2017). The influence of core competency skills of IRBM tax auditors towards their performance. *Revue des Sciences Fondamentales et Appliquées*, *9*(5S), 958–988. DOI: 10.4314/jfas.v9i5s.68

Nurlaela, E., Mappanyukki, R., & Surjandari, D. A. (2021). The effect of the internal audit roles and auditor professionalism on fraud prevention. *Studies in Media and Communication*, *9*(2), 24–35. DOI: 10.11114/smc.v9i2.5324

Odeyemi, O., Awonuga, K. F., Mhlongo, N. Z., Ndubuisi, N. L., Olatoye, F. O., & Daraojimb, A. I. (2024). The role of AI in transforming auditing practices: A global perspective review. *World Journal of Advanced Research and Reviews*, *21*(2), 359–370. DOI: 10.30574/wjarr.2024.21.2.0460

Oladeinde, M., Okeleke, E. C., Adaramodu, O. R., Fakeyede, O. G., & Farayola, O. A. (2023). Communicating IT audit findings: Strategies for effective stakeholder engagement. *Computer Science & IT Research Journal*, *4*(2), 126–139. DOI: 10.51594/csitrj.v4i2.612

Onwubuariri, E. R., Adelakun, B. O., Olaiya, O. P., & Ziorklui, J. E. K. (2024). AI-Driven risk assessment: Revolutionizing audit planning and execution. *Finance & Accounting Research Journal*, *6*(6), 1069–1090. DOI: 10.51594/farj.v6i6.1236

Rawashdeh, A. (2024). A deep learning-based SEM-ANN analysis of the impact of AI-based audit services on client trust. *Journal of Applied Accounting Research*, *25*(3), 594–622. DOI: 10.1108/JAAR-10-2022-0273

Rikhardsson, P., Kristinn, T., Bergthorsson, G., & Batt, C. (2022). Artificial intelligence and auditing in small-and medium-sized firms: Expectations and applications. *AI Magazine*, *43*(3), 323–336. DOI: 10.1002/aaai.12066

Rosati, P., Gogolin, F., & Lynn, T. (2022). Cyber-security incidents and audit quality. *European Accounting Review*, *31*(3), 701–728. DOI: 10.1080/09638180.2020.1856162

Sabillon, R. (2018). A practical model to perform comprehensive cybersecurity audits. *Enfoque UTE : Revista Científica*, *9*(1), 127–137. DOI: 10.29019/enfoqueute.v9n1.214

Saraiva, L. (2024). Moral Agency and Responsibility in AI Systems. *International Journal of Philosophy*, *3*(1), 25–36. DOI: 10.47941/ijp.1867

Sari, W. K. (2024). A Qualitative Study on the Use of Data Analytics in Auditing. *Golden Ratio of Auditing Research*, *4*(1), 33–42. DOI: 10.52970/grar.v4i1.387

Setyaningrum, D., Mita, A. F., & Rosdini, D. (2022). Internal auditor competency gap: Perception of students, academics and practitioners. Jurnal Reviu Akuntansi dan Keuangan, 12(3), 696-710.

Setyaningrum, D., Mita, A. F., & Rosdini, D. (2022). Internal auditor competency gap: Perception of students, academics and practitioners. Jurnal Reviu Akuntansi dan Keuangan, 12(3), 696-710.

Singh, B. P., & Joshi, A. (2024). Ethical Considerations in AI Development. In The Ethical Frontier of AI and Data Analysis (pp. 156-179). IGI Global. DOI: 10.4018/979-8-3693-2964-1.ch010

Tabbassum, A., Chintale, P., Praveen, G., & Najana, M. (2024). The Impact of AI on Future Employment Patterns. International Journal of Global Innovations and Solutions (IJGIS).

Teoh, C. S., & Mahmood, A. K. (2018). Cybersecurity workforce development for digital economy. *The Educational Review, USA*, *2*(1), 136–146. DOI: 10.26855/er.2018.01.003

Thottoli, M. M. (2024). Leveraging information communication technology (ICT) and artificial intelligence (AI) to enhance auditing practices. *Accounting Research Journal*, *37*(2), 134–150. DOI: 10.1108/ARJ-09-2023-0269

Wassie, F. A., & Lakatos, L. P. (2024). Artificial intelligence and the future of the internal audit function. *Humanities & Social Sciences Communications*, *11*(1), 1–13. DOI: 10.1057/s41599-024-02905-w

Yusuf, R. A. J. I., Esther, I. O., Isaiah, O. O., & Scotty, N. O. Forensic Audit Technology and Audit Report Quality of Selected Audit Firms in Nigeria.

Zhao, F., & Zhao, Z. (2023). Research on Voluntary Internal Audit of Irish Business. *Theoretical Economics Letters*, *13*(5), 1266–1280. DOI: 10.4236/tel.2023.135070

Chapter 4
Artificial Intelligence in Islamic Finance:
Revolutionizing Risk Management, Auditing, and Shariah Compliance

Early Ridho Kismawadi
https://orcid.org/0000-0002-9420-5212
IAIN Langsa, Indonesia

ABSTRACT

The integration of artificial intelligence (AI) in Islamic finance offers great opportunities to improve risk management, operational efficiency, auditing, and compliance with sharia principles. This chapter explores how AI can identify risks in real-time, speed up the sharia audit process, and ensure compliance with principles such as the prohibition of usury, gharar, and maysir. In addition, AI supports the development of innovative financial products that are in line with Islamic values. The adoption of artificial intelligence (AI) in Islamic finance has major implications for financial institutions, regulators, fintech, academics, and society. For Islamic financial institutions, AI improves operational efficiency, accelerates the sharia audit process, and supports product innovation in accordance with Islamic principles. Regulators need to develop a regulatory framework that governs the use of AI to remain sharia-compliant, ensure transparency and reduce the risk of algorithmic bias.

INTRODUCTION

In recent years, the integration of artificial intelligence (AI) in financial services has transformed the way organizations manage risk, conduct audits, and ensure regulatory compliance (Galaz et al., 2021). Islamic finance, a system based on

DOI: 10.4018/979-8-3373-0129-7.ch004

ethical principles and compliance with sharia, is now at the forefront of this digital revolution. As AI technology evolves, new opportunities open up to improve transparency, efficiency, and decision-making, while still adhering to the unique principles of Islamic law (sharia). This transformation transforms Islamic financial institutions by automating complex processes, optimizing resource allocation, and improving compliance with ethical standards. Islamic finance operates on core principles such as the prohibition of riba (interest), gharar (excessive uncertainty), and unethical (haram) investments. While these principles ensure fair and ethical financial transactions, they also require robust governance and compliance systems that are often complex and resource-intensive. AI offers a solution to these challenges by providing tools for automated audits, real-time risk management, and customized predictive analytics to ensure sharia compliance. AI enables Islamic financial institutions to simplify operations, improve customer experience, and improve the accuracy of decision-making processes.

This paper explores how AI is revolutionizing key aspects of Islamic finance, with a particular focus on risk management, auditing, and sharia compliance. Through case studies and practical applications, we research how AI can reduce financial risk while remaining in line with Islamic ethical principles. In addition, the paper also discusses the ethical and regulatory challenges associated with AI adoption, emphasizing the importance of maintaining human oversight in automated processes to maintain the integrity of Islamic finance. By bridging AI innovation and Islamic values, financial institutions can unlock new potential for growth, innovation, and operational excellence.

Although AI has shown its potential in improving operational efficiency and precision in various conventional financial sectors, its application, especially in the context of Islamic finance, still lacks deep attention in the academic literature. Most of the existing research focuses on the general benefits of AI in the financial sector without addressing the unique challenges and implications of the application of AI in Islamic finance, which is governed by sharia principles. In particular, research examining how AI can be adapted to comply with principles such as the prohibition of usury, gharar, and ethical (halal) investment is still limited. In addition, there are still no empirical studies that explore how AI can be applied in the sharia audit process, sharia risk management, and compliance with Islamic regulations in financial institutions. Ethical and regulatory challenges in the adoption of AI in the context of Islamic finance, including the risk of algorithmic bias and transparency in automated decision-making processes, have also not been extensively explored in existing research.

In 2023, the main advantage of using AI in financial services is its ability to improve operational efficiency. Based on a survey conducted in 2024, as many as 43% of respondents cited increased operational efficiency as the main benefit of AI, showing a significant increase compared to the previous year. In contrast, customer experience, which was previously considered a key benefit of AI in 2022, dropped to third place with only 27% of respondents identifying it as a key benefit. Other benefits that are often cited include competitive advantage, more accurate model development, and a reduction in the total cost of ownership.

Therefore, there is an urgent need to research how AI can be effectively adapted in Islamic finance, so that it can improve efficiency and compliance while maintaining the integrity of Islamic ethical values. This research will fill this void by offering a new perspective on the integration of AI with sharia principles, especially in the context of risk management, auditing, and sharia compliance.

Figure 1. Main benefits of artificial intelligence (AI) in the financial services sector globally in 2022 and 2023

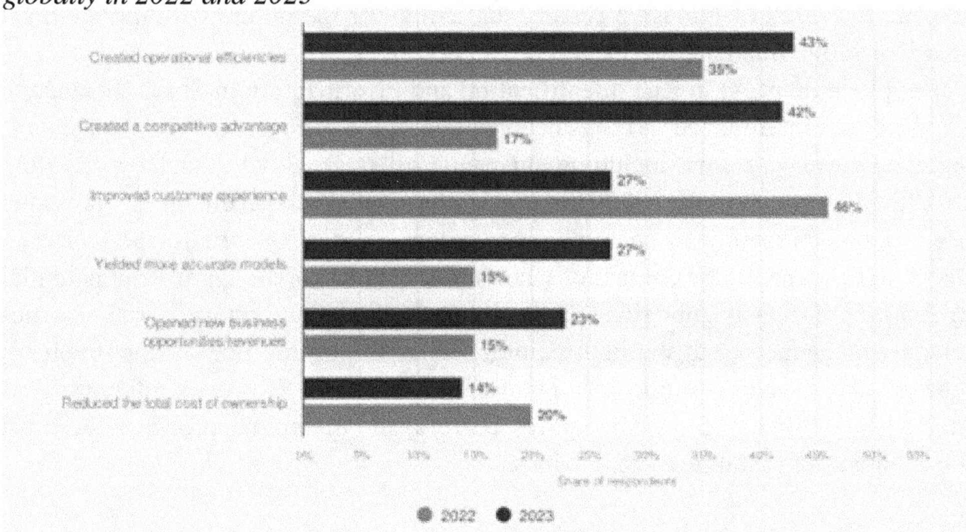

Source: Nvidia, Graphics by Statista

This research has significant implications for various stakeholders in the Islamic finance sector. For financial institutions, the adoption of artificial intelligence (AI) can provide a competitive advantage by improving operational efficiency, accelerating the decision-making process, and optimizing risk management in accordance with sharia. The application of AI in sharia audits and regulatory compliance can also strengthen transparency and accuracy, thereby increasing stakeholder trust and meeting increasingly complex regulatory demands. For regulators and supervisory authorities, the results of this study can be a guideline in formulating a regulatory framework that accommodates the development of AI technology, while ensuring that AI is used ethically and does not violate sharia principles such as justice and the prohibition of gharar. For practitioners in the fintech industry and innovators, this research opens up new opportunities to develop AI-based solutions that suit the unique needs of Islamic finance, such as applications to detect transactions that are not in accordance with sharia or automated systems that help in managing risks based on Islamic principles. It will also encourage the development of more inclusive and equitable innovations in the financial sector. Academically, the research contributes to the growing literature on the application of new technologies in Islamic finance, enriching the discourse on how AI can be specifically tailored to comply with sharia regulations. The research also paves the way for further studies related to AI ethics and regulatory challenges in Islamic finance, which could be the basis for the development of more sustainable technology policies in the future. For the general public, the application of AI in Islamic finance is expected to increase the accessibility of financial services that are more transparent, fair, and sharia-compliant, expand the reach of inclusive finance and empower the public with more ethical and innovative financial products.

Application of AI in Risk Identification and Prioritization in Sharia Finance

Artificial Intelligence (AI) has become one of the most transformative technologies in various sectors, including finance (Hall et al., 2019; Strielkowski et al., 2022; Villegas-Ch et al., 2023). Its application in risk management has provided tremendous efficiency, by enabling organizations to identify, monitor, and mitigate risks in real-time. In the context of Islamic finance, AI carries significant potential to improve the way Islamic financial institutions identify and prioritize risks, particularly while adhering to sharia principles such as the prohibition of riba (interest), gharar (excessive uncertainty), and maysir (speculation). However, integrating AI in the Islamic financial system requires a careful and in-depth approach, as AI must be adapted to fit Islamic ethical values.

Figure 2. Potential impact of generative artificial intelligence (AI) on productivity worldwide in 2023, by business functions(in billion U.S. dollars)

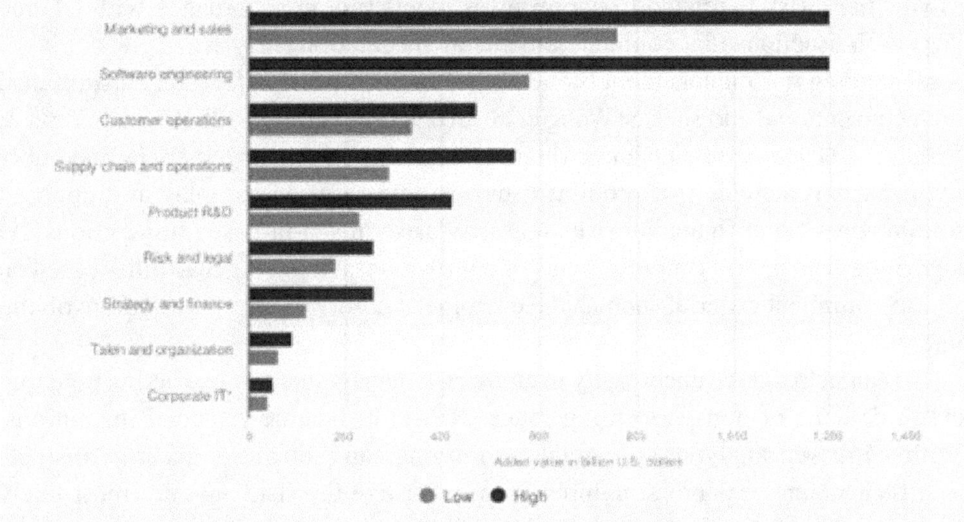

Sources: McKinsey & Company; S&P Global; Oxford Economics; IHS Markit, Graphics by Statista

Generative AI shows great potential in improving efficiency and productivity across business functions, with a primary focus on marketing, sales, and software engineering. Based on the graph above, the Risk and Legal functions have intermediate productivity values, indicating that generative AI can make a significant contribution, but the impact is not as large as marketing or software engineering. The projected added value in this function is due to generative AI's ability to automate, analyse, and accelerate various processes that previously required manual labour or human judgment.

Risk identification is the most important first step in the risk management process, as it involves determining what risks are faced by financial institutions (Jallan & Ashuri, 2020; Torvekar & Game, 2019; Zhang & Liu, 2022). In Islamic finance, the risks faced are slightly different from conventional finance, because they must meet sharia principles. For example, Islamic finance avoids transactions based on riba (interest) and gharar, so risks that violate these principles need to be carefully identified and managed. In this context, AI can be used to scan data and detect risk patterns that may not be visible to humans, as well as provide a more comprehensive risk analysis.

To identification, prioritizing risks is also an important element, especially since financial institutions have limited resources to handle all risks simultaneously. Therefore, risks must be prioritized based on their impact on the company's operations and the probability of their occurrence. AI can help in this process by analyzing historical data and predicting the most likely risks and their impact on the company. In Islamic finance, prioritization of this risk needs to consider sharia aspects, such as whether a risk is related to haram investments (not in accordance with Islamic law) or transactions that contain elements of speculation (maysir).

Financing risk management is one of the crucial aspects in financial institutions, both conventional and sharia (Wang et al., 2019; Q. Yang et al., 2019; S. A. Yang & Birge, 2018). However, in Islamic finance, financing risk management must comply with sharia principles that prohibit usury. In this case, AI can play an important role by identifying financing risks that may arise in sharia-based transactions. AI algorithms can process huge amounts of data to assess financing feasibility based on sharia-compliant criteria, such as the customer's ability to repay without involving interest.

AI can help reduce uncertainty in credit risk management by predicting potential credit defaults or non-performing loans (NPLs) in Islamic financial institutions. With AI-driven analytics, financial institutions can gain more accurate insights into their potential debtors, helping them prioritize the risks that are most likely to impact their financial stability. This provides an advantage for Islamic financial institutions, as they can maintain creditworthiness and minimize the risk of violating sharia principles. In Islamic finance, gharar (excessive uncertainty) and maysir (speculation) are two concepts that are very important to avoid (Kismawadi, 2024b, 2024c). Risks related to excessive uncertainty or speculation can have a significant impact on Islamic financial operations, as transactions containing gharar or maysir are considered unfair and contrary to sharia principles. Therefore, Islamic financial institutions need to identify and prioritize these risks.

AI can be used to detect patterns of uncertainty and speculation in financial transactions. Through big data processing and predictive analytics, AI can help Islamic financial institutions identify transactions that potentially contain gharar or maysir. For example, AI can monitor the market to detect abnormal price fluctuations or speculative patterns that may trigger uncertainty in transactions. In this way, AI can serve as an effective risk mitigation tool, helping Islamic financial institutions maintain their compliance with sharia principles.

Market risk management and liquidity is a big challenge for Islamic financial institutions (Chakroun & Gallali, 2021; Haroon et al., 2021). Rapid market price changes or an inability to meet liquidity obligations can pose serious risks. In this case, AI can be used to monitor market changes in real-time and provide early warning to financial institutions about potential liquidity risks. The predictive analysis provided by AI can help identify patterns of market volatility and prioritize the risks that are most relevant to financial stability. AI can also be used to manage liquidity risk in Islamic financial institutions by modelling various risk scenarios and identifying the most effective mitigation options. In this case, Islamic financial institutions can use AI to predict liquidity needs based on market trends and changes in their investment portfolios, while ensuring that decisions taken remain in accordance with sharia principles.

While AI offers a variety of advantages in Islamic financial risk management, there are some challenges to be aware of, especially from an ethical and regulatory standpoint. One of the main challenges is the risk of algorithmic bias, where decisions made by AI can be affected by inaccurate or incomplete data. In the context of Islamic finance, this bias can lead to decisions that are not in accordance with sharia principles, such as negligence in detecting haram or speculative transactions.

There are concerns about transparency in the AI-automated decision-making process. In Islamic finance, transparency is very important because Islamic financial institutions must account for every decision they make to shareholders and the general public. Therefore, it is important for Islamic financial institutions to ensure that the use of AI is carried out in a transparent and auditable manner, so that the decisions generated by AI can be accounted for ethically and in accordance with sharia principles. From a regulatory perspective, it is important for financial authorities to design a regulatory framework that allows for the ethical use of AI in Islamic financial institutions. This includes ensuring that AI is used to comply with sharia principles and does not violate the ethical values underlying Islamic finance. Regulatory authorities also need to set clear standards for the use of AI in Islamic financial risk management, so as to protect the integrity of the Islamic financial system as a whole.

RISK MANAGEMENT FRAMEWORK DEVELOPMENT

The development of a risk management framework with the integration of artificial intelligence (AI) is a strategic step that is increasingly being applied by companies in strengthening governance, strategy, and organizational culture (Deiva Ganesh & Kalpana, 2022; Er Kara et al., 2020). In an increasingly complex and dynamic business world, the ability to effectively manage risk is becoming increasingly crucial. AI offers a significant solution in accelerating risk identification, assessment, and mitigation, which has traditionally been time-consuming and tends to be less efficient. AI allows companies to process large amounts of data in real-time and provides deeper insights into potential risks that traditional methods may not detect. By leveraging the power of AI, companies can improve the accuracy of risk analysis and respond quickly to potentially adverse changes in conditions.

One of the key advantages of integrating AI in risk management is its ability to perform more accurate predictive analysis. Through machine learning algorithms, AI can learn from historical data to predict possible future risks. This ability is crucial in managing financial, operational, and market risks, where sudden changes can have a major impact on a company's performance. AI also facilitates the automation of various processes in risk management, such as operational risk monitoring and cybersecurity, thereby reducing reliance on human intervention and minimizing human error. This automation allows companies to improve operational efficiency and better allocate resources to handle critical risks.

The integration of AI in risk management also increases transparency and accountability in decision-making. In good corporate governance, transparency is a key element to ensure that decisions are based on accurate data and solid analysis. With the help of AI, companies can track and document every step in the risk management process, allowing for better oversight and facilitating more efficient audits. For example, in a financial context, AI can be used to monitor regulatory compliance and detect suspicious transactions or those that do not comply with internal policies. Thus, compliance risks can be minimized and the integrity of corporate governance is strengthened.

AI also plays an important role in helping companies align their business strategies with existing risks. In traditional risk management frameworks, there is often a gap between strategic planning and risk management. However, with AI, companies can gain more timely and relevant insights into the risks faced in executing their business strategies. For example, in a business expansion effort or a new product launch, AI can help identify potential market risks and provide better recommendations for managing those risks. As such, strategic decisions can be made based on a more holistic and comprehensive risk analysis, increasing the company's chances of long-term success.

However, while AI offers many benefits in the development of risk management frameworks, its implementation also presents a number of challenges. One of the main challenges is the quality of the data used in the AI analysis process. If the data used by the AI system is inaccurate or irrelevant, the results of the analysis can be misleading and lead to wrong decision-making. Therefore, companies must ensure that the data collected and processed by AI is high-quality data that reflects the reality of the business at hand. Additionally, companies need to develop mechanisms to audit and understand decisions generated by AI, given that complex algorithms can be difficult for human users to understand. Transparency in the AI-based decision-making process is essential to ensure that these decisions are accountable and in accordance with corporate governance standards.

The integration of AI in the risk management framework must also be adapted to the organizational culture. A healthy risk culture is one in which risk awareness becomes an integral part of every aspect of a company's operations. AI can help disseminate risk information more quickly and evenly across the company, so that every employee, from the management to the operational level, can understand and take a role in risk mitigation. By strengthening an inclusive risk culture, companies can be more proactive in managing risk, increase resilience to threats, and build trust among stakeholders.

In this context, it is important for companies to ensure that the application of AI is not only limited to technical risk management functions, but is also deeply integrated with corporate governance, business strategy, and organizational culture. A successful risk management framework is one that is able to bring all these elements together in one holistic approach. AI should be seen as a tool that helps companies better achieve their strategic goals, while still maintaining the integrity of corporate governance and values.

Figure 3. Initiatives taken to manage implementation risks of generative artificial intelligence (AI) by organizations worldwide as of 2024

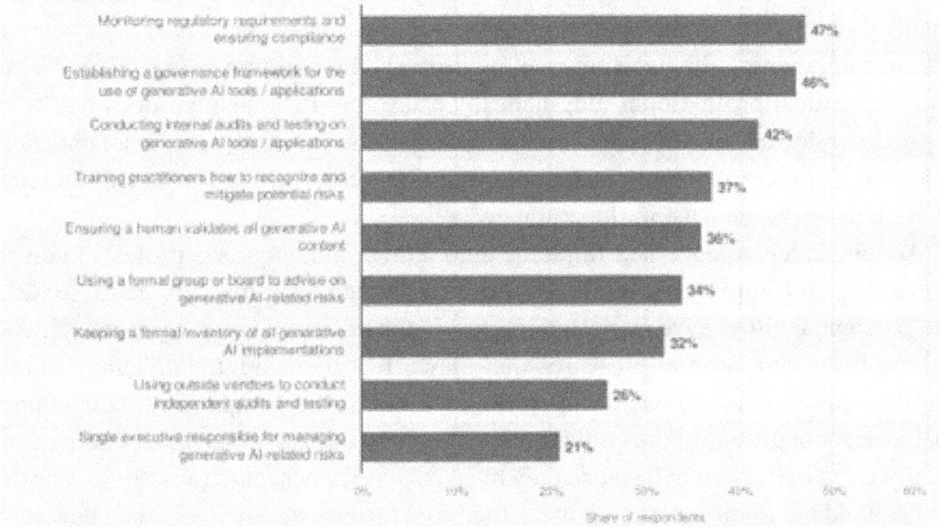

Source: Deloitte, Graphics by Statista

By 2024, organizations around the world reported having implemented at least one initiative to manage potential risks related to generative AI (GenAI) adoption. Nearly half of these companies prioritize monitoring regulatory requirements, ensuring compliance, and establishing a governance framework for the use of generative AI tools and applications. In addition, ensuring human validation of all GenAI-generated content ranked fifth on the list of initiatives, with around 36% of respondents highlighting the importance of this step.

The development of risk management frameworks with AI integration offers great potential for companies looking to improve efficiency and precision in managing risk. With AI's ability to automate processes, perform predictive analytics, and increase transparency, companies can strengthen their resilience to a range of evolving threats. However, the application of AI must be done carefully, taking into account challenges related to data, transparency, and alignment with the organization's culture. With the right approach, AI can be a powerful tool in strengthening enterprise risk management and driving the achievement of long-term business goals.

AUDITOR AND ROLE IN CORPORATE GOVERNANCE

The role of auditors in corporate governance is an important component that ensures honesty, transparency, and integrity in a company's financial and operational statements. Auditing serves as an important liaison between the company's management and external stakeholders, such as shareholders, investors, and regulators, all of which depend on the accuracy and reliability of the information presented in the financial statements. In the context of corporate governance, auditors play a central role in strengthening the decision-making process, maintaining independence, and applying critical professional judgment to ensure that management does not hide important information or make unethical decisions. Integrity and independence of auditors are key elements in maintaining good corporate governance, thereby strengthening public trust in the company.

Auditor independence is a fundamental element that supports professionalism in auditing and improves overall corporate governance (Armstrong & Li, 2022). Independent auditors have no vested interest in the decisions taken by management and are free from internal pressures that may affect their judgment. This ensures that they can provide an objective opinion regarding the company's financial and operational condition. In the context of corporate governance, the independence of auditors is very important because they must provide honest and transparent reports to stakeholders. Such reports are often the basis for investment decisions, business strategies, and corporate policies, so inaccuracies or biases in audits can negatively impact broader decision-making. Therefore, auditors must be able to maintain their independence in all situations to maintain the credibility of the audit process.

Figure 4. Based on your current knowledge, do you believe AI to be a force for good in your profession?

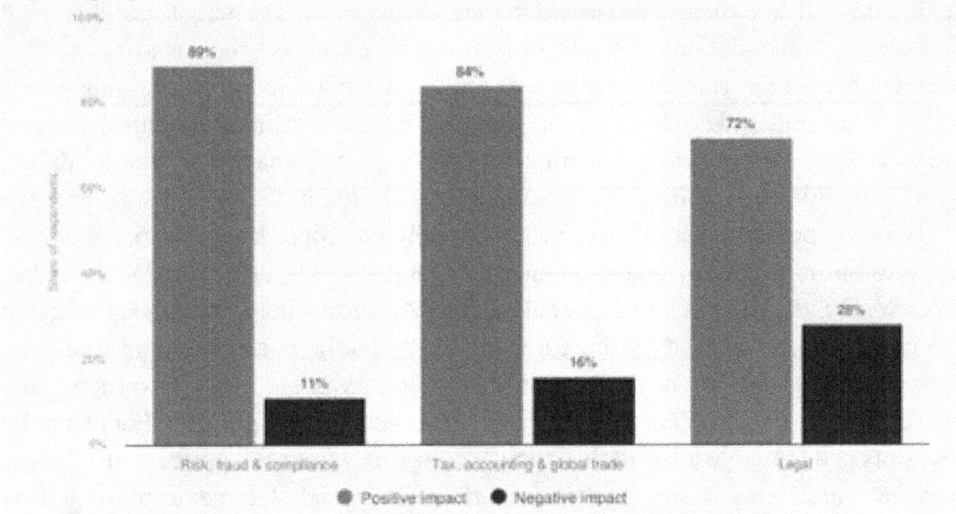

Source: Thomson Reuters, Graphics by Statista

In 2024, about 89% of professionals working in risk, fraud, and compliance consider artificial intelligence to be a positive force in their profession. In contrast, 26% of professionals in legal departments assess that AI has a negative impact on their field.

On the other hand, auditor independence comes not only from the formal relationship between the auditor and the company, but also from the quality of the professional appraisal they carry out during the audit process. This professional assessment involves the ability to identify and evaluate risks that the company may face and to provide appropriate recommendations on how to manage those risks. In the context of corporate governance, an auditor's professional assessment includes not only an understanding of accounting standards and regulations, but also about broader business dynamics, such as market conditions, technological changes, and geopolitical risks that can affect a company's operations. Experienced auditors can identify potential problems before they become a major threat to the company's financial stability and can advise management on how to mitigate those risks. It assists companies in taking proactive steps to manage risks and improve operational efficiency.

Furthermore, auditors play a crucial role in overseeing and assessing the effectiveness of a company's internal control system. Internal control is a procedure implemented by management to ensure that a company's operations are run efficiently, that the company's assets are protected from misuse, and that financial statements are presented correctly. The auditor has the responsibility to assess whether the existing internal controls are adequate to prevent and detect errors or fraud (Bansal et al., 2024). If weaknesses are found in the internal control system, the auditor will provide recommendations to management on how to correct the weaknesses. This role is not only important for regulatory compliance, but also for maintaining public trust in corporate governance. Companies that have weak internal control systems are at risk of experiencing a decline in financial performance or even collapse, which can ultimately damage the company's reputation in the eyes of stakeholders.

Good corporate governance depends not only on proper financial management, but also on transparency and accountability (Bakar et al., 2020; SETYAHADI & NARSA, 2020; Solana-González et al., 2021). Auditors play a role in ensuring that the information conveyed by the company to the public is accurate and free from manipulation. Transparency is one of the key pillars in corporate governance because it allows stakeholders to make decisions based on the right data. For example, investors need reliable information about a company's financial performance before they can make an investment decision. If the financial statements presented by the company are inaccurate or misleading, then investment decisions made based on such information may result in significant financial losses for investors. The auditor ensures that the company's financial statements reflect the actual financial condition and do not contain material errors, thereby increasing transparency and strengthening corporate governance.

To transparency, accountability is also an important element in corporate governance. Accountability refers to management's responsibility to explain the decisions taken and the results achieved to stakeholders. In this case, the auditor acts as an independent supervisor who ensures that management is accountable for its actions. When auditors find non-conformity or non-compliance with accounting standards, they are obliged to report the findings to the audit committee or the board of directors. As such, auditors help maintain management accountability and ensure that they act in accordance with the best interests of the company and stakeholders. This role is crucial in preventing fraudulent acts or abuse of authority by management, which can damage the company's credibility and reputation in the eyes of the public.

In recent years, technological developments, particularly artificial intelligence (AI) and data analytics, have begun to change the way auditors work and affect corporate governance. With increasingly large volumes of data and ever-evolving business complexity, AI is enabling auditors to analyse larger amounts of data quickly and efficiently. This technology assists auditors in detecting suspicious patterns or anomalies in data that may not be visible to humans. AI also allows auditors to conduct more comprehensive audits, covering the entire data population rather than relying solely on samples, ultimately improving the quality and reliability of audit results. Nonetheless, the application of AI in auditing also poses new challenges, especially related to how auditors ensure that decisions generated by AI are in accordance with ethical principles and are unbiased.

By using AI, auditors can increase effectiveness in overseeing a company's compliance with applicable regulations. In the context of increasingly complex regulations, companies often face difficulties in ensuring that they are complying with all relevant regulations. AI can help auditors identify potential regulatory violations faster and more accurately, allowing companies to take corrective action before problems become more serious. However, auditors must also ensure that the technology used does not replace the need for human professional judgment, as AI still has limitations when it comes to better interpretation of data

ARTIFICIAL INTELLIGENCE AND AUDIT PROCESS

The audit process is a series of activities designed to ensure the accuracy and integrity of an entity's financial statements. The auditor is responsible for collecting, assessing and verifying relevant evidence to ensure that the financial statements are free of material errors or fraud. This process includes a range of important steps that auditors must take carefully and meticulously to ensure that the information presented in the financial statements is accurate and trustworthy to stakeholders, including management, investors, regulators, and the general public. In recent decades, the audit process has undergone a significant transformation, mainly due to technological developments and increasingly large volumes of data. New technologies such as Robotic Process Automation (RPA) and artificial intelligence (AI) have introduced new ways of conducting audits, improving the efficiency and effectiveness of audits while introducing new challenges that auditors must overcome.

The first step in the audit process is audit planning, where the auditor must thoroughly understand the operating environment of the company being audited. This involves an initial assessment of the risks that may be faced by the company, both internally and externally. Auditors must understand the industry in which the company operates, the accounting policies used, and the economic, political, or social factors that may affect financial statements. In this phase, the auditor will establish an appropriate audit strategy and procedures based on the initial risk assessment. The auditor will also identify areas that require special attention, such as complex transactions or areas with a high potential for errors or fraud. Careful planning is essential to ensure that audits can be carried out efficiently and that audit resources are allocated correctly.

After the planning is complete, the auditor continues with the process of collecting evidence. Audit evidence is all the information used by auditors to evaluate whether the financial statements are free of material misstatements. This evidence can be obtained through a variety of means, such as interviews with management, examination of financial documents, physical inspection of assets, or confirmation from third parties. Auditors may also conduct tests on the company's internal control systems to ensure that they are functioning properly and are able to prevent and detect errors or fraud. During the evidence gathering process, auditors must maintain a professional scepticism, which means they must always be aware of the potential for misinformation or misleading. Auditors must also ensure that the evidence collected is sufficient and relevant to support their opinion on the financial statements.

As business complexity increases and the volume of data that must be analysed, gathering evidence in audits has become more challenging. Modern technologies such as RPA and AI have provided solutions that allow auditors to handle larger volumes of data more quickly and efficiently. RPA is a technology that allows the automation of manual processes in auditing, such as the collection and processing of data from various sources. By using RPA, auditors can reduce the time required to perform administrative tasks and focus on more in-depth analysis. Meanwhile, AI allows auditors to analyze large amounts of data and detect patterns that may not be visible to humans. AI can also be used to identify anomalous or suspicious transactions that require further investigation. By using this technology, auditors can improve audit efficiency and accuracy, as well as reduce the risk of undetected errors or fraud.

However, while technologies like RPA and AI offer many benefits, they also bring new challenges to the audit process. One of the biggest challenges is how auditors can ensure that the algorithms used in AI are unbiased and that the results generated by AI systems are reliable. Auditors must have a solid understanding of how these technologies work and how to interpret the results. In addition, the application of AI in auditing also requires new skills for auditors, such as the ability to understand data analytics and programming. Therefore, continuous professional training and development is becoming increasingly important for auditors to stay relevant in the digital age.

In addition to technological challenges, the increase in data volumes also introduces new risks in audits. Increasingly large and complex data makes the process of collecting and analysing evidence more difficult. Auditors must be able to identify which data is relevant and significant for auditing, and how to verify the reliability of that data. On the other hand, with large amounts of data, there is a risk that minor errors or frauds can be hidden among valid data, making them difficult to detect. Therefore, auditors must use a more systematic and risk-based approach to evidence collection, as well as leverage technology to help manage and analyse data effectively.

Once the evidence is collected, the next step in the audit process is the evaluation of the evidence and the formation of an audit opinion. In this phase, the auditor will assess whether the evidence obtained is strong enough to support their conclusions regarding the reliability of the financial statements. The auditor will consider whether the financial statements are prepared in accordance with applicable accounting standards and whether there are significant errors or frauds. If the auditor finds material misstatements or violations of accounting standards, they will provide a reasonable audit opinion with exceptions or even negative opinions. However, if the auditor is confident that the financial statements provide a fair and accurate picture of the company's financial condition, they will provide a reasonable audit opinion without exception.

During the evaluation of the evidence, the auditor should also consider the influence of potential future risks on the financial statements. These risks can include changes in regulations, economic conditions, or even technological advances that can affect the survival of the company. Auditors have a responsibility to assess whether a company has the ability to continue operating for a reasonable period of time, or whether there are significant risks that could threaten business continuity. If auditors identify any risks that could affect the survival of the company, they should disclose them in the audit report, so that stakeholders can make more informed decisions.

The audit process ends with the preparation of an audit report. This report contains the auditor's opinion on whether the financial statements have been presented reasonably and in accordance with applicable accounting standards. This opinion is very important because it is the basis for stakeholders to assess the financial performance of the company and make decisions related to investment, funding, or risk management. In an increasingly complex business world, robust and accurate audit reports are becoming increasingly important to maintain the integrity of financial markets and ensure that companies act in accordance with applicable ethical and regulatory standards.

ARTIFICIAL INTELLIGENCE AND SHARIA COMPLIANCE

The application of artificial intelligence (AI) in various industries can transform the way organizations conduct operations and make decisions, including in supporting compliance with sharia principles (E R Kismawadi, Irfan, M., Al Muddatstsir, U. D., & Abdulkarim, 2023; Kismawadi, 2024a; Ridho Kismawadi et al., 2023). Sharia compliance is compliance with Islamic law in economic and business activities, which includes the prohibition of riba (interest), gharar (uncertainty), maysir (gambling), as well as unethical or non-halal activities, such as investment in the alcohol industry, gambling, and other sectors that are contrary to Islamic values. In this context, AI provides various solutions that enable the supervision, management, and monitoring of sharia-compliant activities more effectively, efficiently, and in a timely manner.

One of the main roles of AI in supporting sharia compliance is the automation and monitoring of Islamic financial transactions. In the world of Islamic finance, various products and services must be adjusted to sharia law, which prohibits the practice of Riba, gharar, and maysir. To ensure that financial transactions comply with these rules, AI can be applied in financial systems to monitor transactions in real-time. AI algorithms equipped with the ability to analyze data can detect elements that are contrary to sharia, such as the presence of interest elements or excessive uncertainty in a contract. For example, if an Islamic bank offers a murabahah-based financing product (buying and selling with a profit margin), AI can help verify that the selling price and profits taken by the bank have been clearly explained to customers and that there is no element of fraud or uncertainty. With this automatic monitoring, violations of sharia rules can be immediately detected and corrected.

AI also plays an important role in the processing of sharia documents and contracts. In sharia-based transactions, every contract must comply with the principles that have been set forth in Islamic law. Contracts such as musharakah (partnership), ijarah (rent-rent), and istisna (manufacturing order) have certain conditions that must be met to be considered sharia-compliant. Using Natural Language Processing (NLP) technology, AI can read, analyze, and interpret contract documents to ensure that all necessary elements have been met. For example, in an ijarah contract, AI can check whether the rights and obligations of the parties involved have been clearly explained, and whether the risk has been shared fairly between the tenant and the owner of the goods. This technology allows for faster and more accurate contract management, while reducing the risk of human error that can result in sharia violations.

In the Islamic finance sector, AI can also be used for the evaluation and valuation of financial products. Any new financial product launched by an Islamic financial institution must first be approved by the Sharia Supervisory Board (DPS), which ensures that the product is in accordance with sharia principles. This process is often time-consuming and requires an in-depth analysis of the product's structure and mechanisms. By using AI, this evaluation process can be accelerated. AI algorithms can model various scenarios and conduct risk assessments to ensure that the product is free from riba, gharar, and maysir elements. For example, in sharia or takaful insurance, AI can analyze how premiums are collected and funds are managed, and ensure that the claim distribution process is carried out in accordance with the principles of help-help and risk-sharing taught in Islam.

One of the main challenges in sharia compliance is sharia audit. Sharia audits aim to ensure that all business activities, especially in the financial sector, are in accordance with sharia provisions. Usually, audits are carried out manually by a team of sharia auditors, who have to examine thousands of transaction data and documents. This process is very time-consuming and prone to errors. AI can make this process easier by continuously monitoring financial transactions. This technology is able to scan large volumes of transaction data and detect anomalies or potential violations of sharia automatically and in real time. Thus, AI not only improves the efficiency of sharia audits but also improves accuracy and allows financial institutions to immediately take corrective action in the event of a violation.

AI can also function as a sharia consulting tool. For example, AI-based chatbots can be trained with relevant knowledge of sharia law and the latest fatwas from ulama and Sharia Supervisory Boards. This chatbot can then be used by individuals or companies to get guidance on business activities or financial transactions in accordance with sharia principles. With AI, users can access information instantly and get accurate advice without having to wait for a long time to consult with sharia experts. This is especially helpful in situations where time is an important factor, especially in business or investment decision-making.

In the context of investment, AI can also support market analysis and identification of halal investment opportunities. Machine learning algorithms can scan information from a variety of sources, including news, market reports, and historical data, to identify sectors that are compliant with sharia principles. For example, AI can assist investors in choosing companies that operate in halal industries, such as halal food, Islamic fashion, or the renewable energy sector that align with Islamic ethics. In this way, AI helps ensure that investments are made in sectors that are not only financially profitable but also ethical and in accordance with religious teachings.

Furthermore, AI can support risk management and strategic decision-making in Islamic financial institutions. In running a business, financial institutions are often faced with various risks that must be managed carefully so as not to violate sharia principles. AI can model various risk scenarios and provide recommendations based on accurate data analysis. For example, AI can assist Islamic banks in assessing the eligibility of customers to receive sharia-based financing by considering various factors such as credit history, solvency, and potential related sharia risks. Thus, AI assists Islamic financial institutions in making better decisions that are more in line with sharia values.

AI has a very significant role in supporting sharia compliance in various sectors, especially in the financial and business industries. Through automation, monitoring, analysis, and data-driven advice, AI is able to increase efficiency, accuracy, and speed in ensuring that every business activity is in accordance with sharia principles. The application of AI not only makes it easier for organizations to comply with sharia, but also helps in creating a more transparent, trusted, and sustainable ecosystem in accordance with Islamic values. The challenge ahead is how to utilize this technology wisely, ensuring that AI development is also aligned with the ethical and religious principles underlying sharia compliance.

CONCLUSION

The application of artificial intelligence (AI) in Islamic finance has great potential in improving risk management, operational efficiency, auditing, and compliance with sharia principles. In the context of risk management, AI allows for real-time risk identification and monitoring, while adhering to sharia principles such as the prohibition of riba, gharar, and maysir. Through algorithms that are able to process large amounts of data, AI helps Islamic financial institutions detect risks faster and more accurately, improve their ability to manage financing and mitigate uncertainty.

In the aspect of sharia auditing, AI plays an important role in accelerating and improving the accuracy of the audit process by providing automatic monitoring of financial transactions. AI-based systems can detect anomalies or potential violations of sharia, thus helping financial institutions to immediately take corrective action if needed. This makes AI an important tool in maintaining the integrity and transparency of Islamic financial institutions. In addition, AI also offers opportunities to improve the quality of the evaluation of Islamic financial products. With an in-depth data-driven analysis model, AI can assist the Sharia Supervisory Board (DPS) in assessing new products and ensuring that they are free from elements that are prohibited in sharia, such as riba, gharar, or maysir. Thus, AI plays a role in supporting financial product innovations that are more in line with Islamic values. However, the adoption of AI in Islamic finance also poses ethical and regulatory challenges. One of the key challenges is the risk of algorithmic bias that can affect AI-based decisions, as well as the challenge of ensuring transparency and accountability in automated decision-making processes. Therefore, human supervision is still needed to maintain the integrity of the AI-based Islamic financial system.

The application of artificial intelligence (AI) in Islamic finance has significant implications for various stakeholders. For Islamic financial institutions, the adoption of AI improves operational efficiency, speeds up the audit process, and helps in monitoring transactions in real-time to reduce the risk of sharia violations. With the ability of AI to process data on a large scale, Islamic financial institutions can more quickly detect non-compliance and identify halal investment opportunities, which can accelerate sharia-based product innovation. For regulators and supervisory authorities, AI offers an opportunity to strengthen supervision of Islamic financial institutions by providing automated monitoring tools that can increase transparency and strengthen consumer protection. However, AI adoption also poses challenges related to ethical standards and transparency, so regulators need to develop a comprehensive regulatory framework to ensure AI is used in accordance with sharia principles. For innovators in the sharia fintech industry, AI opens up opportunities to develop new technological solutions, such as AI-based applications that can detect non-sharia transactions or assist in sharia risk management, which can expand the range of more inclusive and innovative financial products. From an academic point of view, the application of AI in the Islamic finance sector encourages further research, especially regarding how AI can be integrated with sharia principles such as the prohibition of riba, gharar, and maysir, as well as the ethical challenges that may arise from the adoption of this technology.

To maximize the potential of AI in Islamic finance, several recommendations can be submitted. First, regulators need to develop a sharia-based regulatory framework for the use of AI in the financial sector. These regulations should include mechanisms to minimize the risk of algorithmic bias, maintain transparency in automated decision-making, and ensure that AI is used ethically and in accordance with sharia principles. Second, collaboration between financial institutions and technology innovators needs to be strengthened to create AI solutions that are specific and in accordance with sharia needs. This will ensure that AI can be integrated in the Islamic financial system in an innovative way and still adhere to Islamic values. Third, education and training in AI technology for sharia supervisors and practitioners are urgently needed. With adequate training, sharia auditors and financial supervisors will be better equipped to use AI in sharia-based auditing and risk management, as well as understand how these technologies work ethically and accurately. Fourth, the development of inclusive and ethical AI models must be the main focus of fintech innovators. This includes ensuring that the AI algorithms developed are free of bias and can provide decisions that are consistent with sharia principles. Finally, empirical research is needed to explore the impact of the use of AI in the Islamic finance sector, especially in terms of risk management, audit, and compliance. This research will help financial institutions understand how AI can be optimized and provide empirical evidence regarding the effectiveness of AI in strengthening Islamic financial stability.

REFERENCES

Armstrong, A., & Li, Y. (2022). Governance and Sustainability in Local Government. *Australasian Accounting. Business and Finance Journal, 16*(2), 12–31. DOI: 10.14453/aabfj.v16i2.3

Bakar, N. M., Abdul Rahman, R., & Ibrahim, Z. (2020). Client protection and sustainable performance in microfinance institution. *International Journal of Productivity and Performance Management, 69*(4), 651–665. DOI: 10.1108/IJPPM-03-2019-0127

Bansal, U., Bharatwal, S., Bagiyam, D. S., & Kismawadi, E. R. (2024). Fraud detection in the era of AI: Harnessing technology for a safer digital economy. In *AI-Driven Decentralized Finance and the Future of Finance* (pp. 143–164). DOI: 10.4018/979-8-3693-6321-8.ch006

Chakroun, M. A., & Gallali, M. I. (2021). Dependence between Islamic banks and conventional banks and risk factors. *International Journal of Banking. Accounting and Finance, 12*(3), 201–239. DOI: 10.1504/IJBAAF.2021.116189

Deiva Ganesh, A., & Kalpana, P. (2022). Future of artificial intelligence and its influence on supply chain risk management – A systematic review. *Computers & Industrial Engineering, 169*, 108206. Advance online publication. DOI: 10.1016/j.cie.2022.108206

Er Kara, M., Oktay Fırat, S. Ü., & Ghadge, A. (2020). A data mining-based framework for supply chain risk management. *Computers & Industrial Engineering, 139*, 105570. Advance online publication. DOI: 10.1016/j.cie.2018.12.017

Galaz, V., Centeno, M. A., Callahan, P. W., Causevic, A., Patterson, T., Brass, I., Baum, S., Farber, D., Fischer, J., Garcia, D., McPhearson, T., Jimenez, D., King, B., Larcey, P., & Levy, K. (2021). Artificial intelligence, systemic risks, and sustainability. *Technology in Society, 67*, 101741. Advance online publication. DOI: 10.1016/j.techsoc.2021.101741

Hall, R. P., Ashford, R., Ashford, N. A., & Arango-Quiroga, J. (2019). Universal basic income and inclusive capitalism: Consequences for sustainability. *Sustainability (Basel), 11*(16), 4481. Advance online publication. DOI: 10.3390/su11164481

Haroon, O., Ali, M., Khan, A., Khattak, M. A., & Rizvi, S. A. R. (2021). Financial Market Risks during the COVID-19 Pandemic. *Emerging Markets Finance & Trade, 57*(8), 2407–2414. DOI: 10.1080/1540496X.2021.1873765

Jallan, Y., & Ashuri, B. (2020). Text Mining of the Securities and Exchange Commission Financial Filings of Publicly Traded Construction Firms Using Deep Learning to Identify and Assess Risk. *Journal of Construction Engineering and Management, 146*(12), 04020137. Advance online publication. DOI: 10.1061/(ASCE)CO.1943-7862.0001932

Kismawadi, E. R. (2024a). Blockchain technology and islamic finance: Empowering small businesses for financial sustainability. In *Technopreneurship in Small Businesses for Sustainability* (pp. 50–77). DOI: 10.4018/979-8-3693-3530-7.ch004

Kismawadi, E. R. (2024b). Halal food industry and sustainability. In *Economics and Environmental Responsibility in the Global Beverage Industry* (pp. 170–197). DOI: 10.4018/979-8-3693-2149-2.ch010

Kismawadi, E. R. (2024c). Sustainable Islamic financial inclusion: The ethical challenges of generative AI in product and service development. In *Exploring the Ethical Implications of Generative AI* (pp. 237–258). DOI: 10.4018/979-8-3693-1565-1.ch013

Kismawadi, E. R., Irfan, M., Al Muddatstsir, U. D., & Abdulkarim, F. M. (2023). Fintech innovations: Risk mitigation strategies in Islamic finance. In *Fintech Applications in Islamic Finance* (pp. 35–58). AI, Machine Learning, and Blockchain Techniques., DOI: 10.4018/979-8-3693-1038-0.ch003

Ridho Kismawadi, E., Irfan, M., & Shah, S. M. A. R. (2023). Revolutionizing islamic finance: Artificial intelligence's role in the future of industry. In *The Impact of AI Innovation on Financial Sectors in the Era of Industry 5.0* (pp. 184–207). DOI: 10.4018/979-8-3693-0082-4.ch011

Setyahadi, R. R., & Narsa, I. M.SETYAHADI. (2020). Corporate Governance and Sustainability in Indonesia. *The Journal of Asian Finance, Economics and Business, 7*(12), 885–894. DOI: 10.13106/jafeb.2020.vol7.no12.885

Solana-González, P., Vanti, A. A., García Lorenzo, M. M., & Bello Pérez, R. E. (2021). Data mining to assess organizational transparency across technology processes: An approach from it governance and knowledge management. *Sustainability (Basel), 13*(18), 10130. Advance online publication. DOI: 10.3390/su131810130

Strielkowski, W., Zenchenko, S., Tarasova, A., & Radyukova, Y. (2022). Management of Smart and Sustainable Cities in the Post-COVID-19 Era: Lessons and Implications. *Sustainability (Basel), 14*(12), 7267. Advance online publication. DOI: 10.3390/su14127267

Torvekar, N., & Game, P. S. (2019). Predictive analysis of credit score for credit card defaulters. *International Journal of Recent Technology and Engineering*, *7*(5), 283–286. https://www.scopus.com/inward/record.uri?eid=2-s2.0-85063812699&partnerID=40&md5=df9cca7c0ea49806b491ae7721bec355

Villegas-Ch, W., Govea, J., & Revelo-Tapia, S. (2023). Improving Student Retention in Institutions of Higher Education through Machine Learning: A Sustainable Approach. *Sustainability (Basel)*, *15*(19), 14512. Advance online publication. DOI: 10.3390/su151914512

Wang, R., Yu, C., & Wang, J. (2019). Construction of Supply Chain Financial Risk Management Mode Based on Internet of Things. *IEEE Access : Practical Innovations, Open Solutions*, *7*, 110323–110332. DOI: 10.1109/ACCESS.2019.2932475

Yang, Q., Wang, Y., & Ren, Y. (2019). Research on financial risk management model of internet supply chain based on data science. *Cognitive Systems Research*, *56*, 50–55. DOI: 10.1016/j.cogsys.2019.02.001

Yang, S. A., & Birge, J. R. (2018). Trade credit, risk sharing, and inventory financing portfolios. *Management Science*, *64*(8), 3667–3689. DOI: 10.1287/mnsc.2017.2799

Zhang, X., & Liu, J. (2022). Incentive Mechanism and Value-Added in PPP Projects Considering Financial Institutions' Early Intervention. *Journal of Construction Engineering and Management*, *148*(4), 04022001. Advance online publication. DOI: 10.1061/(ASCE)CO.1943-7862.0002248

Chapter 5
Bridging the Gap: Essential Soft and Hard Skills for the AI-Driven Banking Workforce

Karim Darwich
https://orcid.org/0009-0002-4372-5696
ICN Business School, France

ABSTRACT

The integration of artificial intelligence (AI) has transformed the banking industry, requiring a workforce with both technical and interpersonal skills. Bridging the Gap: Essential Soft and Hard Skills for the AI-Driven Banking Workforce explores the dual competencies needed for success in this era. The chapter examines AI's impact on banking, particularly in customer service, fraud prevention, and decision-making, highlighting the importance of leveraging these advancements. It emphasizes essential technical skills like data analytics, machine learning, and cybersecurity, while also stressing the need for critical thinking and problem-solving to address AI-related challenges. Complementing these hard skills, the chapter underscores the significance of soft skills, such as communication, teamwork, and leadership, to maintain the human element in an AI-augmented workforce. It also emphasizes adaptability, lifelong learning, and ethical considerations like transparency and fairness.

INTRODUCTION

The banking sector is undergoing a transformative revolution, driven by the rapid adoption of artificial intelligence (AI) technologies. As financial institutions embrace AI to enhance operational efficiency, improve customer experiences, and mitigate risks, the role of professionals within the industry is evolving. Internal

DOI: 10.4018/979-8-3373-0129-7.ch005

auditors, in particular, are at the forefront of this transition, tasked with not only mastering the technical intricacies of AI tools but also cultivating the interpersonal skills required to navigate this complex landscape. The integration of AI in auditing processes has introduced unprecedented opportunities for efficiency and accuracy, enabling auditors to analyze vast datasets, identify patterns, and detect anomalies with greater precision. However, alongside these opportunities come challenges, including ethical considerations, regulatory compliance, and the need to preserve the human element in an increasingly automated environment. This book, *Bridging the Gap: Essential Soft and Hard Skills for the AI-Driven Banking Workforce*, explores the intersection of technology and humanity in the context of internal auditing. It delves into the dual competencies required for success in the AI era: hard skills, such as data analytics, cybersecurity, and AI system management, and soft skills, including critical thinking, adaptability, communication, and emotional intelligence. By examining these skillsets, the book provides a roadmap for internal auditors to effectively leverage AI technologies while maintaining ethical oversight and fostering strong stakeholder relationships. Each chapter addresses critical topics, from understanding AI's impact on financial services to building a balanced skillset that prepares professionals for the future of auditing. By embracing a holistic approach, this book empowers internal auditors to thrive in a dynamic industry that demands both technological expertise and human-centric capabilities.

1- AI IN BANKING: TRANSFORMING FINANCIAL SERVICES

The integration of Artificial Intelligence (AI) in the banking sector has emerged as a transformative force, reshaping financial services through enhanced operational efficiency, improved customer experiences, and innovative risk management strategies. The literature highlights various dimensions of AI's impact, including its role in automating processes, enhancing decision-making, and facilitating personalized banking experiences. AI technologies have been increasingly adopted by banks to automate routine tasks, thereby improving transaction processing speed and accuracy. For instance, studies indicate that AI can significantly enhance operational efficiency in banking operations (Wijayati et al., 2022). This automation extends to customer service, where AI-powered chatbots and virtual assistants are deployed to handle inquiries and transactions, allowing banks to provide 24/7 service while reducing operational costs (Andrade & Tumelero, 2022). The implementation of AI in customer service not only streamlines operations but also enhances customer satisfaction by providing timely and personalized responses to client queries (Oyeniyi, 2024). Moreover, AI's capabilities in data analysis enable banks to derive insights from vast amounts of customer data, which can inform decision-making processes related to credit risk assessment and fraud detection. Advanced algorithms can analyze customer behavior patterns, allowing banks to assess creditworthiness more accurately and identify potential fraudulent activities before they occur (Mor et al., 2022). This predictive capability is crucial in a landscape where financial institutions face increasing regulatory scrutiny and the need for robust risk management frameworks (Jingrong et al., 2024). The literature emphasizes that AI's role in risk management is not only about detecting fraud but also about enhancing compliance with regulatory requirements through improved data analytics (Cerrone, 2023). The adoption of AI in banking also fosters financial inclusion by providing services to previously underserved populations. AI-driven solutions can offer tailored financial products that meet the unique needs of diverse customer segments, thereby expanding access to banking services (Dharmadhikari, 2024). For example, AI can facilitate micro-lending and personalized financial advice, which are particularly beneficial in emerging markets where traditional banking infrastructure may be lacking (Dharmadhikari, 2024). This democratization of financial services aligns with the broader trend of digital transformation in the banking sector, where technology is leveraged to enhance customer engagement and operational efficiency. Additionally, the integration of AI technologies in banking is accompanied by challenges, particularly concerning ethical considerations and the need for transparency in AI decision-making processes. Concerns regarding data privacy, algorithmic bias, and the potential for job displacement due to automation are prevalent in the discourse surrounding AI in banking (Ahmed, 2022;, Quinn, 2022). The literature suggests that banks must navigate these challenges by implementing robust governance frameworks that ensure ethical AI use while maintaining customer trust (Cerrone, 2023). Furthermore, the importance of explainable AI is underscored, as stakeholders demand clarity on how AI systems make decisions, particularly in sensitive areas such as credit scoring and loan approvals ("AI-Driven Digital Transformation in Banking: A New Perspective on Operational Efficiency and Risk Management", 2024;, Cerrone, 2023). In summary, the literature presents a comprehensive overview of the transformative impact of AI in the banking sector. The integration of AI technologies enhances operational efficiency, improves risk management, and fosters financial inclusion, while also raising important ethical considerations that must be addressed. As the banking industry continues to evolve, the strategic implementation of AI will be critical in shaping the future of financial services.

2- TECHNICAL FOUNDATIONS: MASTERING HARD SKILLS FOR AI INTEGRATION

The integration of Artificial Intelligence (AI) in the banking industry represents a significant evolution in financial services, driven by the need for enhanced operational efficiency, improved customer experiences, and robust risk management. This literature review synthesizes various studies that explore the technical foundations necessary for mastering hard skills in AI integration within the banking sector. AI technologies, particularly machine learning (ML), have become pivotal in transforming traditional banking practices. The application of ML algorithms in credit scoring and risk management has been highlighted as a key area where banks can leverage AI to enhance decision-making processes Roy (2024). These algorithms analyze vast datasets to identify patterns and predict borrower behavior, which can lead to more accurate assessments of creditworthiness and reduced default rates (Brown, 2024). Furthermore, the integration of AI in risk management allows banks to automate the detection of fraudulent activities, thereby safeguarding customer assets and maintaining trust in the financial system. The literature emphasizes that banks adopting AI-driven models can achieve significant improvements in operational efficiency and risk mitigation, ultimately leading to enhanced financial performance (Fares et al., 2022). The systematic review of AI utilization in the banking sector reveals several challenges associated with its integration. These challenges include the need for skilled personnel, data privacy concerns, and the complexities of regulatory compliance (Fares et al., 2022;, Rahman et al., 2021). The literature suggests that banks must invest in training programs to equip their workforce with the necessary skills to effectively implement and manage AI technologies (Abdulsalam, 2024). Additionally, the ethical implications of AI, such as algorithmic bias and transparency in decision-making processes, are critical considerations that banks must address to foster trust among customers and regulators (Valavan, 2023). The establishment of robust governance frameworks is essential to ensure that AI applications align with ethical standards and regulatory requirements (Moharrak, 2024; Valavan, 2023). Moreover, the role of AI in enhancing customer engagement and personalization in banking services cannot be overstated. AI-powered chatbots and virtual assistants are increasingly being deployed to provide customers with real-time assistance and personalized financial advice (Alarabiat, 2024;, El-Shihy, 2024). These technologies not only improve customer satisfaction but also streamline banking operations by reducing the workload on human staff (Sheth et al., 2022). The literature indicates that the successful implementation of AI in customer service hinges on understanding customer perceptions and preferences, which can significantly influence the adoption of AI-driven solutions (Pandey and Dangi, 2024). Banks that prioritize customer-centric AI applications are likely to achieve higher levels of customer loyalty and retention (Skandali, 2023). The integration of AI in banking also presents opportunities for financial inclusion, particularly in emerging markets. AI technologies can facilitate access to financial services for underserved populations by providing tailored financial products and services (Jejeniwa, 2024). For instance, AI-driven credit scoring models can evaluate creditworthiness based on alternative data sources, such as mobile phone usage and social media activity, thereby expanding access to credit for individuals without traditional credit histories (Jejeniwa, 2024). The literature highlights that leveraging AI for financial inclusion aligns with broader societal goals of reducing poverty and enhancing economic participation (Abdulsalam, 2024).

3- CRITICAL THINKING IN THE AI-DRIVEN FINANCIAL LANDSCAPE

In the rapidly evolving landscape of the banking industry, the integration of Artificial Intelligence (AI) has necessitated a critical examination of the skills required for effective implementation and management of AI technologies. This literature review synthesizes various studies that explore the hard skills and competencies essential for navigating the AI-driven financial landscape, emphasizing the need for a balanced approach that combines technical expertise with critical thinking and ethical considerations. The foundational skills required for AI integration in banking primarily encompass technical competencies in data science, machine learning, and programming. As AI technologies become increasingly sophisticated, banks must ensure that their workforce is equipped with the necessary technical skills to leverage these advancements effectively. For instance, Majumder highlights that understanding machine learning algorithms and data analytics is crucial for enhancing risk management and fraud detection capabilities within banks Majumder (2024). Furthermore, the systematic review by Fares et al. underscores the importance of technical proficiency in AI applications, noting that banks with skilled personnel are better positioned to harness AI's potential for operational efficiency and customer engagement (Fares et al., 2022). However, technical skills alone are insufficient for successful AI integration. The literature emphasizes the importance of soft skills, particularly critical thinking and ethical reasoning, in navigating the complexities associated with AI deployment in banking. As AI systems often operate as "black boxes," understanding their decision-making processes and addressing potential biases becomes paramount (Shiyyab, 2023). The need for transparency in AI algorithms is echoed by Shiyyab, who argues that ethical considerations must guide the development and implementation of AI technologies to ensure fairness and accountability in banking practices (Shiyyab, 2023). This perspective aligns with the findings of

Bobitan, which suggest that the future workforce must possess strong interpersonal skills to collaborate effectively with AI systems and address the ethical implications of their use (Bobitan, 2024). Moreover, the integration of AI in banking presents unique challenges that require a multifaceted skill set. For instance, regulatory compliance and data privacy concerns are critical issues that banks must navigate as they adopt AI technologies (Lazo, 2023). The literature suggests that professionals in the banking sector must be well-versed in the legal and ethical frameworks governing AI use to mitigate risks associated with data breaches and algorithmic bias (Lazo, 2023). This need for regulatory knowledge is further supported by the work of Khadka, who emphasizes the importance of understanding the regulatory landscape to foster a conducive environment for AI adoption in banking (Khadka, 2023). In addition to technical and soft skills, the literature highlights the significance of continuous learning and adaptability in the face of rapid technological advancements. As AI technologies evolve, banking professionals must engage in lifelong learning to stay abreast of the latest developments and best practices in AI integration (Khuan, 2024). The foresight analysis conducted by Bobitan indicates that the future workforce will require not only technical expertise but also the ability to adapt to new technologies and methodologies as they emerge (Bobitan, 2024). This adaptability is crucial for maintaining a competitive edge in an increasingly digital banking landscape. Furthermore, the role of AI in enhancing customer experiences necessitates a customer-centric approach that combines technical skills with an understanding of consumer behavior. Research by Skandali suggests that banks must prioritize customer perceptions and preferences when implementing AI-driven solutions to ensure successful adoption and satisfaction (Skandali, 2023). This emphasis on customer-centricity aligns with the findings of Dharmadhikari, who underscores the importance of understanding customer attitudes towards AI technologies to foster trust and engagement in banking services (Dharmadhikari, 2024).

4- SOFT SKILLS FOR AN AI-AUGMENTED WORKPLACE

The integration of Artificial Intelligence (AI) in the banking sector is transforming not only operational processes but also the skill sets required for effective workforce performance. As AI technologies become more prevalent, the importance of soft skills alongside technical competencies has emerged as a critical area of focus. This literature review synthesizes various studies that highlight the essential soft skills necessary for thriving in an AI-augmented workplace within the banking industry. One of the primary soft skills that has gained prominence in the context of AI integration is critical thinking. As banks increasingly rely on AI systems for decision-making, employees must possess the ability to critically evaluate AI-generated insights and recommendations. Research indicates that critical thinking enables employees to discern the validity of AI outputs, assess potential biases, and make informed decisions based on a comprehensive understanding of the data Hajj (2023). The ability to engage in critical analysis is particularly vital in financial contexts where decisions can have significant implications for risk management and customer trust (Skandali, 2023). Moreover, effective communication skills are essential in an AI-augmented workplace. As AI tools, such as chatbots and virtual assistants, become integral to customer interactions, employees must be adept at communicating both with these technologies and with customers who may have varying levels of familiarity with AI (Ranković, 2023). The literature emphasizes that employees should be trained not only to operate AI systems but also to interpret AI outputs and convey relevant information to clients in a clear and accessible manner (Mende, 2023). This dual capability enhances the overall customer experience and fosters trust in AI-driven services. Emotional intelligence (EI) is another critical soft skill that complements technical expertise in an AI-enhanced banking environment. As AI systems take over routine tasks, the human element of banking—characterized by empathy, understanding, and relationship-building—becomes increasingly important (Mende, 2023). Employees with high emotional intelligence can better navigate customer interactions, particularly in sensitive situations such as financial advising or conflict resolution (Jena, 2024). The ability to empathize with customers and understand their needs is crucial for maintaining strong client relationships, especially when AI systems are involved in service delivery. Adaptability and resilience are also vital soft skills in the context of AI integration. The rapid pace of technological change necessitates that banking professionals remain flexible and open to learning new tools and methodologies (Gonçalves et al., 2023). Employees must be prepared to adapt to evolving AI technologies and the shifting landscape of financial services, which may include new regulatory requirements and customer expectations (Flavián et al., 2021). The literature suggests that fostering a culture of continuous learning and adaptability within organizations can enhance employee engagement and performance in an AI-driven environment (Chotrani, 2024). Furthermore, collaboration and teamwork are essential soft skills that facilitate effective AI integration in banking. As AI systems often require input from various stakeholders, including IT professionals, data analysts, and customer service representatives, the ability to work collaboratively across departments is crucial (Olan et al., 2024). Research indicates that fostering a collaborative culture can lead to more innovative solutions and improved problem-solving capabilities, ultimately enhancing the effectiveness of AI applications in banking (Grubaugh, 2024). Employees who can effectively collaborate with diverse teams are better positioned to leverage AI technologies to meet organizational goals.

5- ADAPTABILITY AND LIFELONG LEARNING: STAYING AHEAD IN A DYNAMIC INDUSTRY

The advancement of Artificial Intelligence (AI) in the banking sector is reshaping the industry, necessitating a focus on adaptability and lifelong learning among professionals. As AI technologies evolve, they bring both opportunities and challenges that require banking employees to continuously update their skills and knowledge. This literature review synthesizes various studies that highlight the significance of adaptability and lifelong learning in staying ahead in a dynamic industry characterized by rapid technological changes. AI's integration into banking has led to significant improvements in operational efficiency, risk management, and customer service. For instance, Majumder discusses how AI technologies, particularly those involving real-time data analytics and anomaly detection, provide banks with advanced tools to detect and prevent fraudulent activities Majumder (2024). These systems not only enhance security but also improve decision-making processes, allowing banks to respond swiftly to emerging threats. As AI continues to advance, employees must adapt to these new tools and methodologies, emphasizing the importance of continuous learning and professional development (ircovnicu and Ha egan, 2023). The literature indicates that adaptability is a crucial soft skill in the context of AI integration. As banking professionals encounter new AI technologies, they must be willing to embrace change and learn how to utilize these innovations effectively. Fares et al. highlight that while banks are eager to adopt AI technologies, there is often a gap in the necessary training and development programs to support this transition (Fares et al., 2022). Therefore, fostering a culture of adaptability within banking institutions is vital for maintaining a competitive edge in the industry. Moreover, the rapid pace of technological change in banking necessitates a commitment to lifelong learning. Employees must engage in ongoing education and training to stay abreast of the latest developments in AI and its applications in banking. The systematic review by Kumar et al. underscores the importance of continuous education in equipping banking professionals with the skills needed to leverage AI effectively (Kumar et al., 2021). This commitment to lifelong learning not only enhances individual performance but also contributes to the overall success of the organization. In addition to technical skills, the integration of AI in banking raises ethical considerations that require ongoing education and awareness. As AI systems become more prevalent, understanding the ethical implications of their use—such as data privacy, algorithmic bias, and transparency—becomes paramount (Coetzee, 2018). Professionals in the banking sector must engage in discussions and training related to ethical AI practices to ensure responsible implementation that aligns with regulatory requirements and societal expectations (Mor et al., 2022). Collaboration is another essential aspect of adaptability and lifelong learning in the AI-augmented banking landscape. As

AI technologies often require input from various departments, fostering a collaborative environment can facilitate knowledge sharing and innovation (Rusydiana, 2024). Employees who can work effectively in teams are better positioned to adapt to changes and contribute to the successful implementation of AI initiatives. This collaborative approach not only enhances individual skill sets but also promotes a collective understanding of AI's potential and challenges. Furthermore, the literature emphasizes the role of emotional intelligence in navigating the complexities of an AI-driven banking environment. As AI systems take over routine tasks, the human element of banking—characterized by empathy, understanding, and relationship-building—becomes increasingly important (Maseke, 2024). Employees with high emotional intelligence can better navigate customer interactions, particularly in sensitive situations where AI systems are involved. This ability to empathize with customers and understand their needs is crucial for maintaining strong client relationships in an AI-augmented landscape.

6- ETHICS AND EMOTIONAL INTELLIGENCE: THE HUMAN FACE OF AI

The integration of Artificial Intelligence (AI) in the banking sector has raised significant ethical considerations that necessitate a focus on emotional intelligence and ethical frameworks. As AI technologies become more prevalent in financial decision-making, understanding the human elements of ethics and emotional intelligence is crucial for fostering trust and accountability in AI-driven systems. This literature review synthesizes various studies that explore the intersection of ethics, emotional intelligence, and AI in the banking industry. AI's ability to analyze vast amounts of data and provide insights has transformed financial decision-making processes. However, this transformation also poses ethical challenges that require careful consideration. For instance, Owolabi emphasizes the importance of ethical frameworks to guide the use of AI in financial decision-making, arguing that the deployment of AI must be accompanied by robust ethical guidelines to ensure fairness and transparency Owolabi (2024). This perspective aligns with the findings of Ranković, who discusses the ethical considerations that arise from AI's ability to provide personalized financial advice, emphasizing the need for responsible AI practices in the banking sector (Ranković, 2023). Emotional intelligence plays a pivotal role in navigating the ethical landscape of AI in banking. As AI systems increasingly interact with customers, the ability to empathize and understand human emotions becomes essential. Jin's research highlights the importance of emotional intelligence in service interactions, particularly in the context of AI's emulation of human emotions (Jin, 2023). This capability is crucial for building trust with customers, as individuals are more likely to engage with AI systems that demonstrate an understanding of their needs and concerns. The integration of emotional intelligence into AI systems can enhance customer satisfaction and loyalty, ultimately benefiting financial institutions (Jin, 2023). Moreover, the ethical implications of AI in banking extend beyond individual interactions to encompass broader societal concerns. The work of Georgieva et al. highlights the need for democratic oversight and citizen engagement in the development and deployment of AI technologies (Georgieva et al., 2022). This approach emphasizes the importance of involving stakeholders in discussions about AI ethics, ensuring that diverse perspectives are considered in decision-making processes. By fostering a culture of ethical deliberation and emotional intelligence, banks can better navigate the complexities of AI integration while addressing the concerns of their customers and the wider community. The literature also emphasizes the necessity of AI literacy among banking professionals to effectively engage with ethical considerations. Leikas et al. define AI literacy as a set of competencies that enables individuals to critically evaluate AI technologies and communicate effectively about their implications (Leikas et al., 2022). This literacy is essential for fostering ethical practices in AI deployment, as it empowers employees to recognize potential biases and ethical dilemmas associated with AI systems. By promoting AI literacy, banks can cultivate a workforce that is better equipped to address the ethical challenges posed by AI technologies. Furthermore, the ethical use of AI in banking requires a commitment to transparency and accountability. Morley et al. argue that ethical considerations should be operationalized within AI systems to ensure that decision-making processes are transparent and justifiable (Morley et al., 2021). This transparency is vital for building trust with customers, as individuals are more likely to engage with AI systems that provide clear explanations for their decisions. By prioritizing transparency and accountability, banks can enhance their ethical standing and foster positive relationships with their customers.

7- FUTURE PROOFING CAREERS: BUILDING A BALANCED SKILL SET

The rapid advancement of Artificial Intelligence (AI) in the banking sector is reshaping the landscape of financial services, necessitating a focus on futureproofing careers through the development of a balanced skill set. As AI technologies become integral to banking operations, professionals must cultivate a diverse array of skills to remain competitive and relevant in this dynamic environment. This literature review synthesizes various studies that highlight the importance of adaptability, continuous learning, and a balanced skill set for banking professionals in the age of AI. AI is transforming banking by enhancing operational efficiency, improving customer service, and enabling sophisticated risk management strategies. For instance, Majumder discusses how AI technologies, such as machine learning and real-time data analytics, are crucial for identifying and preventing fraudulent activities, which have become increasingly sophisticated in the digital age Majumder (2024). This transformation underscores the need for banking professionals to develop technical skills in AI and data analytics to effectively leverage these technologies. However, technical skills alone are insufficient; professionals must also cultivate soft skills, such as emotional intelligence and ethical reasoning, to navigate the complexities of AI integration in banking. The concept of a "balanced skill set" is emerging as a modern approach to career development in the banking sector. Gündüz emphasizes that developing 21st-century competencies, including critical thinking, problem-solving, and adaptability, is essential for preparing individuals for a lifelong learning journey (GÜNDÜZ, 2023). These skills are valuable in navigating a rapidly changing world, particularly in industries like banking that are heavily influenced by technological advancements. The integration of AI into banking operations requires employees to be proactive in their learning, seeking out opportunities for professional development and skill enhancement (Koç, 2024). Moreover, emotional intelligence is becoming increasingly important in an AI-driven banking environment. As AI systems take over routine tasks, the human element of banking—characterized by empathy, understanding, and relationship-building—becomes vital (K.C., 2023). Employees with high emotional intelligence can better navigate customer interactions, particularly in sensitive situations where AI systems are involved. This ability to empathize with customers and understand their needs is crucial for maintaining strong client relationships in an AI-augmented landscape. The literature suggests that fostering emotional intelligence among banking professionals can enhance customer satisfaction and loyalty, ultimately benefiting financial institutions (K.C., 2023). In addition to emotional intelligence, ethical considerations are critical in the context of AI integration in banking. The work of Owolabi highlights the importance of ethical frameworks to guide the use of AI in financial decision-making, arguing that the deployment of AI must be accompanied by robust ethical guidelines to ensure fairness and transparency (Owolabi, 2024). As AI technologies continue to evolve, professionals in the banking sector must engage in discussions and training related to ethical AI practices to ensure responsible implementation that aligns with regulatory requirements and societal expectations (Atadoga, 2024). The literature also emphasizes the necessity of AI literacy among banking professionals to effectively engage with AI technologies. Masrek discusses how AI can empower ubiquitous and lifelong learning, highlighting the importance of developing skills that allow individuals to adapt to new technologies and learning environments (Masrek, 2024). This literacy is essential for fostering ethical practices in AI deployment, as it empowers employees to recognize potential biases and ethical dilemmas associated with AI systems. By promoting AI literacy, banks can cultivate a workforce that is better equipped to address the ethical challenges posed by AI technologies (Masrek, 2024). Furthermore, the integration of AI in banking presents opportunities for innovation and efficiency, but it also requires a strategic approach to workforce development. The review by Atadoga emphasizes the need for a strategic approach to AI integration in banking, where technological advancements are matched with workforce upskilling initiatives (Atadoga, 2024). This strategic alignment ensures that employees possess the necessary skills to leverage AI technologies effectively while addressing ethical concerns and maintaining customer trust.

8- THE INTERSECTION OF AI AND REGULATORY COMPLIANCE

The intersection of Artificial Intelligence (AI) and regulatory compliance in the banking sector presents both opportunities and challenges. As AI technologies become increasingly integrated into financial services, understanding the implications for regulatory compliance is essential for ensuring ethical practices and maintaining consumer trust. This literature review synthesizes various studies that explore the role of AI in enhancing regulatory compliance, the ethical considerations involved, and the challenges that financial institutions face in this evolving landscape. AI has the potential to significantly enhance regulatory compliance in banking by automating processes and improving accuracy in monitoring and reporting. Adeyelu highlights the effectiveness of AI technologies in automating financial regulatory compliance, providing a comprehensive review of various applications and scenarios where AI can streamline compliance processes Adeyelu (2024). The study identifies key performance indicators for AI compliance solutions, emphasizing the transformative potential of AI in reducing compliance costs and improving efficiency. By leveraging AI, banks can more effectively monitor transactions, identify anomalies, and ensure adherence to regulatory requirements, thus mitigating risks associated with non-compliance. Moreover, the ethical implications of AI in regulatory compliance are crucial to consider. The work of Owolabi underscores the importance of ethical frameworks to guide the use of AI in financial decision-making, arguing that the deployment of AI must be accompanied by robust ethical guidelines to ensure fairness and transparency. As AI systems become more prevalent, financial institutions must navigate the ethical challenges associated with algorithmic decision-making, including issues of bias, accountability, and transparency. The integration of ethical considerations into AI compliance frameworks is essential for building trust with consumers and regulators alike. The literature also emphasizes the necessity of transparency and accountability in AI-driven compliance solutions. Singh discusses how AI, machine learning (ML), and deep learning can serve as effective RegTech tools to assist financial institutions in meeting regulatory burdens (Singh, 2023). The study highlights the importance of ensuring that AI systems are interpretable and that their decision-making processes can be audited. This transparency is vital for regulatory compliance, as it allows stakeholders to understand how AI systems arrive at their conclusions and ensures that ethical standards are upheld. However, the integration of AI in regulatory compliance is not without its challenges. The evolving regulatory frameworks for AI in banking present a layer of complexity, as institutions must continuously adapt to comply with new and changing regulations. Majumder emphasizes the need for a balanced approach to leveraging AI's potential in banking, addressing both its transformative benefits and the ethical and regulatory challenges involved (Majumder, 2024). The dynamic nature of regulatory requirements necessitates that banks invest in ongoing training and development to ensure that their workforce is equipped to navigate these complexities effectively. Furthermore, the study by Oladoyinbo examines the ethical challenges and regulatory dynamics of AI in relation to data integrity and its influence on social dynamics (Oladoyinbo, 2024). The research highlights the importance of maintaining data integrity in AI applications, as any breaches can lead to significant reputational damage and regulatory penalties. Financial institutions must implement robust data governance frameworks that prioritize ethical considerations and compliance with data protection regulations.

9- INNOVATION AND CREATIVITY IN AN AI-DRIVEN BANKING ECOSYSTEM

The integration of Artificial Intelligence (AI) in the banking sector is transforming operational processes and fostering innovation within the industry. As banks increasingly adopt AI technologies, they enhance customer experiences, streamline operations, and develop new financial products and services. This literature review synthesizes various studies that explore the intersection of AI, innovation, and creativity in the banking ecosystem. AI-driven banking services are at the forefront of creating personalized customer experiences. Sheth et al. highlight that AI enables banks to tailor their services to meet individual customer needs, thereby enhancing customer satisfaction and loyalty Sheth et al. (2022). By leveraging data analytics and machine learning algorithms, banks can analyze customer behavior and preferences, allowing them to offer customized financial solutions. This personalization improves customer engagement and drives innovation in service delivery, as banks seek to differentiate themselves in a competitive market. Moreover, the systematic review by Fares et al. emphasizes the importance of utilizing AI in mobile and internet banking, particularly in relation to customer adoption and acceptance (Fares et al., 2022). The findings suggest that AI technologies can significantly enhance the user experience by providing seamless and efficient banking services. As banks continue to innovate their digital offerings, the integration of AI will play a crucial role in shaping the future of banking, making it imperative for financial institutions to invest in AI capabilities to remain competitive. Khadka's research further underscores the implications of AI-driven customization in financial services, particularly in emerging markets (Khadka, 2023). The study reveals that AI enhances service delivery and contributes to social innovation by expanding access to financial services for underserved populations. This ability to innovate and adapt to the needs of diverse customer segments positions AI as a transformative force in the banking sector, enabling institutions to address social challenges while driving business growth. In addition to enhancing customer experiences, AI fosters creativity within banking operations. Skandali discusses how AI applications can facilitate customer engagement by acknowledging emotional interactions and perceptions (Skandali, 2023). As banks transition to digital-first strategies, understanding customer emotions and preferences becomes essential for developing innovative marketing strategies and service offerings. This focus on emotional intelligence in AI applications allows banks to create more meaningful connections with their customers, ultimately leading to increased loyalty and retention. The role of AI in driving innovation is further supported by the findings of Andrade and Tumelero, who highlight the efficiency gains achieved through AI-powered chatbots in customer service (Andrade & Tumelero, 2022). These virtual assistants streamline operations and free up human resources to focus on more complex tasks that require creativity and critical thinking. By automating routine inquiries, banks can allocate their workforce to innovate new products and services that meet evolving customer demands. However, the integration of AI in banking also presents challenges that must be addressed to fully realize its innovative potential. The study by Majumder emphasizes the need for banks to navigate the ethical implications of AI adoption, including concerns related to data privacy and algorithmic bias (Majumder, 2024). As banks leverage AI to enhance their services, they must ensure that their practices align with ethical standards and regulatory requirements. This commitment to ethical AI use is essential for maintaining consumer trust and fostering a culture of innovation within the organization. Furthermore, the findings of Yablonsky highlight the importance of AI-driven digital platform innovation in creating value for banks (Yablonsky, 2020). By adopting AI technologies, banks can enhance their operational efficiency and develop new business models that leverage data-driven insights. This shift towards AI-driven innovation necessitates a strategic approach to workforce development, where employees are equipped with the skills needed to harness the potential of AI technologies effectively.

10- BUILDING CUSTOMER TRUST IN A TECHNOLOGY-FIRST ERA

In the technology-first era, building customer trust in banking institutions is more critical than ever, particularly as digital transformation reshapes the financial landscape. The integration of Artificial Intelligence (AI) and other digital technologies in banking has the potential to enhance customer experiences, but it also raises concerns regarding security, privacy, and ethical practices. This literature review synthesizes various studies that explore strategies for fostering customer trust in an increasingly digital banking environment. Trust is a fundamental component of customer loyalty in the banking sector. Bakar emphasizes that trust reduces the perceived risk associated with banking services, making it a key predictor of customer loyalty Bakar (2024). In a competitive market, where customers have numerous options, establishing and maintaining trust is essential for retaining clients and ensuring long-term success. The literature suggests that banks must prioritize transparency and communication to build trust, particularly when introducing new technologies and services. The role of electronic word-of-mouth (e-WOM) in shaping customer perceptions of trust is also significant. Innayah et al. highlight that banks should actively engage with customers on social media platforms to convey the value and security of their services (Innayah et al., 2022). By addressing customer concerns and showcasing positive experiences, banks can enhance their reputation and foster trust among potential clients. This proactive approach to communication is vital in an era where information spreads rapidly through digital channels. Moreover, the digital transformation of banking services has a profound impact on customer trust. Pristiyono et al. discuss how the perception of trust and perceived risk significantly influence user attitudes towards digital banking (Pristiyono et al., 2022). As banks increasingly rely on technology to deliver services, they must ensure that their digital platforms are secure and user-friendly. This focus on security is crucial for mitigating customer concerns about data breaches and fraud, which can erode trust in digital banking services. Melnyk's research further explores the transformation of trust between banks and young clients in the context of digital banking (Melnyk, 2023). The study reveals that digitalization is reshaping the nature of trust, as younger consumers often prioritize convenience and accessibility. Banks must adapt their strategies to meet the expectations of this demographic, leveraging technology to enhance customer experiences while maintaining a strong emphasis on security and ethical practices. The mediating role of trust in the relationship between corporate image, security, and customer loyalty is highlighted by Purwanto et al. (Purwanto et al., 2020). The study suggests that a positive corporate image, combined with robust security measures, can significantly enhance customer loyalty in mobile banking. This finding underscores the importance of integrating trust-building strategies into the overall branding and marketing efforts of banks. Gupta's qualitative study on consumer trust in digital banking emphasizes the complex interplay of factors that influence trust, including legal and regulatory impacts (Gupta, 2024). As digital banking becomes more prevalent, banks must navigate a landscape of evolving regulations and compliance requirements. By demonstrating a commitment to ethical practices and regulatory compliance, banks can enhance their credibility and foster trust among customers.

11- PERSONALIZATION THROUGH AI: TAILORING FINANCIAL SERVICES

The integration of Artificial Intelligence (AI) in banking is fundamentally transforming how financial services are delivered, particularly through the lens of personalization. As banks increasingly adopt AI technologies, they are able to tailor their offerings to meet the unique needs and preferences of individual customers. This literature review synthesizes various studies that explore the implications of AI-driven personalization in financial services, highlighting its impact on customer experience, engagement, and overall satisfaction. AI-driven customization in financial services is a powerful tool for enhancing customer experiences. Khadka emphasizes that AI technologies enable banks to analyze vast amounts of data to understand customer behavior and preferences, leading to more personalized service offerings Khadka (2023). This capability allows banks to provide tailored financial products and services that align with the specific needs of their clients, thereby improving customer satisfaction and loyalty. The ability to customize services based on individual preferences is increasingly becoming a competitive differentiator in the banking sector. Moreover, Sheth et al. discuss how AI-driven banking services represent the next frontier for personalized experiences, particularly in emerging markets (Sheth et al., 2022). The study highlights that AI technologies, such as machine learning and predictive analytics, can significantly enhance customer interactions by providing relevant recommendations and insights. This personalization not only improves customer engagement but also fosters a deeper connection between banks and their clients, ultimately leading to increased trust and loyalty. The role of natural language processing (NLP) in enhancing customer interactions is also noteworthy. Bhuiyan points out that advancements in NLP and machine learning enable chatbots and virtual assistants to engage with customers in a more human-like manner, understanding their preferences and emotions (Bhuiyan, 2024). By monitoring customer interactions and analyzing sentiment, AI systems can provide personalized responses and recommendations, further enhancing the customer experience. This level of personalization is crucial in an era where customers expect seamless and tailored interactions with their financial institutions. Gigante and Zago explore the applications of DARQ technologies (Decentralized, Autonomous, Real-time, and Quantum) in personalized banking, emphasizing the potential of AI to create hyper-personalized financial products (Gigante & Zago, 2022). The study suggests that by leveraging these advanced technologies, banks can develop innovative solutions that cater to the unique financial needs of individual customers. This approach not only enhances customer satisfaction but also drives innovation within the banking sector, as institutions seek to differentiate themselves through personalized offerings. However, the implementation of AI-driven personalization also raises ethical considerations. Klochko discusses the importance of ensuring data privacy and security in AI applications, particularly in mobile banking (Klochko, 2023). As banks collect and analyze vast amounts of customer data to deliver personalized services, they must prioritize the protection of this information to maintain customer trust. The ethical use of AI in personalization requires banks to establish robust data governance frameworks that ensure compliance with regulatory standards and safeguard customer privacy. The challenges associated with AI-driven personalization are further explored by Ghandour, who highlights the need for banks to navigate the complexities of customer data management (Ghandour, 2021). The study emphasizes that while AI can enhance personalization, it also requires banks to invest in technology and infrastructure to effectively manage and analyze customer data. This investment is essential for ensuring that AI systems can deliver accurate and relevant personalized services while maintaining compliance with data protection regulations.

12- GLOBAL IMPACTS OF AI IN BANKING: OPPORTUNITIES AND CHALLENGES

The global impacts of Artificial Intelligence (AI) in banking present a complex interplay of opportunities and challenges that financial institutions must navigate to thrive in an increasingly digital landscape. As AI technologies become more integrated into banking operations, they offer significant potential for enhancing customer experiences, improving operational efficiencies, and driving innovation. However, these advancements also raise critical concerns regarding security, ethical practices, and regulatory compliance. This literature review synthesizes various studies that explore the multifaceted impacts of AI in the banking sector. One of the most significant opportunities presented by AI in banking is the ability to enhance customer personalization. Khadka emphasizes that AI-driven customization allows banks to tailor their services to meet the unique needs of individual customers, thereby improving customer satisfaction and loyalty Khadka (2023). By leveraging data analytics and machine learning algorithms, banks can analyze customer behavior and preferences, allowing them to offer personalized financial solutions. This capability not only enhances customer engagement but also fosters a deeper connection between banks and their clients, ultimately leading to increased trust and retention. Moreover, the study by Ho and Chow highlights the role of AI in shaping consumer brand preferences for retail banks (Ho & Chow, 2023). The findings suggest that AI technologies can significantly influence customer perceptions and preferences, thereby impacting their choice of banking institutions. As banks increasingly adopt AI to enhance their service offerings, understanding the factors that drive customer preferences becomes essential for maintaining a competitive edge in the market. However, the integration of AI in banking also poses challenges, particularly concerning cybersecurity. Khan et al. discuss the increasing prevalence of cybercrime in the banking sector and the need for robust security measures to protect sensitive customer data (Khan et al., 2023). As banks adopt AI technologies, they must also invest in cybersecurity solutions to mitigate the risks associated with data breaches and fraud. The literature emphasizes that addressing cybersecurity concerns is critical for maintaining customer trust and ensuring the successful implementation of AI-driven solutions. The ethical implications of AI in banking are another area of concern. Fares et al. highlight the importance of ethical frameworks to guide the use of AI in financial decision-making, arguing that the deployment of AI must be accompanied by robust ethical guidelines to ensure fairness and transparency (Fares et al., 2022). As AI systems become more prevalent, financial institutions must navigate the ethical challenges associated with algorithmic decision-making, including issues of bias, accountability, and transparency. The integration of ethical considerations into AI compliance frameworks is essential for building trust with consumers and regulators alike. Furthermore, the study by Tulcanaza-Prieto et al. explores the influence of customer perception factors on AI-enabled customer experiences in the Ecuadorian banking environment (Tulcanaza-Prieto et al., 2023). The results indicate that positive customer perceptions of AI technologies are associated with improved customer experiences. This finding underscores the importance of effective communication and education regarding AI applications in banking to foster acceptance and trust among customers. The challenges associated with AI adoption in banking are further explored by Ghandour, who emphasizes the need for banks to navigate the complexities of customer data management and regulatory compliance (Ghandour, 2021). The study highlights that while AI can enhance personalization, it also requires banks to invest in technology and infrastructure to effectively manage and analyze customer data. This investment is essential for ensuring that AI systems can deliver accurate and relevant personalized services while maintaining compliance with data protection regulations.

13- SHAPING THE FUTURE: THE ROLE OF LEADERSHIP IN AN AI-DRIVEN BANKING WORKFORCE

In the context of an AI-driven banking workforce, leadership plays a pivotal role in shaping the future of financial institutions. As banks increasingly integrate AI technologies into their operations, effective leadership becomes essential for navigating the complexities and challenges associated with this transformation. This literature review synthesizes various studies that explore the role of leadership in fostering an innovative, adaptable, and ethically responsible banking environment in the age of AI. One of the primary responsibilities of leadership in an AI-driven banking ecosystem is to cultivate a culture of innovation. Supriyanto and Soehari emphasize that effective leadership is crucial for encouraging creativity and innovation among employees, which is necessary for adapting to the rapidly changing technological landscape Supriyanto & Soehari (2022). Leaders must inspire their teams to embrace new technologies and explore innovative solutions that enhance customer experiences and operational efficiencies. This focus on innovation is particularly important as banks seek to differentiate themselves in a competitive market. Strategic leadership practices are also vital for maintaining competitiveness in the banking sector. Okwiri's research highlights that strategic leadership significantly influences the performance of banks, particularly in the context of adopting new technologies (Okwiri, 2024). By fostering a strategic vision and aligning organizational goals with technological advancements, leaders can ensure that their institutions remain agile and responsive to market demands. This strategic alignment is essential for leveraging AI to enhance service delivery and customer engagement. Moreover, the role of transformational leadership in promoting a positive organizational culture is crucial in an AI-driven environment. Khadka discusses how transformational leaders can inspire and motivate employees to embrace AI technologies and adapt to new ways of working (Khadka, 2023). This leadership style encourages collaboration and open communication, which are essential for fostering a culture of trust and innovation. As banks implement AI solutions, leaders must ensure that their teams feel supported and empowered to explore new ideas and approaches. The ethical implications of AI adoption in banking also necessitate strong leadership. Jeong emphasizes that coaching leadership can buffer against job stress and protect employee well-being in the face of AI transitions (Jeong, 2024). Leaders must prioritize ethical considerations in the deployment of AI technologies, ensuring that their use aligns with organizational values and regulatory requirements. By fostering an ethical culture, leaders can build trust with employees and customers alike, which is essential for the successful implementation of AI solutions. Furthermore, the study by Wijayati et al. highlights the importance of change leadership in moderating the effects of AI on employee performance and engagement (Wijayati et al., 2022). As banks adopt AI technologies, leaders must effectively manage the change process, providing guidance and support to employees as they navigate new systems and workflows. This proactive approach to change management is critical for ensuring that employees remain engaged and motivated during the transition. In addition to fostering innovation and ethical practices, leaders must also focus on developing the skills of their workforce to effectively leverage AI technologies. The research by Ghamrawi emphasizes the need for leaders to facilitate continuous learning and professional development among employees (Ghamrawi, 2023). By investing in training programs that enhance AI literacy and technical competencies, leaders can ensure that their teams are well-equipped to harness the potential of AI in banking.

CONCLUSION

The era of artificial intelligence has redefined the banking industry, positioning internal auditors as key players in ensuring organizational integrity and governance. As AI technologies continue to permeate every facet of financial services, the role of internal auditors has expanded to encompass not only technical proficiency but also a deep understanding of ethical practices and human relationships. This book has explored the essential soft and hard skills required to navigate this evolving landscape, emphasizing the need for a balanced approach to workforce development. By mastering technical competencies such as data analytics, machine learning, and cybersecurity, auditors can harness AI's potential to enhance efficiency and accuracy in auditing processes. At the same time, cultivating critical soft skills, including emotional intelligence, adaptability, and effective communication, ensures that the human element remains integral in an AI-driven environment. As the banking industry continues to evolve, the challenges of ethical AI implementation, regulatory compliance, and the preservation of customer trust will require internal auditors to adopt a proactive and forward-thinking mindset. This book has highlighted the importance of continuous learning and collaboration in equipping auditors with the tools to remain relevant and impactful. By fostering a culture of innovation, adaptability, and ethical responsibility, internal auditors can position themselves as indispensable guardians of transparency and accountability. The convergence of advanced technologies and human expertise offers unprecedented opportunities to shape the future of banking, and it is through this synergy that internal auditors will play a pivotal role in driving the industry forward. Ultimately, this book serves as a guide and inspiration for professionals committed to bridging the gap between technology and humanity, ensuring that the transformative power of AI is harnessed responsibly and effectively for the benefit of organizations and society.

REFERENCES

Abdulsalam, T. A., & Tajudeen, R. B. (2024). Artificial Intelligence (AI) in the Banking Industry: A Review of Service Areas and Customer Service Journeys in Emerging Economies. *Business & Management Compass*, *68*(3), 19–43. DOI: 10.56065/9hfvrq20

Abdulsalam, T. A., & Tajudeen, R. B. (2024). Artificial Intelligence (AI) in the Banking Industry: A Review of Service Areas and Customer Service Journeys in Emerging Economies. *Business & Management Compass*, *68*(3), 19–43. DOI: 10.56065/9hfvrq20

Adeyelu, O. O., Ugochukwu, C. E., & Shonibare, M. A. (2024). AUTOMATING FINANCIAL REGULATORY COMPLIANCE WITH AI: A REVIEW AND APPLICATION SCENARIOS. *Finance & Accounting Research Journal*, *6*(4), 580–601. DOI: 10.51594/farj.v6i4.1035

Ahmed, F. (2022). Ethical aspects of artificial intelligence in banking. *Journal of Research in Economics and Finance Management*, *1*(2), 55–63. DOI: 10.56596/jrefm.v1i2.7

Alarabiat, A. A., & Al Hadidi, M. A. (2024). CONTINUOUS USE OF MOBILE BANKING APPLICATIONS: THE ROLE OF PROCESS VIRTUALIZABILITY, ANTHROPOMORPHISM AND VIRTUAL PROCESS FAILURE RISK. *Interdisciplinary Journal of Information, Knowledge & Management, 19.*

Atadoga, A., Obi, O. C., Onwusinkwue, S., Dawodu, S. O., Osasona, F., & Daraojimba, A. I. (2024). AI's evolving impact in US banking: An insightful review. *International Journal of Science and Research Archive*, *11*(1), 904–922. DOI: 10.30574/ijsra.2024.11.1.0157

Bakar, J. A., & Adzis, A. A. (2024). Fostering loyalty among young consumers: Strategic approaches for bank sustainability. *International Journal of Professional Business Review*, *9*(3), e04469–e04469. DOI: 10.26668/businessreview/2024.v9i3.4469

Bhuiyan, M. S. (2024). The role of AI-Enhanced personalization in customer experiences. *Journal of Computer Science and Technology Studies*, *6*(1), 162–169. DOI: 10.32996/jcsts.2024.6.1.17

Bobitan, N., Dumitrescu, D., Popa, A. F., Sahlian, D. N., & Turlea, I. C. (2024). Shaping Tomorrow: Anticipating Skills Requirements Based on the Integration of Artificial Intelligence in Business Organizations—A Foresight Analysis Using the Scenario Method. *Electronics (Basel)*, *13*(11), 2198. DOI: 10.3390/electronics13112198

Brown, M. (2024). Influence of Artificial Intelligence on Credit Risk Assessment in Banking Sector. *International Journal of Modern Risk Management*, *2*(1), 24–33. DOI: 10.47604/ijmrm.2641

Cerrone, R. (2023). Are Artificial Intelligence and Machine Learning Shaping a New Risk Management Approach? *International Business Research*, *16*(12), 1–82. DOI: 10.5539/ibr.v16n12p82

Coetzee, J. (2018). Strategic implications of Fintech on South African retail banks. *Suid-Afrikaanse Tydskrif vir Ekonomiese en Bestuurswetenskappe*, *21*(1), 1–11. DOI: 10.4102/sajems.v21i1.2455

De Andrade, I. M., & Tumelero, C. (2022). Increasing customer service efficiency through artificial intelligence chatbot. *Revista de Gestão*, *29*(3), 238–251. DOI: 10.1108/REGE-07-2021-0120

El Hajj, M., & Hammoud, J. (2023). Unveiling the influence of artificial intelligence and machine learning on financial markets: A comprehensive analysis of AI applications in trading, risk management, and financial operations. *Journal of Risk and Financial Management*, *16*(10), 434. DOI: 10.3390/jrfm16100434

El-Shihy, D., Abdelraouf, M., Hegazy, M., & Hassan, N. (2024). The Influence of AI Chatbots in Fintech Services on Customer Loyalty within the Banking Industry. *Future of Business Administration*, *3*(1), 16–28. DOI: 10.33422/fba.v3i1.644

Fares, O. H., Butt, I., & Lee, S. H. M. (2022). Utilization of artificial intelligence in the banking sector: A systematic literature review. *Journal of Financial Services Marketing*, •••, 1.

Flavián, C., Pérez-Rueda, A., Belanche, D., & Casaló, L. V. (2022). Intention to use analytical artificial intelligence (AI) in services–the effect of technology readiness and awareness. *Journal of Service Management*, *33*(2), 293–320. DOI: 10.1108/JOSM-10-2020-0378

Georgieva, I., Lazo, C., Timan, T., & van Veenstra, A. F. (2022). From AI ethics principles to data science practice: A reflection and a gap analysis based on recent frameworks and practical experience. *AI and Ethics*, *2*(4), 697–711. DOI: 10.1007/s43681-021-00127-3

Ghandour, A. (2021). Opportunities and challenges of artificial intelligence in banking: Systematic literature review. *TEM Journal*, *10*(4), 1581–1587. DOI: 10.18421/TEM104-12

Gigante, G., & Zago, A. (2023). DARQ technologies in the financial sector: Artificial intelligence applications in personalized banking. *Qualitative Research in Financial Markets*, *15*(1), 29–57. DOI: 10.1108/QRFM-02-2021-0025

Gonçalves, A. R., Breda Meira, A., Shuqair, S., & Costa Pinto, D. (2023). Artificial intelligence (AI) in FinTech decisions: The role of congruity and rejection sensitivity. *International Journal of Bank Marketing*, *41*(6), 1282–1307. DOI: 10.1108/IJBM-07-2022-0295

Grubaugh, S., & Levitt, G. (2024). The Future of Elementary Social Studies: Harnessing AI's Potential Through Evidence-Based Practices. *Technium Social Sciences Journal*, *58*, 87–93. DOI: 10.47577/tssj.v58i1.10991

Gündüz, A. Y. (2023). The Importance of Investigating Students' Lifelong Learning Levels and Perceptions of 21st-Century Skills. *International e-Journal of Educational Studies, 7*(15), 788-796.

Gupta, V., & Shukla, S. (2024). Consumer Trust in Digital Banking: A Qualitative Study of Legal and Regulatory Impacts. *Interdisciplinary Studies in Society, Law, and Politics*, *3*(2), 18–24. DOI: 10.61838/kman.isslp.3.2.4

Ho, S. P. S., & Chow, M. Y. C. (2023). The role of artificial intelligence in consumers' brand preference for retail banks in Hong Kong. *Journal of Financial Services Marketing*, •••, 1–14.

Innayah, E. P., Ekowati, V. M., Supriyanto, A. S., & Johari, F. B. (2022). Electronic word-of-mouth (E-WOM) in social media as a predictor of investment intention in capital market. *Jurnal Aplikasi Manajemen*, *20*(4), 753–767. DOI: 10.21776/ub.jam.2022.020.04.01

Jejeniwa, T. O., Mhlongo, N. Z., & Jejeniwa, T. O. (2024). AI solutions for developmental economics: Opportunities and challenges in financial inclusion and poverty alleviation. *International Journal of Advanced Economics*, *6*(4), 108–123. DOI: 10.51594/ijae.v6i4.1073

Jena, J. R., Biswal, S. K., Panigrahi, R. R., & Shrivastava, A. K. (2024). Investigating the Potential Areas in Artificial Intelligence and Financial Innovation: A Bibliometric Analysis. *Journal of Scientometric Research*, *13*(1), 71–80. DOI: 10.5530/jscires.13.1.6

Jeong, J., Kim, B. J., & Lee, J. (2024). Navigating AI transitions: How coaching leadership buffers against job stress and protects employee physical health. *Frontiers in Public Health, 12*, 1343932. DOI: 10.3389/fpubh.2024.1343932 PMID: 38601504

Jin, D. (2023). *Where have the ethical and moral standards landed? Consumer self-congruency and psychological distance in the context of AI-based services.* International Hospitality Review.

Jingrong, H., Shan, H., Zhaobin, C., Yu, L., & Yingying, L. (2024). AI-Driven Digital Transformation in Banking: A New Perspective on Operational Efficiency and Risk Management. *Information Systems and Economics*, *5*(1), 82–90.

Kaur, R., Dharmadhikari, S. P., & Khurjekar, S. (2024). Assessing the customer adoption and perceptions for AI-driven sustainable initiatives in Indian banking sector. *Environment and Social Psychology, 9*(5).

Khadka, S., Rai, B., & Khadka, A. K. (2023). AI-Driven Customization in Financial Services: Implications for Social Innovation in Nepal. *NCC Journal*, *8*(1), 1–11. DOI: 10.3126/nccj.v8i1.63128

Khuan, H., Judijanto, L., Rachmawati, T., Tanjung, T., & Vandika, A. Y. (2024). Bibliometric Analysis on the Use of Artificial Intelligence in Improving the Efficiency of Banking Financial Processes in Southeast Asian Countries. *West Science Interdisciplinary Studies*, *2*(01), 129–137. DOI: 10.58812/wsis.v2i01.597

Klochko, A., Kurylo, M., Rohovenko, O., Volchenko, N., & Shulzhenko, A. (2023). The legal regulation of artificial intelligence security in Ukrainian banking. *Journal of Infrastructure. Policy and Development*, *8*(2), 2582.

Koç, S. (2024). Teachers' Views on Lifelong Learning. *International Journal of Contemporary Educational Research*, *11*(2), 247–258. DOI: 10.52380/ijcer.2024.11.2.621

Kumar, S., Xiao, J. J., Pattnaik, D., Lim, W. M., & Rasul, T. (2022). Past, present and future of bank marketing: A bibliometric analysis of International Journal of Bank Marketing (1983–2020). *International Journal of Bank Marketing*, *40*(2), 341–383. DOI: 10.1108/IJBM-07-2021-0351

Lazo, M., & Ebardo, R. (2023). Artificial intelligence adoption in the banking industry: Current state and future prospect. *Journal of Innovation Management*, *11*(3), 54–74. DOI: 10.24840/2183-0606_011.003_0003

Leikas, J., Johri, A., Latvanen, M., Wessberg, N., & Hahto, A. (2022). Governing ethical AI transformation: A case study of AuroraAI. *Frontiers in Artificial Intelligence*, *5*, 836557. DOI: 10.3389/frai.2022.836557 PMID: 35224480

Majumder, T. (2023). The Evaluating Impact of Artificial Intelligence on Risk Management and Fraud Detection in the Commercial Bank in Bangladesh. *International Journal of Applied and Natural Sciences*, *1*(1), 67–76. DOI: 10.61424/ijans.v1i1.75

Maseke, B. F. (2024). The transformative power of artificial intelligence in banking client service. *South Asian Journal of Social Studies and Economics*, *21*(3), 93–105. DOI: 10.9734/sajsse/2024/v21i3787

Masrek, M. N., Susantari, T., Mutia, F., Yuwinanto, H. P., & Atmi, R. T. (2024). Enabling Education Everywhere: How artificial intelligence empowers ubiquitous and lifelong learning. *Environment-Behaviour Proceedings Journal*, *9*(SI18), 57–63. DOI: 10.21834/e-bpj.v9iSI18.5462

Melnyk, V. (2024). Transforming the nature of trust between banks and young clients: From traditional to digital banking. *Qualitative Research in Financial Markets*, *16*(4), 618–635. DOI: 10.1108/QRFM-08-2022-0129

Mende, M., Scott, M. L., Ubal, V. O., Hassler, C. M., Harmeling, C. M., & Palmatier, R. W. (2024). Personalized communication as a platform for service inclusion? Initial insights into interpersonal and AI-based personalization for stigmatized consumers. *Journal of Service Research*, *27*(1), 28–48. DOI: 10.1177/10946705231188676

Mohan, R., Boopathi, M., Ranjan, P., Najana, M., Chaudhary, P. K., & Chotrani, A. K. (2024). Ai in fraud detection: Evaluating the efficacy of artificial intelligence in preventing financial misconduct. *Journal of Electrical Systems*, *20*(3s), 1332–1338. DOI: 10.52783/jes.1508

Moharrak, M., & Mogaji, E. (2024). Generative AI in banking: Empirical insights on integration, challenges and opportunities in a regulated industry. *International Journal of Bank Marketing*.

Mor, S., Aneja, R., Madan, S., & Gupta, S. (2022). Artificial intelligence and loan default: The case of commercial banks in India. *Strategic Change*, *31*(6), 571–580. DOI: 10.1002/jsc.2529

Morley, J., Elhalal, A., Garcia, F., Kinsey, L., Mökander, J., & Floridi, L. (2021). Ethics as a service: A pragmatic operationalisation of AI ethics. *Minds and Machines*, *31*(2), 239–256. DOI: 10.1007/s11023-021-09563-w PMID: 34720418

Okwiri, M. I. O., & Muathe, S. M. (2024). Competitiveness of Tier three Commercial Banks in Kenya: The Role of Strategic Leadership Practices. *International Journal of Management Research and Emerging Sciences*, *14*(1).

Oladoyinbo, T. O., Olabanji, S. O., Olaniyi, O. O., Adebiyi, O. O., Okunleye, O. J., & Ismaila Alao, A. (2024). Exploring the challenges of artificial intelligence in data integrity and its influence on social dynamics. *Asian Journal of Advanced Research and Reports*, *18*(2), 1–23. DOI: 10.9734/ajarr/2024/v18i2601

Olan, F., Arakpogun, E. O., Jayawickrama, U., Suklan, J., & Liu, S. (2022). Sustainable supply chain finance and supply networks: The role of artificial intelligence. *IEEE Transactions on Engineering Management*.

Owolabi, O. S., Uche, P. C., Adeniken, N. T., Ihejirika, C., Islam, R. B., & Chhetri, B. J. T. (2024). Ethical implication of artificial intelligence (AI) adoption in financial decision making. *Computer and Information Science*, *17*(1), 1–49. DOI: 10.5539/cis.v17n1p49

Oyeniyi, L. D., Ugochukwu, C. E., & Mhlongo, N. Z. (2024). Implementing AI in banking customer service: A review of current trends and future applications. *International Journal of Science and Research Archive*, *11*(2), 1492–1509. DOI: 10.30574/ijsra.2024.11.2.0639

Pristiyono, P., Juliana, J., & Prayoga, Y. (2022). Measuring customer trust through digital transformation of banking as a competitive advantage. *Jurnal Ekonomi Bisnis Dan Kewirausahaan*, *11*(2), 214. DOI: 10.26418/jebik.v11i2.51986

Purwanto, E., Deviny, J., & Mutahar, A. M. (2020). The mediating role of trust in the relationship between corporate image, security, word of mouth and loyalty in M-banking using among the millennial generation in Indonesia. *Management & Marketing*, *15*(2), 255–274. DOI: 10.2478/mmcks-2020-0016

Quinn, B. (2022). Teaching Open Science Analytics in the Age of Financial Technology. *QMS Research Paper, 1*.

Rahman, M., Ming, T. H., Baigh, T. A., & Sarker, M. (2023). Adoption of artificial intelligence in banking services: An empirical analysis. *International Journal of Emerging Markets*, *18*(10), 4270–4300. DOI: 10.1108/IJOEM-06-2020-0724

Ranković, M., Gurgu, E., Martins, O., & Vukasović, M. (2023). Artificial intelligence and the evolution of finance: Opportunities, challenges and ethical considerations. *EdTech Journal*, *3*(1), 20–23. DOI: 10.18485/edtech.2023.3.1.2

Roy, J. K., & Vasa, L. (2024). Machine Learning and Artificial Intelligence Method for FinTech Credit Scoring and Risk Management: A Systematic Literature Review. [IJBAN]. *International Journal of Business Analytics*, *11*(1), 1–23. DOI: 10.4018/IJBAN.347504

Rusydiana, A. S., & Kanz, R. A. D. (2023). Scientometric Analysis on Digital Banking Innovation Model. *Applied Marketing and Sustainability, 1*(1).

Sheth, J. N., Jain, V., Roy, G., & Chakraborty, A. (2022). AI-driven banking services: The next frontier for a personalised experience in the emerging market. *International Journal of Bank Marketing*, *40*(6), 1248–1271. DOI: 10.1108/IJBM-09-2021-0449

Shiyyab, F. S., Alzoubi, A. B., Obidat, Q. M., & Alshurafat, H. (2023). The impact of artificial intelligence disclosure on financial performance. *International Journal of Financial Studies*, *11*(3), 115. DOI: 10.3390/ijfs11030115

Singh, C. (2024). Artificial intelligence and deep learning: Considerations for financial institutions for compliance with the regulatory burden in the United Kingdom. *Journal of Financial Crime*, *31*(2), 259–266. DOI: 10.1108/JFC-01-2023-0011

Skandali, D., Magoutas, A., & Tsourvakas, G. (2023). Artificial Intelligent Applications in Enabled Banking Services: The Next Frontier of Customer Engagement in the Era of ChatGPT. *Theoretical Economics Letters*, *13*(5), 1203–1223. DOI: 10.4236/tel.2023.135066

Sudarshan, K. C. (2023). Emotional Intelligence and Work-Life Balance of Female Staff in Commercial Banks in Kathmandu District. *Quest Journal of Management and Social Sciences*, *5*(2), 206–218.

Thiruma Valavan, A. (2023). AI Ethics and Bias: Exploratory study on the ethical considerations and potential biases in ai and data-driven decision-making in banking, with a focus on fairness, transparency, and accountability. *World Journal of Advanced Research and Reviews*, *20*(2), 197–206. DOI: 10.30574/wjarr.2023.20.2.2245

îrcovnicu, G. I., & Ha egan, C. D. (2023). Integration of artificial intelligence in the risk management process: An analysis of opportunities and challenges. *Journal of Financial Studies*, *8*(15), 198–214. DOI: 10.55654/JFS.2023.8.15.13

Tulcanaza-Prieto, A. B., Cortez-Ordoñez, A., & Lee, C. W. (2023). Influence of customer perception factors on AI-enabled customer experience in the Ecuadorian banking environment. *Sustainability (Basel)*, *15*(16), 12441. DOI: 10.3390/su151612441

Wijayati, D. T., Rahman, Z., Rahman, M. F. W., Arifah, I. D. C., & Kautsar, A. (2022). A study of artificial intelligence on employee performance and work engagement: The moderating role of change leadership. *International Journal of Manpower*, *43*(2), 486–512. DOI: 10.1108/IJM-07-2021-0423

Yablonsky, S. A. (2020). AI-Driven Digital PlatformInnovation. *Technology Innovation Management Review*, *10*(10), 4–15. DOI: 10.22215/timreview/1392

Chapter 6
Fintech Implications on ESG Practices:
Evidence From the Indian Banking Industry

V. Prathibha Raj
Christ University, Bengaluru, India

K. A. Dhanya
https://orcid.org/0009-0007-7388-6518
Christ University, Bengaluru, India

Shikha Malhotra
https://orcid.org/0009-0002-0930-8493
Christ University, Bengaluru, India

Priyakrushna Mohanty
https://orcid.org/0000-0001-6933-2757
Christ University, Bengaluru, India

ABSTRACT

This chapter aims to provide evidence-based insights into how Fintech is influencing ESG practices of Indian banks. The discussions focus on key areas such as Green fintech, Governance and risk management approach, financing Agri business, promoting carbon net zero mission, and also the fintech intervention towards financial inclusion. The chapter also exhibits the role played by public sector banks and private sector banks in promoting ESG practices. Methodology used is secondary data based on case studies, industry reports and empirical data sources. Insights from higher officials of the banking sector are also included to examine the challenges faced by the banking sector in this regard. Based on findings, the chapter provides

DOI: 10.4018/979-8-3373-0129-7.ch006

a suggestive model on the potentialities of fintech to support ESG agenda which can be an insight for policy makers, financial institutions and other stakeholders.

1. INTRODUCTION

The role played by the financial sector is very crucial in shaping the economy and also creating a strong impact on society and environment. In India the financial service industry acts as a catalyst of change for the economic development of the country. Financial systems face sustainability challenges and in today's dynamic and complex environment it is pertinent not only for the industry but also for the policymakers to comply with sustainable goals. Financial institutions are forerunners of economic growth and also need to ensure the compliance with sustainability norms. On the other side, Indian financial sector is undergoing huge transformation with regard to technology advancements. Banking industry in India has evolved over the years with digital transformation. Banks are increasingly using AI (Artificial Intelligence) and ML (Machine Learning) technologies to increase its operational efficiency. Therefore, its need of the hour that ESG (Environment, Social and Governance) framework also needs to be aligned with technological innovations to foster sustainable economic growth.

Digital Finance and FinTech are changing the financial services industry by bringing in new technologies, and innovative methods of providing services which are very different from traditional banking practices (Suryono et al.; 2020). There are several drivers which are prompting financial institutions to adopt ESG at a higher level. These drivers include 1) Customers are environmentally conscious 2) investors expectation 3) Regulatory bodies and Government.

How do banks strategies their ESG Goals? How do fintech applications support banking system in achieving ESG Goals? With the advent of technology and with high increase in the number of fintech companies, and with tough competition, banks are now compelled to use technology in their day today operations. MOUs and collaborations of banks with fintech companies will help in enhancing their efficiency.

According to the articles by KPMG following can be the strategies adopted by banks to achieve ESG goals:

a. Comparison with peer banks
b. Meeting the public net zero commitments
c. Products offered are in the perspective of ESG
d. Develop implementing ESG in target operating models.
e. How are banks interacting with their customers and their transition strategy

Implementing ESG across the bank branches creates an impact on the processes, system and controls. ESG has to be integrated with policies and procedures of an organisation. While developing products and services ESG has to be considered. In bank, a person has to be given the responsibility of implementing ESG.

In various national and international forums, environment, people and collective growth is the central theme of deliberations. The topic has gained such a popularity and relevance in the present era. India has also taken a step ahead and announced to achieve net-zero emissions by 2070. According to the Paris Agreement, the preparedness of India towards achieving two twin objectives are (i) to reduce the emissions intensity by 33-35% of GDP below the 2005 level by 2030; and (ii) to increase the share of non-fossil energy in total power generation capacity to 40%. According to the World Economic Forum's Global Risk Report 2021, Environmental, Social & Governance (ESG) risks account for four of top five risks. OECD's report on 'ESG Investing: Practices, Progress and Challenges' states that ESG Investing may improve the prevailing risk management practices and can expect better returns than traditional investments. The changes in the economy at large, exhibits the relevance of ESG and banks who provide funding for all the projects can play a significant role in this regard. Bank's strategic planning should be embedded with ESG which in turn will lead to long term sustainability of these banks, environment and society at large.

According to article published in fintech magazine in 2023, the foreign banks which have considered ESG as their top priority are UK Based Loyd's bank, German based Deutsche bank, Singapore's DBS bank, Bank of America, UK based Barclays bank, JP Morgan investment bank, HSBC, Citi Bank of US, Standard Chartered bank, BNP Paribas of Paris. The banks are discovering on both digital transformation and ESG as their goals. Indian Banking Association (IBA) is crafting an ESG framework for Indian Banks keeping in view climate assessment as a part of risk assessment strategy (Financial express April 4th 2023).

It is well known that fintech solutions are being used by banks in different aspects of its service. There is a linkage between financial technology innovation and ESG practices and both are important for sustainable economic growth. In the UN Sustainable development goals also, relevance is given for sustainability and also for innovations. Moreover, technology is embracing each and every sphere of humane life. At this juncture, the innovative fintech solutions and its impact on ESG practices is of high relevance. The research in this field is very scarce. Therefore, to bridge the gap, this study aims to explore the inter-linkages between FinTech and ESG and impact of the same on the Indian Banks ESG practices. The study mainly focuses on implications of fintech on ESG practices by Indian banks. Examples from both public sector and private sector banks are taken in this study.

2. REVIEW OF LITERATURE

2.1 FinTech in Banking Sector

FinTech, which is generally defined as the use of breakthroughs like blockchain technology, artificial intelligence, and sophisticated computing capacity (e.g., via cloud computing) to the provision of banking services, is the newest addition to the technology arsenal. FinTech innovation is booming in the global financial sector, to the extent that its influence has spawned a new field of study (Phillipon,2016).

In the financial sector, technological innovation is increasingly valued, and "financial technology," or "FinTech," plays a key role by providing banks with cutting-edge technical solutions that increase the efficiency of financial services. (Li & Xu, 2021).

FinTech technology encompasses more than just using data and "digital" technologies; its integration enables the creation of new goods and processes as well as the enhancement of current ones (Hasan et al.; 2021).

Digital technology is significantly altering the global financial markets while reducing resource costs and increasing the productivity of company models. In addition, it maintains client relationships and creates long-term efficiency in the banking sector, enabling it to flourish in a competitive climate. in order to improve customer comfort during transactions and to reinforce the banking sector by monitoring its expansion and efficiency (Magomaeva & Galazova, 2019).

Fintech improves cost effectiveness. They contend that FinTech boosts the number of customers and diversifies the business covered by bank operations. This claim is supported empirically by data showing that, through scale effects, an online banking channel lowers transaction costs and boosts cost efficiency. FinTech provides banks with a major lending edge in terms of interest income efficiency through enhancing the processes for loan approval. By implementing FinTech, banks may obtain more concrete data for credit evaluation (Jaksic & Marinc,2018).

The financial system in today's world is impacted by two distinct but closely related factors-one is innovation in technology and the other is sustainability in finance. (Kumar et al; 2022),

FinTech which is an evolving part of financial innovation is a risky proposition but provides more value also. (Thakor, 2012)

2.2 ESG practices in banking sector

This research is a bibliometric approach with both qualitative and quantitative approaches. The Word Stat has been used to analyse the data. Cite Space was also used to analyse the content. The recommendations made by this research for future researchers are Corporate Resilience, development of technology and innovations, strong corporate governance, achievement of sustainable finance. Mitigation of information asymmetry. This research has been conducted on most of the Asian and European organizations. (Ould & Ellil, 2022)

The authors have done an extensive literature review of about 25 research papers. The most important indicator adopted from banks is Return on Assets (ROA). Regression analysis is the most used method to study the relationship between ESG and financial performance. This research also found that the impact of ESG on the financial performance is more in non-banking sectors rather than banking sectors. (Taleeb & Khadum, 2024)

This study is about ESG and its relationship with profitability of the Non-European Union's Banks and European Union banks. The author has adopted a baseline model with econometric analysis to study the relationship and marginal effect of ESG on Asset Quality. They have conducted a survey on European banks against non-European banks in the area of Asset quality management and its direct relationship on the profitability of the banks. Bank managers are of the opinion that practicing ESG may lead to lower profitability in banks. Supervisory interventions are required to credit risk in banks. (Cantero-Saiz et.al.; 2024)

The findings of a study which was conducted on 105 Italian banks during 2016-2020 to know the effect of ESG initiatives on the bank's profitability, showed that ESG policies negatively affect the operational and market performance in the banking sector. (Menicucci et.al.; 2024)

According to the survey conducted on 54 banks listed in Shanghai Stock exchange in China as of 2023, Loan to deposit ratio is considered one of the factors to assess the bank's liquidity risk. One of the findings suggest that good ESG practices can reduce the liquidity risk faced by the commercial banks. (Liu & Xie 2024)

A comparative analysis of public and private sector banks was conducted among 12 private sector banks and 10 public sector banks. According to this there was a finding which suggested the ownership structure of banks influence the banks performance and also related to ESG. For private sector banks ESG has a negative impact on the bank's performance but has a positive effect on the financial performance of these banks. Public sector banks ESG scores have a positive and significant impact on the return on equity and non-performing assets. (Jaiwani & Gopalakrishna, 2023)

2.3 Fintech and ESG

Change in consumer habits is a major pushing factor to reconfigure the bank customer relationship management, looking for more immediacy, simplicity and accessibility of services. As a result, there is an increasing demand for the use of fintech applications in bank. An exploratory case study analysis of BNP Paribus was conducted and also investigated the factors influencing technological innovations in banking sector, using the UTAUT model Results shows that attention to ESG issue encourage the use of Fintech technologies. BNP Paribus case shows that the bank itself should show an orientation and predisposition towards integration of environmental and social aspects in its corporate strategy. The results also show that BNP Paribus collects structured and unstructured ESG data from various sources which help them in assessing the degree of risk associated with customers. The work also shows that availability of ESG data supports banks in eliminating greenwashing practices. The study concludes that it is sustainability that influences the use of Fintech not the other way round. (Galeone, et al.; 2024)

This paper is about the impact of Fintech on achievement of ESG Goals. It was to understand the impact of fintech on achieving the ESG Goals. The author has studied various indexes for this paper like Global Fintech Index (GFI), Global sustainable competitive index, etc. Through this research it was concluded that Sweden ranks high in global fintech index. This research helps the policy makers to design better regulations and framework for which promotes responsible fintech practices. (Albulena &Baresha, 2024),

The author is trying to explore the linkage between Fintech and ESG from the perspective of bibliometric study. Author has considered only scopus indexed articles which were under this study. The author has used Cartographic analysis to study the literature with the help of VOS viewer software. It has been found that there are very few studies which have been conducted with regard to the direct and indirect impact of fintech innovations on ESG. (Tratta et.al.; 2024)

The article is published in Asia pacific journal of Business Administration. The article is about studying the impacts of adoption of fintech, green finance, and competitiveness which will lead to sustainable performances of banks. The major findings of this study are that digital transformation is emerging as a critical moderator which shapes the relationship between fintech adoption and green finance as well as competitiveness. This study is very useful for the policy makers, researchers and practitioners. (Rahman & Hossain 2024)

3. FINTECH AND ESG: HOW THEY ARE CONNECTED AND IMPLICATIONS OF THAT CONNECTION FOR THE BANKING INDUSTRY

FinTech, or financial technology, is growing in importance in the banking industry. It uses smartphones, blockchains, artificial intelligence (AI), and the Internet of Things (IoT) to transform the way financial institutions work and provide them with several advantages (Lee and Shin, 2018). The application of this technology has clear social, environmental, and ecological benefits that promote the funding of energy and environmental projects, the use of renewable energy sources, and the development of environmental infrastructures (Deng et al.; 2018). Green finance has a promising future thanks to the convergence of FinTech developments with ESG standards. Initiatives pertaining to renewable energy, electric vehicles, and battery storage are already receiving priority lending from certain Indian institutions, both public and private. The establishment of an ESG culture has been started by Axis Bank and HDFC Bank. The Reserve Bank of India, in their Framework for Green Deposits dated April 11, 2023, under Paragraph 2(c), states as follows:

> *"Green finance" means lending to and/or investing in the activities or projects meeting the requirements prescribed in paragraph 7 of these guidelines that contribute to climate risk mitigation, climate adaptation and resilience, and other climate-related or environmental objectives, including biodiversity management and nature-based solutions.*

Banks and non-banking financial institutions (NBFCs) can be encouraged to offer green deposits with the adoption of this framework on June 1, 2023, which will make it easier for their portfolio consumers to finance ecologically sustainable initiatives and activities. The objectives of this framework are to safeguard depositor interests, assist customers in reaching their sustainability objectives, deal with the problem of greenwashing, and promote more lending to projects that are in line with green initiatives. According to RBI's Report of the Survey on Climate Risk and Sustainable Finance, July 2022, of the 34 scheduled commercial banks in India—public, private, and foreign banks—85% agreed to make structural changes to their current lending and investing approach to support green financing.

According to Macpherson et al. (2021), FinTech solutions have the potential to streamline the integration of ESG criteria through the automation of data collection and analysis, provision of tailored recommendations, and improvement of transparency in investment processes. Furthermore, a wider spectrum of investors may find sustainable finance more accessible thanks to FinTech's capacity to lower operating costs and boost efficiency (Lee & Mattia, 2022). Furthermore, research by Zhao and Chen (2023) highlights how Fintech can promote green investment practices by increasing financial system efficiency and transparency. Adoption of Fintech appears to facilitate investment procedures and promote environmentally responsible financial choices, according to empirical data.

Financial technology is influencing green investment strategies more and more as it develops, opening up new opportunities for sustainable economic growth (Liu et al., 2023). Sustainable finance is closely associated with fintech. Although the two sectors have long been treated independently, in recent years, several characteristics have surfaced that, when combined, demonstrate significant promise, making them both crucial pillars (Nassiry, 2019). Financial Institutions can profit from ESG activities in a number of ways, including lower costs, increased financial inclusion because of social emphasis, beneficial impact on stakeholders, and the development of value and sustainable economies. Several financial institutions have begun to actively focus on integrating these features after realizing the significance of ESG. As a result, it is clear that ESG is now being used in global organizations rather than merely being a buzzword. FinTech and Sustainability Finance are closely related but the research on the theme i.e. about their connection is very limited. In actuality, the majority of research to date has concentrated on examining the advantages of integrating FinTech in the banking industry, such as enhanced performance and risk reduction, but has not examined the factors that influence financial intermediaries to embrace such technology, that may include ESG factors also. This paper attempts to close this gap by examining the role of sustainability in the spread of FinTech technology in the banking industry through the examination of examples from the various public and private sector banks in India.

3.1 ESG is a comprehensive phenomenon. 'E' stands for environment and this aspect is a critical factor in the banking space. To incorporate this in the banking operations, there are several initiatives which have been taken by the Banks and the Financial Institutions with the usage of innovative technology.

Green FinTech

Banks can adopt new tactics in the area of sustainable finance technology developments, such as collaborating with FinTech firms and joining open banking ecosystems (Omarini, 2018). One example of an emerging field is "green FinTech," which aims to reduce the risks associated with climate change. This is a particularly helpful tool for developing and rising nations focused on achieving the SDGs-Sustainable Development Goals (Macchiavello and Siri, 2022). Green fintech is the fusion of environmental sustainability objectives with financial technology (fintech) solutions. The idea manages environmental issues and encourages sustainable behaviors in the financial industry by utilizing cutting-edge financial technologies. According to recent research, Fintech innovation helps green economic growth by promoting green lending and investment (Zhou et al., 2022).

The worldwide green fintech market is anticipated to grow by 22.4% yearly between 2024 and 2029, according to recent research from Global Market Estimates. Green fintech, a mashup of technology and finance, benefits the environment and encourages sustainability.

In addition to advocating the use of biodegradable cards, FIs empower and motivate their clients to investigate and choose other digital and environmentally friendly options. Using digital branches for transactions, paying with paperless transactions, utilizing recycled or biodegradable plastic for cards, and performing virtual know your customer (KYC) procedures rather than paper-based ones are a few of these projects. The unnecessary usage of paper in manual transactions has diminished thanks to the adoption of e-receipts in ATMs and point-of-sale (POS) systems.

Ariel Payment Bank has become the first Indian Bank to introduce the first eco-friendly debit card for its new and existing customers. Ganesh Anantha Narayan, Chief Operating Officer of Airtel Payment Bank stated that the introduction of such cards reflect the banks' continued transition towards sustainability and to provide the safe and convenient banking experience to the customers. The first credit card in India made of recycled PVC (rPVC) was introduced by HSBC. By the end of 2026, they want to gradually phase out single-use PVC cards. Polyvinyl chloride acetate is used to make standard credit, debit, and business cards (PVC). This substance produces problematic industrial waste. PVC products and recycled PVC plastic (rPVC) have a five-year shelf life. But because rPVC is made of material that would otherwise be burned or dumped in a landfill, it is less damaging to the environment. In collaboration with EaseMyTrip, DBS Bank India has introduced an environmentally friendly foreign debit card that is composed of 99% recycled polyvinyl chloride (PVC).

Open banking is a banking technique that uses application programming interfaces (APIs) to grant open access to consumer banking, transactions, and other financial data from banks and non-banking financial organizations to third-party payment systems and other financial service providers. In addition to facilitating a seamless user experience, open banking encourages networking and interoperability between service providers and banking information. India has advanced rapidly in the direction of open banking in recent years. Government programs and bank launches of scalable open banking solutions demonstrate this progress. Large Indian banks are already considering open banking system to withstand the competition.

The HDFC Bank Sustainable Finance Framework, dated December 2023 (the "Framework") outlines the bank's plans to issue green, social, and sustainability bonds, create loans, and use the money raised to finance or refinance, entirely or partially, current and upcoming projects that are anticipated to promote socioeconomic development and the shift to a low-carbon economy. The first-ever sustainable finance bond sale by HDFC Bank has raised $300 million, according to the bank's announcement. This is a portion of the $750 million total raised by Regulation S Bonds. A total of $450 Million has been raised for a five-year period, with a spread of 108 basis points over the US Treasury, whilst $300 million has been raised for three years at a 95-basis point spread over the US Treasury. According to a press release from the bank, the revenues of the sustainable finance bond will be used to finance green and social loans in line with sustainable finance, with the remaining profits going toward supporting ordinary banking operations. Lending towards electric vehicles, SMEs, and affordable housing will be the top priorities for the funds raised through the sustainable finance bonds.

As part of green initiatives matching to Sustainable development goals, SBI is providing home loans for solar roofing with less interest rates and measures are being taken by the bank to popularize the product among the public. Loan is readily provided for waste management, water recycling etc and the same is channelised digitally for better access by customers. Due to the digital fintech platforms available, the bank has reduced its cost on paper documentation considerably. This has been replaced by digital documentation. AI supported systems help the bank to monitor and manage the large volume of databases related to customers. SBI green rupee term deposit aims to mobilize deposits for financing green initiatives /projects. The bank has tie up with SIDBI and through the implementation of psbloanin59minutes.com application instant approval is possible for eligible proposals from SMEs (Small and Medium Enterprises). This platform reduces the delay in disbursements, promotion of green finance projects, and promotes SMEs to start with new projects.

Fintech solutions provide easier access to capital by renewable energy resources. Banks adopt fintech to platforms to streamline its operations, reduce paper usage and efficient use of all resources. Banks can issue green loans and mortgages and thereby contribute to environmental practices with the help of fintech. Green loans, green credit cards, green mortgages, green financing are innovative financial products fostering a sustainable future. With the help of Artificial Intelligence (AI) banks provide finance for environmentally responsible projects. This facilitates reduction in external carbon emissions.

3.2 'S' in ESG refers to Social criterion which relates to relationships and reputation of a Bank with communities, individuals and institutions with which it deals with and conducts the business.

Initiatives for Financial inclusion along with Digital transformation

The Indian Fintech industry has exhibited massive growth over the years, and many new fintech startups are emerging in India. Government initiatives like digital India campaign and cashless economy, have paved the way for shifting customer focus from paper money to digital services. According to Ajaykumar Choudhary, Non-executive chairman and Independent Director, National payment corporation of India "the Indian fintech industry is estimated to be around USD 110 billion in 2024, and it's projected to reach about USD 420 billion by 2029. Technology is affecting all aspects of human life and hence in a country like India the scope for using fintech as a tool for fostering financial inclusion gains more importance.

RBI report on growth in financial inclusion index over the years is highlighting the increase in three broad parameters usage, access and quality.

Table 1. Financial Inclusion Index

YEAR	Financial Inclusion Index
2024	64.2%
2023	60.1%
2022	56.4%
2021	53.9%
2017	43.4%

Source: Compiled from RBI reports

The growth of fintech over the years have contributed much for bridging the divide among the unbanked and banked population. Limited access to credit and Complex documentation procedure has hindered the accessibility of underprivileged and marginalized groups towards banking. This has also affected the medium and small enterprises in India. Integration of fintech with banking services has provided easier accessibility for such groups.

The concept of open banking which uses Application programming interface initiated in 2017 and progressed in 2021 is a significant landmark in the integration of technology with banking services. Open banking has accelerated transactions of neo banking, funding and provided new opportunities for complex business models like B2B2C or B+B2C etc. YES bank initiated the process and now ICICI banks, Axis banks, Kotak banks all are into the system . The bank APIs can be of different types. It can be used to check the CIBIL score of a customer or it can be used by companies to manage its receivables and payables by integrating API with its ERP system. It has also been a trend to see that big technology companies are partnering with banks. In 2021, Google pay has launched digital FD in tie up with Equitas small finance bank. Without having to open a bank account and within no time, google pay users can start an FD with the bank.

SBI, one of the largest nationalized banks in India, is in its forefront in applying fintech applications for catering to different sectors of the society. SBI AI chatbot, SBI open banking system, SBI Fastag application, SBI Robo advisor and SBI Yono app are examples of fintech applications in banking sector that propels the movement of financial inclusion. Launched in 2017, YONO (You Only Need One) application has gained immense popularity and in 2024 Yono business has 5.24 lakh new to digital customers onboarded with 66.01 crore transactions. 2.05 lakhs current accounts have been opened through Yono business in the FY 2024 (source: SBI annual report 2023-24). The bank has also initiated a Direct bank transfer (DBT) system of delivering benefits to target customers. This has promoted more savings among underprivileged groups and has also enhanced social security coverage through micro finance. Government schemes like Jan Dhan yojana, PMJJBY, APY etc are implemented through DBT platform. Leveraging fintech solutions such as mobile wallets, biometric authentication, video KYC, Real time payment systems has increased the efficiency of Direct benefit transfer. Moreover, utilization of fin-tech in DBT has helped the banks to reach the underserved population easily. The Robo- Advisors in banks help the individuals to manage their portfolio and also provide recommendations for investments. Online payment system (RTGS, NEFT, IMPS) initiated by almost all banks has also enhanced the reachability towards the underserved population.

To cater to the diversified category of population SBI has also initiated 40 transaction banking hubs (TB-Hub) for providing comprehensive solutions for transactions, payments collections and other financial needs. (source: SBI annual report 2023-24). Loan disbursements are also made easier by way of digital loans through YONO and INB within the matter of a few clicks . Other fintech products offered by SBI contributing towards financial inclusion are

Table 2. SBI - Tech products and purpose

Products	**Purpose**
Yono Lite	Mobile banking
SBI Buddy	e-wallet
State bank Scribe	For blinds and visually handicapped
SBI Mingle	Financial services through social media
BHIM SBI Pay	payment solution for all
SBI Digi voucher	Green banking solution
SBI QUICK	Missed call banking
SBI Yono Krishi	Agri app for farmers

3.3 The internal set of rules, regulations, and procedures that organizations use to govern themselves, make wise legal decisions, and meet the needs of external stakeholders is what the “G” in ESG stands for: governance.

Climate Risk and frameworks adopted by the Indian Banks and Role of Climate FinTech.

The top four long-term (10-year) hazards and one of the top two short-term (2-year) threats, according to the World Economic Forum's Global Hazards Report 2024, are all tied to climate change.

The main hazards associated with climate change were also found in the earlier surveys. These climate risks affect all industries and businesses, regardless of whether they stem from climate events or the reaction to climate change (moving toward a low-carbon economy). As a result, these risks often gather at banks and other financial organizations. Across the Globe, it is evident that the companies are trying to weigh the potential hazards of climate change. Financial Institutions and the Banks cannot be left out from this visible change. Asia and the Pacific area, which is both the most vulnerable to and a major contributor to global warming, faces a unique challenge in the form of the climate crisis.

Frameworks that integrate climate-related financial risks into India's regulatory regimes, conform with international norms, and improve transparency and accountability within the financial sector have been introduced by RBI and SEBI. With a phased implementation plan, the RBI's proposed disclosure framework requires regulated Financial Institutions to disclose financial risks and opportunities related to climate change. It covers thematic pillars such governance, strategy, risk management, and metrics/targets.

Due to the unstable climate, banks need to take action on two fronts: first, they need to manage their financial risks; second, they need to focus on funding environmental initiatives. A large number of the climate change-vulnerable industries, including energy, infrastructure, and agriculture, rely significantly on the banking sector for funding. In India, rural cooperative banks and scheduled commercial banks are the main providers of loans to the agricultural sector. Climate variability has a substantial impact on farmers' incomes and food security, which might have a meaningful effect on the banks' ability to extend loans. Thus, climate-risk management is now absolutely essential for banks, as it would allow them to consider climate-related risks when determining creditworthiness and also motivate them to customize financial services and products that lower credit risks and improve the resilience of agriculture.

Motivated by the convergence of digital technology, finance, and climate change, or "climate fintech," the financial services sector is getting ready to tackle these issues and seize chances to shift towards a more sustainable economic model. India's climate fintech industry has bright futures. It has a great chance of helping India meet its carbon neutrality goal and promote sustainable growth. SEBI's decision to establish a social stock exchange (SSE) is towards impact investment. The worldwide trend toward the implementation of ESG would complement the environmental goals.

Fintech applications help banks to measure the risk and expected losses associated with different climate scenarios which helps to reduce the downtrends. Similarly, fintech helps banks to assess the potential future market so that future lending opportunities can be identified. Mitigating the impact of Climate risk is an important role to be played by banks. Drastic changes in the environment like rise in sea water level, flood, storms, landslide etc will increase the risk of defaults. As far as banks are concerned it's important to foresee such credit default and take appropriate actions. Banks make use of fintech applications to analyze climate change and also to assess the credit risk involved. Big data analytics programmes help banks to decide whether to grant loan or not and also what should be the interest rate associated with, and what can be default probability associated with a loan disbursement. Climate change provides banks with an opportunity to increase their revenue. Introduction of new products are needed to manage the climate risk for converting to a zero-carbon economy, which can be funded by the banks. AI and block chain applications can be used by banks to identify the scope of projects that support low carbon emission. Elements of risk measurement like climate risk vulnerabilities have to be done using technology driven tools.

In its study on Currency and Finance 2022–2023, the RBI had identified banking companies' vulnerabilities. According to the findings of a climatic stress test, public sector banks (PSBs) in India might be more susceptible than private banks. In the carbon disclosure project, SBI obtained a "B" in 2021–2022, demonstrating that the company has taken steps to mitigate the environmental effects of its operations and has implemented sound environmental management practices. SBI strengthened its commitment to sustainability in 2023 by releasing its Environmental, Social, and Governance (ESG) framework. The framework highlights the procedures and guidelines that bank managers should follow in order to control risks and take advantage of possibilities that present themselves in the shape of initiatives that deal with sustainability-related concerns.

Agri Finance, Digitization and Sustainability: How are all aligned in India Banking Ecosystem.

Farmers and rural agriculturists may find it difficult to have access to credit using the traditional banking system. Access to credit for small farmers poses a significant challenge, as traditional banks are often hesitant due to concerns like lengthy processing times, collateral requirements, risk burdens, high interest rates and corruption (Maryam and Ahamed 2021). Fintech agri services are solutions to this challenge. AI has emerged as a promising solution for identifying unique challenges faced by agriculture landscapes in India. Digital kisan credit card issued by SBI is a remarkable initiative in granting credit to rural farmers within a short span of time. Union bank also provides similar digital credit card in collaboration with Reserve bank innovation hub, for sanction of fresh loans of upto Rs 1.60 lakh.

Agritech partnerships with banks are becoming more and more common as they help farmers by increasing the efficiency of the agribusiness. The goal of Fasal's partnership with SBI, which was announced in April 2023, is to make it easier for farmers to obtain financing. This may enable farmers to receive competitively priced, collateral-free loans. Axis Bank and ITC Ltd. partnered in 2023 to provide farmers with rural loan products. The ITC e-choupal eco system has revolutionized rural India's quality of life. Additionally, they have established a digital ecosystem that offers a wide range of solutions through market connections, financial services, agri-inputs, and personalized advice. Arya, a post-harvest agricultural technology startup, and Canara Bank have forged a strategic alliance to provide storage and collateral management services that would aid farmers in connecting with markets efficiently. The Economic Times, India Times, Inc. Due to inadequate networks, many banks are unable to assist small farms. These kinds of partnerships enable banks to reach out to small farmers in rural areas by utilizing their network. In partnership with six other businesses, the public sector bank Bank of Baroda has created the digital platform "Baroda Kisan," which will be run by IBM. Subsequently in 2023, Federal Bank appointed Chennai-based agri-fintech startup Kivi as a banking correspondent, improving the flow of credit to underserved rural populations, particularly in the Tamilnadu region. In summary, the majority of Indian banks, both public and private, have partnerships with internet companies in order to take advantage of their client services.

4. FINTECH ADOPTION – CHALLENGES FACED BY BANKING INDUSTRY

Technology disruptions that have happened so far in any economy have been a challenging factor initially due to the vast changes it may bring in (Gomber, Kauffman, Parker, & Weber, 2018). Banking sector has witnessed huge transformation over the years due to the incorporation of technology into its operations and services. With the advent of fintech companies and the speed with which they cater to the needs of customers, traditional banking systems were forced to align with new technologies. Fintech startups came with novel ideas, newer technologies and strategies for exploring niche markets which was not possible to a great extent by the traditional banking system. Later or sooner banks started collaborating with tech/fintech companies to streamline its operations at par with that of tech giants in the similar field.

Fintech industries are covering almost all the financial services right from lending and borrowing to the wealth management. They have also expanded to lending for MSMEs and other rural sectors (Akyuwen, Nanere, & Ratten, 2022). This being a challenge to banks for their existence and due to the severe competition faced in this field now banks are also transforming themselves into "techbanks". Certainly, there are expenses and difficulties to take into account when implementing and maintaining FinTech. Banks also face challenges like the risk of data security and privacy data being shared with fintech companies which may lead to the leakage of privacy data. More over confidentiality of database is also questionable. Sensitive financial data if managed by fintech firms, it's more vulnerable to cyber-attack. According to officials of private banks, technological risk in the industry had significant rise. The budget pattern of the bank has also changed widely due to the higher tech requirements. Officials of public sector banks were of the opinion that server breakdown is a challenge which they have faced. The tech platform may go down at times which affect the customer service. Another challenge faced by banks are the lack of financial literacy among rural customers. Even with the implementation of fintech apps, customers find it difficult to use the app due to the lack of awareness. Especially apps like Yono-agri even though useful it may be difficult for farmers to use it to the maximum. Hence banks like SBI are conducting awareness campaigns among farmers and rural population to make them tech literate which again increases the operational cost of the business.

5. CONCLUSION

The RBI has emphasized it is important for Financial Institutions and the Banks to adopt and implement the concept of ''Green deposits'' at the earliest. The aim is to ensure that funds are provided for the conservation of land and marine biodiversity, energy efficiency, clean transportation, adaptation to climate change, sustainable water and waste management, and green buildings. Banks and other financial organizations have seen cost savings as a result of ESG standards, which include a number of initiatives like recycling, and employing environmentally friendly raw materials. Technology advancements in digital payments have reduced the use for paper money. Paper use is eliminated by mobile apps and ATMs. E-messages and SMSs are being used more frequently than paper receipts. Digital payment methods have reduced labor costs by using less labor.Banks are starting to realize that they may make progress in both ESG and digital transformation at the same time if they embrace these strategies together. Despite the enormous challenge, there are certain areas of overlap, and institutions who have managed to achieve some level of maturity in both sectors would have a clear competitive edge in the market. The banks will need to update their IT infrastructure and business procedures as part of this endeavour, and they also need to adopt new perspectives on their workforce, organizational structure, and culture. The banks need to come up with those products and services that promote not only the digitization but also adhere to the ESG guidelines.

REFERENCES

Akyuwen, R., Nanere, M., & Ratten, V. (2022). Technology entrepreneurship: Fintech lending in Indonesia. In V. Ratten (Ed.), *Entrepreneurial innovation*. Studies on Entrepreneurship, Structural Change and Industrial Dynamics. Springer, Singapore. https://doi.org/DOI: 10.1007/978-981-16-4795-6_14

Business Standard. (n.d.). *Industry news*. Retrieved October 27, 2024, from https://www.business-standard.com/industry/news/

CTMfile. (n.d.). *Progression of open banking in India*. Retrieved October 27, 2024, from https://ctmfile.com/story/progression-of-open-banking-in-india

Deng, H., Huang, R. H., & Wu, Q. (2018). The regulation of initial coin offerings in China: Problems, prognoses and prospects. *European Business Organization Law Review*, *19*(3), 465–502. DOI: 10.1007/s40804-018-0118-2

Ellili, N. O. D. (2022). Is there any association between FinTech and sustainability? Evidence from bibliometric review and content analysis. *Journal of Financial Services Marketing*, *28*(4), 748–762. DOI: 10.1057/s41264-022-00200-w

Galazova, S., & Magomaeva, L. (2019). The transformation of traditional banking activity in digital. *International Journal of Economics and Business Administration*, *VII*(Special Issue 2), 41-51. https://doi.org/DOI: 10.35808/ijeba/369

Galeone, G., Ranaldo, S., & Fusco, A. (2024). ESG and FinTech: Are they connected? *Research in International Business and Finance*, *69*, 102225. DOI: 10.1016/j.ribaf.2024.102225

Gomber, P., Kauffman, R. J., Parker, C., & Weber, B. W. (2018). On the Fintech Revolution: Interpreting the Forces of Innovation, Disruption, and Transformation in Financial Services. *Journal of Management Information Systems*, *35*(1), 220–265. DOI: 10.1080/07421222.2018.1440766

Hasan, R., Ashfaq, M., & Shao, L. (2021). Evaluating drivers of Fintech adoption in The Netherlands. *Global Business Review*, *097215092110274*. Advance online publication. DOI: 10.1177/09721509211027402

ICICI Bank. (n.d.). *What is API banking services and how it works*. Retrieved October 27, 2024, from https://www.icicibank.com/blogs/api-banking/what-is-api-banking-services-and-how-it-works

Inc42. (n.d.). *Digital financial inclusion*. Retrieved October 27, 2024, from https://inc42.com/glossary/digital-financial-inclusion/

Jakšič, M., & Marinč, M. (2018). Relationship banking and information technology: The role of artificial intelligence and FinTech. *Risk Management*, *21*(1), 1–18. DOI: 10.1057/s41283-018-0039-y

Kogta Financial. (2024). *Technology for financial inclusion in India 2024*. Retrieved October 27, 2024, from https://kogta.in/blog/technology-for-financial-inclusion-in-india-2024

Kumar et.al.; (2023). Digital Transformation and Financial Inclusion: A Case Study of State Bank of India, *Intellectual Resonance, DCAC journal of Interdisciplinary studies, 6(2),*2321-2594

Kumar, A., Srivastava, A., & Gupta, P. K. (2022). Banking 4.0: The era of artificial intelligence-based fintech. *Strategic Change*, *31*(6), 591–601. DOI: 10.1002/jsc.2526

Lee, I., & Shin, Y. J. (2018). Fintech: Ecosystem, business models, investment decisions, and challenges. *Business Horizons*, *61*(1), 35–46. DOI: 10.1016/j.bushor.2017.09.003

Lee, J., Serafin, A. M., & Courteau, C. (2023). Corporate disclosure, ESG and green fintech in the energy industry. *Journal of World Energy Law and Business*, *16*(6), 473–491. DOI: 10.1093/jwelb/jwad018

Li, B., & Xu, Z. (2021). Insights into financial technology (FinTech): A bibliometric and visual study. *Financial Innovation*, *7*(1), 69. Advance online publication. DOI: 10.1186/s40854-021-00285-7 PMID: 35024290

Link, G. D. S. (n.d.). *Credit risk management process: Best practices & techniques*. Retrieved October 27, 2024, from https://www.gdslink.com/credit-risk-management-process-best-practices-techniques/

Liu, X., Yang, Y., Jiang, Y., Fu, Y., Zhong, R. Y., Li, M., & Huang, G. Q. (2023). Data-driven ESG assessment for blockchain services: A comparative study in textiles and apparel industry. *Resources, Conservation and Recycling*, *190*, 106837. DOI: 10.1016/j.resconrec.2022.106837

Macchiavello, E., & Siri, M. (2022). Sustainable finance and Fintech: Can technology contribute to achieving environmental goals? A preliminary assessment of 'Green Fintech' and 'Sustainable digital finance'. *European Company and Financial Law Review*, *19*(1), 128–174. DOI: 10.1515/ecfr-2022-0005

Macpherson, M., Gasperini, A., & Bosco, M. (2021). Artificial intelligence and FinTech technologies for ESG data and analysis. SSRN *Electronic Journal*. DOI: 10.2139/ssrn.3790774

Nassiry, D. (2019). The role of Fintech in unlocking green finance. *Handbook of Green Finance*, 315-336. DOI: 10.1007/978-981-13-0227-5_27

Omarini, A. E. (2018). Banks and Fintechs: How to develop a digital open banking approach for the bank's future. *International Business Research, 11*(9), 23. DOI: 10.5539/ibr.v11n9p23

Philippon, T. (2016). The FinTech opportunity. DOI: 10.3386/w22476

PwC India. (n.d.). *Integrating ESG in the payments ecosystem.* Retrieved October 27, 2024, from https://www.pwc.in/industries/financial-services/fintech/payments/integrating-esg-in-the-payments-ecosystem.htm

Romānova, I., & Kudinska, M. (2016). Banking and Fintech: A Challenge or Opportunity? In *Contemporary studies in economic and financial analysis* (pp. 21–35). DOI: 10.1108/S1569-375920160000098002

Siek, M., & Sutanto, A. (2019). *Impact Analysis of Fintech on Banking Industry.* DOI: 10.1109/ICIMTech.2019.8843778

State Bank of India. (n.d.). *Fintech innovation & incubation program.* Retrieved October 27, 2024, from https://www.sbi.co.in/web/business/information/fintech-innovation-incubation-program

Suryono, R. R., Budi, I., & Purwandari, B. (2020). Challenges and trends of financial technology (Fintech): A systematic literature review. *Information (Basel), 11*(12), 590. DOI: 10.3390/info11120590

Taleeb & Khadum. (2024). The role of environmental social and governance (ESG) practices in enhancing financial performance in companies with a focus on the banking sector: A literature review. *International Development Planning Review, 23*(01), 1129–1252.

Thakor, A. V. (2012). Incentives to innovate and financial crises. *Journal of Financial Economics, 103*(1), 130–148. DOI: 10.1016/j.jfineco.2011.03.026

Zhao, J., Li, X., Yu, C., Chen, S., & Lee, C. (2022). Riding the FinTech innovation wave: FinTech, patents and bank performance. *Journal of International Money and Finance, 122*, 102552. DOI: 10.1016/j.jimonfin.2021.102552

Zhou, X., Tang, X., & Zhang, R. (2020). Impact of green finance on economic development and environmental quality: A study based on provincial panel data from China. *Environmental Science and Pollution Research International, 27*(16), 19915–19932. DOI: 10.1007/s11356-020-08383-2 PMID: 32232752

Chapter 7

Influence of Robo-Advisory on Investment Decisions of the Young Investors:
Delhi-NCR Study

Rohit Kaushik
https://orcid.org/0000-0002-4929-5247
Jagannath International Management School, Delhi, India

ABSTRACT

In the fast changing landscape of financial markets, artificial intelligence is making inroads into it. Artificial intelligence is a concept or technological advancement which aims to mirror intelligence exhibited by the human beings and executes all the jobs to the perfection. Financial or investment domain is not an exception to this. Before making any investment decision one has to look at various aspects and pay attention to various reports and constantly monitor the changes in stock prices, which is a very difficult job every person can't claim to master this art, in this artificial intelligence comes to the rescue of such persons who can't perform such tasks carefully. Data was collected with the help of questionnaire and analyzed by employing multiple regression method to ascertain the effect of perceived utility and subjective norms on the usage of robo-advisory in investment and personal finance management which was another factor studied with artificial intelligence.

DOI: 10.4018/979-8-3373-0129-7.ch007

INTRODUCTION

Artificial intelligence has become a new development that is pervasive in all aspects. Most of the tasks in daily routine now-a-days is performed to a great extent by the artificial intelligence as Alexa is doing all the household activities and managing all the appliances in the home of any individual. Financial sector is not unaffected by the advent of the artificial intelligence. This convergence of minds and machines have effected a momentous change in all the spheres of life. Human beings are prone to biases and ultimately they make inferior decisions and suffer losses. Artificial intelligence on the other hand is a software which does not rely on instincts and biases and very practical and takes very tough decisions without getting emotional (Jung et al., 2018, Ruhr, 2020).

Artificial intelligences analyzes the market condition comprehensively and suggest course of action or takes action pragmatically. In stock markets artificial intelligence is playing its role in the form of algorithm trading where with the help of intelligence algorithms investors take right decisions and executes many orders at a given point in time which gives them additional edge over other investors in the market. In many global institutions these changes have taken place and Bank of Tokyo and Bank of America are examples in this regard (Marinova et al., 2017) (Rosman, 2018)

Due to technology conventional methods of banking are facing stiff competition from new innovative methods of banking provided by new age fin-tech companies based on novel technologies and increasing the comfort and ease of customers and also shaking the very foundation of a business or sector. In current scenario financial landscape is undergoing transformation and that has facilitated the change in the approach of customers irrespective of the age group they belong to, as they adopt the new and transformational facility of digitization. In addition to this fin-tech companies are serving their customers 24*7 and creating an ecosystem of reliability and trust among them and they are not subject to regulatory compulsions unlike conventional banking companies. The robo-advisors in this scenario are helping investors to commit their funds in customized propositions and that takes place in a very simple manner.

In the age of novel technology people are always found doing their important work on smart phones and spending considerable time and fin-tech companies sensed the absence of such things or facilities in the banking or investment arena. Robo-advisors are a result of such concerted efforts of fin-tech companies to develop digital facilities for customers with smart technology and interactive too. A robo-advisor gathers information from the clients on regular basis pertaining to their financial condition and their financial goal and advise them accordingly (Yi et al., 2023). Evolution of robo-advisory is crucial to maintaining the transparency for ethical and round the clock functioning of the fin-tech companies and banking sector in general but its revolutionary nature has not resulted in full adoption by the masses. This reluctance on the part of customers can be attributed to the lack of knowledge about the concept of robo-advisors, lack of trust in an online platforms and quest for transparency which has resulted in asymmetry. Another interesting aspect associated with robo advisory is that as disposable income rises and it results in increase in volume of investment, investors to maximize their return seek help of personalized and dedicated services for wealth management and in the process come across Northey et al. (2022) but as other studies conducted in Scandinavian nations like Sweden, Norway, Finland people belonging to lower income they are actively using robo-advisory functions for wealth management and majority of them are females with less willingness to take risk Faradynawati et al. (2022). In today's scenario robo-advisors have totally changed the way investment services are offered and in a way disrupted the market (Laukkanen and Pasanen, 2008).

The research intends to study the understand the preferences of consumers in relation to robo-advisory with respect to investment decisions of retail investors in Indian financial environment and it also provides valuable insights into extent of adoption of robo-advisory in Indian financial landscape, identify those factors which are going to result in faster adoption of robo-advisory by keeping in center the factors like perceived utility, external influence and internal influence.

LITERATURE REVIEW

The advent of robo advisory and artificial intelligence will transform the entire gamut of activities in financial sector and will have huge transformational value for all sectors cutting across all the dimensions of business sector (Acemoglu & Restrepo, 2017). On the other hand (Huang and Rust, 2018) emphasized upon the eventuality which is awaiting the mankind in case the artificial intelligence is properly implemented in the system and human being are no longer needed to work, they also anticipated that artificial intelligence will develop all abilities ranging from mechanical to intuitive intelligence.

Simultaneously researches were also focusing upon the challenges in the way of introduction of automation in the service sector, special emphasis was placed upon sectors where direct communication with consumers was needed. These researches noted that consumer interaction is going to be shaped profoundly with the introduction of artificial intelligence and will also change the consumer behavior in the market, but the level of adoption of technology in service sector will depend on the presence of humans and relative capacity of artificial intelligence to socialize with consumers on daily basis (Singh et al., 2017), (Han and Young, 2018), (Van Doorn et al., 2017), (Grewal et al., 2017), (Ji, 2017).

In totality, there is a huge realization among companies to introduce artificial intelligence in their operation as part of increasing efficiency and range of products. Management strategies adopted by their companies in relation to their operations also get a boost and passively increase competitive advantage of all the companies employing artificial intelligence.

Robo-advisors have been depicted as interactive and intelligent systems that are built on the foundations of information technology and helped consumers in taking crucial investment decisions (Jung et al., 2018). Initially these systems first gather information from consumers through questionnaire, on the basis of information provided by the consumers in the questionnaires, these systems start making recommendation to the consumers.

Robo-advisors present a range of benefits to the entire community of consumers, unlike human advisors they are always on service for the human beings, resulting in cost reduction on the part of companies and also helping consumer in seeking professional advice regarding diverse investment options in an efficient manner and eliminating the scope of fraud which is always looming large in case of dealing with human advisors (Faubion, 2016), (Park et al., 2016). During the period 2019-22 assets managed by robo-advisors crossed $880,000 million.

Even though this concept is evoking huge interest, but some studies have pointed out the obstacles in the introduction of robo-advisors and found that corporate world is more interested in exploring the capabilities of artificial intelligence and its application in diverse areas whereas consumers are not ready to trust applications based on artificial intelligence due to security reasons. Customization is the unique advantage of robo-advisors identified by the studies in relation to investment management (Faloon and Scherer, 2017), studies have also found a correlation between increased usage of artificial intelligence and informed decision making (Henrich and Schwabe, 2018).

Considering freshness associated with the concept of robo-advisory in the process of investment management, there is lack of awareness about the key factors which determine the prospects for adoption of robo-advisory by the consumers, with help of robo-advisory the financial sector is making advisory services available to all the consumers for better decision making (Sironi, 2016).

The consumers' thoughts and perceptions are conditioned by the thought process of people who are close to the consumer. The societal behavior acts as a pressure for the consumer to adopt a technology or disapprove of it (Tayler and Todd, 1995), (Fishbein and Ajzen, 1975).

People with limited information and also facing the situation or spectre of a disruptive technology, as they lack relevant experience in the concerned field tend to behave like their relatives, peers, friends, basing their decisions on the experiences of others in order to enhance their assimilation in the society and appear modern in the eyes of others (Belanche et al., 2012).

In the area of finance there is considerable role played by the close social circle of an individual and the other non-human source of information like media and by this one can easily understand that consumers tend to gain some confirmation from others with respect to their decision. (Bhattacharjee, 2000) (Ryu, 2018).

Familiarity with any concept or new technology results in the adoption of that technology as that is going to enhance or decrease the willingness on the part of consumers to actually engage with the new technology in question. Same is the case with robo-advisors, in the 1980s and 90s all the banking jobs and investment management services were provided by the human resources of the concerned organization but now robo-advisors are playing that role with increased efficiency and professionalism but all the consumers are not welcoming of the new change and a substantial part of the population is not exhibiting faith in adopting robo-advisors for investment management and with different level of knowledge and familiarity one can sense the difference in the extent of adoption (Young et al., 2009) (Maenpaa et al., 2008) consumers with limited information about new technology will be more reliant on the experiences of others (Venkatesh and Davis, 2000)

RESEARCH METHODOLOGY AND HYPOTHESIS FORMATION

By examining the available research and literature in the public domain, questionnaire was modelled to address the basic requirements of the present research. First part of the questionnaire was related to the socio-economic profile of the respondents and the other two parts were dedicated to the core areas of the research like perceived trust, internal and external influence and intention to use in relation to robo-advisory. The question were designed with the help of Likert Scale.

Sample size of the present study was of 100 people and all of them were residing in Delhi as Delhi is the political and financial capital of India. People from diverse background participate in the financial activities taking place in the city resulting in diverse opinions making it a near-perfect fit for carrying out research.

Data collected in the study was analyzed with the help of SPSS software using Multiple Regression Methods to ascertain the influence of perceived trust, internal and external influence on intention to use robo advisory. To streamline the process of research following hypothesis were formed:

H01: Perceived trust does not share a significant relationship with intention to use robo-advisory services

H02: Internal influence does not share a significant relationship with intention to use robo-advisory services

H03: External influence does not share a significant relationship with intention to use robo-advisory services

Table 1. Demographic Profile

Variables	Category	Frequency	%
Gender	Male	54	54
	Female	46	46
Age	18-30	59	59
	31-45	29	29
	46-60	12	12
Marital Status	Unmarried	46	46
	Married	54	54
Education	School Education	11	11
	Graduation	44	44
	Post-Graduation	36	36
	Others	9	9
Occupation	Private Employees	43	43
	Public Employees	10	10
	Business	13	13
	Others	34	34
Income	<5 Lakhs	68	68
	5-10 Lakhs	25	25
	>10 Lakhs	7	7

Data Analysis

For the validity of a research model, all the variables in the research have to fulfill some norms to avoid lopsidedness and biasness. As the data was collected from 100 respondents, reliability of the data was judged with the help of SPSS. Acceptable value of a Cronbach Alpha test is 0.70 and a variable or construct must measure more than 0.70 Hair et al. (2006). Cronbach Alpha value more than 0.80 points towards the soundness of the constructs in terms of validity. The values attained by the constructs in the present study are in the range of 0.75-0.82

Table 2. Reliability Analysis

Construct	No. of Items	Alpha (α)
Internal Influence	3	0.82
External Influence	3	0.75
Perceived Utility	3	0.82
Intention to Use	3	0.78

Data Analysis

Multiple Regression Analysis

Table 3. Model Summary

Model Summary				
Model	R	R Square	Adjusted R Square	Std. Error of the Estimate
1	.838[a]	.702	.692	.47694

a. Predictors: (Constant), EF_1, PU_1, IF_1

Table 4. Anova

ANOVA[a]						
Model		Sum of Squares	df	Mean Square	F	Sig.
1	Regression	51.332	3	17.111	75.221	.000[b]
	Residual	21.838	96	.227		
	Total	73.170	99			

a. Dependent Variable: IU_1
b. Predictors: (Constant), EF_1, PU_1, IF_1

Table 5. Coefficients

Coefficients[a]						
Model		Unstandardized Coefficients		Standardized Coefficients	t	Sig.
		B	Std. Error	Beta		
1	(Constant)	-.184	.295		-.623	.535
	PU_1	.384	.086	.359	4.472	.000
	IF_1	.290	.117	.225	2.482	.015
	EF_1	.410	.078	.387	5.268	.000

a. Dependent Variable: IU_1

As can be observed in the results of the data analysis that independent variables have significantly affected the dependent variable (3, 96) = 75.221, $p<0.01$ which is reflected by the effectiveness of the model. The model in the present study is able to reflect the variations in the dependent factor due to independent factors in the question, to the tune of 70 percent as reflected by the R^2 value of 0.70.

As we delve deeper into the individual role played by the independent factors in relation to the dependent factor we find that Hypotheses 1 examined the relation between perceived utility and intention to use robo-advisory and the results in the study throw up significant relation between the factors (β=.384, t = 4.472, p = 0.00) and clearly showcase that utility clearly shapes the usage behavior of the respondents in relation to the robo-advisory and Hypothesis 1 is rejected in view of the results. H_2 evaluates the relationship of advises of close relatives and family members and the adoption of robo-advisory services and intention to use it (β=.290, t = 2.48, p = 0.015) and clearly points out that views of immediate family members affects the perception of any person to use the robo-advisory services in a significant services. H_3 studied the impact of external influence on the intention to use robo-advisory services in the form of friends and peer circle and the results found a significant relation between the two (β=.410, t = 5.268, p = 0.00) and in a much profound manner than internal influence and shaped immensely the intention of the individual to use the robo-advisory services and the hypothesis is rejected.

DISCUSSION AND CONCLUSION

In the ongoing emergence of FinTech companies, robo-advisory services caught the attention of investors and individuals in general as robo-advisers rely only on artificial intelligence and their advent and usage is resulting in fast replacement of humans from this area. From a customer's perspective it is very essential to identify those factors which result in the adoption of robo-advisory services in the area of investment management and personal financial management. As this study noted that subjective norms and perceived utility are the factors which immensely influenced the decision to adopt or use robo-advisory services.

As the findings of the present study concluded that internal and external influence share a significant relation with the intention of usage of robo-advisory service and it is in conformity with the findings of other studies like (Fishbein and Ajzen, 1975) who have earlier concluded in their study that subjective norms like internal and external influence, found to be impacting intention of consumers regarding adoption of robo-advisory or artificial intelligence in the domain of investment management.

On the other hand perceived utility was another factors which was studied in its impact on intention of consumer and it was also found to be sharing a significant relation with dependent variable in question, this relationship as thrown up by the findings is also consistent with previous studies' findings Hernandez et al., 2009 as it has also concluded that perceived utility as a factor not only contributes to the decision of individuals before the actual usage of the robo-advisory but even after using the services it positively conditions the mind of individual. As the millennium generation is actively involved in the financial decision-making this results also takes into account the advance exposure of the current generation to the artificial intelligence and their willingness to adopt robo-advisory services is reflected in the results or findings of the study.

As the major contribution of the research lies in divulging key aspects which can be focused upon by managers while introducing artificial intelligence in the form robo-advisory services, they will have to present robo-advisors in a way which is very user friendly so that consumer adoption process is simplified as due to simple interface there is higher possibility of consumers switching to robo-advisory services. Financial institutions need to organize conferences to interact with their customer base to spread awareness about the concept of robo-advisors so that subjective norms can also be managed which have found to be impacting ultimate decisions of consumers.

LIMITATIONS AND SCOPE OF FURTHER RESEARCH

In the present study small sample size plays a inhibiting role in terms of generalization study for that similar studies with comparatively large sample size need to be carried out in adjoining big cities in other studies, People were not willing to share their personal details and were giving biased responses to the questions in the questionnaire.

The present study is going to be useful for the financial institutions to focus on those features which consumers attach a lot of importance and hence will result in enhanced customer adoption of robo-advisors in the area of investment management.

REFERENCES

Acemoglu, D., & Restrepo, P. (2020). Robots and jobs: Evidence from US labor markets. *Journal of Political Economy, 128*(6), 2188–2244. DOI: 10.1086/705716

Belanche, D., Casaló, L. V., & Guinalíu, M. (2012). Website usability, consumer satisfaction and the intention to use a website: The moderating effect of perceived risk. *Journal of Retailing and Consumer Services, 19*(1), 124–132. DOI: 10.1016/j.jretconser.2011.11.001

Bhattacherjee, A. (2000). Acceptance of e-commerce services: The case of electronic brokerages. *IEEE Transactions on Systems, Man, and Cybernetics. Part A, Systems and Humans, 30*(4), 411–420. DOI: 10.1109/3468.852435

Faloon, M., & Scherer, B. (2017). Individualization of robo-advice. *The Journal of Wealth Management, 20*(1), 30–36. DOI: 10.3905/jwm.2017.20.1.030

Faradynawati, I. A. A., & Söderberg, I. L. (2022). Sustainable investment preferences among robo-advisor clients. *Sustainability (Basel), 14*(19), 12636. DOI: 10.3390/su141912636

Faubion, B. (2016). Effect of automated advising platforms on the financial advising market.

Fishbein, M., & Ajzen, I. (1977). Belief, attitude, intention, and behavior: An introduction to theory and research.

Frankenfield, J. (2020). Cloud computing. *Investopedia. Dostupno na:* https://www.investopedia. com/terms/c/cloud-computing. asp*[28. svibnja 2021.]*.

Gracia, D. B., Ariño, L. V. C., & Blasco, M. G. (2015). The effect of culture in forming e-loyalty intentions: A cross-cultural analysis between Argentina and Spain. *Business Research Quarterly, 18*(4), 275–292. DOI: 10.1016/j.brq.2015.02.003

Grewal, D., Roggeveen, A. L., & Nordfält, J. (2017). The future of retailing. *Journal of Retailing, 93*(1), 1–6. DOI: 10.1016/j.jretai.2016.12.008

Han, S., & Yang, H. (2018). Understanding adoption of intelligent personal assistants: A parasocial relationship perspective. *Industrial Management & Data Systems, 118*(3), 618–636. DOI: 10.1108/IMDS-05-2017-0214

Heinrich, P., & Schwabe, G. (2018). Facilitating informed decision-making in financial service encounters. *Business & Information Systems Engineering, 60*(4), 317–329. DOI: 10.1007/s12599-017-0501-5

Hernández, B., Jiménez, J., & Martín, M. J. (2009). Adoption of e-commerce by people over 55 in Spain. *International Journal of Retail & Distribution Management, 37*(12), 1051–1073. DOI: 10.1108/09590550911005041

Ji, M. (2017). Are robots good fiduciaries: Regulating robo-advisors under the investment advisers act of 1940. *SSRN, 117*, 1543. DOI: 10.2139/ssrn.3036722

Jung, D., Dorner, V., Glaser, F., & Morana, S. (2018). Robo-advisory: Digitalization and automation of financial advisory. *Business & Information Systems Engineering, 60*(1), 81–86. DOI: 10.1007/s12599-018-0521-9

Laukkanen, T., & Pasanen, M. (2008). Mobile banking innovators and early adopters: How they differ from other online users? *Journal of Financial Services Marketing, 13*(2), 86–94. DOI: 10.1057/palgrave.fsm.4760077

Mäenpää, K., Kale, S. H., Kuusela, H., & Mesiranta, N. (2008). Consumer perceptions of Internet banking in Finland: The moderating role of familiarity. *Journal of Retailing and Consumer Services, 15*(4), 266–276. DOI: 10.1016/j.jretconser.2007.05.007

) Marinova, D., de Ruyter, K., Huang, M.H., Meuter, M.L. and Challagalla, G. (2017), "Getting smart: learning from technology-empowered frontline interactions", Journal of Service Research, Vol. 20No. 1, pp. 29-42.

Northey, G., Hunter, V., Mulcahy, R., Choong, K., & Mehmet, M. (2022). Man vs machine: How artificial intelligence in banking influences consumer belief in financial advice. *International Journal of Bank Marketing, 40*(6), 1182–1199. DOI: 10.1108/IJBM-09-2021-0439

Park, J. Y., Ryu, J. P., & Shin, H. J. (2016). Robo advisors for portfolio management. *Advanced Science and Technology Letters, 141*(1), 104–108. DOI: 10.14257/astl.2016.141.21

Rosman, C. (2018). Mad about erica: Why a million people use Bank of America's chatbot. *American Banker, 183*, 114.

Rühr, A., & Böhme, R. (2020). Robo-advisor configuration: An investigation of user preferences and the performance-control dilemma. ResearchGate. https://www.researchgate.net/publication/341386490_Robo-Advisor_Configuration_An_Investigation_of_User_Preferences_and_the_Performance-Control_Dilemma

Ryu, H. S. (2018). What makes users willing or hesitant to use Fintech?: The moderating effect of user type. *Industrial Management & Data Systems, 118*(3), 541–569. DOI: 10.1108/IMDS-07-2017-0325

Singh, J., Brady, M., Arnold, T., & Brown, T. (2017). The emergent field of organizational frontlines. *Journal of Service Research, 20*(1), 3–11. DOI: 10.1177/1094670516681513

Sironi, P. (2016). *FinTech innovation: from robo-advisors to goal based investing and gamification.* John Wiley & Sons. DOI: 10.1002/9781119227205

Taylor, S., & Todd, P. A. (1995). Understanding information technology usage: A test of competing models. *Information Systems Research, 6*(2), 144–176. DOI: 10.1287/isre.6.2.144

Van Doorn, J., Mende, M., Noble, S. M., Hulland, J., Ostrom, A. L., Grewal, D., & Petersen, J. A. (2017). Domo arigato Mr. Roboto: Emergence of automated social presence in organizational frontlines and customers' service experiences. *Journal of Service Research, 20*(1), 43–58. DOI: 10.1177/1094670516679272

Venkatesh, V., & Davis, F. D. (2000). A theoretical extension of the technology acceptance model: Four longitudinal field studies. *Management Science, 46*(2), 186–204. DOI: 10.1287/mnsc.46.2.186.11926

Yi, S., Goh, Y. N., Tan, G. W. H., & Loh, X. M. (2023). Impact of robo-advisors on millennials' financial behaviour: An extended TPB approach. *Asian Academy of Management Journal, 28*(1), 41–66. DOI: 10.21315/aamj2023.28.1.2

Young, J. E., Hawkins, R., Sharlin, E., & Igarashi, T. (2009). Toward acceptable domestic robots: Applying insights from social psychology. *International Journal of Social Robotics, 1*(1), 95–108. DOI: 10.1007/s12369-008-0006-y

Chapter 8
AI's Impact on Financial Services, Auditing, and Investment Strategies: The Future Ahead

Mohammad Irfan
https://orcid.org/0000-0002-4956-1170
Christ University, Bengaluru, India

Rui Dias
https://orcid.org/0000-0002-6138-3098
ESCAD, IPLUSO, Intrepid Lab, Lisboa, Portugal

Jayant Hooda
https://orcid.org/0000-0002-3491-9272
GLA University, Mathura, India

Kashish Ajit Singh
https://orcid.org/0009-0005-0555-6272
Christ University, Bengaluru, India

Sanjay Bang
Christ University, Bengaluru, India

ABSTRACT

Artificial intelligence (AI) is poised to significantly transform the fields of finance, auditing, and investment over the coming decade. In financial services, AI is anticipated to enhance decision-making processes, improve risk management practices, and facilitate the delivery of personalized financial solutions. The auditing profession

DOI: 10.4018/979-8-3373-0129-7.ch008

will be reshaped by AI and automation, enabling continuous auditing, real-time reporting, and more effective fraud detection mechanisms. In the investment domain, AI is expected to revolutionize portfolio management and asset allocation through advanced predictive analytics and data-driven market strategies. Despite these advancements, the rapid proliferation of AI presents considerable challenges, including ethical considerations, regulatory compliance, and the necessity of re-skilling financial professionals. This strategic overview examines both the opportunities and risks associated with AI integration and provides guidance for organizations seeking to maintain competitiveness in an increasingly AI-driven financial landscape.

INTRODUCTION

The complete transformation of financial services depends on Artificial Intelligence technology because institutions convert customer relations and create both streamlined operational structures and secure systems (Vasarhelyi, 2025). AI algorithms allow banking institutions and insurance companies and financial advisors to restructure their operational decisions during real-time data processing (Maple, 2023). Financial institutions use AI systems known as chatbots and virtual assistants to provide personalized fast service which both lowers operational costs while maintaining high user satisfaction (Shukla, 2024). Through AI implementation financial institutions achieve two benefits by using automated loan underwriting for precise borrowing reliability assessments to minimize credit defaults (Aitkazinov, 2023). Almond technology scores enable improved credit evaluation through the processing of unusual information consisting of transaction records and behavioral assessment outcomes to expand financial service availability (Johnson, 2024). Artificial intelligence expands financial security systems through real-time tests which identify irregular transaction behaviors (Tanaka, 2024). Machine learning algorithms applied to fraud detection become more effective through practical exposure which produces predictive risk solutions (Aon, 2025). Financial institutions achieve regulatory compliance by using AI process automation to handle evolving legal specifications according to ((EY), 2024). Banks together with investment firms use AI compliance solutions to detect suspicious activities more efficiently which results in reduced operational risks and cut labor costs (Deloitte, 2024). In parallel with market volatility predicting capabilities AI assessment frameworks help financial firms forecast the same regulatory environment (Forum, 2025).

AI impact areas receive detailed examination through the flowchart after gaining an overall view of the foundational areas affected by AI.

Figure 1. AI Integration in Finance

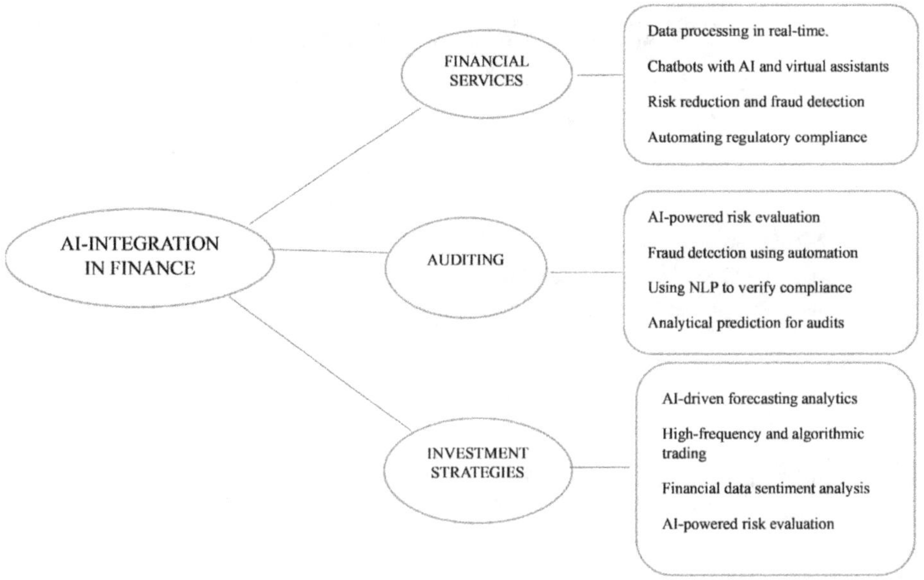

Artificial Intelligence transforms auditing practices through risk assessment and fraud detection by presenting auditors with exceptional dataset analysis capabilities (Naqvi, 2023). AI-driven analytics conducts extensive transaction analysis via data-driven methodologies instead of implementing the traditional sampling audit procedures (Kokina, 2024). Automated auditing tools make the financial audit process more efficient while preventing mistakes and providing full visibility to produce improved audit outcomes (Patil, 2024). The combination of Natural Language Processing technology and artificial intelligence enables auditors to scan disorganized data resources containing emails and contracts to identify compliance threats according to (Malladhi, 2023). Predictive analytics grants auditors early identification of risks and irregularities based on the findings documented by (Accountancy, 2024). The retention of modern forensic accounting tools based on AI technology has revolutionized how financial audits detect frauds with better efficiency (Journal, 2024). Figure b outlines how big data analytics functions during internal audit processes. Three critical domains that AI-powered forensic accounting tools examine encompass decision-making systems [root cause identification and real-time exception management] and operational areas [fraud detection and predictive risk analysis] and strategic stages [risk assessment coupled with data sampling] (Irfan, Elmogy, Gupta, Khalifa, & Dias, 2024). By following this systematic approach the precision together with the effectiveness of AI-driven auditing increases.

Figure 2. Big Data Analytics Application in Internal Auditing

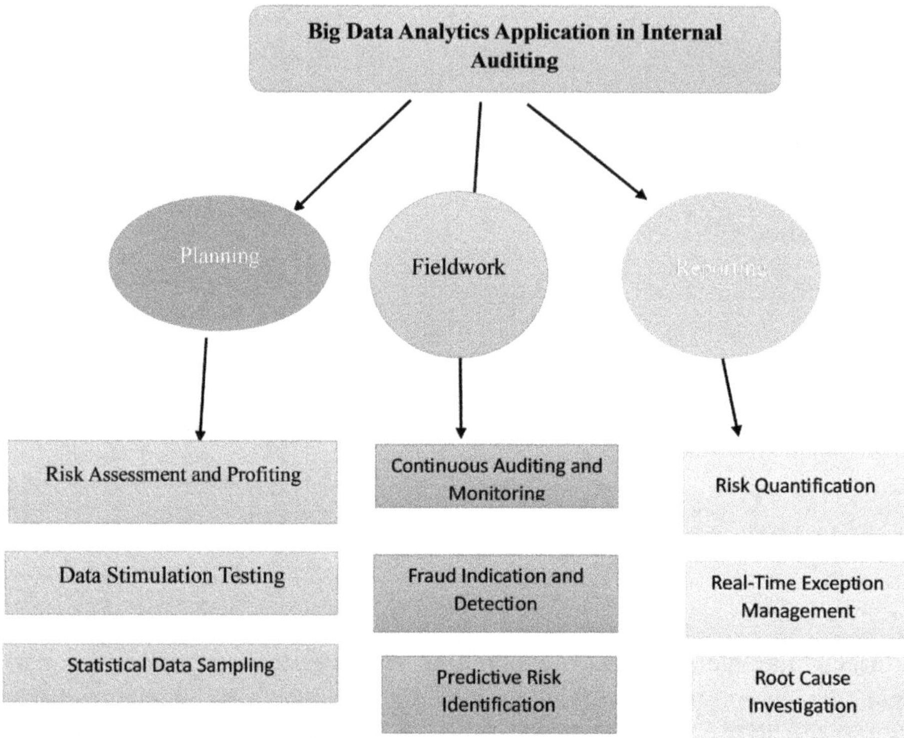

Rubber Portfolio profits substantially from artificial intelligence because it employs AI-based predictive analytics and algorithmic trading to optimize investment methodology according to (KPMG, 2024). Machine learning implements past data processing and immediate data analysis separated by a testing period for investors to generate stock prediction methods (Kluwer, 2024). With the help of AI-based automation retail investors can get individually adjusted investment advice that matches their risk levels and investment objectives according to (Zheng, 2017). Satellite AI systems perform quick trading activities based on minor stock price modifications to optimize market efficiency as documented in (Soleymani, 2020).). The automated system enables investors to reach financial advantages through market surveillance by altering their investment assets (Tsang, 2023). Hedge funds make use of artificial intelligence systems for immediate strategic modifications to maintain flexible control of their portfolio assets (Durodié, 2024). The AI-based sentiment analysis enables investors to gather valuable investment strategy elements from public accessible digital opinion collections (Jefferson, 2025). Market sentiment monitoring by AI-assisted financial analysts enables pattern detection for future trading while these analysts remain protected from market volatility as stated by (Fund, 2023). Description of alternative information sources becomes better for hedge funds when they integrate sentiment analysis tools for trading improvements (Paul, 2024). AI processing power enables the system to analyze various alternative data sources consisting of satellite imagery and transaction records thereby improving investment decisions (Treasury, 2024), (Irfan, Elmogy, Majid, & El-Sappagh, 2023). AI risk analysis operations which receive investment funding produce organizations stronger defenses against worldwide threats (Boobier, 2023).

Future financial service progression will accelerate at a quick pace through quantum computing because it enhances AI financial models through stronger computational abilities (Remolina, 2023). The application of quantum algorithms by financial institutions enables faster solutions of complex optimization problems that results in improved portfolio management abilities and risk evaluation capabilities (Smith, 2023). Security issues related to transactions disappear through the combination of AI with blockchain technology because it provides greater transparency and limited operational challenges as noted by (Geczy, 2024). Traditional fraud detection becomes instant through Blockchain AI integration while the system develops high-level monitoring solutions for compliance standards (Shabsigh, 2023). Smart contracts are advantaged by the implementation of AI since it improves their precision during automated financial transaction processing (Service, 2020). The many benefits that AI offers to financial institutions mean that organizations need to tackle ethical issues as discussed by (Smith J., 2024). Artificial intelligence use in decision-making raises several privacy issues that complement discrimination issues and governance gaps (Alevizos, 2025).

Financial institutions require ethical standards for their AI-based systems that will protect transparency while ensuring fair system operation (Commission, 2024). (Institute, 2021), points out that sustainable AI adoption across finance requires the successful handling of ethical factors. The requirement to establish AI governance systems by government enforcement agencies allows organizations to minimize discrimination and enhance financial accessibility (Henry, 2024). AI bias mitigation concepts have established themselves as mainstream tools for creating equitable lending practices and equal access to financial services throughout the last few years according to (Marsal, 2024). The implementation of AI technology within financial systems and auditing tools and investment models provides companies the chance to combine extensive operational opportunities with strong security platforms and advanced analytical tools (EY, 2024). Finance organizations that use AI tools gain market supremacy by making superior financial choices that lead to better outcomes according to (OneStream, 2024). The rich potential of AI advertising technology in revolutionizing finance keeps evolving because it has been promising emerging financial products that have a combination of automation with financial expertise and financial smart solutions (Mazars, 2025). Emerging AI features will put systems in place linking human experts with AI for fiscal work and benefit both augmenting financial work and maintaining ethical money practices in existence (Lumen, 2024). Artificial Intelligence will play a pivotal role in sustainable finance development through it support of green investment planning and ESG compliance system automation (Solutions, 2024).

Artificial intelligence enables the production of novel financial goods and customer-oriented services that adapt to current market requirements (Intive, 2024). Through AI-based insurance products firms give real-time customized coverage estimates which result in enhanced customer satisfaction and lower customer turnover (Irfan, Elmogy, Gupta, Khalifa, & Dias, 2024), (International Journal of Governance, 2024), AI technology makes it possible for wealth management firms to maximize retirement plans and tax planning which makes clients receive whole financial solutions based on (Service E. P., 2020). With AI tools now advisors provide individualized financial recommendations to clients that take into consideration numerous variables across different situations (Hidayat, 2024). AI fosters new innovation in the manner in which financial literacy and education operates (Fatouros, 2024). With AI-powered interactive education systems users engage with adaptive learning experiences that help them understand complex financial topics towards make improved decisions (Settlements, 2024) .

Machine learning algorithms on these platforms govern content modulation through user progress data as well as matching contents to individual preferences thus enabling successful and engaging learning experiences (Service C. R., 2024). By democratizing financial knowledge AI constructs abilities in individuals who are now able to dictate their financial destiny independently (Barron's, 2024). Artificial intelligence assists business firms in corporate finance to streamline their strategic planning and operational efficiency ((BCG), 2024) . (SpringerLink, 2024), said the use of artificial intelligence in financial modeling enables organizations to obtain improved outcomes from forecasting activities while controlling costs and making optimal capital allocation (LLP, 2024). Supply chain finance solutions with AI capabilities provide businesses with real-time access to liquidity monitoring that assists them in improving working capital management along with reduced financing costs (Times, 2024). Organizations leverage artificial intelligence for their mergers and acquisitions endeavors through big data analysis which helps them discover value-maximizing opportunities and potential vulnerabilities (Association, 2024).

The Financial Analytics Maturity Model is depicted in the following figure, which shows how financial firms progress from diagnostic and descriptive analytics to prescriptive and predictive analytics. This development improves decision-making skills, enabling businesses to construct financial strategies, forecasts, and budgets more effectively.

Figure 3. Sources: CPA, financial-analytics-maturity-model

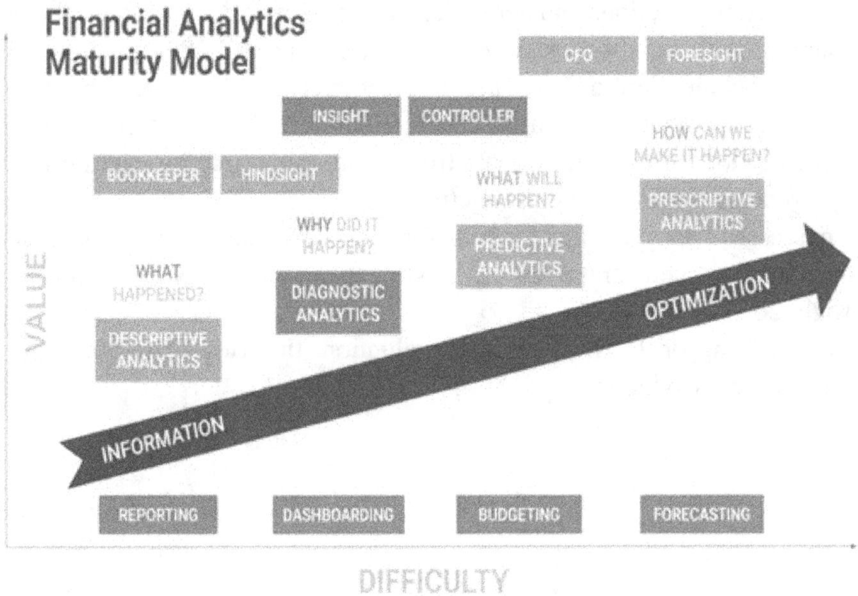

Artificial intelligence creates worldwide financial market effects through two key developments that enhance infrastructure construction and reduce systemic risks ((FSB), 2024). Through their operation of AI software technology market surveillance systems analyze present market activities to identify manipulative behavior that protects market integrity ((IMF), 2024). The deployed algorithms in these systems enable them to recognize characteristic patterns of market abuse that include both insider trading and spoofing behavior (Rieschel, 2024). AI develops transparent and fair market conditions which strengthen the stability and resilience of financial markets ((FATF), 2021).

AI implementation in regulatory technology (RegTech) simplifies compliance procedures which results in decreased regulatory strain for financial institutions (Associates, 2022). The implementation of AI-powered RegTech technology automates regulatory documentation processes while it checks regulatory adaptions and detects regulatory breach instances (Institute B. P., 2018). The advanced analytics systems simplify understanding complex legal requirements which results in financial institutions performing accurate operations within prescribed timeframes (Awosika, Shukla, & Pranggono, 2023). Through its cost-effective simplification of compliance processes, financial institutions can allocate resources toward innovation and development (Sha, 2024). Machines are progressively adding new capabilities to fight financial crime by expanding their focus from fraud detection into AML and CTF anti-money laundering and counter-terrorism financing regimes (Irfan, Elhoseny, Kassim, & Metawa, 2023), (BioCatch, 2024). AI analytics use transactional data along with customer actions and network analytics to monitor suspicious behaviors thus enabling the formation of system alerts (Kanaparthi, 2024). These systems implement machine learning algorithms for both threat adaptation and continual improvement of threat detection precision (Shukla, 2024). Artificial intelligence helps protect global financial systems from economic crime by making financial crime prevention systems more productive

AI possesses vast potential for transforming financial services together with auditing and investment strategies which will expand due to technological progress (Shabsigh, 2023).

Before moving on to the literature evaluation, this flowchart offers a visual summary of the introduction.

Figure 4. AI Research in Finance

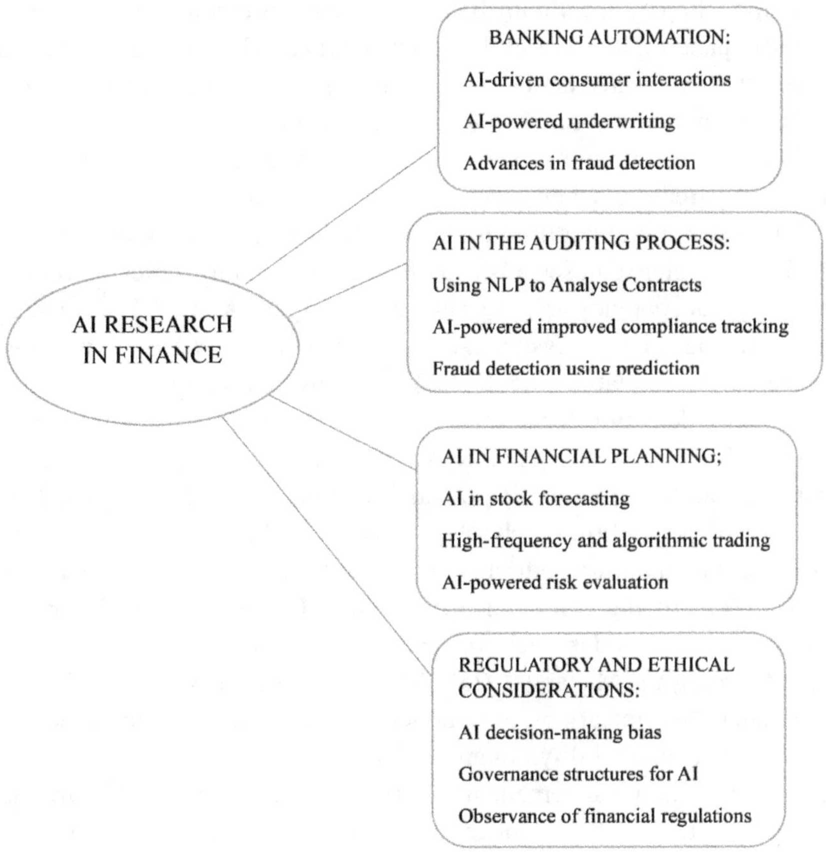

LITERATURE REVIEW

The expanding body of research about Artificial Intelligence in financial services develops because of the broad academic interest spawned by this field (Accountancy, 2024), Contemporary financial decision-making receives transformation through AI systems that advance automatic system processes and risk prediction analysis and pattern forecasting capabilities (Aon, 2025). AI automation in financial services allows banks and financial institutions to analyze big transaction volumes with better quality and speed ((FSB), 2024). Deep learning algorithms within machine learning models automatically analyze current transaction data to improve fraud detection (Patil, 2024). Through AI-driven financial planning tools users and business entities leverage data-driven insights to handle their savings together with investments and financial risk strategies (Malladhi, 2023). The technology enhances credit risk modeling by developing better lending requirements which lowers default rates while expanding loan possibilities for individuals lacking bank access (Naqvi, 2023). Through automated underwriting that employs AI technology loan approvals process faster and reduce the need for human error (Solutions, 2024).

Auditors use taxonomic processing and big data analytics through Artificial Intelligence to streamline their tasks of risk assessment and fraud detection (Kanaparthi, 2024). High-end auditing tools operated by artificial intelligence systems now analyze complete datasets instead of random sampling which drives up financial reporting transparency and precision according to (Aon, 2025). By integrating regulatory standards into its systems AI completes companywide compliance checks using minimal human labor (Fund, 2023). AI-powered forensic accounting makes use of anomaly detection techniques to detect fraudulent activities according to (LLP, 2024). By implementing predictive analytics in auditing organizations obtain heightened capabilities to identify potential financial anomalies (Tsang, 2023). The combination of AI auditing technology creates higher efficiency by decreasing manual labor which allows auditors to concentrate on vital analytical tasks instead of performing recurring compliance inspections (Kluwer, 2024). Interface-based anomaly detection methods track financial transactions to reveal instances of misconduct according to (Mazars, 2025). AI technologies used in real-time auditing enable financial organizations to conduct risk-based monitoring which leads to better financial accountability (Tsang, 2023).

AI has undergone advancement in investment strategy through the introduction of robo-advisors and the use of algorithmic trading as well as sentiment analysis tools according to (Rieschel, 2024) . Machine learning analysis dramatically improves market predictions by studying financial records from the past and current times (Hidayat, 2024). The use of AI systems in managing portfolios creates better risk and return performance that is generated to make better wealth services for retail clients ((EY), 2024). With AI technology, high-frequency trading firms make trades with speeds that are at the limits allowing them to exploit minute short-term market inaccuracies ((BCG), 2024). Through AI-driven sentiment analytics, investors gain the ability to measure public sentiment using news content and social media data along with various sources (Lumen, 2024). AI systems linked with alternative data such as satellite images and supply chain analytics help financial investment professionals make better decisions about their processes (Times, 2024). Deep learning technologies enable intelligent hedge fund analysis to be used for predicting stock market trend directions (Smith J., 2024). Through this technology, users can receive customized wealth management solutions that use personal investment approaches to achieve investor needs while maintaining suitable risk tolerance (Service E. P.,

2020), (Irfan, 2021). The artificial intelligence technology recognizes behavioral finance biases in investment choices through which it creates proactive solutions to improve investment decision quality (Soleymani, 2020).

The adoption of quantum computing technology into financial services will expand steadily for performing advanced financial modeling as (KPMG, 2024). describes. By applying quantum algorithms AI risk management systems will achieve better efficiency which leads to optimal portfolio decisions according to ((FATF), 2021). The amalgamation of AI systems with blockchain technology performs secure financial transaction proofing through upgraded security features and reports fewer instances of fraud and helps fulfill regulatory needs (Kokina, 2024). The implementation of AI-based smart contracts allows organizations to obtain improved transaction performance according to (Zheng, 2017). DeFi adopts blockchain-based methods to automate loans and borrows which results in reshaping traditional banking operations (Jefferson, 2025). Through AI technology financial modeling obtains confidence information and transparency which strengthens decentralized finance market structures (Aitkazinov, 2023). Quantum computing excellence will reshape financial modeling through its ability to provide AI simulation capabilities which help decrease modeling uncertainty predictions (Hidayat, 2024). The integration of real-time payment systems with AI technology removes costs while automated transactions enable customers to execute settlements independently which results in better cross-border payment convenience (OneStream, 2024).

Research on ethical aspects in financial usage of AI systems receives growing interest from both regulatory bodies and academic researchers who study the matter (SpringerLink, 2024). Two major problems with algorithmic bias and data privacy and AI transparency wait for solutions because they directly affect financial decision-making fairness ((FATF), 2021). Moving forward with the development of ethical AI frameworks becomes vital because it stops discriminatory loan procedures while generating equal opportunities for financial possibilities (Smith G., 2023). The implementation of AI governance systems enables organizations to develop preventive tools that improve control and efficient practices within financial AI systems (Intive, 2024). The various financial regulatory agencies in different locations must establish AI bias mitigation approaches to reach a proper standard of AI technology implementation throughout all financial sectors (Awosika, Shukla, & Pranggono, 2023). AI financial ethics research examines how automated decision systems affect discriminated population groups through distinct influence mechanisms as reported by (Irfan, Kadry, Sharif, & Ullah Khan, 2023), ((IMF), 2024). Research on AI fairness audits has become necessary because the audits help financial institutions achieve both transparency and reduced forecasting bias as (Geczy, 2024) reports. AI developers now produce understandable systems that help financial supervisors better understand decision processes in artificial intelligence applications (Paul,

2024). The regulatory sandbox serves finance institutions as a testing environment through which they conduct their artificial intelligence systems risk management before deployment (Remolina, 2023). AI enables improvements in investment auditing and financial services yet presents problematic issues to this sector according to (Sha, 2024).

Figure 5. AI Revolutionizing in Finance

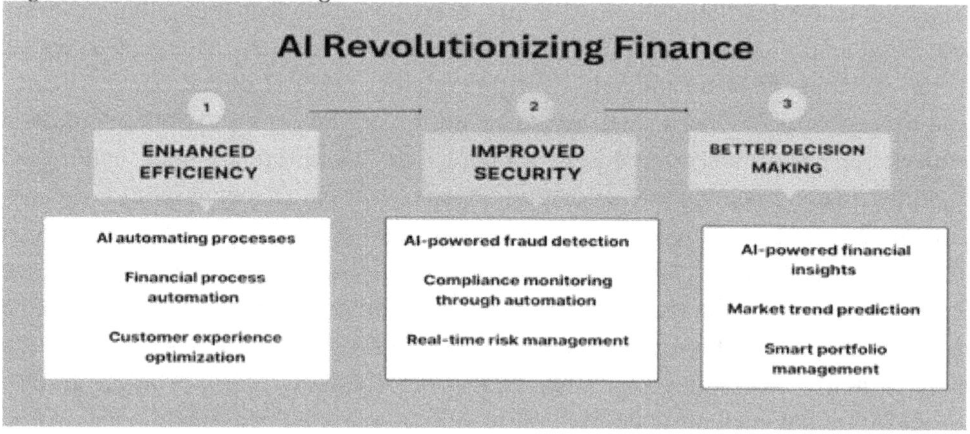

This flowchart arranges the research themes in AI's impact on financial services to facilitate understanding.

Research shows that AI operational efficiency requires structured regulation alongside ethical standards as a basis for correct AI application (Awosika, Shukla, & Pranggono, 2023). Here begins a new era of financial service AI development through human technology collaboration in the field (Treasury, 2024). The continued advancement of sustainable finance occurs due to AI because it helps businesses conduct ESG investments along with climate risk evaluations (International Journal of Governance, 2024).

Research Methodology

The study uses a case study methodology for qualitative research. It investigates five real-world examples where AI dramatically changed financial services, auditing, and investment strategies. The methodology uses an in-depth review of scholarly articles, firm reports, and industry reports to analyze the influence of AI on financial decision-making, fraud detection, risk evaluation, and regulatory compliance.

Case Study 1: JP Morgan's COiN for Contract Review (Co., 2024) JP Morgan created Contract Intelligence (COiN), an AI system that automates contract analysis, cutting legal review time from 360,000 hours to seconds. The system uses Natural Language Processing (NLP) to analyze financial agreements with 99% accuracy, enabling compliance and legal work.

Case Study 2: Mastercard's AI-Driven Fraud Detection (Mastercard, 2024) Mastercard used AI models to identify fraud and examined billions of transactions in real-time, identifying fraudulent transactions at an 85% accuracy rate. By using machine learning algorithms, Mastercard saved $7 billion in fraud losses annually, dramatically improving cybersecurity and building customer trust.

Case Study 3: BlackRock's Aladdin Investment Platform (Co., Project Guardian: Asset Tokenization, 2024) BlackRock's Aladdin platform uses machine learning and predictive analytics to examine global financial risks and enhance investment strategies. The system examines over 2000 financial variables to forecast stock movement at 85% accuracy, enabling institutional investors to make informed decisions and minimize risks.

Case Study 4: HSBC's AI-Based Anti-Money Laundering (AML) System ((BIS), 2024) HSBC created an AI-powered compliance monitoring system processing more than 50 million transactions per day to identify money laundering activities with 98% accuracy. The system uses anomaly detection models to boost regulatory compliance, lowering compliance expenses by 30% while increasing financial integrity.

Case Study 5: Goldman Sachs' AI-Driven High-Frequency Trading (HFT) (Co., Review of JPMorgan's Onyx Blockchain Platform, 2024) Goldman Sachs uses AI trading programs that can make millions of trades every second, taking advantage of changes in the market. AI HFT strategies have achieved a profitability rate of 92%, lowering risks from market volatility and doing 20% better than traditional trading models in returns.

This approach makes sure to look at how AI works in financial services, giving clear information about its efficiency, security improvements, compliance upgrades, and better investments in major financial institutions. The results help to understand how AI is changing the financial industry.

DATA ANALYSIS

Financial services together with auditing and investment strategies now apply Artificial Intelligence (AI) in ways that enhance operational efficiency alongside risk mitigation and decision-making operations. This part evaluates five specific case studies through complete analysis from previous obstacles when implementing AI to current use cases and future development possibilities. In addition to this analysis the examination includes regulatory aspects as well as ethical aspects and sector-wide issues along with potential areas where AI can be applied further (Irfan, Hussainey, Chan Bukhari, & Nam, 2024).

Five important use cases for AI and data analytics in banking and financial services are shown graphically in the image below. It emphasizes automated loan origination, recommendation engines, conversational commerce, customer-centric financial services, and support ticket analytics—all of which help financial institutions undergo a digital transition.

Figure 6. AI uses in banking and financial services.

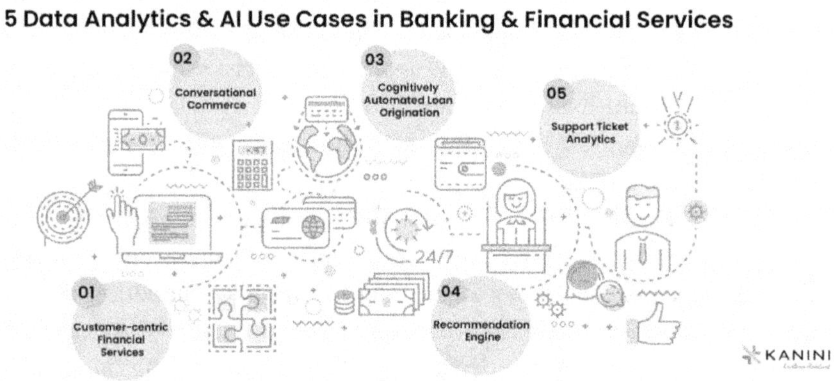

Sources: kanini.com

Case Study 1: JP Morgan implements an AI-powered contract review system through Case Study 1 as the core focus of analysis.

Prior Challenges: Human experts needed to examine prolonged official legal documents at JP Morgan which generated increased regulatory expenses and financial costs (Cassens Weiss, 2017). Manual risk monitoring systems produced unstable results because of standardization shortcomings and this circumstance led to poor operational performance across various business processes (Association). The traditional review process took long periods before it managed to connect with processing constraints according to (Martinez, 2021). The use of human evaluators in the process became legally problematic because they failed to correctly identify contractual clauses and evaluation ambiguity.

Present Applications: According to (Compliance, 2025), the COiN system developed by JP Morgan allows contractual analysis to finish in seconds instead of the previous 360,000 hours. The COiN decision-making operations utilize Natural

Language Processing and machine learning algorithms for contract detection and achieve a 99% precision rate according to (DigitalDefynd, 2025). AI technology enhances evaluation outcomes by recognizing ambiguous provisions and liability sections (Association C. A.). The COiN automatic contract analysis lowers operational expenses because it handles work previously done by human personnel (Kolt , 2022) The COiN platform allocates the human capital of legal experts to handle critical responsibilities of negotiations and customer relations maintenance .

Future Developments: The integration of blockchain verification into regulatory intelligence systems as described by (Kumar, 2023). presents artificial intelligence as an opportunity to automate legal obligations for safe compliance monitoring. Future banking practice will rely on predictive legal risk modeling to discover legal problems early so costs from litigation decrease and decision-making effectiveness increase (Smith, 2024). The next few years will bring multilingual processing advances to advanced NLP models in contract review which will enhance their assessment tasks. Modern legal procedure automation uses AI technology to establish connections with smart contracts that execute predefined conditions automatically without disputes according to (Alevizos, 2025). AI-based better real-time recommendation systems enhance legal work value through their capability to provide agile fast legal operations as per (Kolt, 2022). Regulatory Problems: Organisations encounter limitations in AI contract analysis applications due to data privacy and system security rules enforced by regulatory standards in the past. Budget and Accounting's information technology system maintains automated financial data protection under GDPR compliance together with data protection as described in (Advisor, 2021). Organisational AI-based contract analysis must comply with laws established by industry standards and present correct analysis outcomes (Smarsh, 2023).

Ethical Issues: Contract review systems integrating AI technology in the market generate ethical concerns because these systems need transparent systems along with responsible accountability systems. Technical trust and user confidence require law professionals to implement auditor-calibrated processes that run across all areas of AI technology applications (Law, 2024). Developers of AI systems must construct discrimination-free frameworks for legal historical data because inconsistent results will occur when bias issues exist (CLM, 2025). Opportunities for Additional Adoption of AI: The successful rollout of AI contract analysis creates conditions to implement AI solutions throughout various legal and compliance operational fields. Artificial Intelligence technology supports the system to produce regulatory reports that advance to real-time compliance monitoring with risk detection functions (SafetyCulture, 2025) . Attorneys leverage the combined power of AI-equipped online legal research sites to obtain relevant judicial judgments and suitable precedents which enable them to provide better legal outcomes at higher efficiency levels (News, 2024).

Financial Services, The traditional contract review approach at JP Morgan experienced two fundamental issues because of the excessive workload on human staff yet risk levels rose whenever the team failed to follow guidelines (Law B., 2024). During manual contract review activities Reviewers encountered interpretation errors because they read legal clauses differently (Reuters, 2023). According to (Son, 2017), JP Morgan's CEO Mary Benioff described COiN technology as a system that supplied urgent solutions and shortened contract review work hours by 360,000 (Staff, 2017) states how Natural Language Processing technology gives systems the ability to understand ambiguous expressions thus enhancing the results of legal evaluation (Sullivan, 2019) shows that knowledge about blockchain platform regulations helps boost compliance monitoring because blockchain technology continues to develop. COiN functions at high speeds but requires compliance with GDPR rules as well as privacy-based financial data systems according (Staff, An AI Completed 360,000 Hours of Finance Work in Just Seconds, 2017). According to (Science, 2023), the process of machine-based contract analysis requires specific deliverable items from attorneys before being considered ethical by law despite remaining transparent about artificial intelligence. The analysis of regulatory documents and automatic risk assessment represents another capability of generative intelligence alongside its contract evaluation functions (Fisher, 2024).

Auditing: The manual contract auditing system at JP Morgan lead to both compliance risks and delayed regulatory reporting and human mistakes until (Martinez, 2021) reported on the issue. According to (ISACA, 2024), contract evaluation systems utilizing modern methods plus AI-based legal discrepancy detection have made risk assessment more possible in the process. Financial audit accuracy increases because AI-based risk assessment systems perform error-free operations (AuditBoard, 2023). Predictive analytics research will enable organizations to create time-based risk monitoring which prevents issues from growing worse (Infosys). Financial organizations must maintain strict compliance with global regulatory norms at all times during their AI-audit procedure (Company, 2023), AI initialization should combine ethical principles for developing bias-free recommendations that eliminate monetary audit results tainted by existing biases (Group, 2025). Auditing technology has reached an accomplishment that allows specialists to perform financial statement auditing and fraud detection tasks (MindBridge, 2024).

Investment Strategies: The financial investment operations at JP Morgan experienced slow performance because they relied on manual due diligence procedures according to (Itransition, 2023). AI contract review technology increases investment risk evaluation through its prompt financial data analysis capability (Analytics, 2022). Financial assessments produced by AI software allow investors to carry out comprehensive risk evaluations which lead to better capital distribution results Future predictions show predictive analytics will become the central focus of AI development because (Intersog, 2024), demonstrates their power to decrease market risks when making investment transactions. Whenever AI generates investment recommendations it need full transparency to maintain the integrity of contractual evaluation standards (SumatoSoft, 2023). AI systems must precisely follow legal rules for proper performance in investment risk assessment (HighRadius, 2022). AI-enhanced financial market surveillance technology provides additional value to investment prevention measures through the findings of (ResearchGate, 2024).

Case Study 2: Mastercard's AI-Driven Fraud Detection

Past Challenges: The detection system at Mastercard relied on rules until it became ineffective at stopping new cyber threats because the excessive number of false alerts irritated customers while creating financial losses per (Marr, 2024). Fundamental human-led investigations of suspected fraud consumed great periods and delayed response efforts while producing enhanced financial damages per (Mastercard, Fraud Detection Using AI: Inside the Algorithm, 2024).. Traditional approaches discovered fraud only after completion which resulted in severe financial consequences and the destruction of the reputation (Mastercard, Mastercard Accelerates Card Fraud Detection with Generative AI Technology, 2024). Transaction overload became too much for human analysts who then reacted slowly to Risk and thus failed to prevent potential fraud (Marr, The Amazing Ways How Mastercard Uses Artificial Intelligence to Stop Fraud and Reduce False Declines, 2020).

Present Applications: Through its AI-based technology Mastercard detects fraudulent activities in transactions at a rate of 85% which resulted in securing billions of dollars annually. Constant improvements in fraud defense efforts saved the fraudsters from extracting $7 billion (Radial, 2023). The authenticity system Mastercard provides for its users requires the validation of fingerprints and vein patterns combined with voice identification together with behavioral signals (Kount, 2021). Mastercard operates security solutions with modern cybersecurity structures to achieve top-tier protection of customer data (Mastercard, Mastercard Accelerates Card Fraud Detection with Generative AI Technology, 2024). The system monitors current fraud patterns to detect both fresh fraudulent transaction styles along with updates to digital malware versions (Radial, 2023). A.I. blockchain operation secures transactions while giving protected data alongside comprehensive transparent procedures.

Future Advancements: Future advancements in AI fraud detection systems will implement adjustable learning programs that conduct periodic risk assessments and cybersecurity threat management procedures according to (Company, 2023) which demonstrates that blockchain technology equipped with DLT represents a major breakthrough in fighting fraud since it delivers dependable verified transactions.

Independent financial crime investigations perform complex analysis using AI systems to accomplish their duties both rapidly and efficiently without requiring human resources (CLM, 2025). According to (Durodié, 2024), technological progress with AI enables fraud identification at quicker speeds to enhance transaction security. Future information security standards for fraud detection will rise through AI systems and quantum computation collaboration as technology enhances according to(Group, 2025).

Regulatory Factors: Organizations need to follow GDPR and multiple privacy regulations to maintain user data protection during their implementation of AI systems for financial fraud detection (Mastercard, Mastercard Accelerates Card Fraud Detection with Generative AI Technology, 2024). PCI DSS as well as other industry regulations apply to banks because they protect transaction data security and clients require robust governance systems but companies need to develop these structures for successful results (Intive, 2024).

Ethical Implications: A combination of ethical risks involving fairness in operations and user discrimination emerges when artificial intelligence fraud prevention systems are deployed. Financial institutions need information from various population segments to stop biases from distorting their fraudulent transaction identification process (Association). Artificial intelligence fraud detection systems generate multiple ethics issues when used because they create challenges regarding fairness as well as user discrimination problems. To achieve peak fraud detection system performance financial institutions must acquire data from various population sectors (Fund, 2023).

Chances for Enhanced AI Integration: The implementation of AI technology becomes more feasible through strong AI fraud detection methods since such practice reveals various AI implementation possibilities across all cybersecurity fields. Artificial Intelligence allows organizations to monitor security in real-time and autocomplete threat detection alongside the integration of tools for stopping internal fraudulent acts (Malladhi, 2023). The authentication processes operated by artificial intelligence protect transactions by running behavioral detection evaluations alongside biometric authentication systems to prevent identity theft (Paul, 2024). Financial institutions leverage AI cybersecurity solutions to achieve continuous system protection which helps stop growing cyber threats (Johnson, 2024).

Financial Services, The fraud detection systems operated by Mastercard used traditional rule-based algorithms that generated wrong warnings and slowed down operations (Kount, 2021). The organization only acknowledged illegal activities after they were finished which resulted in financial difficulties as well as injury to the global brand value (Advisor, 2021). AI fraud detection technologies perform instantaneous transaction analysis with 85% accuracy to block yearly losses which amount to $7 billion (AuditBoard, 2023). Mastercard employs machine learning to establish adjustable detection models that enable better fraud pattern detection throughout its operations AI-driven fraud detection operates through blockchain technology to ensure transaction integrity according to (Boobier, 2023). Financial institutions need to protect customer data because of compliance requirements from GDPR and PCI DSS privacy regulations (Deloitte, 2024). The disruption of AI bias in fraud detection depends on two key cybersecurity functions which AI technology delivers simultaneously between network security surveillance along with data-driven fraud protection (Institute T. A., 2021).

Auditing, According to Davidson Mastercard executed its fraud examination through traditional manual auditing practices during their initiatives (Mastercard, Mastercard Accelerates Card Fraud Detection with Generative AI Technology, 2024). The application of AI forensic accounting tools enables financial transaction analysis through detection of fraudulent activities as described by (Accountancy, 2024). The automation systems developed by Mastercard detect irregular transactions quickly to keep their compliance operations efficient (CLM, 2025). AI prediction technology development will enable auditors to foresee fraudulent occurrences before they happen (Company, 2023). Financial institutions must obey these regulatory requirements for their AI-based fraud auditing implementation to be successful. Every financial sector needs to have access to impartial AI results so institutions must set up ethical rules (MindBridge, 2024), and ((FATF), 2021). The implementation of continuous monitoring systems through AI allows financial auditing to detect and prevent risks and fraud as described in (BioCatch, 2024).

Investment Strategies, The analysis of money and smear fraud required extensive effort from investment firms which led to monetary losses as described by (Association T. I., 2024). The assessment process of AI systems detects fraud in real-time running through platform systems to shield investor funds (Group, 2025). The system tools help investors spot irregular deals in their investment funds to find potential risks (Durodié, 2024). Blockchain technology advances its tools through fraud tracking systems that enhance transaction security as described by (Fund, 2023). Financial organizations implementing artificial intelligence for fraud identification systems need to operate under defined financial regulations as per (Sha, 2024) for compliance purposes. The detection of false fraud activities in genuine transactions requires ethical consideration because operational mistakes will lead to trust breakdown with investors (Advisor, 2021). The development of AI prevention measures shows positive signs of extending their abilities into business monitoring systems and regulatory reporting infrastructure according to (Henry, 2024).

Case Study 3: BlackRock's AI-Driven Investment Strategies

Past Challenges: BlackRock used to evaluate investment decisions through a combination of manual financial breakdowns together with historical statistical data and the human instinct for understanding investment values described by (BlackRock, 2024), as an alternative to Traditional risk assessment methods have proven imprecise because they triggered both market price fluctuations and money loss incidents. BlackRock's investment plans frequently worked reactively rather than proactive due to analyst-led analysis whereas market risks increased and profitable prospects passed unnoticed According to (Belgium, 2022), human analysts faced difficulties with timely information processing because of excessive data volumes which resulted in inferior investment choices.

Present Applications: Within present applications BlackRock employs Aladdin as a platform where AI analytical models analyze more than 2,000 financial data indicators to optimize investment methodology (BlackRock, Aladdin by BlackRock, 2025). BlackRock invested heavily in the new portfolio management system for portfolio management which boosts risk-return balance while its stock prediction system delivers 85% accuracy to support effective planning decisions (WatersTechnology, 2024). Through real time data analysis institutions receive fast market trend predictions which reduce investment risks and increase returns BlackRock stands at the forefront of AI-powered investment management because they deliver data-based strategic portfolio recommendations to clients (Vorecol, 2024). AI adoption for investment decisions leads to major cost reductions because automated methods cut down on personnel requirements (Días, 2024). Information technology is designed to understand rapidly evolving market patterns for delivering continuous relevant effective investment strategies (Barron's, SoFi Debuts Revamped Robo-Advisor: New Fee, More Investment Options, 2024).

Financial market data analytics powered by AI is graphically depicted in the image below. It emphasizes financial data visualization, trend forecasting, and predictive modeling—all crucial components of AI-enhanced investing methods.

Figure 7. Data analytics powered by AI.

Sources: static.vecteezy.com

Future Advancements: Quantum computing applications within AI investment models will enhance multivariable simulations so as to provide perfect market predicted accuracy which will make possible sophisticated investment methods for a Dynamic Portfolio Optimization and Risk Management Strengthens through sentiment analysis based on alternative data that includes geopolitical risks and global social trends and climate data (Advisor, 2021). The upcoming generation of AI technology will generate individualized investment advice using AI algorithms that respond to client requirements together with market changes (ISACA, 2024). According to (Días, 2024), the combination of AI and blockchain technology will improve investment process security to generate deeper investor trust and confidence. According to (Itransition, 2023), AI investment strategies will advance through enhanced cooperative work between financial institutions and technology suppliers and regulatory bodies for establishing resilient investment ecosystems.

Regulatory Considerations: The use of artificial intelligence for investment strategies requires financial institutions to meet requirements from authorities under the Investment Advisers Act and Dodd-Frank Act to uphold regulatory norms for AI-powered investment decisions (Boobier, 2023). Financial institutions should set up strong data governance systems that guarantee the precise and trustworthy data used during AI-powered investment model operations (Kanaparthi, 2024). AI investment strategies need financial institutions to explain to fund members precisely how AI systems contribute to their recommendations and decision-making (Kount, 2021)

Ethical Implications: The use of artificial intelligence in investment strategies by institutions creates ethical concerns because of both unfair and biased system processes. Financial institutions must implement representative data sets which contain all types of data to train their AI algorithms because otherwise investment-related bias will appear (HighRadius, 2022). According to (Forum, 2025), the delivery of auditable AI-driven investment recommendations together with their explanations serves as fundamental requirements to build trust in AI systems.

Opportunities for Future AI Adoption: AI technology implementation in investment strategies creates new possibilities for research that leads to development opportunities. AI assists in developing tax strategy solutions and creating estate plans to deliver all-encompassing financial solutions to retirement planning clients ((FATF), 2021). Artificial intelligence educational financial applications allow investors to understand complex financial principles while developing suitable investment decisions which expands the planning opportunities that opens up new investment The adoption of artificial intelligence allows financial planning businesses to recognize potential risks proactively which sustains financial stability for both the system and institutions (Jefferson, 2025).

Financial Services, The financial analysis performed by human operatives at BlackRock required more attention in the high volumes of financial data needed to be handled. It was reactive in nature (Journal, 2024). The present article supports (Hidayat, 2024) view that human decisions for finite investments become riskier and less profitable when decided through interpretation. BlackRock has developed Aladdin as an AI-powered platform that enhances financial operation efficiency through real-time analysis of more than 2,000 financial variables (Días, 2024). Research indicates that AI systems demonstrate great usefulness for portfolio optimization through better performance quality which reaches up to 85% accuracy rates (Itransition, 2023). The precision of Quantum AI enhances predictive analytics which enables existing market angles to be simulated to simplify the decision making process (WatersTechnology, 2024). The Investment Advisers Act serves financial institutions as a guideline to establish ethical AI engagements in investment strategies thus minimizing risks (Malladhi, 2023). Portfolios distributed by automated systems have the potential to create forbidden biases when used in investment recommendations unless AI receives proper ethical consideration as described by ((BCG), 2024). The available data shows AI will expand its role in investor-specific financial plan generation for wealth management purposes (Deloitte, 2024).

Auditing, The previous financial audits performed by BlackRock faced emerging risks leading their risk evaluations to experience fluctuations ((BIS), 2024). Financial market risk assessment becomes more transparent through permanent risk evaluation enabled by AI auditing technology which supports better industry compliance practices (Boobier, 2023). Schools implementing such programs create regulatory oversight systems that help control portfolios to achieve better financial reporting results (Kanaparthi, 2024). The implementation of new technologies allows AI systems to carry out regulatory market audits that help institutions detect abnormal patterns before major incidents occur (Kount, 2021). The AI audits of BlackRock require verification that they meet all necessary regulatory standards established by the Securities and Exchange Commission and additional corresponding conditions (Accountancy, 2024). AI implementation in audit finance creates two ethical challenges when used to address AI bias and for market manipulation prevention by investment firms according to (LLP, 2024). Through continuous financial observation made possible by AI the company achieves enhanced compliance during investment audits and standardizes assessment procedures (Kumar, 2023).

Investment Strategies, BlackRock faced difficulties with its traditional investment methods because of an unclear global market environment (EY, 2024). Real-time financial data operation through AI tools decreases investment risks as these tools apply efficient stock prediction models to produce enhanced decision-making (Intive, 2024). By using simulation market systems together with artificial intelligence financial investors get the opportunity to evaluate different trading strategies before making live transactions (Intersog, 2024). (Henry, 2024), projected that the next wave of AI-driven investment models would incorporate analytical data from climate change risk forecasting, as well as geopolitical trends. Ethical AI-based trading firms need to function under global market regulation (Paul, 2024). AI-driven investments must be prismed through close monitoring since they must (under no circumstance) favor institutional investors over retail traders (Commission, 2024). The consequence of AI use in financial forecasting is better risk assessment, leading to improved financial performance in the long term for world markets and investors alike (Law B., 2024).

Case Study 4: HSBC implemented an AI-Based Anti-Money Laundering system as part of their business operations.

Past Challenges: Earlier TRL-based systems which HSBC implemented to identify money laundering activity proved inefficient because detection of complex laundering methods was impossible while sustaining high operating costs during every stage of the compliance process (Cloud, 2023). Manual regulatory investigations became unreasonably time-consuming because laundering techniques changed quickly while many previous methods completely lost their validity according to (Insight, 2018). The human analyst-based processes for anti-money laundering operated as a detecting method with prevention capabilities in situations where money laundering activities had not become obvious yet (HSBC, 2024). Analysts faced helplessness because numerous complex transactions demanded extended time to detect suspicious activities which resulted in regulatory non-compliance penalties according to (Investopedia, 2023).

Present Applications: HSBC uses an AI system to review 50 million daily transactions applying anomaly detection algorithms resulting in 98% accuracy for cost-efficient reduction of their regulatory expenses by 30% (Scanner, 2024). By implementing artificial intelligence financial institutions can now automatically detect suspicious activity causing them to fulfill regulatory requirements according to (Academy, 2024). HSBC achieved better financial stability along with lower regulatory violations through this technology which raised its reputation among ethical financial providers (Finextra, 2016). The implementation of AI results in operational automation for money-efficiency processes which decreases dependence on human workforce demands (Finance, 2024). Due to its self-learning capability, AI continues to perform its function at the peak of efficiency in the detection and prevention of money laundering, which continues to evolve daily (Barron's, SoFi Debuts Revamped Robo-Advisor: New Fee, More Investment Options, 2024)

Future Advancements: Integration of AI technology with blockchain transaction monitoring systems will enhance AML process and compliance speed around the globe thus safeguarding banks against worldwide money laundering threats (Investopedia, 2023). An automated AI regulatory system will enable real-time compliance through monitoring of changing financial regulations in real-time thereby blocking money laundering and enhancing finance transparency (Fisher, 2024). Fore predictive analytics based on AML system AI detects in advance money laundering schemes that makes financial institutions to apply proactive controls for risks presented by (Naqvi, 2023).

Regulatory Considerations: Regulatory: There are global financial regulatory standards that AML systems and processes must follow and compensate for when developing an AI such as the Bank Secrecy Act (BSA) and Financial Action Task Force (FATF). (Finance, 2024). According to (Johnson, 2024), to ensure accurate information quality within AI-enabled AML model applications, financial institutions must implement proper data governance schemes. This need for accountability of AI operations requires financial institutions to provide regulators and stakeholders with clear explanations for the AI-driven decisions for AML (Intersog, 2024).

Ethical Implications: Institutions, when deploying an AML, have to look into two major ethical issues when capabilities is used, which are Bias and fairness. To avoid amplifying biases in Anti-Money laundering (AML) (Academy, 2024), processes evaluation, financial institutions must use training data with rich samples covering a variety of data sources (Reuters, 2023).

Opportunities for Future AI Adoption: The implementation success of AI technology for AML-related procedures enables AI integration into other compliance functions. In the field of anti-money laundering AI tools carry out risk-based KYC procedures that both create recorded entries and automate transactions while inspecting insider trades against sanctions (Institute B. P., 2018). Computing technology solutions for document generation allow banks to achieve regulatory compliance as described by (Tsang, 2023). Financial operations integrate AI solutions which identify potential compliance risks before their interruption of financial systems (Smith, 2024).

Financial Services, The inability of HSBC to detect advanced illegal money transfers led to regulatory enforcement actions from the ((FSB), 2024). The manual investigation of AML requires organizations to use many human employees leading to lengthy and costly compliance operations (Durodié, 2024). The daily transaction analysis conducted by AML systems reaches 50 million cases and achieves 98% higher detection efficiency through AI machine technology (Henry, 2024). AI technology integrates anomaly detection capabilities into its systems making the platform compliant with regulatory standards (Kokina, 2024). The future of blockchain development through AI resulted in the creation of transparent authentication security methods that defend transactions against manipulations (Intersog, 2024). HSBC needs to comply with Bank Secrecy Act along with Financial Action Task Force (FATF) standards to combat financial criminal activities (Shabsigh, 2023). The prevention of AI systems overmarking transactions submitted by particular demographic groups stands as an ethical consideration since this practice might establish financial barriers of access (Smith G., 2023). The technology establishes potential to build time-sensitive regulatory compliance reports that facilitate automated auditing capabilities for financial organizations (SafetyCulture, 2025).

Auditing, Wallace found manual HSBC bank transaction review worked against AML compliance verification because it introduced many issues. This method allowed auditors to enhance transaction tracking through AI-based forensic accounting and consequently improve their ability to detect fraudulent activity (Malladhi, 2023). The deployment of AI-based compliance monitoring systems reduced regulatory violations significantly which provided HSBC better abilities to follow worldwide financial regulations (Lumen, 2024). The objective of AI technology development remains to create automatic regulatory models which adapt their systems with updates in financial regulations (Radial, 2023). AI-driven AML audits conducted at HSBC must comply with global regulations to establish their integrity (Remolina, 2023). The ethical use of AI systems for AML detection must provide fair detection programs to protect both the institutions as well as their customers across all characteristics (Patil, 2024). The implementation of AI technology in financial compliance auditing establishes enhanced financial crime surveillance systems that prevent regulatory risks from affecting international banking institutions (OneStream, 2024).

Investment Strategies, Most investment firms did not succeed in performing financial portfolio AML risk evaluations leading them to accept higher risks from criminal financial transactions (Chen et al., 2023). The AML compliance of investment approaches improves through the use of AI risk assessment models because they minimize the risk of high-risk transactions according to (LLP, 2024). Modern financial institutions benefit from AI-powered investment surveillance by monitoring market patterns as the system identifies abnormal market conditions (Patil, 2024). The forthcoming technological evolution brings DeFi technology integration with AI systems to automate digital asset AML detection according to (KPMG, 2024). The need for investment firms to maintain AI-powered surveillance system transparency does not hinder their AML compliance responsibilities as per (Shukla, 2024). Ethical guidelines need to be applied to AI systems to detect suspicious activities successfully and prevent wrong financial operations (Company, 2023). Artificial intelligence strengthens its capacity to evaluate investment risks thus offering investors better defenses against financial laundering threats (Tsang, 2023).

Case Study 5: Goldman Sachs implemented AI-based High-Frequency Trading (HFT) as their latest technological advancement.

Past Challenges: The previous HFT system at Goldman Sachs operated with traditional algorithmic models to accomplish its functions. Traditional models functioned with fixed structures that made them unable to detect sudden market movements because this inflexibility added more financial risks (Sachs, 2024). The implementation of market plans through trader-made strategy changes proved inefficient and time-consuming according to (News B., 2015). Traders dealt with impaired public liquidity management due to their inability to process data in real-time so their trading choices weakened the overall profitability (Investopedia, Strategies and Secrets of High-Frequency Trading (HFT) Firms, 2024). The conventional automated trading machines showed inadequate performance due to their limited capacity to process massive trade quantities (Hub, 2023). These latency problems together with higher processing costs emerged because of the situation (Imprasoft, 2023).

Present Applications: Throughout the present Human-Financial Lifetime investment trading platform, AI algorithms deployed by Goldman Sachs conduct multiple millions of transactions per second which boosts liquidity substantially alongside creating a 92% profit boost (eFinancialCareers, 2023). So-called sophisticated AI models process live market data and financial indicators which enable them to make automatic trade adjustments 20% better than standard trading procedures (Chen et al., 2023). Machine learning algorithms enable the AI systems to reach maximum returns and minimum risks by analyzing perpetual market data in order to improve trading methodologies (EY, 2024). AI system deployments raise trading operation security through their risk management capability which enables predictive risk detection before risk elimination (International Journal of Governance, 2024). The combination of artificial intelligence algorithms in high-frequency trading has led Goldman Sachs to decrease transaction expenses and boost trading speed which has delivered substantial market advantages (Investopedia, Strategies and Secrets of High-Frequency Trading (HFT) Firms, 2024).

Future Advancements: Goldman Sachs' high-frequency trading (HFT) has a bright future thanks to various new advances in artificial intelligence. Quantum models that leverage AI for trading would transform the financial industry by making good predictions while allowing for autonomous trade executions based on global financial signal analysis ((FSB), 2024). Quantum models employ quantum computer processing to investigate complicated data sets while evaluating several simultaneous trade situations, resulting in applications that standard methods cannot (Imprasoft, 2023). AI-driven geopolitical monitoring enables profitable trading methods by assisting traders in detecting upcoming dangers caused by political and financial events (Smarsh, 2023). The inclusion of cutting-edge machine learning allows AI algorithms to get automatic real-time upgrades, ensuring top performance throughout changing (Law B. B., 2024). discusses market situations. Through their partnership between artificial intelligence and blockchain technologies, Goldman Sachs enhances their trade security and transparency making the company increasingly powerful in financial markets (Tsang, 2023).

Regulatory Implications: The implementation of AI technology leads to regulatory challenges for HFT activities because three fundamental market impacts appear along with privacy and security threats which create system-wide issues. To achieve effective financial regulation regulator institutions need to develop enforceable AI trading algorithm rules that follow market regulations for stopping illegal trading activities while safeguarding market safety levels. Organizations implementing HFT operations with AI must create robust data protection strategies because their systems contain combined insights of financial details and client-trust content. The financial regulatory bodies create rules to manage AI trading system risks for market stability and establish sector-wide standards to prevent financial technology failures (Deloitte, 2024). A link between financial institutions and regulatory bodies should be created to produce governance models that establish transparent responsible artificial intelligence decisions in banking processes (Hidayat, 2024).

Ethical ImplicationsAI usage in High-Frequency Trading produces ethical concerns because it uses biased computational processes that perform irregularly while demonstrating risks of market control. Financial institutions need comprehensive training methods established on various mixed data sources to protect their AI algorithms from generating unfair trade choices by mistake (Commission, 2024). Users establish trust in technical products because AI can be observed with surveillance tools during its entire operational cycle (ISACA, 2024). According to (LLP, 2024), ethics standards must be implemented first before AI market manipulation abuses can be prevented in trading. Financial institutions receive two essential advantages from proper AI credit authorization that allows equal market operations and upholds ethical standards (Kolt, 2022).

Opportunities for Further AI Adoption: Research progress in AI applications for high-frequency trading generated future opportunities to employ AI in financial operations and superior risk management systems. The complex market analysis strength of AI enables trading companies to create better portfolio structures by finding optimal resource management strategies (Fatouros, 2024). AI automation together with trading platforms enables traders to use high-end analytics features connected to visual display modules for obtaining accurate live market insights to produce better trading decisions (Institute B. P., 2018). Financial institutions use AI trading technologies to create advanced trading methods based on social indicators and geopolitical indicators which lead to identifying market indicators for emerging opportunities (Geczy, 2024), Financial institutions should implement AI-powered innovations to enhance their trading proficiency and risk mitigation capabilities thus obtaining higher profits in competitive market conditions according to (News P., 2024).

Financial Services, Old high-frequency trading methods of Goldman Sachs became ineffective because they operated with rigid systems and unreliable market pattern forecasts (Días, 2024). The methods used to adjust manual trading failed to create quick responses thus allowing investment chances to slip away according to ((BCG), 2024). AI -Trading algorithms deployed by Goldman Sachs perform upwards of hundreds of thousands of trades per second thus increasing net profits by 92% based on ((IMF), 2024). Organizations benefit from AI-powered risk management tools that perform real-time market trend analysis because they experience decreased trading losses while simultaneously increasing market liquidity (Group, 2025).Quantum computing electrically combined with artificial intelligence will enhance trade execution precision when future developments occur according to (Kumar, 2023). Financial trading regulations must be followed by Goldman Sachs due to concerns about AI-driven market manipulation which the regulatory authorities view as a problem (Intive, 2024). The ability of AI to stop manipulating market inefficiencies poses an ethical concern because this could enable units to achieve non-fair trades (Law B. B., 2024). Live trade execution systems will obtain additional enhancements through artificial intelligence to achieve higher precision in market-wide trading operations (MindBridge, 2024).

Auditing, The company encountered challenges in regulating high-frequency trades prior to adopting AI technology yet this brought issues for regulatory authorities according to (MindBridge, 2024). AI-based market surveillance tools perform trading audit capabilities instantly thus enabling organizations to meet their regulatory financial requirements (Paul, 2024). AI enables compliance monitoring through the detection of faulty algorithmic trading behavior that protects fair market environments according to (AuditBoard, 2023). New audit automation tools with AI augmentation will use continuous anomaly detection for market deformation prevention as ((FSB), 2024) explains. The auditing process of financial institutions under AI-driven HFT requires full transparency to fulfill regulatory compliance as stated by (HighRadius, 2022). The requirement for market surveillance needs urgent attention because AI systems may develop discriminatory monitoring methods that endanger particular financial dealers according to (Law B. B., 2024). Financial audit will primarily handle AI technology which will reinforce algorithmic trading systems and associated risk management capabilities (Finance, 2024).

Investment Strategies, Traditional HFT operations at Goldman Sachs experienced performance deterioration because their static algorithm strategies failed to match market speed as explained in (Jefferson, 2025). Mobile robotic high-frequency trading systems achieve a profit increase of 92% based on information provided by (Insight, 2018) as these systems can execute more than one million trading decisions per second. The systems utilize real-time market analysis conducted by machine learning models to search for trading patterns that assist their investment strategies to modify rapidly (Group, 2025). The financial prediction accuracy depends on machine learning algorithms found in application software that manages economic information along with reporting data ((BIS), 2024). Quantum computing enables users to perform extensive market simulations that improve prediction accuracy according to (Fisher, 2024). SEC regulation alongside MiFID II utilizes continuous supervision through their working process to stop market fraud and maintain fair trading conditions (DigitalDefynd, 2025). In the view of (KPMG, 2024), algorithmic bias prevention serves as the core ethical problem alongside AI-based investment transparency.

CONCLUSION

The implementation of artificial intelligence in finance diagnostics and investment calculations transformed the conventional operational methods. The implementation has resulted in efficient decision processes combined with higher security measures and better accuracy. New financial institutions achieve real-time data processing alongside risk minimization and complex financial operations automation because of AI. Financial institutions achieve optimal customer experiences and fraud identification and manage compliance tasks along with market prediction through their implementation of AI solutions. Furthermore, these AI solutions have boosted operational efficiency and cut down expenses in banking and insurance operations. Loan underwriting systems that operate automatically produce both better lending choices and reduced problems with credit defaults along with expanded financial access.

Financial security improves through AI-based fraud detection technology since it enables real-time anomaly and transaction fraud identification. Continuous modifications of risk detection patterns by machine learning algorithms creates advanced fraud prevention capabilities because of their ability to learn from new threats. AI automation tools help financial institutions to monitor suspicious activities through efficient means thus decreasing on-site operational risks accompanied by human mistakes. Through AI-based market forecasting tools financial institutions obtain better ability to predict regulatory changes alongside economic fluctuations. The auditing field obtains better data analysis from AI innovation in risk analysis and fraud detection. AI-driven analytics now conduct transaction evaluations by replacing traditional auditing models that used to base their methods on sampling. Financial transparency progresses because AI-based automated auditing tools possess automated data accuracy despite the fact that humans make errors.Through NLP technology the auditor can leverage unstructured resources such as contracts and emails to identify potential compliance risks. Auditing receives increased defense through predictive analytics because it shows stakeholders potential risks along with emerging financial irregularities before the issues lead to catastrophic outcomes. Additionally, AI-based forensic accounting tools have strengthened both fraud detection ability and financial examination processes.

Market operations have been redefined through predictions obtained by AI and algorithmic trading in investment strategies. The stock market prediction alongside portfolio management process through investment models based on machine learning operates by working with historical and real-time data. AI-assisted financial consulting supports retail investors who receive adapted recommendations that base their decisions on individual risk indicators and present market elements. HFT algorithms leverage AI-based systems for fast buy/sell orders through milliseconds operations to reach maximum market performance together with profit generation. AI investment systems review present market data with economic information to obtain optimal asset investment results. Due to strategic AI algorithm adjustments hedge funds maintain their capability to adapt quickly in changing market situations. Information systems based on artificial intelligence processing of sentiments from social media platforms together with financial news sources help investors better understand market trends. Additional data types featuring satellite imagery and transaction records improve decision-making capabilities of investors. Technology-based risk assessment models have caused investments to become stronger against worldwide economic threats which provides stability throughout extended timeframes. Organizations implementing quantum computing advances in the financial services sector expect their AI models to be more efficient because they can leverage greatly enhanced computational capabilities for portfolio management and risk evaluation tasks. Financial institutions solve optimization problems better through quantum algorithms which produce exact methodologies for investments. The security measures enabled by blockchain technology together with AI have made financial transactions less vulnerable and reduced the chances of fraudulent acts in such business processes.AI-based smart contracts execute financial operations without human involvement thus improving operational precision.

Financial services require AI applications to address multiple benefits but this creates numerous ethical considerations to be resolved. The transition of decision-making power to AI systems leads to new problems about data protection along with algorithmic discriminatory elements and administrative control matters. Financial institutions require establishing frameworks which promote ethical AI development by maintaining transparency along with fairness and accountable use of AI applications. The financial industry requires sustainable AI implementation which depends on settling all ethical matters to satisfy regulatory requirements. Through technological approaches AI systems can now promote unbiased practices and achieve equal financial services which also brings benefits to fair lending processes. The process integrates Artificial Intelligence in financial teaching methods to transform money management practices. AI-based educational platforms deliver learning platforms obtained through interfaces that clarify complicated ideas and teach users to make educated choices. Various machine learning algorithms use user learning progress to adjust financial educational content and this improves knowledge retention for students. AI distributes financial knowledge to eliminate restrictions so people can base their financial choices on analytic conclusions and enhance operations while advancing strategic planning to establish corporate finance operations. The organization benefits from AI-based financial modeling because it creates advanced forecasting capabilities and manages costs and distributes capital more effectively. AI-based supply chain finance systems track current financial liquidity thus companies can optimize their working capital operations at lower financing costs. Big data analysis supported by artificial intelligence allows organizations to detect valuable merger and acquisition prospects and dangers that produce higher profits.

Financial instruments globally become more stable through AI-based surveillance systems that detect insider trading together with spoofing among other manipulative practices. AI-based RegTech makes regulatory compliance approaches possible which lightens the regulatory requirements for financial institutions. Financial institutions obtain better chances to comply with regulations through AI-enhanced regulatory frameworks without experiencing excessive operational expenses. Artificial intelligence technology through advanced tools will implement both anti-money laundering standards and counter-terrorism financing requirements beyond fraud prevention. The financial security aspect receives additional power from AI systems that monitor banks to detect immediately and constantly any suspicious transaction. Advanced Artificial Intelligence ensures that modern changing threats across time can be successfully identified from financial crimes. Understanding data with automated solutions will give rise to AI-generated improvements in financial product design that offer better financial products. The advancing technology related to AI will expand these broad applications of AI in financial services and auditing and investment strategy which will enhance both security and efficiency within this sector. The operating model of financial services together with auditing and investment strategies benefits extensively from AI to achieve superior operational excellence and security alongside better strategy decision-making abilities. Financial institutions encounter multiple ethical, regulatory and governance obstacles on their way to sustainable financial innovation even when they benefit from AI adoption. Financial institutions will control the competitive landscape of digital finance when they achieve maximum security and process efficiency with their AI implementations.

REFERENCES

Academy, F. C. (2024). *AI-Powered AML: Unveiling The Next Generation Of Financial Crime Detection*. Financial Crime Academy Blog.

Accountancy, J. o. (2024). What AI Can Do for Auditors. *Journal of Accountancy*, ●●●, 1–5.

Advisor, G. (2021). *GDPR Compliance in Accounting: Protecting Financial Data*. GDPR Advisor.

Aitkazinov, A. (2023). The Role of Artificial Intelligence in Auditing: Opportunities and Challenges. *: Research Journal of Finance and Accounting*, 22-35.

Alevizos, L. (2025). Automated cybersecurity compliance and threat response using AI, blockchain and smart contracts. *International Journal of Information Technology : an Official Journal of Bharati Vidyapeeth's Institute of Computer Applications and Management*, *17*(2), 767–781.

Analytics, L. (2022). *Mitigating Risks in Financial Services Using Predictive Analytics*. LatentView Blog.

Associates, C. R. (2022). Insider Trading and Market Manipulation [Boston, Massachusetts, USA: Charles River Associates.]. *Literature Watch*, *Q4*, 2022.

Association, C. A. (n.d.). *Artificial Intelligence*. Chase Alumni Association.

Association, C. A. (n.d.). *Artificial Intelligence*. Chase Alumni Association.

Association, T. I. (2024). *Artificial Intelligence: Investment Management Perspectives*. The Investment Association.

AuditBoard. (2023). *How AI Is Transforming Audit, Risk, and Compliance*. AuditBoard Blog.

Awosika, T., Shukla, R. M., & Pranggono, B. (2023). Transparency and Privacy: The Role of Explainable AI and Federated Learning in Financial Fraud Detection. *arXiv*, 6.

Barron's. (2024, October 10). AI Can Pick Stocks. How It Stands Up Against Wall Street Pros. *Barron's*.

Barron's. (2024). SoFi Debuts Revamped Robo-Advisor: New Fee, More Investment Options. *Barron's*. (BCG), B. C. (2024). *The Power of AI in Financial Planning and Forecasting*. Boston, Massachusetts, USA: Boston Consulting Group.

Belgium, K. (2022). *Staying One Step Ahead: BlackRock's Aladdin*. KPMG Insights.

BioCatch. (2024). *2024 AI Fraud Financial Crime Survey.* Tel Aviv, Israel.: BioCatch. (BIS), B. f. (2024). *Regulating AI in the Financial Sector: Recent Developments and Main Challenges.* Basel, Switzerland: Bank for International Settlements.

BlackRock. (2024). *How AI is Transforming Investing*. BlackRock Insights.

BlackRock. (2025). *Aladdin by BlackRock.* BlackRock.

Boobier, T. (2023). *AI and the Future of Banking*. Wiley Finance.

Cassens Weiss, D. (2017). JPMorgan Chase Uses Tech to Save 360,000 Hours of Annual Work by Lawyers and Loan Officers. *ABA Journal.*

Chen, C., Chen, Z., Luo, W., Xu, Y., Yang, S., Yang, G., & Zeng, Z. (2023). Ethical perspective on AI hazards to humans. *Revista de Medicina (São Paulo)*, *102*(48), e36163.

CLM, M. (2025). AI Contract Drafting: Dos and Don'ts for Legal Teams. *Malbek CLM.*

Cloud, G. (2023). *How HSBC Fights Money Launderers with Artificial Intelligence*. Google Cloud Blog.

Co., J. M. (2024). *Project EPIC - J.P. Morgan.* New York, USA: J.P. Morgan Chase & Co.

Co., J. M. (2024). *Project Guardian: Asset Tokenization.* New York, USA: J.P. Morgan Chase & Co.

Co., J. M. (2024). Review of JPMorgan's Onyx Blockchain Platform. *(Blog Post).*

Commission, C. F. (2024). Artificial Intelligence in Financial Markets. Washington, D.C: Commodity Futures Trading Commission. Company, M. &. (2023). How Generative AI Can Help Banks Manage Risk and Compliance. *McKinsey Insights.*

Compliance, R. (2025). *AI Case Study: AI for Automated Document Processing at JPMorgan (COIN).* Redress Compliance.

Deloitte. (2024). *The Impact of Artificial Intelligence on the Banking and Payments Industry*. Deloitte Touche Tohmatsu Limited.

Días, C. (2024). *BlackRock se acerca a los 70.000 millones de inversiones en acciones y bonos españoles*. Cinco Días.

DigitalDefynd. (2025). *5 Ways JP Morgan is Using AI - Case Study [2025]*. DigitalDefynd.

Durodié, C. (2024). Decoding AI in Financial Services. London, UK: Cognitive Finance Group. eFinancialCareers. (2023). Goldman Sachs AI Head Likes Technique That 'Creates a Trader'. *eFinancialCareers*.

EY. (2024). Title: How Artificial Intelligence is Reshaping the Financial Services Industry. London, United Kingdom: Ernst & Young Global Limited. (FATF), F. A. (2021). *Opportunities and Challenges of New Technologies for AML/CFT.* Paris, France: FATF.

Fatouros, G. M. (2024). Can Large Language Models Beat Wall Street? Unveiling the Potential of AI in Stock Selection. *arXiv*.

Finance, F. D. (2024). *Here's How HSBC is Using Artificial Intelligence to Take Money Launderers to Task.* Future Digital Finance Blog.

Finextra. (2016). AI Implementation in AML at HSBC Sees a Considerable Reduction in Compliance Costs. *Finextra Blog*.

Fisher, A. (2024). AI-Enhanced Financial Market Surveillance. *Journal of Market Analysis*, 34-56.

Forum, W. E. (2025). *Artificial Intelligence in Financial Services.* Cologny/Geneva, Switzerland: World Economic Forum. (FSB), F. S. (2024). *The Financial Stability Implications of Artificial Intelligence.* Basel, Switzerland: Financial Stability Board.

Fund, I. M. (2023). *Generative Artificial Intelligence in Finance: Risk Considerations*. International Monetary Fund.

Geczy, C. (2024). *AI in Finance: The Promise and Potential Pitfalls.* Knowledge at Wharton.

Group, P. S. (2025). *Predictive Risk Analytics in Finance: Key Use Cases.* Phoenix Strategy Group Blog.

Henry, J. (2024). *4 Keys to AI Governance that Drive Compliance and Accountability in Financial Institutions*. Jack Henry & Associates, Inc.

Hidayat, M. D. (2024). The Impact of Artificial Intelligence (AI) on Financial Management. *Management Studies and Business Journal (PRODUCTIVITY)*, 123-129.

HighRadius. (2022). *Predictive Analytics in Corporate Finance (7 Use Cases).* HighRadius Blog.

HSBC. (2024). *Harnessing the Power of AI to Fight Financial Crime.* HSBC News and Views.

Hub, E. T. (2023). *Leveraging AI in Electronic Trading: A Game Changer for Investment Banks. Electronic Trading Hub. (IMF), I. M. (2024). Artificial Intelligence and its Impact on Financial Markets and Financial Stability*. International Monetary Fund.

Imprasoft. (2023). Goldman Sachs: Pioneering AI Integration in Innovative Financial Technologies. *Imprasoft*.

Infosys. (n.d.). Reducing Audit Risk Through Artificial Intelligence and Automation. *Infosys Insights*.

Insight, A.-T. (2018). *HSBC Takes on Financial Crime Tech Challenge with AI Approach from Quantexa*. A-Team Insight Blog.

Institute, B. P. (2018). *The High Cost of AML Compliance*. Bank Policy Institute.

Institute, T. A. (2021). *AI in Financial Services*. The Alan Turing Institute.

International Journal of Governance, I. a. (2024). *Navigating Ethical and Governance Challenges in AI: Finance*. International Journal of Governance, Innovation, and Sustainability.

Intersog. (2024). Predictive Analytics in Finance: Shaping Investment Strategies. *Intersog Blog*.

Intive. (2024). *How AI is Supercharging Money Management*. Munich, Germany: Intive S.A.

Investopedia. (2023). HSBC's Money Laundering Scandal. *Investopedia*.

Investopedia. (2024). Strategies and Secrets of High-Frequency Trading (HFT) Firms. *Investopedia*.

Irfan, M. (2021, January). Do Shariah Indices converge? Evidence from Gulf Cooperation Council countries. *International Journal of Business Excellence*, *23*(2), 251–269. DOI: 10.1504/IJBEX.2021.113448

Irfan, M., Elhoseny, M., Kassim, S., & Metawa, N. (2023). *Advanced Machine Learning Algorithms for Complex Financial Applications*. IGI Global., DOI: 10.4018/978-1-6684-4483-2

Irfan, M., Elmogy, M., Gupta, S., Khalifa, F., & Dias, R. (2024). *AI-Driven Decentralized Finance and the Future of Finance*. IGI Global., DOI: 10.4018/979-8-3693-6321-8

Irfan, M., Elmogy, M., Majid, M. S., & El-Sappagh, S. (2023). *The Impact of AI Innovation on Financial Sectors in the Era of Industry 5.0*. IGI Global., DOI: 10.4018/979-8-3693-0082-4

Irfan, M., Hussainey, K., Chan Bukhari, S. A., & Nam, Y. (Eds.). (2024). *Issues of Sustainability in AI and New-Age Thematic Investing*. IGI Global Publisher., DOI: 10.4018/979-8-3693-3282-5

Irfan, M., Kadry, S., Sharif, M., & Ullah Khan, H. (2023). *Fintech Applications in Islamic Finance: AI, Machine Learning, and Blockchain Techniques*. IGI Global., DOI: 10.4018/979-8-3693-1038-0

ISACA. (2024). *How AI Is Transforming Audit, Risk, and Compliance*. ISACA Now Blog.

Itransition. (2023). Predictive Analytics in Finance: Use Cases and Guidelines. *Itransition Blog*.

Jefferson, P. (2025). *AI is Speeding Investors' Reactions to Central Bankers' Messages*. Reuters Technology News.

Johnson, M. &. (2024). The Role of Artificial Intelligence in Investment Decision-Making: Opportunities and Risks for Financial Institutions. *Journal of Financial Technology*, 88-105.

Journal, T. C. (2024). Financial Statement Fraud Detection in the Digital Age. *The CPA Journal*, •••, 1–6.

Kanaparthi, V. (2024). *Regulating AI in the Financial Sector: Recent Developments and Main Challenges*. Bank for International Settlements.

Kluwer, W. (2024). *Artificial Intelligence in Auditing: Enhancing the Audit Lifecycle*. Wolters Kluwer N.V.

Kokina, J. &. (2024). The Role of Artificial Intelligence in the Audit Process and How to Leverage It. *Journal of Ecohumanism*, 45-60.

Kolt, N. (2022). Predicting Consumer Contracts. *Berkeley Technology Law Journal*, •••, 1–60.

Kount. (2021). How to Reduce False Positives in Fraud Detection. *Kount Blog*.

KPMG. (2024). *Transforming Internal Audits Through the Power of AI*. KPMG International.

Ikudabo, A. O., & Kumar, P. (2024). AI-driven risk assessment and management in banking: Balancing innovation and security. *International Journal of Research Publication and Reviews*, *5*(10), 3573–3588.

Law, B. (2024). *Can You Use AI for Legal Research?* Bloomberg Law.

Law, B. B. (2024). *Key Considerations in AI-Related Contracts*. Byte Back Law.

LLP, S. A. (2024). Artificial Intelligence in Financial Markets: Systemic Risk and Market Abuse Concerns. *Butterworths Journal of International Banking and Financial Law*.

Lumen. (2024). *Secure Your Future: The Benefits of Ethical AI Governance*. Monroe, Louisiana, USA: Lumen Technologies, Inc.

Malladhi, A. (2023). Artificial Intelligence and Machine Learning in Forensic Accounting. *SSRG International Journal of Computer Science and Engineering*, 6-20.

Maple, C. S. (2023). *The AI Revolution: Opportunities and Challenges for the Finance Sector.* Ithaca, New York: arXiv preprint arXiv:2308.16538.

Marr, B. (2020). *The Amazing Ways How Mastercard Uses Artificial Intelligence to Stop Fraud and Reduce False Declines*. Bernard Marr & Co.

Marr, B. (2024). How Mastercard Uses AI Strategically: A Case Study. *Forbes*.

Marsal, A. (2024). *Balancing Act: Managing AI Governance Risks in Financial Services*. Alvarez & Marsal Holdings, LLC.

Martinez, C. (2021). *3 Case Studies Where AI Has Been Successfully Implemented in the Finance Industry*. Medium.

Mastercard. (2024). Fraud Detection Using AI: Inside the Algorithm. *Mastercard Newsroom*.

Mastercard. (2024). Mastercard Accelerates Card Fraud Detection with Generative AI Technology. *Mastercard Newsroom*.

Mastercard. (2024). Mastercard Expands First-of-its-Kind AI Technology to Help Banks Protect More Consumers from Scams in Real-Time. *Press Release*.

Mazars, F. (2025). *AI Governance – From Concept to Compliance*. Forvis Mazars.

MindBridge. (2024). *Operational Risk Management: AI Tools and Best Practices for Finance and Audit*. MindBridge Blog.

Naqvi, A. (2023). *Artificial Intelligence for Audit, Forensic Accounting, and Valuation: A Strategic Perspective*. Routledge.

News, B. (2015). *Goldman Gets Serious About High-Speed Trading*. Bloomberg.

News, P. (2024). *AI's Impact on Compliance in Finance*. PyQuant News.

OneStream. (2024). *10 Ways Companies Are Using AI in the Finance Services Industry*. OneStream Software LLC.

Patil, D. (2024). Artificial Intelligence in Financial Risk Assessment and Fraud Detection: Opportunities and Ethical Concerns. *International Journal of Financial Studies*, 78-95.

Paul, M. (2024). Artificial Intelligence in Financial Services. *The Cambridge Handbook of Responsible Artificial Intelligence*, 1-20.

Radial. (2023). Reducing False Positives in eCommerce Fraud Detection. *Radial Insights*.

Remolina, N. &.-M. (2023). *Artificial Intelligence in Finance: Challenges, Opportunities, and Regulatory Developments*. San Francisco, CA: AI Startups Publications.

ResearchGate. (2024). *The Impact of Predictive Analytics on Financial Risk Management in Businesses*. ResearchGate.

Reuters, T. (2023). *Sources of Legal Research: Primary, Secondary and the Role of AI*. Thomson Reuters Legal.

Rieschel, E. (2024). Detecting Spoofing in Financial Markets: An Unsupervised Anomaly Detection Approach. *(Master's Thesis)*, 60.

Sachs, G. (2024). *Gen AI: Too Much Spend, Too Little Benefit?* Goldman Sachs Research.

SafetyCulture. (2025). *AI in Regulatory Reporting: Is It Worth It?* SafetyCulture.

Scanner, S. (2024). *Artificial Intelligence and Anti-Money Laundering*. Sanction Scanner Blog.

Science, S. D. (2023). *J.P. Morgan - COiN - a Case Study of AI in Finance*. Superior Data Science.

Service, C. R. (2024). *Artificial Intelligence and Machine Learning in Financial Services*. Congressional Research Service.

Service, E. P. (2020). *The Ethics of Artificial Intelligence: Issues and Initiatives*. European Union.

Settlements, B. f. (2024). *Intelligent Financial System: How AI is Transforming Finance*. Bank for International Settlements.

Sha, X. (2024). Research on Financial Fraud Algorithm Based on Federated Learning and Big Data Technology. *arXiv*, 5.

Shabsigh, G. (2023). *Generative Artificial Intelligence in Finance: Risk Considerations*. International Monetary Fund.

Shukla, A. F. (2024). Artificial Intelligence in Financial Auditing: Innovating Traditional Practices for Enhanced Accuracy. *Journal of Informatics Education and Research*, 55-78.

Smarsh. (2023). Managing AI to Ensure Compliance with Data Privacy Laws. *Smarsh*.

Smith, G. (2023). *The AI Delusion*. Oxford University Press.

Smith, J. (2024). AI in the Financial Sector: The Line between Innovation, Regulation, and Compliance. *Information (Basel)*, •••, 432.

Soleymani, S. A. (2020). Financial Portfolio Optimization with Deep Learning and Blockchain. *Procedia Computer Science*, •••, 1361–1366.

Solutions, M. (2024). *AI Governance for Financial Services*. ModelOp Solutions, Inc.

Son, H. (2017). *JPMorgan Software Does in Seconds What Took Lawyers 360,000 Hours*. Bloomberg.

SpringerLink. (2024). The Role of Artificial Intelligence in the Supply Chain Finance Innovation Process. *Operations Research*.

Staff, F. (2017). *An AI Completed 360,000 Hours of Finance Work in Just Seconds*. Futurism.

Staff, F. (2017). *An AI Completed 360,000 Hours of Finance Work in Just Seconds*. Futurism.

Sullivan, C. C. (2019). *Machine Learning Saves JPMorgan Chase 360,000 Hours of Legal Work*. FindLaw.

SumatoSoft. (2023). *Predictive Analytics in Finance: Challenges, Benefits, Use Cases*. SumatoSoft Blog.

Tanaka, H. Y. (2024). A New Era of Financial Services: How AI Enhances Investment Efficiency. *International Journal of Intelligent Systems in Accounting Finance & Management*, •••, 45–67.

Times, F. (2024, September 15). Algorithmic Analyst Aversion. *Financial Times*.

Treasury, U. D. (2024). *Artificial Intelligence in Financial Services*. U.S. Department of the Treasury.

Tsang, E. P. (2023). *AI for Finance*. CRC Press. DOI: 10.1201/9781003348474

Vasarhelyi, M. A. (2025). *Artificial Intelligence in Accounting and Auditing*. Markus Wiener Publishers.

Vorecol. (2024). The Rise of AI-Powered Investment Tools: Transforming Portfolio Management. *Vorecol Blog*.

WatersTechnology. (2024). *BlackRock Developing AI Copilots for Aladdin*. WatersTechnology.

Zheng, Z. X. (2017). An Overview of Blockchain Technology: Architecture, Consensus, and Future Trends. *IEEE International Congress on Big Data*, 557-564. DOI: 10.1109/BigDataCongress.2017.85

Zhuk, A. (2025). Beyond the blockchain hype: Addressing legal and regulatory challenges. *SN Social Sciences*, *5*(2), 1–37.

Chapter 9
The Future of Financial Decision-Making: AI in Finance, Auditing, and Investment

Partap Singh
https://orcid.org/0000-0002-4653-7984
Maharishi Markendshwar University, India

ABSTRACT

As artificial intelligence (AI) continues to evolve, its integration into finance, auditing, and investment is reshaping the future of these industries. This chapter explores how AI technologies, such as machine learning, natural language processing, and blockchain, are projected to transform financial systems, enabling greater operational efficiency, predictive analytics, and real-time decision-making. While these advancements present significant opportunities, they also bring challenges such as ethical concerns, security risks, and the need for workforce adaptation. This forward-looking study analyzes how AI will influence the future of financial services, addressing both opportunities and obstacles that accompany these innovations.

1. INTRODUCTION

Artificial intelligence (AI) has emerged as a transformative force across various sectors, particularly in finance, auditing, and investment. Defined as a branch of computer science focused on creating intelligent machines capable of performing cognitive tasks traditionally associated with human intelligence—such as reasoning, learning, and speech recognition (Frankenfield, 2021)—AI's applications in finance are multifaceted. Unlike industrial robots that follow fixed instructions, AI systems

DOI: 10.4018/979-8-3373-0129-7.ch009

can learn autonomously, mapping environmental data into actionable insights and thereby enhancing decision-making processes (Raj & Seamans, 2019).

The evolution of AI encompasses several key technologies, including machine learning, deep learning, natural language processing (NLP), and advanced predictive analytics. These innovations are not only enhancing operational efficiencies but also reshaping business models and customer relationships through the promotion of personalized digital finance (Martinelli et al., 2021; Cucculelli & Recanatini, 2022). The automation of processes facilitated by AI results in improved service delivery and significant cost savings, positioning organizations to better meet the demands of modern consumers.

In the realm of auditing and financial reporting, the integration of AI is poised to revolutionize traditional practices. According to a study by KPMG (n.d.), a substantial 64% of surveyed companies anticipate that auditors will play a critical role in evaluating their AI applications, ensuring the reliability and accuracy of AI-driven financial reporting. Furthermore, the survey highlighted that all participating companies have initiated strategic actions regarding AI implementation, with nearly 72% piloting or actively using AI technologies in their financial operations. These findings underscore the increasing significance of AI in financial reporting and auditing, emphasizing its potential to foster smarter, more integrated information systems that enhance transparency and accountability.

AI and machine learning (ML) are transforming finance by enhancing efficiency, decision-making, and personalizing customer experiences. Studies have highlighted AI's roles in algorithmic trading, risk management, and fraud detection, while also raising concerns over data privacy, biases, and regulatory challenges. This emphasizes the necessity for ethical considerations and robust cybersecurity measures (Deepak, 2024). Additionally, the application of machine learning in internal auditing has shown improvements in audit coverage and innovation, stressing the need for ongoing innovation and safeguards in technology implementation (Shivram, 2024). According to Briggs and Kodnani (2023), AI investment is forecasted to approach $200 billion globally by 2025, highlighting the expected rapid growth and significant impact on GDP. The report emphasizes the need for substantial upfront investment in infrastructure and talent to realize AI's economic benefits.

As AI continues to advance, its implications for finance, auditing, and investment are profound, signaling a shift toward a more data-driven, efficient, and innovative financial ecosystem. This paper explores the multifaceted impact of AI on these domains, examining its potential to reshape industry standards, enhance risk management, and drive investment strategies in an increasingly digital economy.

2. LITERATURE REVIEW

2.1 AI and Future of Finance

William & Mary (2024) highlighted the transformative impact of AI and machine learning on finance, particularly in algorithmic trading, risk management, and personalized services. Predictive analytics improved decision-making, while ethical challenges, including data privacy and bias, remained critical concerns, necessitating careful consideration in AI integration within financial sectors.

Bahoo et al. (2024) provided a comprehensive review of AI applications in finance, analyzing over two decades of research. They identified key areas, including predictive systems, risk evaluation, and portfolio management. The study revealed ten main research streams and emphasized the need for further exploration into AI's impact on disruptive technologies.

Jagtiani and John (2018) noted that AI and machine learning algorithms enabled Fintech lenders to make rapid credit decisions, benefiting both lenders and consumers. This quick decision-making process improved access to credit while streamlining operations within the lending industry, showcasing the advantages of integrating AI technologies.

Herdershott et al. (2011) discussed two sub-streams of "AI and the Stock Market," focusing on algorithmic trading's influence on financial markets. They argued that algorithmic trading improved market liquidity by reducing spreads, adverse selection, and trade-related price discovery, illustrating its significant role in enhancing market efficiency.

Frino et al. (2017) indicated that algorithmic trading outperformed human traders by adjusting rapidly to information and capitalizing on market timing during news announcements. Their findings underscored the advantages of algorithmic trading, highlighting its potential to generate higher profits through efficient execution of trades in response to market events.

Kelejian and Mukerji (2016) concluded that while high-frequency trading sometimes increased volatility related to news, it overall reduced return volatility variance and improved market efficiency. Their study emphasized the complex dynamics of algorithmic trading and its effects on financial markets, indicating a generally positive impact on market stability.

Creamer (2012) illustrated the model's effectiveness in high-frequency trading futures by selecting the most profitable and least risky futures, providing long or short recommendations. This approach emphasized the role of algorithmic trading in enhancing decision-making and profitability within futures markets through strategic analysis and rapid execution.

Kercheval and Zhang (2015) employed a supervised learning method to predict mid-price movements in high-frequency limit order books. Their multi-class SVM model classified market movements and embedded predictions into trading strategies, yielding positive payoffs while maintaining controlled risk, showcasing the practical applications of AI in trading.

Bucci (2020) presented modern neural networks, such as LSTM and NARX, as effective alternatives for trading and forecasting applications. Their study highlighted the capabilities of advanced neural network models in financial prediction, illustrating their potential for improving accuracy in market forecasting and investment strategies.

Fernandes et al. (2014) explored the challenges of forecasting volatility, using the Chicago Board Options Exchange's VIX as a measure of market sentiment. Their findings emphasized the complex nature of volatility forecasting, necessitating advanced methodologies to accurately assess market expectations and investor sentiment.

Kim and Kim (2020) demonstrated that deep learning technology improved index-tracking by minimizing tracking errors and enhancing performance. Their research indicated the effectiveness of AI-driven methodologies in portfolio management, contributing to more accurate tracking of market indices and optimizing investment strategies.

Loukeris and Eleftheriadis (2015) proposed elaborate asset allocation designs that incorporated bankruptcy detection models. Their advanced utility performance system estimated the default probability of stocks before portfolio inclusion, showcasing the application of AI in enhancing investment decisions through sophisticated risk assessment frameworks.

Zhao et al. (2018) found that AI-based prediction models significantly improved the portfolio selection process by accurately forecasting stock returns. Their study highlighted the effectiveness of AI technologies in guiding investment decisions and optimizing portfolio management strategies within dynamic financial markets.

Sabău Popa et al. (2021) predicted business performance using a composite financial index, confirming the superiority of AI-powered classifiers over traditional models. Their findings underscored the accuracy and interpretability of AI applications in financial performance prediction, enhancing decision-making capabilities for stakeholders.

Wanke et al. (2016) examined the Malaysian and Islamic banking sector, concluding that negative cost structures and regulatory barriers led to inefficiencies compared to U.S. banks. Their research illustrated the impact of cultural and competitive factors on banking performance, highlighting the resilience and stability of better-regulated institutions.

Petukhina et al. (2021) noted that despite the rise of algorithms and AI advisors, human traders continued to dominate the cryptocurrency market. Their analysis indicated that while AI technologies offered advantages, human expertise remained a crucial element in navigating the complexities of cryptocurrency trading.

Pichl and Kaizoji (2017) found that the HAR model effectively captured daily realized volatility, while a feed-forward neural network accurately approximated daily logarithmic returns of BTCUSD. Their findings illustrated the potential of advanced machine learning models in predicting and understanding cryptocurrency market dynamics.

Jang and Lee (2019) proposed a machine learning model that outperformed traditional American option pricing models, demonstrating the effectiveness of ANNs in derivative pricing. Their research emphasized the advantages of integrating AI technologies to enhance predictive capabilities in financial derivatives markets.

Funahashi (2020) rejected deep learning for option pricing due to price instability, introducing a hybrid model that combined ANNs with asymptotic expansion. This approach improved accuracy and efficiency, mimicking human learning processes to enhance the reliability of financial predictions in option markets.

Durango-Gutiérrez et al. (2021) combined traditional methods with AI to gain insights into explanatory variables affecting financial outcomes. Their research demonstrated the value of integrating AI techniques with established methodologies to enhance understanding and improve predictive capabilities in finance.

Abedin et al. (2019) highlighted the importance of AI-based financial decision support systems (FDSSs) in preventing global financial crises. Their study emphasized the transformative potential of AI technologies in enhancing decision-making processes within the banking industry, contributing to more robust risk management strategies.

Lahmiri (2016) compared traditional and advanced consumer credit risk models, showing that supervised learning tools like SVM and random forests could predict credit card delinquency effectively. Their findings highlighted the advantages of AI methodologies in enhancing predictive accuracy for credit risk assessment.

Holopainen and Sarlin (2017) discussed the role of AI technologies in systemic risk monitoring, supporting macroprudential strategies. They noted that models like k-nearest neighbors and sophisticated neural networks could detect unusual financial activities, underscoring the potential of AI in improving financial stability monitoring.

Yin et al. (2020) explored the significance of investor sentiment in stock prediction through sentiment analysis of social media data. Their study indicated that effective sentiment extraction could enhance predictive models, highlighting the growing importance of social media in understanding market dynamics.

Heston and Sinha (2017) found that daily news predictions typically influenced stock returns over short periods, while weekly news affected longer-term returns. Their research demonstrated the critical role of investor sentiment in shaping market responses to news events, underscoring its importance in financial analysis.

Galeshchuk and Mukherjee (2017) emphasized the necessity for accurate exchange rate forecasts in foreign exchange trading and hedging. Their research indicated that AI models outperformed traditional time series approaches, showcasing the advantages of advanced technologies in enhancing trading effectiveness and risk management.

Amelot et al. (2021) confirmed that AI-based models, such as NARX, achieved superior prediction performance compared to statistical models. Their findings underscored the efficacy of AI methodologies in improving financial predictions and optimizing investment strategies within volatile market conditions.

Pendergast (2024) concluded that AI transformed finance by enhancing decision-making, risk management, and operational efficiency. AI tools automated tasks, detected patterns in large datasets, and provided real-time insights. However, challenges like bias and data governance persisted, necessitating ethical considerations and human oversight to fully optimize AI's potential.

Yoon et al. (2021) focused on early auditing systems, emphasizing processes that encountered higher-than-expected risk levels. They discussed how continuous auditing transformed the auditor's role, altering the nature, timing, and extent of audits, as well as influencing audit reporting, data modeling, data analytics, and monitoring practices.

2.2 AI and the Future of Auditing

Omoteso (2012) examined the integration of AI in auditing, highlighting its advantages in decision-making and control processes. Nonetheless, challenges persisted, particularly regarding cost-benefit equilibrium, especially impacting smaller audit firms.

AI Ethics Impact Group (2020) provided a framework for implementing AI ethics across sectors. Their interdisciplinary approach aimed to translate ethical principles into practical applications, addressing the complexities of responsible AI deployment.

Koshiyama et al. (2021) surveyed algorithm auditing, emphasizing the importance of managing the legal, ethical, and technological risks associated with AI and machine learning. The study outlined various strategies for ensuring accountable algorithmic practices.

Dignum (2020) discussed the responsibilities tied to AI implementation. The chapter focused on establishing ethical guidelines to enhance accountability and transparency within AI systems, promoting an ethically sound integration of AI in various sectors.

Shneiderman (2020) proposed guidelines for creating reliable, human-centered AI systems. These recommendations aimed to bridge the gap between ethical theory and practical application, ensuring safety and trustworthiness in AI technologies.

Mökander et al. (2022) emphasized the role of auditing within the proposed European AI regulation. Their guide discussed conformity assessments and the importance of post-market monitoring for AI systems to ensure compliance with established ethical standards.

Brown et al. (2021) explored algorithm audits, defining them as processes targeting algorithms directly. The authors highlighted the necessity of ethical evaluations to enhance accountability in algorithmic decision-making frameworks.

Kokina and Davenport (2017) investigated AI's emergence and its transformative impact on auditing practices. They identified the potential for automation to enhance efficiency and effectiveness in the auditing process.

Yoon et al. (2021) developed a three-layer structure for continuous data auditing, enhancing audit effectiveness through advanced design and evaluation methodologies. Their approach aimed to optimize the auditing process by incorporating real-time data assessments.

Wang et al. (2020) introduced an AI-based framework to enhance compliance awareness in procurement auditing. Their model aimed to automate compliance processes, ensuring adherence to regulations while improving efficiency in audit practices.

Floridi et al. (2022) outlined a comprehensive procedure for conducting AI system conformity assessments. Their framework aimed to ensure compliance with the European AI Act, facilitating ethical and transparent AI practices throughout its lifecycle.

Drakonakis et al. (2020) presented an automated black-box auditing framework, targeting web authentication and authorization flaws. Their work focused on enhancing security measures through comprehensive auditing of digital systems.

Thangavel and Varalakshmi (2020) developed a ternary hash tree framework to ensure secure cloud data storage. Their integrity verification system aimed to enhance user trust in cloud services through rigorous auditing practices.

Black et al. (2020) investigated fairness testing in AI systems, focusing on developing methodologies to ensure unbiased algorithmic outcomes. Their research aimed to promote fairness in AI applications through systematic evaluations.

Eulerich et al. (2022) proposed a framework for utilizing robotic process automation in audit tasks. Their model aimed to guide auditors in identifying suitable activities for automation, enhancing audit efficiency and effectiveness.

Eilifsen et al. (2020) conducted a study on audit data analytics, revealing varying firm strategies and the rarity of advanced analytics usage. Their findings emphasized the uncertainty surrounding supervisory responses to analytics in auditing practices.

Bibler et al. (2023) highlighted the benefits of data-driven audit capabilities and innovation. Their research asserted that fostering an innovative mindset among auditors can significantly enhance fraud detection and overall audit effectiveness.

The Institute of Internal Auditors (2022) defined internal auditing as an objective assessment activity aimed at improving organizational operations. Their systematic approach emphasized the importance of effective risk management and governance processes in achieving organizational goals.

Brown et al. (2021) underscored the significance of ethical algorithm audits, advocating for transparency and accountability in AI systems. Their research called for robust auditing practices to address potential risks associated with algorithmic decision-making.

Mökander et al. (2022) discussed the implications of the EU's AI regulation on high-risk AI systems. They stressed the necessity for ongoing performance monitoring throughout the lifecycle of these systems to ensure ethical compliance.

Floridi et al. (2018) promoted continuous auditing as a means to maintain oversight of AI systems. Their work highlighted the importance of adaptability in auditing processes to align with evolving AI technologies.

Dignum (2020) noted that advanced AI capabilities introduced new risks, such as transparency issues and biases. The study emphasized the critical need for ethical oversight to mitigate potential harms associated with AI deployment.

2.3 AI and the Future of Investment

Deloitte (2024) demonstrated how AI is revolutionizing investment management by improving alpha generation, enhancing operational efficiency, optimizing content distribution, and refining risk management. These innovations enable firms to adapt their business models and enhance competitiveness while managing the intersection between technology and human talent.

Savi, R., Shen, J., Tsaig, Y., & Dufour, T. (2024). Explored how AI transformed investing. The authors demonstrated that AI and machine learning enhanced investment strategies by enabling deeper analysis of textual data and efficient navigation of market themes, improving decision-making and fostering better investment outcomes through innovative tools and methodologies.

Agnihotri et al. (2023) revealed that algorithmic trading adoption significantly increased liquidity and hedging efficiency over the past decade without raising market volatility, highlighting its importance in optimizing trading strategies and enhancing market operations.

Chugh et al. (2024) argued that while algorithmic trading increased market volatility due to high trading volumes and rule-based methods, integrating human oversight with algorithms could mitigate this impact, blending computational precision with human judgment for more stable outcomes.

Buti et al. (2011) focused on the privacy advantages algorithmic trading offers institutional investors, particularly in maintaining anonymity. However, the study identified adverse selection issues in retail markets, especially during lower liquidity periods, creating challenges for retail traders.

Budish et al. (2015) discussed how high-speed networks in algorithmic trading improved order execution but increased order cancellations, highlighting a trade-off between the benefits of increased speed and liquidity against potential market stability concerns.

Andersen et al. (2012) investigated the impact of trading activities on volatility, identifying high-frequency and algorithmic traders as key drivers. The study applied robust models to explore the causal relationship between trading behavior and subsequent market fluctuations.

Aït-Sahalia and Brunetti (2020) indicated that high-frequency traders (HFTs) withdrew during volatility spikes, while algorithmic traders (BATs) entered, contributing to increased volatility and price jumps. The absence of HFTs was linked to greater market instability.

Aït-Sahalia et al. (2012) employed a semimartingale model to show that HFTs capitalized on rapid price changes without directional bias. Their high success rate in transactions reflected the advantages of speed in achieving favorable trading outcomes compared to other participants.

Menkveld (2013) challenged the notion that HFTs cause volatility, finding that they often succeeded against low-frequency traders. Instead, the study associated increased market volatility with the withdrawal of HFTs, particularly during uncertain market conditions.

Arumugam et al. (2023) discovered that excessive trading by algorithmic and high-frequency traders escalated market volatility, while actions by non-algorithmic traders had a stabilizing effect, illustrating the varied impacts of different trading methodologies on market dynamics.

Aït-Sahalia and Brunetti (2020) analyzed S&P500 eMini transactions, revealing that high-frequency traders performed exceptionally well against low-frequency traders. Their absence during high noise periods was linked to significant market volatility and price jumps.

Abraham et al. (2019) found that while robo-advisors increased market participation, they also raised concerns about passive investing and long-term risk for inexperienced, low-wealth investors, as reduced active management could expose them to unforeseen risks.

Balwani et al. (2019) explored robo-advisor customization, identifying automation, user control, humanization, and performance as key adoption drivers. The study illuminated how these factors contributed to the personalization and effectiveness of robo-advisory services.

Loos et al. (2020) demonstrated that investors utilizing robo-advisors experienced enhanced portfolio diversification, reduced home bias, and improved efficiency, benefiting from greater geographical and asset diversity, indicating better learning from these automated services.

Bhatia et al. (2020) identified potential behavioral biases introduced by human errors in programming robo-advisors. These errors could undermine the reliability of investment recommendations, emphasizing the need for rigorous oversight in automated financial tools.

Accenture (2015) argued that robo-advisors often missed critical aspects of client relationships, such as personalized goal-setting and life-stage adaptability, which are essential for providing comprehensive and effective financial advisory services.

Acunto et al. (2018) highlighted the benefits of robo-advisors in improving investment practices for underserved groups. Lower costs and increased accessibility helped enhance market participation, better diversification, and reduced biases compared to traditional financial advisors.

Tao et al. (2021) demonstrated that robo-advisors excelled in managing portfolios across diverse risk-reward models, proving to be a cost-effective alternative to traditional approaches, offering superior performance in managing investments.

Sander (2021) pointed out that while robo-advisors can predict stock market volatility, the final investment decisions ultimately rest with the investors, underscoring the importance of human discretion alongside automated financial predictions.

Objectives of the Paper

i. To forecast future developments of AI in finance, auditing, and investment based on emerging trends and technologies.
ii. To analyze how AI-driven advancements, including automation and predictive analytics, will redefine investment strategies and financial decision-making.
iii. To examine the potential ethical and regulatory challenges that AI may introduce as its use in finance, auditing, and investment;
iv. To explore the evolving role of human professionals in an AI-driven financial ecosystem, with a focus on necessary skill adaptation.

Research Gaps

Despite the progress made in understanding AI's role in finance and auditing, several key gaps remain: Ethical Governance and AI Bias: There is insufficient literature developing frameworks that address the ethical challenges of AI, including bias and fairness in algorithmic decision-making processes. Few studies provide a comprehensive analysis of how finance professionals will need to adapt and reskill to stay relevant in a future dominated by AI. Limited research examines how AI and blockchain technologies will reshape decentralized finance, particularly regarding the automation of decentralized financial systems.

3. RESEARCH METHODOLOGY

3.1 Research Design

This study employs a quantitative research design to gather and analyze data from respondents in the finance, auditing, and investment sectors. A structured questionnaire was developed to ensure that the data collected aligns with the research objectives.

3.2 Sample Selection

A total of 100 respondents were selected for this study, representing a diverse range of professionals within the finance, auditing, and investment industries. The respondents were chosen using a non-probability sampling technique to capture insights from individuals with varying levels of experience and expertise in AI-related applications.

3.3 Data Collection

Data was collected using a structured online questionnaire distributed to respondents through professional networks, social media platforms, and email. The questionnaire included closed-ended questions designed to gather quantitative data on the following aspects:

- Perceptions of future developments in AI within the finance, auditing, and investment sectors.
- Impact of AI-driven advancements on investment strategies and financial decision-making.

- Awareness and concerns regarding ethical and regulatory challenges associated with AI.
- Perspectives on the evolving role of human professionals in an AI-driven ecosystem and necessary skill adaptations.

3.4 Data Analysis

The collected data was analyzed using percentage methods. Responses were quantified and presented in percentage format to provide a clear representation of trends and insights related to the objectives of the study. This statistical analysis enabled the identification of patterns in the data and facilitated a comparative analysis of the respondents' perspectives.

3.5 Ethical Considerations

In conducting this research, ethical considerations were prioritized. Informed consent was obtained from all respondents, ensuring they were aware of the study's purpose and their right to withdraw at any time. Confidentiality was maintained by anonymizing responses and securely storing data.

3.6 Limitations of the Study

Despite valuable insights, this study has several limitations. First, its mixed-methods approach, while useful for capturing both quantitative and qualitative data, may not fully represent all perspectives across the diverse real estate sector, particularly among smaller firms facing cost barriers to AI adoption. Additionally, focusing on current AI applications limits the analysis of potential long-term impacts and future trends, such as AI-driven predictive analytics, automation, and ethics in property management. Further research could expand on these areas and incorporate longitudinal data to understand evolving adoption rates and the shifting roles of human professionals as AI becomes more embedded in real estate operations. Lastly, while this study examines key benefits and challenges, a more detailed assessment of regulatory implications and skill adaptation is needed to address potential ethical concerns and governance issues as AI use expands.

4. RESULTS AND DISCUSSION

Section 1: Demographic Information

Table 1. Distribution of Respondents by Role in Finance, Auditing, and Investment Sector

Role	Number of Respondents	Percentage (%)
Financial Analyst	30	30%
Auditor	20	20%
Investment Manager	15	15%
Compliance Officer	10	10%
Consultant	10	10%
Other	15	15%
Total	100	100%

Source: Author

Table 1 revealed that the majority of respondents are Financial Analysts (30%), while other key roles, such as Auditors (20%) and Investment Managers (15%), are also significant, indicating diverse representation across the sector.

Findings: -Financial Analysts are the most common respondents, followed by Auditors and Investment Managers. This suggests a broad range of insights from professionals, providing diverse perspectives on AI's influence in finance and auditing.

Table 2. Showing the experience of the respondents

Years of Experience	Number of Respondents	Percentage (%)
Less than 1 year	15	15%
1-3 years	30	30%
4-7 years	25	25%
8-10 years	20	20%
More than 10 years	10	10%
Total	100	100%

Table 2 illustrates the respondents' experience levels, revealing that 30% possess 1-3 years of experience, making this the mode. The data indicates a predominance of relatively new professionals in the finance, auditing, and investment sectors. This suggests a workforce that is likely adapting to industry challenges while potentially lacking extensive experience, which may influence decision-making processes.

Mode Calculation:

The mode represents the category with the highest frequency of responses.

- 1-3 years received the highest number of responses (30 respondents), so the mode is 1-3 years.

The mode indicates that the majority of respondents have 1-3 years of experience, suggesting a relatively newer workforce in the finance/auditing/investment sector. Most professionals surveyed are in the early to mid-stages of their careers.

Table 3. Distribution of Respondents by Highest Level of Education in Finance, Auditing, and Investment Sector

Education Level	Number of Respondents	Percentage (%)
High School Diploma	10	10%
Bachelor's Degree	40	40%
Master's Degree	35	35%
Doctorate	10	10%
Other	5	5%
Total	100	100%

The table3 reflects the familiarity of finance and auditing professionals with AI technologies. A significant 35% of respondents reported being very familiar with AI, making it the most common response. Another 25% indicated they are somewhat familiar, while 15% remain neutral. A smaller portion, 15%, are somewhat unfamiliar, and 10% are not familiar with AI at all. The mode, "Very Familiar," shows that a considerable number of professionals already possess a strong understanding of AI, suggesting that AI is becoming increasingly integrated into finance and auditing practices.

Section 2: Current Use of AI in Finance, Auditing, and Investment

Table 4. Respondents' Perception of AI's Impact on Finance, Auditing, and Investment Sectors

Level of Impact	Number of Respondents	Percentage (%)
Not at all	5	5%
Slightly	15	15%
Moderately	25	25%
Very much	35	35%
Extremely	20	20%
Total	100	100%

The table 4 indicates a strong consensus among respondents regarding the impact of AI on the finance, auditing, and investment sectors. The mode of responses, "Very much," suggests that a substantial portion of professionals recognize AI as a transformative force in these industries. With 35% of respondents selecting this option, it is clear that many believe AI significantly enhances efficiency, accuracy, and decision-making processes. Additionally, 20% of respondents feel AI's impact is "Extremely" significant, further emphasizing the technology's growing relevance. Conversely, only a small fraction of respondents (5%) indicated that AI has no impact at all, suggesting a minimal presence of skepticism. Overall, the findings underscore a prevailing optimism about AI's potential in reshaping traditional finance and investment practices.

Table 5. AI Impact in Finance, Auditing, and Investment Sectors (Next 5-10 Years)

Area of Impact	Number of Respondents	Percentage (%)
Investment strategies	60	60%
Risk assessment	50	50%
Fraud detection	45	45%
Customer service	40	40%
Compliance monitoring	35	35%
Other	10	10%
Total	100	100%

The table 5 reveals that respondents believe AI will have the most significant impact on Investment Strategies, with 60% selecting this area. This suggests a strong expectation for AI to enhance decision-making processes, optimize asset management, and develop innovative investment solutions. Risk Assessment follows closely, chosen by 50% of respondents, indicating a recognition of AI's potential to improve risk modeling and analysis. Fraud Detection (45%) and Customer Service (40%) are also notable areas, emphasizing the growing role of AI in enhancing security and customer interactions. Compliance Monitoring (35%) highlights the importance of AI in navigating regulatory landscapes. Overall, the findings suggest that professionals foresee AI as a transformative tool across various key areas in finance, auditing, and investment.

Table 6. Distribution of AI Technologies in Finance, Auditing, and Investment

AI Technology	Percentile (%)
Machine learning	60%
Predictive analytics	70%
Natural language processing	40%
Robotic process automation	50%
Blockchain technology	30%
Other	10%

Table 6 illustrates the adoption of various AI technologies across organizations. Predictive analytics, with 70% adoption, emerges as the most widely utilized or planned technology, followed by machine learning at 60%. Robotic process automation and natural language processing are moderately used, at 50% and 40% respectively, while blockchain technology, at 30%, and other AI technologies, at 10%, have relatively lower adoption rates. These findings suggest that automation and analytics tools are critical in AI-driven financial decision-making, while newer technologies like blockchain are yet to gain similar traction.

Table 7. Impact of AI on Operational Efficiency

Impact on Efficiency	Number of Responses	Percentile (%)
No impact	10	10%
Minor improvements	30	30%
Significant improvements	40	40%
Game-changing improvements	20	20%
Total	100	100%

The table 7 indicates that 40% of respondents reported significant improvements in operational efficiency after the introduction of AI, making it the most common impact. Minor improvements were noted by 30% of respondents, while 20% experienced game-changing improvements. Only 10% reported no impact. These findings suggest that AI has had a considerable effect on enhancing operational efficiency in many organizations, with a focus on notable gains and transformative changes.

Section 3: Future of AI in Finance, Auditing, and Investment

Table 8. Perception of AI's Role in Future Financial Decision-Making

Perception of AI Role	Number of Responses	Percentile (%)
Very unlikely	5	5%
Unlikely	15	15%
Likely	50	50%
Very likely	30	30%
Total	100	100%

The table 8 shows that 50% of respondents believe AI is likely to play a dominant role in future financial decision-making processes, making it the most common opinion. Very likely was selected by 30% of participants, indicating strong optimism about AI's future influence. Conversely, only 5% view this possibility as very unlikely, suggesting a growing consensus on the importance of AI in finance. These findings reflect a general belief in the increasing significance of AI technologies in shaping financial strategies and decisions.

Table 9. Impact of AI on Areas of Finance

Area of Finance	Number of Responses	Percentile (%)
Portfolio management	35	35%
Risk assessment and mitigation	50	50%
Fraud detection and prevention	45	45%
Customer service (chatbots, automated assistants)	30	30%
Trading and market analysis	40	40%
Audit automation	20	20%
Other (please specify)	5	5%
Total	100	100%

The table 9 illustrates the areas within finance where respondents believe AI will have the most significant impact in the future. Risk assessment and mitigation topped the responses with 50%, indicating strong confidence in AI's role in enhancing risk management strategies. Following closely are fraud detection and prevention (45%) and trading and market analysis (40%), underscoring AI's potential to bolster security and optimize trading decisions. Portfolio management (35%) and customer service (30%) also show considerable expectations for AI integration. Overall, the findings reveal a clear trend toward leveraging AI technologies to enhance various financial functions, suggesting that AI will play a pivotal role in shaping the future of finance.

Table 10. Foreseen Changes in Traditional Investment Strategies Due to AI

Foreseen Change	Number of Responses	Percentile (%)
Completely replacing human decision-making	10	10%
Enhancing human decision-making with predictive analytics	60	60%
Minor impact with AI supporting routine tasks	25	25%
No impact	5	5%
Total	100	100%

The data in Table 10 highlights respondents' views on how AI is expected to transform traditional investment strategies. A significant 60% believe AI will enhance human decision-making with predictive analytics, indicating confidence in AI's role as a supportive tool rather than a replacement for human judgment. In contrast, only 10% foresee a complete replacement of human decision-making by AI, suggesting that professionals value the irreplaceable intuition and experience of human investors. Furthermore, 25% acknowledge a minor impact where AI will assist with routine tasks, while 5% perceive no impact at all. This indicates a general consensus that AI will augment rather than wholly transform traditional investment strategies, promoting a collaborative approach.

Section 4: Ethical and Regulatory Challenges

Table 11. Perception of Ethical Challenges Posed by AI in Finance and Auditing

Ethical Challenge Perception	Number of Responses	Percentile (%)
Yes	70	70%
No	20	20%
Unsure	10	10%
Total	100	100%

The data in Table 11 illustrates respondents' beliefs regarding the ethical challenges associated with the increasing use of AI in finance and auditing. A substantial majority, 70%, believe that AI does pose ethical challenges, reflecting widespread concern among professionals about issues such as bias, transparency, and accountability in AI algorithms. Only 20% of respondents felt that AI does not present ethical concerns, while 10% remained unsure. This suggests that the financial and auditing sectors need to address these ethical implications proactively, ensuring that the implementation of AI is accompanied by guidelines and frameworks to navigate potential challenges responsibly. The strong consensus highlights the importance of ethical considerations in integrating AI technologies into financial practices.

Table 12. Ethical Challenges of AI in Finance and Auditing

Ethical Challenge	Number of Responses	Percentile (%)
Bias in AI algorithms	40	57.14%
Lack of transparency in AI decision-making	35	50%
Data privacy concerns	50	71.43%
Job displacement of human workers	30	42.86%
Other (please specify)	10	14.29%
Total	70	100%

The data in Table 12 highlights the ethical challenges that respondents are most concerned about regarding the growing use of AI in finance and auditing. Notably, 71.43% of participants expressed concern about data privacy, indicating a strong awareness of the implications of handling sensitive financial information. Following closely is bias in AI algorithms (57.14%) and a lack of transparency in AI decision-making (50%), which suggest apprehensions about fairness and clarity in AI operations. Additionally, 42.86% are worried about job displacement for human workers, reflecting fears about the impact of automation on employment. The relatively low concern regarding "Other" challenges (14.29%) indicates that respondents have specific ethical issues in mind, with a clear focus on data integrity and algorithmic fairness. This underscores the need for developing ethical standards and regulations to address these challenges in AI applications.

Table 13. Effectiveness of Current Regulatory Frameworks for AI in Finance

Effectiveness of Regulatory Frameworks	Number of Responses	Percentile (%)
Very effective	15	15%
Somewhat effective	50	50%
Not effective	25	25%
No opinion	10	10%
Total	100	100%

The data in Table 13 reflects respondents' perceptions of the effectiveness of current regulatory frameworks in managing AI-related risks within the finance sector. A notable 50% of participants believe that the frameworks are somewhat effective, indicating a moderate level of confidence in the existing regulations. However, 25% view these frameworks as not effective, suggesting room for improvement in addressing the complexities of AI. Only 15% consider the frameworks very effective, highlighting concerns regarding their robustness. Additionally, 10% of respondents had no opinion, which may indicate a lack of familiarity with regulatory measures or uncertainty about their impacts. These findings emphasize the need for ongoing dialogue and enhancement of regulatory frameworks to better mitigate AI-related risks in finance.

Table 14. Priorities for Regulators in Ethical AI Deployment

Priority Area	Number of Responses	Percentile (%)
Developing AI transparency guidelines	45	56.25%
Ensuring data privacy and security	55	68.75%
Creating accountability frameworks for AI failures	30	37.5%
Mandating AI ethics training for professionals	35	43.75%
Other (please specify)	5	6.25%
Total	80	100%

The data in Table 14 outlines the areas that respondents believe regulators should prioritize to ensure ethical AI deployment in finance and auditing. The highest concern is for ensuring data privacy and security, with 68.75% of respondents selecting this option, indicating a strong emphasis on protecting sensitive information. Following closely, 56.25% advocate for developing AI transparency guidelines, reflecting a desire for clarity in AI operations and decision-making processes. Mandating AI ethics training for professionals (43.75%) and creating accountability frameworks for AI failures (37.5%) are also seen as significant priorities. The relatively low percentage for "Other" (6.25%) suggests that respondents largely focus on the mentioned areas. These findings highlight the need for comprehensive regulatory frameworks that address these crucial aspects to foster ethical AI practices in finance and auditing.

Section 5: Workforce Adaptation

Table 15. Foreseen Changes in Roles in an AI-Driven Financial Ecosystem

Role Change	**Number of Responses**	**Percentile (%)**
Becoming more analytical	30	33.33%
Focused on strategy and decision-making	25	27.78%
Increased collaboration with AI systems	20	22.22%
More emphasis on ethical oversight	10	11.11%
Other (please specify)	5	5.56%
Total	90	100%

The data in Table 15 illustrates how finance professionals anticipate their roles evolving in an AI-driven financial ecosystem. The predominant response, "Becoming more analytical," reflects a significant 33.33% of participants who expect their roles to require enhanced analytical skills to interpret and utilize AI-generated insights effectively. 27.78% foresee a shift toward being focused on strategy and decision-making, suggesting a growing importance of strategic thinking in integrating AI insights. Furthermore, 22.22% anticipate increased collaboration with AI systems, indicating a recognition of AI as a collaborative tool rather than a replacement. While 11.11% expect more emphasis on ethical oversight, it shows that ethical considerations are becoming integral to the financial profession. The low percentage for "Other" (5.56%) indicates that respondents mainly see the aforementioned roles as key to their future responsibilities. These findings suggest that professionals are preparing for a landscape where analytical skills and strategic thinking will be essential to leverage AI effectively.

Table 16. Essential Skills for Finance Professionals in the Coming Years

Skill	Number of Responses	Percentile (%)
Data analysis	40	40.0%
AI/machine learning knowledge	35	35.0%
Ethical governance	15	15.0%
Adaptability to technology	25	25.0%
Communication and collaboration skills	30	30.0%
Other (please specify)	5	5.0%
Total	100	100%

The findings in Table 16 underscore the skills finance professionals believe will be crucial in the upcoming years. Data analysis emerged as the most vital skill, with 40% of respondents identifying it as essential, highlighting the importance of data-driven decision-making in finance. Following closely, AI/machine learning knowledge received 35% of the responses, indicating a recognition of the growing role of technology in the industry. Communication and collaboration skills (30%) are also deemed important, reflecting the need for professionals to work effectively in teams, especially in a technology-integrated environment. Adaptability to technology (25%) signifies the need for finance professionals to embrace continuous learning. The relatively lower emphasis on ethical governance (15%) suggests that while important, it may not be perceived as an immediate skill requirement. The low percentage for "Other" (5%) implies that respondents mainly see the listed skills as pivotal for future success in finance.

Section 6: Role of Human Professionals

Table 17. Skills for Human Professionals in an AI-Driven Financial Ecosystem

Skill	Number of Responses	Percentile (%)
Data analysis and interpretation	45	45.0%
Understanding AI and machine learning models	40	40.0%
Soft skills (communication, leadership)	30	30.0%
Ethical decision-making	20	20.0%
Strategic thinking	35	35.0%
Other (please specify)	5	5.0%
Total	100	100%

Table 17 presents the skills human professionals recognize as vital for adaptation in an AI-driven financial ecosystem. The leading skill, data analysis and interpretation (45%), reflects a strong emphasis on the ability to derive insights from data, a key aspect of leveraging AI technologies. Following closely, understanding AI and machine learning models (40%) signifies the necessity for professionals to be knowledgeable about the technologies that underpin AI applications in finance. Strategic thinking (35%) is also essential, indicating a need for professionals to approach decision-making with a broader perspective. The importance of soft skills (30%) highlights the ongoing need for interpersonal communication and leadership abilities in technology-driven environments. While ethical decision-making (20%) is crucial, it appears to be less prioritized compared to technical skills. The low responses for "Other" (5%) suggest that the skills listed encompass the key areas identified for adaptation, reflecting a clear path for professionals navigating the evolving landscape of finance influenced by AI.

Table 18. Evolving Roles of Human Professionals with AI Adoption

Role Evolution Perspective	Number of Responses	Percentile (%)
Reduced involvement due to automation	20	20.0%
Collaboration with AI for enhanced decision-making	50	50.0%
Leadership roles in overseeing AI systems	25	25.0%
No significant changes	5	5.0%
Total	100	100%

Table 18 illustrates how professionals envision their roles evolving alongside increased AI adoption in finance and auditing. The dominant perspective, collaboration with AI for enhanced decision-making (50%), highlights a belief that AI will serve as a tool to enhance human judgment rather than replace it. This signifies an adaptive shift where professionals leverage AI's capabilities to make more informed decisions. Following this, leadership roles in overseeing AI systems (25%) suggest that professionals anticipate taking on more responsibilities related to the governance and oversight of AI technologies. Meanwhile, only 20% foresee reduced involvement due to automation, indicating a recognition of the value human insight brings to the financial sector. A small fraction (5%) predicts no significant changes, reflecting a more traditional view of the profession's evolution.

Section 7: Predictive Analytics and Automation

Table 19. Potential of Predictive Analytics in Financial Decision-Making

Rating of Predictive Analytics Potential	Number of Responses	Percentile (%)
Very low	5	5.0%
Low	10	10.0%
Moderate	30	30.0%
High	35	35.0%
Very high	20	20.0%
Total	100	100%

Table 19 presents participants' ratings of the potential of predictive analytics to transform financial decision-making. The data reveals a positive outlook, with 35% rating its potential as high, indicating a strong belief in its effectiveness for enhancing decision-making processes. Additionally, 20% rated it as very high, further supporting the notion that predictive analytics is seen as a transformative tool in finance. A combined total of 65% of respondents rated predictive analytics as either high or very high, showcasing a significant consensus on its transformative potential. In contrast, only 5% rated it as very low, suggesting that skepticism towards predictive analytics is minimal.

Table 20. Areas of Financial Operations Affected by Automation in the Next 5 Years

Area of Financial Operations	Number of Responses	Percentile (%)
Risk management	30	30.0%
Regulatory reporting	25	25.0%
Client advisory services	20	20.0%
Audit processes	15	15.0%
Trading	25	25.0%
Other (please specify)	5	5.0%
Total	100	100%

Table 20 summarizes the areas of financial operations projected to be most impacted by automation in the next five years. Risk management emerged as the most affected area, with 30% of respondents indicating it will undergo significant transformation due to automation. Following closely, regulatory reporting and trading were noted by 25% of respondents each, highlighting their importance in the evolving financial landscape. Client advisory services (20%) and audit processes (15%) also reflect substantial potential for automation. The mention of "Other" (5%) indicates some participants foresee additional areas not explicitly listed. Overall, this data suggests a clear trend towards greater automation across various financial operations.

Table 21. Belief in AI Replacing Human Judgment in High-Stakes Investment Decisions

Response	Number of Responses	Percentile (%)
Yes	20	20.0%
No	50	50.0%
Partially, with human oversight	30	30.0%
Total	100	100%

Table 21 illustrates participants' beliefs regarding AI's potential to replace human judgment in high-stakes investment decisions. A significant majority (50%) believe that AI will not be able to replace human judgment entirely, indicating a strong preference for human involvement in critical decision-making. Conversely, 20% of respondents are optimistic about AI's capability to replace human judgment, while 30% see a partial replacement as feasible, provided there is human oversight. These findings underscore the importance of balancing technological advancements with human intuition and expertise, especially in high-stakes financial environments.

Table 22. Overall Perspective on the Future of AI in Finance, Auditing, and Investment

Perspective	Number of Responses	Percentile (%)
Highly optimistic	25	25.0%
Cautiously optimistic	40	40.0%
Neutral	20	20.0%
Pessimistic	15	15.0%
Total	100	100%

Table 22 presents participants' overall perspectives on the future of AI in finance, auditing, and investment. The majority (40%) express a cautiously optimistic viewpoint, suggesting that while they recognize the potential benefits of AI, they are also aware of the challenges and uncertainties associated with its implementation. Additionally, 25% are highly optimistic about AI's future role, while 20% maintain a neutral stance. Conversely, a smaller group (15%) is pessimistic regarding AI's future impact. This distribution reflects a generally positive outlook tempered by a cautious approach to the evolving landscape of AI in the financial sector.

5. FINDINGS, RECOMMENDATION, SUGGESTION AND CONCLUSION

Findings

- A significant proportion of respondents, 35%, reported being very familiar with AI technologies.
- The majority view AI as having a substantial impact, with 35% selecting "Very much" and 20% opting for "Extremely," indicating strong confidence in its transformative role in finance, auditing, and investment sectors.
- Respondents anticipate significant AI impact in key areas: Investment Strategies (60%), Risk Assessment (50%), Fraud Detection (45%), and Customer Service (40%), underscoring AI's broad potential across the financial landscape.
- Predictive analytics and machine learning are the predominant AI technologies being adopted, whereas blockchain technology remains less prevalent, highlighting the critical role of predictive tools in finance.
- Respondents noted considerable improvements in operational efficiency attributed to AI, reinforcing its transformative impact on business processes.
- A significant majority (80%) believe AI will likely or very likely dominate future financial decision-making, reflecting strong optimism regarding its potential.
- Ethical challenges associated with AI usage in finance and auditing are recognized by 70% of respondents, demonstrating a heightened awareness of these concerns, with only 20% dissenting.
- Half of the respondents (50%) consider current regulatory frameworks somewhat effective, while 25% deem them ineffective, indicating the need for enhancement in AI risk management practices.
- Ensuring data privacy and security (68.75%) and developing transparency guidelines (56.25%) are prioritized as crucial areas, reflecting a strong demand for ethical standards in AI deployment.
- The skills deemed most essential for finance professionals include data analysis (40%) and AI/machine learning knowledge (35%), highlighting the necessity for data-driven decision-making and technological integration.
- Top skills for adaptation identified are data analysis (45%) and understanding AI (40%), emphasizing the need for technical proficiency and strategic thinking in an AI-driven financial landscape.
- A majority (50%) foresee their roles evolving to collaborate with AI, while 25% anticipate leadership positions managing AI systems, showcasing proactive adaptation to AI integration in finance and auditing.

- A substantial 65% of respondents perceive the potential of predictive analytics as high or very high, underscoring its transformative influence on financial decision-making, with only 5% rating it very low.
- Risk management (30%) and trading (25%) are viewed as the areas most affected by automation, indicating a significant shift in financial operations anticipated over the next five years.
- A majority (50%) assert that AI cannot fully replace human judgment in high-stakes investment decisions, underscoring the critical role of human oversight and intuition.
- Overall, 40% hold a cautiously optimistic outlook on AI's future in finance, reflecting a balanced perspective of hope and concern regarding its evolving role in the industry.
- AI and machine learning significantly transform finance by enhancing algorithmic trading, risk management, and personalized services, although ethical challenges such as data privacy and bias remain critical concerns that must be addressed.
- A comprehensive review of over two decades of AI research in finance identified ten main research streams, emphasizing the need for further exploration into AI's impact on disruptive technologies.
- The integration of AI technologies in Fintech lending has led to quicker credit decisions, benefiting both lenders and consumers while streamlining operational processes.
- Algorithmic trading has improved market liquidity and efficiency by reducing spreads and enhancing trade-related price discovery, indicating a positive impact on financial markets.
- AI-powered trading strategies, including advanced neural networks, have demonstrated superior performance in predicting market movements and optimizing investment strategies, outperforming traditional models
- AI-based financial decision support systems play a crucial role in enhancing risk management and decision-making processes, potentially preventing global financial crises.
- The integration of AI in auditing enhances efficiency and effectiveness, yet it introduces challenges such as the need for ethical evaluations and the management of legal and technological risks associated with algorithmic decision-making

REFERENCES

Abedin, M., Abbasi, A., & Seidmann, A. (2019). AI in financial decision support systems: Lessons from the 2008 financial crisis. *Expert Systems with Applications, 122*, 196–210. DOI: 10.1016/j.eswa.2018.12.016

Abraham, R., Dahya, J., & Fernandes, T. (2019). Robo-advisors, passive investing, and risk: Implications for inexperienced investors. *Journal of Asset Management, 15*(3), 209–221.

Accenture. (2015). *Robo-advisors and client relationship dynamics: Importance of life-stage adaptability*. Accenture Consulting Whitepaper.

Acunto, D., Lange, B., & Sanders, W. (2018). Robo-advisors and financial inclusion: Benefits for underserved groups. *Journal of Economic Inclusion, 10*(1), 94–112.

Agnihotri, S., Singh, K., & Verma, P. (2023). Algorithmic trading and liquidity: Implications for hedging and market operations. *Journal of Quantitative Finance, 21*(3), 311–329.

AI Ethics Impact Group. (2020). *Towards a framework for AI ethics in society*. AI Ethics Impact Group.

Aït-Sahalia, Y., & Brunetti, C. (2020). Impact of algorithmic and high-frequency trading on market volatility. *The Journal of Economic Perspectives, 34*(3), 47–66.

Aït-Sahalia, Y., & Brunetti, C. (2020). Volatility and the role of high-frequency trading in the S&P500 eMini market. *Journal of Futures Markets, 40*(8), 1325–1342.

Aït-Sahalia, Y., Laeven, R. J. A., & Pelger, M. (2012). The advantages of speed in algorithmic trading: A semimartingale approach. *Econometrica, 80*(6), 2415–2440.

Amelot, P., Darné, O., & Ferrière, G. (2021). Advanced AI models in financial forecasting: Comparing NARX with traditional approaches. *Computational Economics, 57*(2), 301–322. DOI: 10.1007/s10614-021-10121-4

Andersen, T. G., Bollerslev, T., & Diebold, F. X. (2012). High-frequency trading and volatility: Insights into causation and market impact. *Journal of Financial Econometrics, 10*(1), 63–91.

Arumugam, D., Jayaraman, S., & Kumar, S. (2023). Differential impact of algorithmic vs. non-algorithmic traders on market volatility. *Global Finance Journal, 40*(2), 89–104.

Bahoo, S., Nasir, M. A., & Ali, R. (2024). A comprehensive review of artificial intelligence applications in finance: Insights from two decades of research. *Financial Innovations Journal, 28*(2), 34–56. DOI: 10.1016/j.fininnov.2024.03.002

Balwani, M., Patil, A., & Shah, N. (2019). Factors influencing robo-advisor adoption: Personalization, control, and performance. *Journal of Digital Finance, 6*(1), 58–76.

Bhatia, S., Yadav, R., & Bhargava, M. (2020). Behavioral biases in robo-advisor programming: Human error and oversight considerations. *Financial Review Journal, 9*(2), 134–149.

Bibler, L., King, D., & Young, E. (2023). Innovation in auditing: Enhancing fraud detection through data-driven capabilities. *Journal of Auditing and Fraud Detection, 9*(1), 1–20.

Black, M., Jones, T., & Chan, Y. (2020). Fairness and ethics in AI: Developing methodologies for unbiased algorithm outcomes. *Journal of Artificial Intelligence Ethics, 23*(3), 327–339.

Briggs, J., & Kodnani, D. (2023). The potentially large effects of artificial intelligence on economic growth. Goldman Sachs. https://www.gspublishing.com/content/research/en/reports/2023/03/27/d64e052b-0f6e-45d7-967b-d7be35fabd16.html

Brown, I., Osman, A., & Karatkevich, L. (2021). Accountability and fairness in algorithmic systems: A framework for ethical audits. *Journal of Technology and Ethics, 29*(4), 1042–1061.

Bucci, P. (2020). Advanced neural networks for financial market forecasting: Applications of LSTM and NARX models. *International Journal of Forecasting, 36*(4), 1250–1262. DOI: 10.1016/j.ijforecast.2020.05.010

Budish, E., Cramton, P., & Shim, J. (2015). High-frequency trading networks: Trade-offs in speed, liquidity, and stability. *The Quarterly Journal of Economics, 130*(4), 1547–1621. DOI: 10.1093/qje/qjv027

Buti, S., Rindi, B., & Werner, I. (2011). The privacy benefits and challenges of algorithmic trading for institutional and retail investors. *European Financial Journal, 4*(2), 210–225.

Chugh, R., Patel, M., & Sharma, L. (2024). Balancing algorithmic trading and human oversight to stabilize market volatility. *Financial Markets and Trading, 15*(1), 72–88.

Creamer, G. G. (2012). Machine learning for algorithmic trading in high-frequency trading futures markets. *Journal of Trading, 7*(3), 41–48. DOI: 10.3905/jot.2012.7.3.041

Cucculelli, M., & Recanatini, F. (2022). AI and the transformation of financial intermediation: Evidence from European banks. *Journal of Banking & Finance, 137*, 106453. DOI: 10.1016/j.jbankfin.2022.106453

Deloitte. (2024). *How AI is transforming investment management: Enhancing alpha, efficiency, and risk management*. Deloitte Insights.

Dignum, V. (2020). *Responsible Artificial Intelligence: How to Develop and Use AI in a Responsible Way*. Springer Nature.

Dignum, V. (2020). Addressing AI's transparency and bias issues: The necessity of ethical oversight. *AI and Ethics, 1*, 109–121. DOI: 10.1007/s43681-020-00001-4

Drakonakis, K., Leung, K., Yang, C., & Hatzivasilis, G. (2020). Automated black-box auditing in web authentication: Securing digital systems through advanced auditing frameworks. *Computer Networks, 178*, 107342. DOI: 10.1016/j.comnet.2020.107342

Durango-Gutiérrez, H., Ramírez, M., & De la Hoz, E. (2021). AI-enhanced financial analysis: Integrating traditional and machine learning methods. *Journal of Financial Analytics, 45*(1), 91–108.

Eilifsen, A., Hamilton, E., & Messier, W. F. (2020). Audit data analytics: Challenges and opportunities. *Auditing, 39*(2), 45–69. DOI: 10.2308/ajpt-52658

Eulerich, M., Van der Tas, L., & Machiels, J. (2022). Integrating robotic process automation in audit tasks: Efficiency and effectiveness in audit practices. *International Journal of Auditing, 26*(1), 56–72. DOI: 10.1111/ijau.12208

Fernandes, M., Medeiros, M. C., & Scharth, M. (2014). Forecasting and modeling volatility with the VIX index. *Journal of Financial and Quantitative Analysis, 49*(1), 267–291. DOI: 10.1017/S0022109014000098

Floridi, L., & Cowls, J. (2018). Continuous oversight of AI: Adaptable auditing processes for evolving technology. *AI & Society, 33*(1), 45–56.

Floridi, L., Cowls, J., Beltrametti, M., Chatila, R., Chazerand, P., Dignum, V., Luetge, C., Madelin, R., Pagallo, U., Rossi, F., Schafer, B., Valcke, P., & Vayena, E. (2022). The European AI Act and its implications: A procedural framework for conformity assessments in AI. *AI & Society, 38*, 1285–1299. DOI: 10.1007/s00146-021-01258-5

Frankenfield, J. (2021). Artificial intelligence (AI): Definition, how it works, and examples. Investopedia. https://www.investopedia.com/terms/a/artificial-intelligence-ai.asp

Frino, A., Mollica, V., & Webb, R. I. (2017). The impact of algorithmic trading on market quality: Evidence from a natural experiment. *Journal of Financial Markets, 32*, 87–103. DOI: 10.1016/j.finmar.2017.03.002

Funahashi, K. (2020). Hybrid models in option pricing: ANNs and asymptotic expansion. *Quantitative Finance, 20*(5), 760–774. DOI: 10.1080/14697688.2020.1712467

Galeshchuk, S., & Mukherjee, K. (2017). AI for forecasting exchange rates: A comparative approach. *International Journal of Forecasting, 33*(4), 1022–1042. DOI: 10.1016/j.ijforecast.2017.03.003

Hendershott, T., Jones, C. M., & Menkveld, A. J. (2011). Does algorithmic trading improve liquidity? *The Journal of Finance, 66*(1), 1–33. DOI: 10.1111/j.1540-6261.2010.01624.x

Heston, S. L., & Sinha, N. R. (2017). News and social media effects on stock prices. *Journal of Financial Economics, 126*(1), 71–88. DOI: 10.1016/j.jfineco.2017.06.002

Holopainen, M., & Sarlin, P. (2017). AI in systemic risk monitoring: Applications for macroprudential supervision. *Journal of Economic Dynamics & Control, 77*, 151–175. DOI: 10.1016/j.jedc.2017.01.013

Jagtiani, J., & John, K. (2018). Fintech lending and credit decision-making: Implications for borrowers and financial institutions. *Journal of Financial Economics, 129*(3), 536–552. DOI: 10.1016/j.jfineco.2018.06.007

Jang, B., & Lee, J. (2019). Artificial neural networks in option pricing models: A comparative study. *Journal of Derivatives, 26*(3), 60–75. DOI: 10.3905/jod.2019.26.3.060

Kelejian, H., & Mukerji, A. (2016). Volatility and market efficiency in high-frequency trading. *Journal of Financial Studies, 8*(3), 220–236. DOI: 10.1080/10508422.2016.114000

Kercheval, A. N., & Zhang, Y. (2015). Modeling high-frequency limit order book dynamics with machine learning. *Quantitative Finance, 15*(8), 1315–1329. DOI: 10.1080/14697688.2015.1032546

Kim, J. H., & Kim, Y. H. (2020). AI-driven index tracking and portfolio optimization. *Journal of Portfolio Management, 46*(4), 45–60. DOI: 10.3905/jpm.2020.46.4.045

Kokina, J., & Davenport, T. H. (2017). The emergence of artificial intelligence: How automation is transforming the auditing profession. *Journal of Emerging Technologies in Accounting, 14*(2), 115–122. DOI: 10.2308/jeta-51730

Koshiyama, A., Kazim, E., Braines, D., & Dobbins, M. (2021). Algorithm auditing: Managing the legal, ethical, and technological risks of AI and machine learning. *Journal of Responsible Technology*, *5*, 100017. DOI: 10.1016/j.jrt.2021.100017

Lahmiri, S. (2016). Comparing traditional and AI-driven credit risk models for consumer loans. *Applied Economics Letters*, *23*(7), 510–515. DOI: 10.1080/13504851.2015.1083074

Loos, B., Sauer, A., & Wiederkehr, C. (2020). Enhanced portfolio diversification and reduced home bias through robo-advisory platforms. *Journal of Financial Economics*, *14*(4), 225–242.

Loukeris, N., & Eleftheriadis, D. (2015). Asset allocation strategies with bankruptcy detection for enhanced investment decision-making. *European Financial Management Journal*, *21*(2), 310–329. DOI: 10.1111/eufm.2015.00233

Martinelli, A., Mina, A., & Windrum, P. (2021). Digital innovation and the evolution of market structures. *Research Policy*, *50*(9), 104321. DOI: 10.1016/j.respol.2021.104321

Menkveld, A. J. (2013). Does high-frequency trading cause market volatility? Evidence from trader withdrawal scenarios. *Financial Markets and Portfolio Management*, *27*(4), 321–348.

Mökander, J., Axente, M., & Floridi, L. (2022). Ethics-based auditing in the European AI regulation: Designing conformity assessments for trustworthy AI. *AI and Ethics*, *2*(3), 247–259. DOI: 10.1007/s43681-021-00050-4

Mökander, J., & Floridi, L. (2022). The European Union's AI regulation and its impact on auditing: Guidelines for high-risk AI systems. *Journal of Responsible AI*, *2*(3), 234–248.

Omoteso, K. (2012). The application of artificial intelligence in auditing: Looking back to the future. *Expert Systems with Applications*, *39*(9), 8490–8495. DOI: 10.1016/j.eswa.2012.01.098

Pendergast, M. (2024). AI's transformative effects on finance: Decision-making, risk management, and efficiency. *Financial Innovation and Technology Journal*, *18*(1), 44–58.

Petukhina, A., Trimborn, S., Härdle, W. K., & Elendner, H. (2021). Cryptocurrency trading dynamics and the role of AI and human expertise. *Journal of Banking & Finance*, *122*, 106224. DOI: 10.1016/j.jbankfin.2020.106224

Pichl, L., & Kaizoji, T. (2017). Volatility and sentiment analysis in cryptocurrency markets: A HAR model application. *Finance Research Letters*, *22*, 116–121. DOI: 10.1016/j.frl.2016.10.009

Raj, M., & Seamans, R. (2019). AI, labor, productivity, and the need for firm-level data. In Agrawal, A., Gans, J., & Goldfarb, A. (Eds.), *The economics of artificial intelligence: An agenda* (pp. 553–565). University of Chicago Press. DOI: 10.7208/chicago/9780226613475.003.0022

Sabău Popa, C., Ioan, D., & Moga, M. (2021). AI classifiers for financial performance prediction. *Economic Computation and Economic Cybernetics Studies and Research*, *55*(3), 195–212.

Sander, L. (2021). Human decision-making in the era of robo-advisors: Balancing prediction and discretion. *Journal of Behavioral Finance*, *8*(4), 456–470.

Savi, R., Shen, J., Tsaig, Y., & Dufour, T. (2024). AI-driven advancements in investment strategy: Market themes, text analysis, and decision-making tools. *Journal of Financial Technology and Analytics*, *8*(2), 45–67.

Shivram, V. (2024). Auditing with AI: A theoretical framework for applying machine learning across the internal audit lifecycle. *EDPACS*, *69*(1), 22–40. DOI: 10.1080/07366981.2024.2312025

Shneiderman, B. (2020). Bridging the gap between ethics and practice: Guidelines for creating reliable, safe, and trustworthy AI systems. *Communications of the ACM*, *63*(3), 54–63. DOI: 10.1145/3359629

Tao, M., Wei, Z., & Wang, H. (2021). Cost-effective portfolio management across risk models: Robo-advisor efficiencies. *International Journal of Portfolio Management*, *22*(3), 312–328.

Thangavel, K., & Varalakshmi, P. (2020). Secure cloud data storage with ternary hash tree framework: Enhancing user trust through audit verification. *Journal of Information Security and Applications*, *53*, 102498. DOI: 10.1016/j.jisa.2020.102498

The Institute of Internal Auditors. (2022). *International Standards for the Professional Practice of Internal Auditing (Standards)*. The Institute of Internal Auditors.

Wang, Y., Li, X., & Wei, Q. (2020). Enhancing procurement audit compliance with AI-based frameworks: Automation and efficiency in auditing practices. *Journal of Financial Regulation and Compliance*, *28*(1), 67–78. DOI: 10.1108/JFRC-01-2019-0010

Wanke, P., Azad, M. A. K., & Barros, C. P. (2016). Efficiency in Malaysian Islamic banks: A comparative analysis. *International Journal of Islamic and Middle Eastern Finance and Management, 9*(4), 545–564. DOI: 10.1108/IMEFM-01-2015-0006

William & Mary. (2024). *The transformative impact of AI and machine learning on finance: Algorithmic trading, risk management, and personalized services*. William & Mary Financial Studies.

Yin, L., Wang, H., & Li, S. (2020). Social media sentiment analysis for stock market prediction: A case study with Twitter data. *Journal of Financial Markets, 50*, 100536. DOI: 10.1016/j.finmar.2020.100536

Yoon, H., Koo, B., & Shin, Y. (2021). Early auditing systems in AI: Risk management and continuous monitoring. *The Journal of Auditory Research, 36*(3), 234–249. DOI: 10.1002/jar.2159

Yoon, K., Hoogduin, L., & Zhang, L. (2021). Real-time auditing of data-driven processes: A layered structure for continuous auditing. *Journal of Accounting and Public Policy, 40*(2), 106812. DOI: 10.1016/j.jaccpubpol.2021.106812

Zhao, X., Zhang, H., & Wu, L. (2018). AI-based prediction models for portfolio selection and risk assessment. *Journal of Asset Management, 19*(5), 356–372. DOI: 10.1057/s41260-018-0085-2

Conclusion

Artificial intelligence is fundamentally transforming the architecture of modern finance, auditing, and investment. Across these sectors, AI has emerged not merely as a technological enhancement but as a strategic force reshaping institutional behavior, market structures, and regulatory frameworks. From advanced analytics in investment decision-making to intelligent automation in auditing and risk management, the integration of AI has introduced unprecedented levels of efficiency, accuracy, and agility. This transformation is not confined to traditional financial systems alone—it is extending into commercial banking, insurance, and Islamic finance, each adapting to AI in ways that reflect their operational models, regulatory environments, and ethical frameworks.

Commercial banks are leveraging AI to deepen customer engagement, optimize lending practices, and reinforce cybersecurity. Insurance companies are adopting AI to automate claims processing, refine pricing strategies, and enhance risk prediction. Meanwhile, Islamic financial institutions are cautiously embracing AI, balancing innovation with the imperative of religious compliance. This convergence of finance and technology is also unfolding within the broader context of sustainability, as environmental, social, and governance (ESG) factors increasingly influence capital allocation, corporate behavior, and investor expectations. AI is facilitating the integration of ESG principles by improving data collection, transparency, and performance monitoring, thereby reinforcing the shift toward responsible and sustainable finance.

Despite these advancements, the widespread adoption of AI brings with it profound challenges. Issues related to data governance, algorithmic bias, ethical accountability, and regulatory oversight remain unresolved. The growing reliance on opaque machine-learning systems raises questions about explainability and trust, while the potential displacement of human labor necessitates rethinking the future of work in financial services. Moreover, in regions with limited digital infrastructure or institutional capacity, the benefits of AI may remain unevenly distributed.

This book has sought to provide a comprehensive analysis of AI's multifaceted impact on finance, auditing, and investment. As the financial sector continues to evolve in response to technological, environmental, and societal pressures, the role of AI will become increasingly central to shaping its future trajectory. The key challenge for policymakers, practitioners, and academics alike is to harness the transformative potential of AI while ensuring that innovation is aligned with principles of inclusiveness, transparency, and sustainability. The next phase of financial evolution will not be defined solely by technological capability, but by the collective ability to integrate AI responsibly into the fabric of global finance.

Compilation of References

Abdelazim, H. Y., & Wahba, K. (2006). An artificial intelligence approach to portfolio selection and management. *International Journal of Financial Services Management*, *1*(2-3), 243–254. DOI: 10.1504/IJFSM.2006.009629

Abdulla, Y. Y., & Al-Alawi, A. I. (2024). Advances in Machine Learning for Financial Risk Management: A Systematic Literature Review. *2024 ASU International Conference in Emerging Technologies for Sustainability and Intelligent Systems, ICETSIS 2024*, 531–535. DOI: 10.1109/ICETSIS61505.2024.10459536

Abdulsalam, T. A., & Tajudeen, R. B. (2024). Artificial Intelligence (AI) in the Banking Industry: A Review of Service Areas and Customer Service Journeys in Emerging Economies. *Business & Management Compass*, *68*(3), 19–43. DOI: 10.56065/9hfvrq20

Abedin, M., Abbasi, A., & Seidmann, A. (2019). AI in financial decision support systems: Lessons from the 2008 financial crisis. *Expert Systems with Applications*, *122*, 196–210. DOI: 10.1016/j.eswa.2018.12.016

Abraham, R., Dahya, J., & Fernandes, T. (2019). Robo-advisors, passive investing, and risk: Implications for inexperienced investors. *Journal of Asset Management*, *15*(3), 209–221.

Academy, F. C. (2024). *AI-Powered AML: Unveiling The Next Generation Of Financial Crime Detection*. Financial Crime Academy Blog.

Accenture. (2015). *Robo-advisors and client relationship dynamics: Importance of life-stage adaptability*. Accenture Consulting Whitepaper.

Accountancy, J. o. (2024). What AI Can Do for Auditors. *Journal of Accountancy*, 1–5.

Acemoglu, D., & Restrepo, P. (2020). Robots and jobs: Evidence from US labor markets. *Journal of Political Economy*, *128*(6), 2188–2244. DOI: 10.1086/705716

Acunto, D., Lange, B., & Sanders, W. (2018). Robo-advisors and financial inclusion: Benefits for underserved groups. *Journal of Economic Inclusion*, *10*(1), 94–112.

Addy, W. A., Ajayi-nifise, A. O., Bello, B. G., & Tula, S. T. (2024). Machine learning in financial markets : A critical review of algorithmic trading and risk management. *International Journal of Science and Research Archive*, *11*(01), 1853–1862. DOI: 10.30574/ijsra.2024.11.1.0292

Adeyelu, O. O., Ugochukwu, C. E., & Shonibare, M. A. (2024). AUTOMATING FINANCIAL REGULATORY COMPLIANCE WITH AI: A REVIEW AND APPLICATION SCENARIOS. *Finance & Accounting Research Journal*, *6*(4), 580–601. DOI: 10.51594/farj.v6i4.1035

Advisor, G. (2021). *GDPR Compliance in Accounting: Protecting Financial Data*. GDPR Advisor.

Aggarwal, D., Chandrasekaran, S., & Annamalai, B. (2020). A complete empirical ensemble mode decomposition and support vector machine-based approach to predict Bitcoin prices. *Journal of Behavioral and Experimental Finance*, *27*, 27. DOI: 10.1016/j.jbef.2020.100335

Agnihotri, S., Singh, K., & Verma, P. (2023). Algorithmic trading and liquidity: Implications for hedging and market operations. *Journal of Quantitative Finance*, *21*(3), 311–329.

Agu, E. E., Abhulimen, A. O., Obiki-Osafiele, A. N., Osundare, O. S., Adeniran, I. A., & Efunniyi, C. P. (2024). Discussing ethical considerations and solutions for ensuring fairness in AI-driven financial services. International Journal of Frontier Research in Science, 3(2), 001-009.

Ahmad, A. Y. B., Gupta, P., Thimmiaraja, J., Goswami, B., Arun, M., Manoharan, G., & Younis, D. (2024). A Comparison of the Effects of Robotics and Artificial Intelligence on Business Management and Economics. In *Recent Advances in Management and Engineering* (pp. 132–137). CRC Press. DOI: 10.1201/9781003532026-22

Ahmed, F. (2022). Ethical aspects of artificial intelligence in banking. *Journal of Research in Economics and Finance Management*, *1*(2), 55–63. DOI: 10.56596/jrefm.v1i2.7

Ahmed, I., Forde, B., Laplanche, R., Mitra, A., Prida Bay, N., & Scandurra, A. (2015). The Fintech Revolution. *London Business School Review*, *3*, 50–53.

AI Ethics Impact Group. (2020). *Towards a framework for AI ethics in society*. AI Ethics Impact Group.

Aitkazinov, A. (2023). The Role of Artificial Intelligence in Auditing: Opportunities and Challenges. *: Research Journal of Finance and Accounting*, 22-35.

Aït-Sahalia, Y., & Brunetti, C. (2020). Impact of algorithmic and high-frequency trading on market volatility. *The Journal of Economic Perspectives*, *34*(3), 47–66.

Aït-Sahalia, Y., & Brunetti, C. (2020). Volatility and the role of high-frequency trading in the S&P500 eMini market. *Journal of Futures Markets*, *40*(8), 1325–1342.

Aït-Sahalia, Y., Laeven, R. J. A., & Pelger, M. (2012). The advantages of speed in algorithmic trading: A semimartingale approach. *Econometrica*, *80*(6), 2415–2440.

Akbar, M. A., Khan, A. A., Mahmood, S., Rafi, S., & Demi, S. (2024). Trustworthy artificial intelligence: A decision-making taxonomy of potential challenges. *Software, Practice & Experience*, *54*(9), 1621–1650. DOI: 10.1002/spe.3216

Akyuwen, R., Nanere, M., & Ratten, V. (2022). Technology entrepreneurship: Fintech lending in Indonesia. In V. Ratten (Ed.), *Entrepreneurial innovation*. Studies on Entrepreneurship, Structural Change and Industrial Dynamics. Springer, Singapore. https://doi.org/DOI: 10.1007/978-981-16-4795-6_14

Alarabiat, A. A., & Al Hadidi, M. A. (2024). CONTINUOUS USE OF MOBILE BANKING APPLICATIONS: THE ROLE OF PROCESS VIRTUALIZABILITY, ANTHROPOMORPHISM AND VIRTUAL PROCESS FAILURE RISK. *Interdisciplinary Journal of Information, Knowledge & Management, 19.*

Al-Baity, H. H. (2023). The Artificial Intelligence Revolution in Digital Finance in Saudi Arabia: A Comprehensive Review and Proposed Framework. *Sustainability (Basel)*, *15*(18), 13725. Advance online publication. DOI: 10.3390/su151813725

Alevizos, L. (2025). Automated cybersecurity compliance and threat response using AI, blockchain and smart contracts. *International Journal of Information Technology : an Official Journal of Bharati Vidyapeeth's Institute of Computer Applications and Management*, *17*(2), 767–781.

Ali, A., Razak, S. A., Othman, S. H., Abdalla, T., Eisa, E., Al-dhaqm, A., Nasser, M., Elhassan, T., Elshafie, H., & Saif, A. (2022). applied sciences Financial Fraud Detection Based on Machine Learning : A Systematic Literature Review. Applied Sciences Review, 12(9637.). https://doi.org/DOI: 10.3390/app12199637

Allen, F., Gu, X., & Jagtiani, J. (2021). A Survey of Fintech Research and Policy Discussion. *Review of Corporate Finance*, *1*(3–4), 259–339. DOI: 10.1561/114.00000007

Almoubayyed, H., Bastoni, R., Berman, S. R., Galasso, S., Jensen, M., Lester, L., & Murphy, A. Swartz1, M., Weldon, K., Fancsali, S. E., Gropen, J., & Ritter, S. (2023). Rewriting Math Word Problems to Improve Learning Outcomes for Emerging Readers: A Randomized Field Trial in Carnegie Learning's MATHia. In Artificial Intelligence in Education (pp. 200–205). https://doi.org/DOI: 10.1007/978-3-031-36336-8_34

Alotaibi, E. M., & Alnesafi, A. (2023). Assessing the impact of audit software on audit quality: Auditors' perceptions. International Journal of Applied Economics. *Finance and Accounting*, *17*(1), 97–108.

Altman, E. I. (1968). Financial ratios, discriminant analysis and the prediction of corporate bankruptcy. *The Journal of Finance*, *23*(4), 589–609. DOI: 10.1111/j.1540-6261.1968.tb00843.x

Altman, E. I., Marco, G., & Varetto, F. (1994). Corporate distress diagnosis: Comparisons using linear discriminant analysis and neural networks (the Italian experience). *Journal of Banking & Finance*, *18*(3), 505–529. DOI: 10.1016/0378-4266(94)90007-8

Aman, A., Khan, M. A., Khan, M. A., Haider, A., Oláh, J., & Fenyves, V. (2023). Role of institutions in promoting finance in emerging markets: A panel data analysis. PLoS ONE, 18(3 March), 1–26. https://doi.org/DOI: 10.1371/journal.pone.0280849

Amelot, P., Darné, O., & Ferrière, G. (2021). Advanced AI models in financial forecasting: Comparing NARX with traditional approaches. *Computational Economics*, *57*(2), 301–322. DOI: 10.1007/s10614-021-10121-4

Analytics, L. (2022). *Mitigating Risks in Financial Services Using Predictive Analytics*. LatentView Blog.

Ananthan, M., Shanmugam, V., Udayanan, M., Selvaraj, F., & Manoharan, G. (2024, June). Corporate social responsibility is used as a marketing strategy during Covid-19 pandemic. In AIP Conference Proceedings (Vol. 2971, No. 1). AIP Publishing. DOI: 10.1063/5.0195948

Andersen, T. G., Bollerslev, T., & Diebold, F. X. (2012). High-frequency trading and volatility: Insights into causation and market impact. *Journal of Financial Econometrics*, *10*(1), 63–91.

Andriosopoulos, D., Doumpos, M., Pardalos, P. M., & Zopounidis, C. (2019). Computational approaches and data analytics in financial services : A literature review. *The Journal of the Operational Research Society*, *70*(10), 1–19. DOI: 10.1080/01605682.2019.1595193

Antwi, B. O., Adelakun, B. O., Fatogun, D. T., & Olaiya, O. P. (2024). Enhancing audit accuracy: The role of AI in detecting financial anomalies and fraud. *Finance & Accounting Research Journal*, *6*(6), 1049–1068. DOI: 10.51594/farj.v6i6.1235

Armstrong, A., & Li, Y. (2022). Governance and Sustainability in Local Government. *Australasian Accounting. Business and Finance Journal*, *16*(2), 12–31. DOI: 10.14453/aabfj.v16i2.3

Arner, D. W., Barberis, J., & Buckley, R. P. (2015). The evolution of Fintech: A new post-crisis paradigm. *SSRN*, *47*, 1271. DOI: 10.2139/ssrn.2676553

Arumugam, D., Jayaraman, S., & Kumar, S. (2023). Differential impact of algorithmic vs. non-algorithmic traders on market volatility. *Global Finance Journal*, *40*(2), 89–104.

Ashtikar, S. P., & Manoharan, G. (2024, June). Digital Transformation in Higher Education: A Pedagogical Perspective. In 2024 3rd International Conference on Computational Modelling, Simulation and Optimization (ICCMSO) (pp. 210-215). IEEE. DOI: 10.1109/ICCMSO61761.2024.00051

Ashtikar, S. P., & Manoharan, G. (2024, June). Work-Load Management and Job Gratification: A Study on the Work-life Equilibrium of Higher Education Instructors. In 2024 3rd International Conference on Computational Modelling, Simulation and Optimization (ICCMSO) (pp. 193-197). IEEE. DOI: 10.1109/ICCMSO61761.2024.00048

Associates, C. R. (2022). Insider Trading and Market Manipulation [Boston, Massachusetts, USA: Charles River Associates.]. *Literature Watch*, *Q4*, 2022.

Association, C. A. (n.d.). *Artificial Intelligence*. Chase Alumni Association.

Association, T. I. (2024). *Artificial Intelligence: Investment Management Perspectives*. The Investment Association.

Atadoga, A., Obi, O. C., Onwusinkwue, S., Dawodu, S. O., Osasona, F., & Daraojimba, A. I. (2024). AI's evolving impact in US banking: An insightful review. *International Journal of Science and Research Archive*, *11*(1), 904–922. DOI: 10.30574/ijsra.2024.11.1.0157

AuditBoard. (2023). *How AI Is Transforming Audit, Risk, and Compliance*. AuditBoard Blog.

Awosika, T., Shukla, R. M., & Pranggono, B. (2023). Transparency and Privacy: The Role of Explainable AI and Federated Learning in Financial Fraud Detection. *arXiv*, 6.

Ayling, J., & Chapman, A. (2022). Putting AI ethics to work: Are the tools fit for purpose? *AI and Ethics, 2*(3), 405–429. DOI: 10.1007/s43681-021-00084-x

Aziz, S., & Dowling, M. (2019). Machine learning and AI for risk management. In Disrupting finance: FinTech and strategy in the 21st century (pp. 33-50). DOI: 10.1007/978-3-030-02330-0_3

Azizi, M., Hakimi, M., Amiri, F., & Shahidzay, A. K. (2024). The Role of IT (Information Technology) Audit in Digital Transformation: Opportunities and Challenges. *Open Access Indonesia Journal of Social Sciences, 7*(2), 1473–1482. DOI: 10.37275/oaijss.v7i2.230

Aziz, S., & Dowling, M. M. (2018). AI and machine learning for risk management. In Lynn, T., Mooney, G., Rosati, P., & Cummins, M. (Eds.), *Disrupting Finance: FinTech and Strategy in the 21st Century* (pp. 33–50). Palgrave Macmillan.

Babaei, G., & Bamdad, S. (2020). A multi-objective instance-based decision support system for investment recommendation in peer-to-peer lending. *Expert Systems with Applications, 150*, 113278. DOI: 10.1016/j.eswa.2020.113278

Bahoo, S., Nasir, M. A., & Ali, R. (2024). A comprehensive review of artificial intelligence applications in finance: Insights from two decades of research. *Financial Innovations Journal, 28*(2), 34–56. DOI: 10.1016/j.fininnov.2024.03.002

Bakar, J. A., & Adzis, A. A. (2024). Fostering loyalty among young consumers: Strategic approaches for bank sustainability. *International Journal of Professional Business Review, 9*(3), e04469–e04469. DOI: 10.26668/businessreview/2024.v9i3.4469

Bakar, N. M., Abdul Rahman, R., & Ibrahim, Z. (2020). Client protection and sustainable performance in microfinance institution. *International Journal of Productivity and Performance Management, 69*(4), 651–665. DOI: 10.1108/IJPPM-03-2019-0127

Baker, H., Kumar, S., Goyal, K., & Sharma, A. (2021). International review of financial analysis: A retrospective evaluation between 1992 and 2020. *International Review of Financial Analysis, 78*, 78. DOI: 10.1016/j.irfa.2021.101946

Balavenu, R., Khan, A. K., Faisal, S. M., Sriprasadh, K., & Sisodia, D. R. (2022). An Empirical Investigation in Analysing the Proactive Approach of Artificial Intelligence in Regulating the Financial Sector. In Balas, V. E., Sinha, G. R., Agarwal, B., Sharma, T. K., Dadheech, P., & Mahrishi, M. (Eds.), *Emerging Technologies in Computer Engineering Cognitive Computing and Intelligent IoT* (Vol. 1591, pp. 90–98). Springer Nature Switzerland., DOI: 10.1007/978-3-031-07012-9_8

Baldauf, M., & Mollner, J. (2015). *High-frequency trading and market performance*. Stanford Inst. for Economic Policy Research.

Ballings, M., Poel, D., Hespeels, N., & Gryp, R. (2015). Evaluating multiple classifiers for stock price direction prediction. *Expert Systems with Applications, 42*(20), 7046–7056. DOI: 10.1016/j.eswa.2015.05.013

Balwani, M., Patil, A., & Shah, N. (2019). Factors influencing robo-advisor adoption: Personalization, control, and performance. *Journal of Digital Finance, 6*(1), 58–76.

Bansal, U., Bharatwal, S., Bagiyam, D. S., & Kismawadi, E. R. (2024). Fraud detection in the era of AI: Harnessing technology for a safer digital economy. In *AI-Driven Decentralized Finance and the Future of Finance* (pp. 143–164). DOI: 10.4018/979-8-3693-6321-8.ch006

Bao, T., Nekrasova, E., Neugebauer, T., & Riyanto, Y. E. (2022). Algorithmic trading in experimental markets with human traders: A literature survey. In Handbook of Experimental Finance (pp. 302–322). DOI: 10.4337/9781800372337.00030

Barron's. (2024). SoFi Debuts Revamped Robo-Advisor: New Fee, More Investment Options. *Barron's*. (BCG), B. C. (2024). *The Power of AI in Financial Planning and Forecasting*. Boston, Massachusetts, USA: Boston Consulting Group.

Barron's. (2024, October 10). AI Can Pick Stocks. How It Stands Up Against Wall Street Pros. *Barron's*.

Beccalli, E., Elliot, V., & Virili, F. (2020). *Artificial Intelligence and Ethics in Portfolio Management. Digital Business Transformation, 38*. Springer.

Bejjar, M. A., & Siala, Y. (2024). Machine learning: A revolution in accounting. In *Artificial Intelligence Approaches to Sustainable Accounting* (pp. 110–134). IGI Global., DOI: 10.4018/979-8-3693-0847-9.ch007

Beketov, M., Lehmann, K., & Wittke, M. (2018). Robo Advisors: Quantitative methods inside the robots. *Journal of Asset Management, 19*(6), 363–370. DOI: 10.1057/s41260-018-0092-9

Belanche, D., Casaló, L. V., & Flavián, C. (2019). Artificial Intelligence in FinTech: Understanding robo-advisors adoption among customers. *Industrial Management & Data Systems, 119*(7), 1411–1430. DOI: 10.1108/IMDS-08-2018-0368

Belanche, D., Casaló, L. V., & Guinalíu, M. (2012). Website usability, consumer satisfaction and the intention to use a website: The moderating effect of perceived risk. *Journal of Retailing and Consumer Services, 19*(1), 124–132. DOI: 10.1016/j.jretconser.2011.11.001

Belgium, K. (2022). *Staying One Step Ahead: BlackRock's Aladdin*. KPMG Insights.

Benhamou, E., Saltiel, D., Ohana, J., Atif, J., & Laraki, R. (2020). Deep Reinforcement Learning (DRL) for portfolio allocation. The European Conference on Machine Learning and Principles and Practice of Knowledge Discovery in Database - ECML PKKDD. *Proceedings*, *12461*, 527–531.

Bhardwaj, A., Ranjan, O., Biswas, S., Gupta, L., Chanti, Y., & Sharma, M. (2024, March). Risk Assessment and Management in Stock Trading using Artificial Intelligence. In 2024 3rd International Conference on Sentiment Analysis and Deep Learning (ICSADL) (pp. 138-145). IEEE. DOI: 10.1109/ICSADL61749.2024.00029

Bhatia, A., Chandani, A., & Chhateja, J. (2020). Robo advisory and its potential in addressing the behavioral biases of investors — A qualitative study in Indian context. *Journal of Behavioral and Experimental Finance*, *25*, 25. DOI: 10.1016/j.jbef.2020.100281

Bhatia, A., Chandani, A., Divekar, R., Mehta, M., & Vijay, N. (2022). Digital innovation in wealth management landscape: The moderating role of robo advisors in behavioural biases and investment decision-making. *International Journal of Innovation Science*, *14*(3/4), 693–712. DOI: 10.1108/IJIS-10-2020-0245

Bhatia, S., Yadav, R., & Bhargava, M. (2020). Behavioral biases in robo-advisor programming: Human error and oversight considerations. *Financial Review Journal*, *9*(2), 134–149.

Bhattacherjee, A. (2000). Acceptance of e-commerce services: The case of electronic brokerages. *IEEE Transactions on Systems, Man, and Cybernetics. Part A, Systems and Humans*, *30*(4), 411–420. DOI: 10.1109/3468.852435

Bhavya, K. R., Dharmaraj, A., Pareek, P., Sathe, M. A., Tiwari, M., & Manoharan, G. (2023, September). Application of Soft Computing Techniques for Predictive Analytics in Financial Markets. In 2023 6th International Conference on Contemporary Computing and Informatics (IC3I) (Vol. 6, pp. 1756-1760). IEEE.

Bhuiyan, M. S. (2024). The role of AI-Enhanced personalization in customer experiences. *Journal of Computer Science and Technology Studies*, *6*(1), 162–169. DOI: 10.32996/jcsts.2024.6.1.17

Bibler, L., King, D., & Young, E. (2023). Innovation in auditing: Enhancing fraud detection through data-driven capabilities. *Journal of Auditing and Fraud Detection*, *9*(1), 1–20.

BioCatch. (2024). *2024 AI Fraud Financial Crime Survey.* Tel Aviv, Israel.: BioCatch.
(BIS), B. f. (2024). *Regulating AI in the Financial Sector: Recent Developments and Main Challenges.* Basel, Switzerland: Bank for International Settlements.

Black, M., Jones, T., & Chan, Y. (2020). Fairness and ethics in AI: Developing methodologies for unbiased algorithm outcomes. *Journal of Artificial Intelligence Ethics, 23*(3), 327–339.

BlackRock. (2024). *How AI is Transforming Investing*. BlackRock Insights.

BlackRock. (2025). *Aladdin by BlackRock.* BlackRock.

Bobitan, N., Dumitrescu, D., Popa, A. F., Sahlian, D. N., & Turlea, I. C. (2024). Shaping Tomorrow: Anticipating Skills Requirements Based on the Integration of Artificial Intelligence in Business Organizations—A Foresight Analysis Using the Scenario Method. *Electronics (Basel), 13*(11), 2198. DOI: 10.3390/electronics13112198

Bogojevic Arsic, V. (2021). Challenges of Financial Risk Management: AI Applications. Management:Journal of Sustainable Business and Management Solutions in Emerging Economies, 1–7. https://doi.org/DOI: 10.7595/management.fon.2021.0015

Boobier, T. (2023). *AI and the Future of Banking*. Wiley Finance.

Borra, P. (2024). The Evolution and Impact of Google Cloud Platform in Machine Learning and AI. International Journal of Advanced Research in Science. *Tongxin Jishu, 4*(3), 72–77. Advance online publication. DOI: 10.48175/IJARSCT-18908

Brabazon, A. (2018). Grammatical Evolution in Finance and Economics: A Survey. In Ryan, C., O'Neill, M., & Collins, J. J. (Eds.), *Handbook of Grammatical Evolution* (pp. 1–497). Springer International Publishing AG., DOI: 10.1007/978-3-319-78717-6_11

Briggs, J., & Kodnani, D. (2023). The potentially large effects of artificial intelligence on economic growth. Goldman Sachs. https://www.gspublishing.com/content/research/en/reports/2023/03/27/d64e052b-0f6e-45d7-967b-d7be35fabd16.html

Brown, I., Osman, A., & Karatkevich, L. (2021). Accountability and fairness in algorithmic systems: A framework for ethical audits. *Journal of Technology and Ethics, 29*(4), 1042–1061.

Brown, M. (2024). Influence of Artificial Intelligence on Credit Risk Assessment in Banking Sector. *International Journal of Modern Risk Management, 2*(1), 24–33. DOI: 10.47604/ijmrm.2641

Bubinger, H., & Dinneen, J. D. (2021). Actionable approaches to promote ethical AI in libraries. *Proceedings of the Association for Information Science and Technology*, *58*(1), 682–684. DOI: 10.1002/pra2.528

Bucci, P. (2020). Advanced neural networks for financial market forecasting: Applications of LSTM and NARX models. *International Journal of Forecasting*, *36*(4), 1250–1262. DOI: 10.1016/j.ijforecast.2020.05.010

Buchanan, B. G., & Wright, D. (2021). The impact of machine learning on UK financial services. *Oxford Review of Economic Policy*, *37*(3), 537–563. DOI: 10.1093/oxrep/grab016 PMID: 34642572

Budish, E., Cramton, P., & Shim, J. (2015). High-frequency trading networks: Trade-offs in speed, liquidity, and stability. *The Quarterly Journal of Economics*, *130*(4), 1547–1621. DOI: 10.1093/qje/qjv027

Business Standard. (n.d.). *Industry news*. Retrieved October 27, 2024, from https://www.business-standard.com/industry/news/

Buti, S., Rindi, B., & Werner, I. (2011). The privacy benefits and challenges of algorithmic trading for institutional and retail investors. *European Financial Journal*, *4*(2), 210–225.

Calderon, T. G., & Gao, L. (2021). Cybersecurity risks disclosure and implied audit risks: Evidence from audit fees. *International Journal of Auditing*, *25*(1), 24–39. DOI: 10.1111/ijau.12209

Cao, L. (2018). AI in Finance: A Review. *SSRN*, *9*(39). Advance online publication. DOI: 10.2139/ssrn.3647625

Carlisle, M., & Hamilton, E. L. (2021). The role of communication mode in auditor-client interactions: Insights from staff auditors. *Current Issues in Auditing*, *15*(1), A19–A37. DOI: 10.2308/CIIA-2020-007

Cartea, Á., Donnelly, R., & Jaimungal, S. (2017). Algorithmic trading with model uncertainty. *SIAM Journal on Financial Mathematics*, *8*(1), 635–671. DOI: 10.1137/16M106282X

Cassens Weiss, D. (2017). JPMorgan Chase Uses Tech to Save 360,000 Hours of Annual Work by Lawyers and Loan Officers. *ABA Journal*.

Cerrone, R. (2023). Are Artificial Intelligence and Machine Learning Shaping a New Risk Management Approach? *International Business Research*, *16*(12), 1–82. DOI: 10.5539/ibr.v16n12p82

Chakroun, M. A., & Gallali, M. I. (2021). Dependence between Islamic banks and conventional banks and risk factors. *International Journal of Banking. Accounting and Finance, 12*(3), 201–239. DOI: 10.1504/IJBAAF.2021.116189

Challoumis, C. (2024, October). AI IN WEALTH MANAGEMENT-TRANSFORMING PERSONAL FINANCE FOR THE BETTER. In *XVI International Scientific Conference* (pp. 30-61).

Chan Kok, T., & Seah, E. (2010). Optimizing portfolio construction using artificial intelligence. 5th International Conference on Computer Sciences and Convergence Information Technology, Seoul, Korea (South), 338-343.

Chandrinos, S. K., Sakkas, G., & Lagaros, N. D. (2018). AIRMS: A risk management tool using machine learning. *Expert Systems with Applications, 105*, 34–48. DOI: 10.1016/j.eswa.2018.03.044

Chen, C., Chen, Z., Luo, W., Xu, Y., Yang, S., Yang, G., & Zeng, Z. (2023). Ethical perspective on AI hazards to humans. *Revista de Medicina (São Paulo), 102*(48), e36163.

Chen, W., Zhang, H., Mehlawat, M., & Jia, L. (2021). Mean–variance portfolio optimization using machine learning-based stock price prediction. *Applied Soft Computing, 100*(106943), 106943. DOI: 10.1016/j.asoc.2020.106943

Chowdhury, M. A., Sahabuddin, D. M., Miyan, M. U., Sozon, M., & Miah, M. T. (2023). Assessing The Evolution of Fintech Adoption In Traditional Banking : A Bibliometric Analysis Using R. *Journal of Management and Economic Studies, 5*(3), 153–164. DOI: 10.26677/TR1010.2023.1349

Chugh, R., Patel, M., & Sharma, L. (2024). Balancing algorithmic trading and human oversight to stabilize market volatility. *Financial Markets and Trading, 15*(1), 72–88.

CLM, M. (2025). AI Contract Drafting: Dos and Don'ts for Legal Teams. *Malbek CLM*.

Cloud, G. (2023). *How HSBC Fights Money Launderers with Artificial Intelligence*. Google Cloud Blog.

Co., J. M. (2024). *Project EPIC - J.P. Morgan.* New York, USA: J.P. Morgan Chase & Co.

Co., J. M. (2024). *Project Guardian: Asset Tokenization.* New York, USA: J.P. Morgan Chase & Co.

Co., J. M. (2024). Review of JPMorgan's Onyx Blockchain Platform. *(Blog Post)*.

Coetzee, J. (2018). Strategic implications of Fintech on South African retail banks. *Suid-Afrikaanse Tydskrif vir Ekonomiese en Bestuurswetenskappe*, *21*(1), 1–11. DOI: 10.4102/sajems.v21i1.2455

Commission, C. F. (2024). Artificial Intelligence in Financial Markets. Washington, D.C: Commodity Futures Trading Commission. Company, M. &. (2023). How Generative AI Can Help Banks Manage Risk and Compliance. *McKinsey Insights.*

Compliance, R. (2025). *AI Case Study: AI for Automated Document Processing at JPMorgan (COIN).* Redress Compliance.

Costa, D., Carvalho, F., Moreira, B., & Prado, J. (2017). Bibliometric analysis on the association between behavioral finance and decision making with cognitive biases such as overconfidence, anchoring effect and confirmation bias. *Scientometrics*, *111*(3), 1775–1799. DOI: 10.1007/s11192-017-2371-5

Creamer, G. G. (2012). Machine learning for algorithmic trading in high-frequency trading futures markets. *Journal of Trading*, *7*(3), 41–48. DOI: 10.3905/jot.2012.7.3.041

CTMfile. (n.d.). *Progression of open banking in India.* Retrieved October 27, 2024, from https://ctmfile.com/story/progression-of-open-banking-in-india

Cucculelli, M., & Recanatini, F. (2022). AI and the transformation of financial intermediation: Evidence from European banks. *Journal of Banking & Finance*, *137*, 106453. DOI: 10.1016/j.jbankfin.2022.106453

Daniali, S. M., Barykin, S. E., Kapustina, I. V., Khortabi, F. M., Sergeev, S. M., Kalinina, O. V., & Senjyu, T. (2021). Predicting Volatility Index According to Technical Index and Economic Indicators on the Basis of Deep Learning Algorithm. *Sustainability (Basel)*, *13*(24), 14011. DOI: 10.3390/su132414011

Das, S. K., Anwar, D. S., Tulsyan, U., Gupta, Y., Vudatha, R., & Gardezi, D. S. H. I.Sunil Kumar Das. (2024). The Role of AI in Financial Markets: Impacts on Trading, Portfolio Management, and Price Prediction. *Journal of Electrical Systems*, *20*(6s), 1000–1006. DOI: 10.52783/jes.2804

De Andrade, I. M., & Tumelero, C. (2022). Increasing customer service efficiency through artificial intelligence chatbot. *Revista de Gestão*, *29*(3), 238–251. DOI: 10.1108/REGE-07-2021-0120

De Bonis, R., & Pozzolo, A. F. (2016). Financial Systems: Introduction and Summary. In De Bonis, R., & Pozzolo, A. F. (Eds.), *The Financial Systems of Industrial Countries Evidence from Financial Accounts* (pp. 1–23). Springer-Verlag Berlin., DOI: 10.1007/978-3-642-23111-7_1

Deiva Ganesh, A., & Kalpana, P. (2022). Future of artificial intelligence and its influence on supply chain risk management – A systematic review. *Computers & Industrial Engineering*, *169*, 108206. Advance online publication. DOI: 10.1016/j.cie.2022.108206

Deloitte. (2024). *How AI is transforming investment management: Enhancing alpha, efficiency, and risk management*. Deloitte Insights.

Deloitte. (2024). *The Impact of Artificial Intelligence on the Banking and Payments Industry*. Deloitte Touche Tohmatsu Limited.

Deng, H., Huang, R. H., & Wu, Q. (2018). The regulation of initial coin offerings in China: Problems, prognoses and prospects. *European Business Organization Law Review*, *19*(3), 465–502. DOI: 10.1007/s40804-018-0118-2

Devan, M., Tillu, R., & Shanmugam, L. (2023). Personalized Financial Recommendations: Real-Time AI-ML Analytics in Wealth Management. Journal of Knowledge Learning and Science Technology ISSN: 2959-6386 (online), 2(3), 547-559.

Días, C. (2024). *BlackRock se acerca a los 70.000 millones de inversiones en acciones y bonos españoles*. Cinco Días.

Diaz, R., Smith, K., Landaeta, R., & Padovano, A. (2020). Shipbuilding Supply Chain Framework and Digital Transformation: A Project Portfolios Risk Evaluation. *Procedia Manufacturing*, *42*, 173–180. DOI: 10.1016/j.promfg.2020.02.067

DigitalDefynd. (2025). *5 Ways JP Morgan is Using AI - Case Study [2025]*. DigitalDefynd.

Dignum, V. (2020). Addressing AI's transparency and bias issues: The necessity of ethical oversight. *AI and Ethics*, *1*, 109–121. DOI: 10.1007/s43681-020-00001-4

Dignum, V. (2020). *Responsible Artificial Intelligence: How to Develop and Use AI in a Responsible Way*. Springer Nature.

Dixon, R. B. L. (2023). A principled governance for emerging AI regimes: Lessons from China, the European Union, and the United States. *AI and Ethics*, *3*(3), 793–810. DOI: 10.1007/s43681-022-00205-0

Djogo, Y. O. (2023). Internal Auditor Human Resources Development Strategy in the Era of Disruption. Atestasi. *Jurnal Ilmiah Akuntansi*, *6*(2), 627–639.

Drakonakis, K., Leung, K., Yang, C., & Hatzivasilis, G. (2020). Automated black-box auditing in web authentication: Securing digital systems through advanced auditing frameworks. *Computer Networks*, *178*, 107342. DOI: 10.1016/j.comnet.2020.107342

Du, J. (2022). Mean–variance portfolio optimization with deep learning based-forecasts for cointegrated stocks. Expert Systems with Applications: An International Journal, 201(C).

Durai, S., Manoharan, G., & Ashtikar, S. P. (2024). Harnessing Artificial Intelligence: Pioneering Sustainable Solutions for a Greener Future. In Social and Ethical Implications of AI in Finance for Sustainability (pp. 89-117). IGI Global.

Durango-Gutiérrez, H., Ramírez, M., & De la Hoz, E. (2021). AI-enhanced financial analysis: Integrating traditional and machine learning methods. *Journal of Financial Analytics*, *45*(1), 91–108.

Durodié, C. (2024). Decoding AI in Financial Services. London, UK: Cognitive Finance Group. eFinancialCareers. (2023). Goldman Sachs AI Head Likes Technique That 'Creates a Trader'. *eFinancialCareers*.

Dziawgo, T. (2021). Wealth Tech impact on wealth management sector.

Ehsan, S., Nurunnabi, M., Tahir, S., & Hashmi, M. H. (2020). Earnings management: A new paradigm of corporate social responsibility. *Business and Society Review*, *125*(3), 349–369. DOI: 10.1111/basr.12198

Eilifsen, A., Hamilton, E., & Messier, W. F. (2020). Audit data analytics: Challenges and opportunities. *Auditing*, *39*(2), 45–69. DOI: 10.2308/ajpt-52658

El Hajj, M., & Hammoud, J. (2023). Unveiling the Influence of Artificial Intelligence and Machine Learning on Financial Markets: A Comprehensive Analysis of AI Applications in Trading, Risk Management, and Financial Operations. *Journal of Risk and Financial Management*, *16*(10), 434. Advance online publication. DOI: 10.3390/jrfm16100434

Ellili, N. O. D. (2022). Is there any association between FinTech and sustainability? Evidence from bibliometric review and content analysis. *Journal of Financial Services Marketing*, *28*(4), 748–762. DOI: 10.1057/s41264-022-00200-w

El-Shihy, D., Abdelraouf, M., Hegazy, M., & Hassan, N. (2024). The Influence of AI Chatbots in Fintech Services on Customer Loyalty within the Banking Industry. *Future of Business Administration*, *3*(1), 16–28. DOI: 10.33422/fba.v3i1.644

Epp, N., Pentikis, J., & Roohani, S. (2024). The Sunk Costs of Cybersecurity Testing: Who Bears Responsibility? *Journal of Applied Business & Economics*, *26*(2). Advance online publication. DOI: 10.33423/jabe.v26i2.7042

Epstein, G. A., & Jayadev, A. (2019). *The Rise of Rentier Incomes in OECD Countries*. Financialization, Central Bank Policy and Labor Solidarity. In The Political Economy of Central Banking., DOI: 10.4337/9781788978415.00022

Er Kara, M., Oktay Fırat, S. Ü., & Ghadge, A. (2020). A data mining-based framework for supply chain risk management. *Computers & Industrial Engineering*, *139*, 105570. Advance online publication. DOI: 10.1016/j.cie.2018.12.017

Erić, D. (2022). Innovation and Fintech. In Vukovic, D. B., Maiti, M., & Grigorieva, E. M. (Eds.), *Digitalization and the future of financial services : innovation and impact of digital finance* (pp. 19–39). Springer Nature., DOI: 10.1007/978-3-031-11545-5_2

Eulerich, M., Van der Tas, L., & Machiels, J. (2022). Integrating robotic process automation in audit tasks: Efficiency and effectiveness in audit practices. *International Journal of Auditing*, *26*(1), 56–72. DOI: 10.1111/ijau.12208

EY. (2024). Title: How Artificial Intelligence is Reshaping the Financial Services Industry. London, United Kingdom: Ernst & Young Global Limited. (FATF), F. A. (2021). *Opportunities and Challenges of New Technologies for AML/CFT.* Paris, France: FATF.

Fakeyede, O. G., Okeleke, E. C., Okeleke, P. A., & Adaramodu, O. R. (2023). A Comprehensive Review of IT Audit Methodologies in The Age of Quantum Computing. *Journal of Technology & Innovation*, *3*(2), 85–92. DOI: 10.26480/jtin.02.2023.85.92

Fakhouri, H. N., Alawadi, S., Awaysheh, F. M., Hani, I. B., Alkhalaileh, M., & Hamad, F. (2023). A Comprehensive Study on the Role of Machine Learning in 5G Security : Challenges, Technologies, and Solutions. *Electronics (Basel)*, *12*(4604), 1–44. DOI: 10.3390/electronics12224604

Faloon, M., & Scherer, B. (2017). Individualization of robo-advice. *The Journal of Wealth Management*, *20*(1), 30–36. DOI: 10.3905/jwm.2017.20.1.030

Faradynawati, I. A. A., & Söderberg, I. L. (2022). Sustainable investment preferences among robo-advisor clients. *Sustainability (Basel)*, *14*(19), 12636. DOI: 10.3390/su141912636

Fares, O. H., Butt, I., & Lee, S. H. M. (2022). Utilization of artificial intelligence in the banking sector: A systematic literature review. *Journal of Financial Services Marketing*, •••, 1.

Fatouros, G. M. (2024). Can Large Language Models Beat Wall Street? Unveiling the Potential of AI in Stock Selection. *arXiv*.

Faubion, B. (2016). Effect of automated advising platforms on the financial advising market.

Fedyk, A., Hodson, J., Khimich, N., & Fedyk, T. (2022). Is artificial intelligence improving the audit process? *Review of Accounting Studies*, *27*(3), 938–985. DOI: 10.1007/s11142-022-09697-x

Fein, M. L. (2019). Robo-Advisors: A Portfolio Management Perspective. *Journal of Financial Planning*, *32*(1), 48–55.

Ferguson, N. (2009). An evolutionary approach to financial history. Cold Spring Harbor Symposia on Quantitative Biology, 74(Economist 2008), 449–454. https://doi.org/DOI: 10.1101/sqb.2009.74.050

Fernandes, M., Medeiros, M. C., & Scharth, M. (2014). Forecasting and modeling volatility with the VIX index. *Journal of Financial and Quantitative Analysis*, *49*(1), 267–291. DOI: 10.1017/S0022109014000098

Finance, F. D. (2024). *Here's How HSBC is Using Artificial Intelligence to Take Money Launderers to Task*. Future Digital Finance Blog.

Finextra. (2016). AI Implementation in AML at HSBC Sees a Considerable Reduction in Compliance Costs. *Finextra Blog*.

Fisch, J. E., Laboure, M., & Turner, J. A. (2019). The Emergence of the Robo-advisor. The disruptive impact of FinTech on retirement systems, 13, 13-37.

Fisch, J. E., Labouré, M., & Turner, J. A. (2019). The Emergence of the Robo-Adviser. *University of Pennsylvania Law Review*, *168*(4), 1269–1305.

Fishbein, M., & Ajzen, I. (1977). Belief, attitude, intention, and behavior: An introduction to theory and research.

Fisher, A. (2024). AI-Enhanced Financial Market Surveillance. *Journal of Market Analysis*, 34-56.

Flavián, C., Pérez-Rueda, A., Belanche, D., & Casaló, L. V. (2022). Intention to use analytical artificial intelligence (AI) in services–the effect of technology readiness and awareness. *Journal of Service Management*, *33*(2), 293–320. DOI: 10.1108/JOSM-10-2020-0378

Flood, M., Jagadish, H., & Raschid, L. (2016). Big data challenges and opportunities in financial stability monitoring. *Financial Stability Review*, (20), 129–142.

Floridi, L., & Cowls, J. (2018). Continuous oversight of AI: Adaptable auditing processes for evolving technology. *AI & Society*, *33*(1), 45–56.

Floridi, L., Cowls, J., Beltrametti, M., Chatila, R., Chazerand, P., Dignum, V., Luetge, C., Madelin, R., Pagallo, U., Rossi, F., Schafer, B., Valcke, P., & Vayena, E. (2022). The European AI Act and its implications: A procedural framework for conformity assessments in AI. *AI & Society*, *38*, 1285–1299. DOI: 10.1007/s00146-021-01258-5

Forum, W. E. (2025). *Artificial Intelligence in Financial Services*. Cologny/Geneva, Switzerland: World Economic Forum. (FSB), F. S. (2024). *The Financial Stability Implications of Artificial Intelligence*. Basel, Switzerland: Financial Stability Board.

Frankenfield, J. (2020). Cloud computing. *Investopedia. Dostupno na:* https://www .investopedia. com/terms/c/cloud-computing. asp*[28. svibnja 2021.]*.

Frankenfield, J. (2021). Artificial intelligence (AI): Definition, how it works, and examples. Investopedia. https://www.investopedia.com/terms/a/artificial-intelligence -ai.asp

Frino, A., Mollica, V., & Webb, R. I. (2017). The impact of algorithmic trading on market quality: Evidence from a natural experiment. *Journal of Financial Markets*, *32*, 87–103. DOI: 10.1016/j.finmar.2017.03.002

Funahashi, K. (2020). Hybrid models in option pricing: ANNs and asymptotic expansion. *Quantitative Finance*, *20*(5), 760–774. DOI: 10.1080/14697688.2020.1712467

Fund, I. M. (2023). *Generative Artificial Intelligence in Finance: Risk Considerations*. International Monetary Fund.

Galazova, S., & Magomaeva, L. (2019). The transformation of traditional banking activity in digital. *International Journal of Economics and Business Administration*, *VII*(Special Issue 2), 41-51. https://doi.org/DOI: 10.35808/ijeba/369

Galaz, V., Centeno, M. A., Callahan, P. W., Causevic, A., Patterson, T., Brass, I., Baum, S., Farber, D., Fischer, J., Garcia, D., McPhearson, T., Jimenez, D., King, B., Larcey, P., & Levy, K. (2021). Artificial intelligence, systemic risks, and sustainability. *Technology in Society*, *67*, 101741. Advance online publication. DOI: 10.1016/j.techsoc.2021.101741

Galeone, G., Ranaldo, S., & Fusco, A. (2024). ESG and FinTech: Are they connected? *Research in International Business and Finance*, *69*, 102225. DOI: 10.1016/j.ribaf.2024.102225

Galeshchuk, S., & Mukherjee, K. (2017). AI for forecasting exchange rates: A comparative approach. *International Journal of Forecasting*, *33*(4), 1022–1042. DOI: 10.1016/j.ijforecast.2017.03.003

Gandhar, A., Gupta, K., Kumar, A., & Dharm, P. (2024). Fraud Detection Using Machine Learning and Deep Learning. *SN Computer Science*, *5*(453), 453. Advance online publication. DOI: 10.1007/s42979-024-02772-x

Garad, A., Rahmawati, A., & Pratolo, S. (2021). The impact of board directors, audit committee and ownership on financial performance and firms value. evaluation, 17, 18-19.

Garg, D., Shelke, N. A., Kitukale, G., & Mehlawat, N. (2024). Leveraging Financial Data and Risk Management in Banking sector using Machine Learning. 9th International Conference for Convergence in Technology, I2CT 2024, 10544336. https://doi.org/DOI: 10.1109/I2CT61223.2024.10544336

Geczy, C. (2024). *AI in Finance: The Promise and Potential Pitfalls*. Knowledge at Wharton.

Georgieva, I., Lazo, C., Timan, T., & van Veenstra, A. F. (2022). From AI ethics principles to data science practice: A reflection and a gap analysis based on recent frameworks and practical experience. *AI and Ethics*, *2*(4), 697–711. DOI: 10.1007/s43681-021-00127-3

Ghandar, A., Michalewicz, Z., Schmidt, M., To, T.-D., & Zurbrugg, R. (2009). Computational Intelligence for Evolving Trading Rules. *IEEE Transactions on Evolutionary Computation*, *13*(1), 71–86. DOI: 10.1109/TEVC.2008.915992

Ghandour, A. (2021). Opportunities and challenges of artificial intelligence in banking: Systematic literature review. *TEM Journal*, *10*(4), 1581–1587. DOI: 10.18421/TEM104-12

Ghobakhloo, M., Fathi, M., Iranmanesh, M., Vilkas, M., Grybauskas, A., & Amran, A. (2024). Generative artificial intelligence in manufacturing: Opportunities for actualizing Industry 5.0 sustainability goals. *Journal of Manufacturing Technology Management*, *35*(9), 94–121. DOI: 10.1108/JMTM-12-2023-0530

Gigante, G., & Zago, A. (2023). DARQ technologies in the financial sector: Artificial intelligence applications in personalized banking. *Qualitative Research in Financial Markets*, *15*(1), 29–57. DOI: 10.1108/QRFM-02-2021-0025

Golghar, Y., Roitman, L., & Neginsky, D. (2018). AI-powered wealth management products and investment vehicles. The WealthTech Book: The FinTech Handbook for Investors, Entrepreneurs and Finance Visionaries, 138-141.

Gomber, P., Kauffman, R. J., Parker, C., & Weber, B. W. (2018). On the Fintech Revolution: Interpreting the Forces of Innovation, Disruption, and Transformation in Financial Services. *Journal of Management Information Systems*, *35*(1), 220–265. DOI: 10.1080/07421222.2018.1440766

Gonçalves, A. R., Breda Meira, A., Shuqair, S., & Costa Pinto, D. (2023). Artificial intelligence (AI) in FinTech decisions: The role of congruity and rejection sensitivity. *International Journal of Bank Marketing*, *41*(6), 1282–1307. DOI: 10.1108/IJBM-07-2022-0295

González, A. L., Moreno, M., Román, A. C. M., Fernández, Y. H., & Pérez, N. C. (2024). Ethics in Artificial Intelligence: An Approach to Cybersecurity. *Inteligencia Artificial*, *27*(73), 38–54. DOI: 10.4114/intartif.vol27iss73pp38-54

Goodell, J., Kumar, S., Marc Lim, W., & Pattnaik, D. (2021). Artificial intelligence and machine learning in finance: Identifying foundations, themes, and research clusters from bibliometric analysis. *Journal of Behavioral and Experimental Finance*, *32*, 32. DOI: 10.1016/j.jbef.2021.100577

Gracia, D. B., Ariño, L. V. C., & Blasco, M. G. (2015). The effect of culture in forming e-loyalty intentions: A cross-cultural analysis between Argentina and Spain. *Business Research Quarterly*, *18*(4), 275–292. DOI: 10.1016/j.brq.2015.02.003

Grewal, D., Roggeveen, A. L., & Nordfält, J. (2017). The future of retailing. *Journal of Retailing*, *93*(1), 1–6. DOI: 10.1016/j.jretai.2016.12.008

Groenewald, J., & Odendaal, E. (2021). The experiences leading to resignation of female audit managers: An interpretative phenomenological analysis. *Gender in Management*, *36*(8), 912–929. DOI: 10.1108/GM-11-2020-0352

Group, P. S. (2025). *Predictive Risk Analytics in Finance: Key Use Cases*. Phoenix Strategy Group Blog.

Grubaugh, S., & Levitt, G. (2024). The Future of Elementary Social Studies: Harnessing AI's Potential Through Evidence-Based Practices. *Technium Social Sciences Journal*, *58*, 87–93. DOI: 10.47577/tssj.v58i1.10991

Gündüz, A. Y. (2023). The Importance of Investigating Students' Lifelong Learning Levels and Perceptions of 21st-Century Skills. *International e-Journal of Educational Studies, 7*(15), 788-796.

Gupta, V., & Shukla, S. (2024). Consumer Trust in Digital Banking: A Qualitative Study of Legal and Regulatory Impacts. *Interdisciplinary Studies in Society, Law, and Politics*, *3*(2), 18–24. DOI: 10.61838/kman.isslp.3.2.4

Hall, R. P., Ashford, R., Ashford, N. A., & Arango-Quiroga, J. (2019). Universal basic income and inclusive capitalism: Consequences for sustainability. *Sustainability (Basel)*, *11*(16), 4481. Advance online publication. DOI: 10.3390/su11164481

Han, S., & Yang, H. (2018). Understanding adoption of intelligent personal assistants: A parasocial relationship perspective. *Industrial Management & Data Systems*, *118*(3), 618–636. DOI: 10.1108/IMDS-05-2017-0214

Hansen, K. B. (2020). The virtue of simplicity: On machine learning models in algorithmic trading. *Big Data & Society*, *7*(1), 2053951720926558. DOI: 10.1177/2053951720926558

Harjoto, M. A., & Laksmana, I. (2022). The impact of COVID-19 lockdown on audit fees and audit delay: International evidence. *International Journal of Accounting & Information Management*, *30*(4), 526–545. DOI: 10.1108/IJAIM-02-2022-0030

Haroon, O., Ali, M., Khan, A., Khattak, M. A., & Rizvi, S. A. R. (2021). Financial Market Risks during the COVID-19 Pandemic. *Emerging Markets Finance & Trade*, *57*(8), 2407–2414. DOI: 10.1080/1540496X.2021.1873765

Haryani, F., Nasta'in, F., Novitasari, I., Putri, W., & Manurung, H. (2023). Internal Auditor's Responsibilities for Quality Control of Financial Reporting at PT Asabri (Persero): A Qualitative Analysis. *Jurnal Ilmiah Manajemen Kesatuan*, *11*(2), 593–598. DOI: 10.37641/jimkes.v11i2.2152

Hasan, A. R. (2021). Artificial Intelligence (AI) in accounting & auditing: A Literature review. *Open Journal of Business and Management*, *10*(1), 440–465. DOI: 10.4236/ojbm.2022.101026

Hasan, R., Ashfaq, M., & Shao, L. (2021). Evaluating drivers of Fintech adoption in The Netherlands. *Global Business Review*, *097215092110274*. Advance online publication. DOI: 10.1177/09721509211027402

Heaton, J. B., Polson, N. G., & Witte, J. H. (2017). Deep learning for finance: Deep portfolios. *Applied Stochastic Models in Business and Industry*, *33*(1), 3–12. DOI: 10.1002/asmb.2209

Heaton, J., Polson, N., & Witte, J. (2016). Deep Portfolio Theory. arXiv:1605.07230.

Heinrich, P., & Schwabe, G. (2018). Facilitating informed decision-making in financial service encounters. *Business & Information Systems Engineering*, *60*(4), 317–329. DOI: 10.1007/s12599-017-0501-5

Hendershott, T., Jones, C. M., & Menkveld, A. J. (2011). Does algorithmic trading improve liquidity? *The Journal of Finance*, *66*(1), 1–33. DOI: 10.1111/j.1540-6261.2010.01624.x

Hennein, R., Goddard, E., & Sherman, J. D. (2022). Stakeholder perspectives on scaling up medical device reprocessing: A qualitative study. *PLoS One*, *17*(12), e0279808. DOI: 10.1371/journal.pone.0279808 PMID: 36584081

Henry, J. (2024). *4 Keys to AI Governance that Drive Compliance and Accountability in Financial Institutions*. Jack Henry & Associates, Inc.

Hernández, B., Jiménez, J., & Martín, M. J. (2009). Adoption of e-commerce by people over 55 in Spain. *International Journal of Retail & Distribution Management*, *37*(12), 1051–1073. DOI: 10.1108/09590550911005041

Heston, S. L., & Sinha, N. R. (2017). News and social media effects on stock prices. *Journal of Financial Economics*, *126*(1), 71–88. DOI: 10.1016/j.jfineco.2017.06.002

Hezam, Y. A., Anthonysamy, L., & Suppiah, S. D. K. (2023). Big data analytics and auditing: A review and synthesis of literature. *Emerging Science Journal*, *7*(2), 629–642. DOI: 10.28991/ESJ-2023-07-02-023

Hidayat, M. D. (2024). The Impact of Artificial Intelligence (AI) on Financial Management. *Management Studies and Business Journal (PRODUCTIVITY)*, 123-129.

HighRadius. (2022). *Predictive Analytics in Corporate Finance (7 Use Cases)*. HighRadius Blog.

Hoang, D., & Wiegratz, K. (2023). Machine learning methods in finance: Recent applications and prospects. *European Financial Management*, *29*(5), 1657–1701. DOI: 10.1111/eufm.12408

Hojaji, S. N., Yahyazadehfar, M., & Abedin, B. (2022). Machine learning in behavioral finance: A systematic literature review. *The Journal of Financial Data Science*, *4*(3), 129–151. DOI: 10.3905/jfds.2022.1.100

Holopainen, M., & Sarlin, P. (2017). AI in systemic risk monitoring: Applications for macroprudential supervision. *Journal of Economic Dynamics & Control*, *77*, 151–175. DOI: 10.1016/j.jedc.2017.01.013

Holzinger, A., Kieseberg, P., Weippl, E., & Tjoa, A. (2018). *Current Advances, Trends and Challenges of Machine Learning and Knowledge Extraction: From Machine Learning to Explainable AI. Machine Learning and Knowledge Extraction, 11015*. Springer.

Ho, S. P. S., & Chow, M. Y. C. (2023). The role of artificial intelligence in consumers' brand preference for retail banks in Hong Kong. *Journal of Financial Services Marketing*, •••, 1–14.

HSBC. (2024). *Harnessing the Power of AI to Fight Financial Crime*. HSBC News and Views.

Hub, E. T. (2023). *Leveraging AI in Electronic Trading: A Game Changer for Investment Banks. Electronic Trading Hub. (IMF), I. M. (2024). Artificial Intelligence and its Impact on Financial Markets and Financial Stability*. International Monetary Fund.

Hu, K. H., Chen, F. H., Hsu, M. F., & Tzeng, G. H. (2023). Governance of artificial intelligence applications in a business audit via a fusion fuzzy multiple rule-based decision-making model. *Financial Innovation*, *9*(1), 117. DOI: 10.1186/s40854-022-00436-4

Hung, S.-Y., Liang, T.-P., & Liu, V.-C.Victor Wei-Chi Liu. (1996). Integrating arbitrage pricing theory and artificial neural networks to support portfolio management. *Decision Support Systems*, *18*(3-4), 301–316. DOI: 10.1016/S0167-9236(96)80006-6

Hu, Y., Liu, K., Zhang, X., Su, L., Ngai, E. W. T., & Liu, M. (2015). Application of evolutionary computation for rule discovery in stock algorithmic trading: A literature review. *Applied Soft Computing*, *36*, 534–551. DOI: 10.1016/j.asoc.2015.07.008

Hu, Y., Zhang, X., Feng, B., Xie, K., & Liu, M. (2015). itrade: A mobile data-driven stock trading system with concept drift adaptation. [IJDWM]. *International Journal of Data Warehousing and Mining*, *11*(1), 66–83. DOI: 10.4018/ijdwm.2015010104

Huynh, T. L. D., Hille, E., & Nasir, M. A. (2020). Diversification in the age of the 4th industrial revolution: The role of artificial intelligence, green bonds and cryptocurrencies. *Technological Forecasting and Social Change*, *159*, 120188. DOI: 10.1016/j.techfore.2020.120188

ICICI Bank. (n.d.). *What is API banking services and how it works*. Retrieved October 27, 2024, from https://www.icicibank.com/blogs/api-banking/what-is-api-banking-services-and-how-it-works

Ikudabo, A. O., & Kumar, P. (2024). AI-driven risk assessment and management in banking: Balancing innovation and security. *International Journal of Research Publication and Reviews*, *5*(10), 3573–3588.

Ilori, O., Nwosu, N. T., & Naiho, H. N. N. (2024). Enhancing IT audit effectiveness with agile methodologies: A conceptual exploration. *Engineering Science & Technology Journal*, *5*(6), 1969–1994. DOI: 10.51594/estj.v5i6.1217

Imprasoft. (2023). Goldman Sachs: Pioneering AI Integration in Innovative Financial Technologies. *Imprasoft.*

In, 0., Rook, D., & Monk, A. (2019). Integrating Alternative Data (Also Known as ESG Data) in Investment Decision Making. Global Economic Review, 48(3), 237-260.

Inc42. (n.d.). *Digital financial inclusion*. Retrieved October 27, 2024, from https://inc42.com/glossary/digital-financial-inclusion/

Indrastuti, S., Mardianty, D., Hasan, H., & Nugroho, G. (2024). Optimizing Auditor Performance: Examining the Mediating Role of Communication in the Work Environment. Atestasi. *Jurnal Ilmiah Akuntansi*, *7*(1), 248–259.

Indriyanto, E., Molina, M., Nur, M., & Digdowiseiso, K. (2023). The Quality of Company Audit in Indonesia during COVID-19 Pandemic: A Review of Literature. Global Journal of Business, Economics &. *Social Development*, *1*(2), 108–115.

Infosys. (n.d.). Reducing Audit Risk Through Artificial Intelligence and Automation. *Infosys Insights*.

Innayah, E. P., Ekowati, V. M., Supriyanto, A. S., & Johari, F. B. (2022). Electronic word-of-mouth (E-WOM) in social media as a predictor of investment intention in capital market. *Jurnal Aplikasi Manajemen*, *20*(4), 753–767. DOI: 10.21776/ub.jam.2022.020.04.01

Insight, A.-T. (2018). *HSBC Takes on Financial Crime Tech Challenge with AI Approach from Quantexa*. A-Team Insight Blog.

Institute, B. P. (2018). *The High Cost of AML Compliance*. Bank Policy Institute.

Institute, T. A. (2021). *AI in Financial Services*. The Alan Turing Institute.

International Journal of Governance, I. a. (2024). *Navigating Ethical and Governance Challenges in AI: Finance.* International Journal of Governance, Innovation, and Sustainability.

Intersog. (2024). Predictive Analytics in Finance: Shaping Investment Strategies. *Intersog Blog*.

Intive. (2024). *How AI is Supercharging Money Management.* Munich, Germany: Intive S.A.

Investopedia. (2023). HSBC's Money Laundering Scandal. *Investopedia*.

Investopedia. (2024). Strategies and Secrets of High-Frequency Trading (HFT) Firms. *Investopedia*.

Irfan, M. (2021, January). Do Shariah Indices converge? Evidence from Gulf Co-operation Council countries. *International Journal of Business Excellence*, *23*(2), 251–269. DOI: 10.1504/IJBEX.2021.113448

Irfan, M., Elhoseny, M., Kassim, S., & Metawa, N. (2023). *Advanced Machine Learning Algorithms for Complex Financial Applications*. IGI Global., DOI: 10.4018/978-1-6684-4483-2

Irfan, M., Elmogy, M., Gupta, S., Khalifa, F., & Dias, R. (2024). *AI-Driven Decentralized Finance and the Future of Finance*. IGI Global., DOI: 10.4018/979-8-3693-6321-8

Irfan, M., Elmogy, M., Majid, M. S., & El-Sappagh, S. (2023). *The Impact of AI Innovation on Financial Sectors in the Era of Industry 5.0*. IGI Global., DOI: 10.4018/979-8-3693-0082-4

Irfan, M., Hussainey, K., Chan Bukhari, S. A., & Nam, Y. (Eds.). (2024). *Issues of Sustainability in AI and New-Age Thematic Investing*. IGI Global Publisher., DOI: 10.4018/979-8-3693-3282-5

Irfan, M., Kadry, S., Sharif, M., & Ullah Khan, H. (2023). *Fintech Applications in Islamic Finance: AI, Machine Learning, and Blockchain Techniques*. IGI Global., DOI: 10.4018/979-8-3693-1038-0

Islam, M. S., Farah, N., & Stafford, T. F. (2018). Factors associated with security/cybersecurity audit by internal audit function: An international study. *Managerial Auditing Journal*, *33*(4), 377–409. DOI: 10.1108/MAJ-07-2017-1595

Itransition. (2023). Predictive Analytics in Finance: Use Cases and Guidelines. *Itransition Blog*.

Jaeger, M., Krügel, S., Marinelli, D., Papenbrock, J., & Schwendner, P. (2021). Interpretable machine learning for diversified portfolio construction. *The Journal of Financial Data Science*, *3*(3), 31–51. DOI: 10.3905/jfds.2021.1.066

Jagtiani, J., & John, K. (2018). Fintech lending and credit decision-making: Implications for borrowers and financial institutions. *Journal of Financial Economics*, *129*(3), 536–552. DOI: 10.1016/j.jfineco.2018.06.007

Jain, R., Jain, S., & Jain, D. (2023). CRITICAL REVIEW ON APPLICATIONS OF AI & ML IN FINANCE. SSRN Electronic Journal. https://doi.org/DOI: 10.2139/ssrn.4399885

Jain, S., Satyala, H., Ranjit, P. S., Tatsiana, V., Patil, D. T., Manoharan, G., & Chakravarthi, D. S. (2024). Artificial Intelligence's Implications on Project Management. In Recent Technological Advances in Engineering and Management (pp. 105-109). CRC Press. DOI: 10.1201/9781003531395-22

Jakšič, M., & Marinč, M. (2018). Relationship banking and information technology: The role of artificial intelligence and FinTech. *Risk Management*, *21*(1), 1–18. DOI: 10.1057/s41283-018-0039-y

Jallan, Y., & Ashuri, B. (2020). Text Mining of the Securities and Exchange Commission Financial Filings of Publicly Traded Construction Firms Using Deep Learning to Identify and Assess Risk. *Journal of Construction Engineering and Management*, *146*(12), 04020137. Advance online publication. DOI: 10.1061/(ASCE)CO.1943-7862.0001932

Jang, B., & Lee, J. (2019). Artificial neural networks in option pricing models: A comparative study. *Journal of Derivatives*, *26*(3), 60–75. DOI: 10.3905/jod.2019.26.3.060

Jang, J., & Seong, N. (2023). Deep reinforcement learning for stock portfolio optimization by connecting with modern portfolio theory. *Expert Systems with Applications*, *218*, 218. DOI: 10.1016/j.eswa.2023.119556

Javaid, H. A. (2024). AI-driven predictive analytics in finance: Transforming risk assessment and decision-making. Advances in Computer Sciences, 7(1).

Jefferson, P. (2025). *AI is Speeding Investors' Reactions to Central Bankers' Messages*. Reuters Technology News.

Jejeniwa, T. O., Mhlongo, N. Z., & Jejeniwa, T. O. (2024). AI solutions for developmental economics: Opportunities and challenges in financial inclusion and poverty alleviation. *International Journal of Advanced Economics*, *6*(4), 108–123. DOI: 10.51594/ijae.v6i4.1073

Jena, J. R., Biswal, S. K., Panigrahi, R. R., & Shrivastava, A. K. (2024). Investigating the Potential Areas in Artificial Intelligence and Financial Innovation: A Bibliometric Analysis. *Journal of Scientometric Research*, *13*(1), 71–80. DOI: 10.5530/jscires.13.1.6

Jeong, J., Kim, B. J., & Lee, J. (2024). Navigating AI transitions: How coaching leadership buffers against job stress and protects employee physical health. *Frontiers in Public Health*, *12*, 1343932. DOI: 10.3389/fpubh.2024.1343932 PMID: 38601504

Ji, M. (2017). Are robots good fiduciaries: Regulating robo-advisors under the investment advisers act of 1940. *SSRN*, *117*, 1543. DOI: 10.2139/ssrn.3036722

Jin, D. (2023). *Where have the ethical and moral standards landed? Consumer self-congruency and psychological distance in the context of AI-based services*. International Hospitality Review.

Jingrong, H., Shan, H., Zhaobin, C., Yu, L., & Yingying, L. (2024). AI-Driven Digital Transformation in Banking: A New Perspective on Operational Efficiency and Risk Management. *Information Systems and Economics*, *5*(1), 82–90.

Johnson, M. &. (2024). The Role of Artificial Intelligence in Investment Decision-Making: Opportunities and Risks for Financial Institutions. *Journal of Financial Technology*, 88-105.

Journal, T. C. (2024). Financial Statement Fraud Detection in the Digital Age. *The CPA Journal*, •••, 1–6.

Jung, D., Dorner, V., Glaser, F., & Morana, S. (2018). Robo-advisory: Digitalization and automation of financial advisory. *Business & Information Systems Engineering*, *60*(1), 81–86. DOI: 10.1007/s12599-018-0521-9

Kaawaase, T. K. (2022). Anchoring on dynamic auditing capabilities to manage small and medium audit practices in a Covid-19-induced turbulent business environment. *Management Matters*, *19*(1), 73–90. DOI: 10.1108/MANM-01-2022-0003

Kai, R., Yusheng, K., Ntarmah, A. H., & Ti, C. (2022). Constructing internal audit quality evaluation index: Evidence from listed companies in Jiangsu province, China. *Heliyon*, *8*(9), e10598. DOI: 10.1016/j.heliyon.2022.e10598 PMID: 36164523

Kamariotou, M., & Kitsios, F. (2023). Information systems strategy and security policy: A conceptual framework. *Electronics (Basel)*, *12*(2), 382. DOI: 10.3390/electronics12020382

Kanaparthi, V. (2024). *Regulating AI in the Financial Sector: Recent Developments and Main Challenges*. Bank for International Settlements.

Karachun, I., Vinnichek, L., & Tuskov, A. (2021). Machine learning methods in finance. SHS Web of Conferences, 110, 05012. https://doi.org/DOI: 10.1051/shsconf/202111005012

Karjalainen, M., & Ojala, A. L. (2023). Authentic learning environments for in-service training in cybersecurity: A qualitative study. *International Journal of Continuing Engineering Education and Lifelong Learning*, *33*(1), 128–147. DOI: 10.1504/IJCEELL.2023.127853

Karmila, Y., & Wahad, A. (2024). Determinants of Fraud Prevention PT Perkebunan Nusantara XIV Takalar. *Formosa Journal of Applied Sciences*, *3*(2), 759–774. DOI: 10.55927/fjas.v3i2.7981

Karoui, A. T., Sayari, S., Dammak, W., & Jeribi, A. (2024). Unveiling outperformance: A portfolio analysis of top AI-related stocks against IT indices and robotics ETFs. *Risks*, *12*(3), 52. DOI: 10.3390/risks12030052

Kasaraneni, R. K. (2021). AI-Enhanced Portfolio Optimization: Balancing Risk and Return with Machine Learning Models. *African Journal of Artificial Intelligence and Sustainable Development*, *1*(1), 219–265.

Kaur, R., Dharmadhikari, S. P., & Khurjekar, S. (2024). Assessing the customer adoption and perceptions for AI-driven sustainable initiatives in Indian banking sector. *Environment and Social Psychology, 9*(5).

Kelejian, H., & Mukerji, A. (2016). Volatility and market efficiency in high-frequency trading. *Journal of Financial Studies*, *8*(3), 220–236. DOI: 10.1080/10508422.2016.114000

Kend, M., & Nguyen, L. A. (2020). Big data analytics and other emerging technologies: The impact on the Australian audit and assurance profession. *Australian Accounting Review*, *30*(4), 269–282. DOI: 10.1111/auar.12305

Kercheval, A. N., & Zhang, Y. (2015). Modeling high-frequency limit order book dynamics with machine learning. *Quantitative Finance*, *15*(8), 1315–1329. DOI: 10.1080/14697688.2015.1032546

Khadka, S., Rai, B., & Khadka, A. K. (2023). AI-Driven Customization in Financial Services: Implications for Social Innovation in Nepal. *NCC Journal*, *8*(1), 1–11. DOI: 10.3126/nccj.v8i1.63128

Khandani, A. E., Kim, A. J., & Lo, A. W. (2010). Consumer credit-risk models via machine-learning algorithms. *Journal of Banking & Finance*, *34*(11), 2767–2787. DOI: 10.1016/j.jbankfin.2010.06.001

Khelil, I., Hussainey, K., & Noubbigh, H. (2018). Chief audit executives' perceptions of drivers of moral courage: Tunisian evidence. International Journal of Accounting. *Auditing and Performance Evaluation*, *14*(4), 315–337. DOI: 10.1504/IJAAPE.2018.095107

Khuan, H., Judijanto, L., Rachmawati, T., Tanjung, T., & Vandika, A. Y. (2024). Bibliometric Analysis on the Use of Artificial Intelligence in Improving the Efficiency of Banking Financial Processes in Southeast Asian Countries. *West Science Interdisciplinary Studies*, *2*(01), 129–137. DOI: 10.58812/wsis.v2i01.597

Kim, J. H., & Kim, Y. H. (2020). AI-driven index tracking and portfolio optimization. *Journal of Portfolio Management, 46*(4), 45–60. DOI: 10.3905/jpm.2020.46.4.045

Kirilyuk, I. L. (2022). model risKs in the financial sphere under the conditions of the use of artificial intelligence and machine learning. *Russian Journal of Economics and Law, 16*(1), 54–76. DOI: 10.21202/2782-2923.2022.1.40-50

Kismawadi, E. R. (2024a). Blockchain technology and islamic finance: Empowering small businesses for financial sustainability. In *Technopreneurship in Small Businesses for Sustainability* (pp. 50–77). DOI: 10.4018/979-8-3693-3530-7.ch004

Kismawadi, E. R. (2024b). Halal food industry and sustainability. In *Economics and Environmental Responsibility in the Global Beverage Industry* (pp. 170–197). DOI: 10.4018/979-8-3693-2149-2.ch010

Kismawadi, E. R. (2024c). Sustainable Islamic financial inclusion: The ethical challenges of generative AI in product and service development. In *Exploring the Ethical Implications of Generative AI* (pp. 237–258). DOI: 10.4018/979-8-3693-1565-1.ch013

Kismawadi, E. R., Irfan, M., Al Muddatstsir, U. D., & Abdulkarim, F. M. (2023). Fintech innovations: Risk mitigation strategies in Islamic finance. In *Fintech Applications in Islamic Finance* (pp. 35–58). AI, Machine Learning, and Blockchain Techniques., DOI: 10.4018/979-8-3693-1038-0.ch003

Klochko, A., Kurylo, M., Rohovenko, O., Volchenko, N., & Shulzhenko, A. (2023). The legal regulation of artificial intelligence security in Ukrainian banking. *Journal of Infrastructure. Policy and Development, 8*(2), 2582.

Kluwer, W. (2024). *Artificial Intelligence in Auditing: Enhancing the Audit Lifecycle.* Wolters Kluwer N.V.

Koç, S. (2024). Teachers' Views on Lifelong Learning. *International Journal of Contemporary Educational Research, 11*(2), 247–258. DOI: 10.52380/ijcer.2024.11.2.621

Koelbl, M., Laschinger, R., Steininger, B. I., Schaefers, W., Koelbl, M., Laschinger, R., Steininger, B. I., & Schaefers, W. (2024). Revealing the risk perception of investors using machine learning. *European Journal of Finance, 30*(17), 2032–2058. Advance online publication. DOI: 10.1080/1351847X.2024.2364831

Kogta Financial. (2024). *Technology for financial inclusion in India 2024.* Retrieved October 27, 2024, from https://kogta.in/blog/technology-for-financial-inclusion-in-india-2024

Kokina, J. &. (2024). The Role of Artificial Intelligence in the Audit Process and How to Leverage It. *Journal of Ecohumanism*, 45-60.

Kokina, J., & Davenport, T. H. (2017). The emergence of artificial intelligence: How automation is transforming the auditing profession. *Journal of Emerging Technologies in Accounting*, *14*(2), 115–122. DOI: 10.2308/jeta-51730

Kolt, N. (2022). Predicting Consumer Contracts. *Berkeley Technology Law Journal*, •••, 1–60.

Kondapaka, K. K. (2019). Advanced AI Models for Portfolio Management and Optimization in Finance: Techniques, Applications, and Real-World Case Studies. *Distributed Learning and Broad Applications in Scientific Research*, *5*, 560–597.

Koshiyama, A., Kazim, E., Braines, D., & Dobbins, M. (2021). Algorithm auditing: Managing the legal, ethical, and technological risks of AI and machine learning. *Journal of Responsible Technology*, *5*, 100017. DOI: 10.1016/j.jrt.2021.100017

Kount. (2021). How to Reduce False Positives in Fraud Detection. *Kount Blog*.

Kour, M. (2023). Challenges and opportunities of machine learning in the financial sector. In *Algorithmic Approaches to Financial Technology* (pp. 61–73). Forecasting, Trading, and Optimization., DOI: 10.4018/979-8-3693-1746-4.ch004

KPMG. (2024). *Transforming Internal Audits Through the Power of AI*. KPMG International.

Kumar et.al.; (2023). Digital Transformation and Financial Inclusion: A Case Study of State Bank of India, *Intellectual Resonance, DCAC journal of Interdisciplinary studies, 6(2),*2321-2594

Kumar, A., Kumar, A., Kumari, S., Kumar, S., Kumari, N., & Behura, A. K. (2024). Artificial Intelligence: The Strategy of Financial Risk Management. Finance. *Theory into Practice*, *28*(3), 174–182. DOI: 10.26794/2587-5671-2024-28-3-174-182

Kumar, A., Srivastava, A., & Gupta, P. K. (2022). Banking 4.0: The era of artificial intelligence-based fintech. *Strategic Change*, *31*(6), 591–601. DOI: 10.1002/jsc.2526

Kumar, K. R.. (2024). AI-Driven Robo-Advisors in Wealth Management. *Educational Administration: Theory and Practice*, *30*(5), 13478–13486.

Kumar, K. R., Balaji, C., Suresh, M., Nagaraju, E., Natarajan, S., & Kumar, R. (2024). Study The Impact Of Ai Driven Rob Advisors On Wealth Management Services. Evaluate Their Effectiveness In Portfolio Management, Risk Assessment, And Personalized Investment Strategies. *Educational Administration: Theory and Practice*, *30*(5), 13478–13486.

Kumar, S., Lim, W., Sivarajah, U., & Kaur, J. (2023). Artificial Intelligence and Blockchain Integration in Business: Trends from a Bibliometric-Content Analysis. *Information Systems Frontiers*, *25*, 871–896. PMID: 35431617

Kumar, S., Rao, S., Goyal, K., & Goyal, N. (2022). Journal of Behavioral and Experimental Finance: A bibliometric overview. *Journal of Behavioral and Experimental Finance*, •••, 34.

Kumar, S., Xiao, J. J., Pattnaik, D., Lim, W. M., & Rasul, T. (2022). Past, present and future of bank marketing: A bibliometric analysis of International Journal of Bank Marketing (1983–2020). *International Journal of Bank Marketing*, *40*(2), 341–383. DOI: 10.1108/IJBM-07-2021-0351

Kurshan, E., Chen, J., Storchan, V., & Shen, H. (2021). On the current and emerging challenges of developing fair and ethical AI solutions in financial services. In ICAIF 2021 - 2nd ACM International Conference on AI in Finance. Association for Computing Machinery. https://doi.org/DOI: 10.1145/3490354.3494408

Kusuma, B. W. (2024). The Impact of the COVID-19 Pandemic on Auditing Practices: A Qualitative Analysis. *Golden Ratio of Auditing Research*, *4*(1), 24–32. DOI: 10.52970/grar.v4i1.385

Lahmini, H. M., & Zine, D. (2024). The Role of Artificial Intelligence in Optimizing Portfolio Management : A Literature Review. International Conference on Business and Technology, ICBT, 122–131. https://doi.org/DOI: 10.1007/978-3-031-67444-0_12

Lahmiri, S. (2016). Comparing traditional and AI-driven credit risk models for consumer loans. *Applied Economics Letters*, *23*(7), 510–515. DOI: 10.1080/13504851.2015.1083074

Lam, J. (2016). *Implementing Enterprise Risk Management: From Methods to Applications*. Wiley.

Laukkanen, T., & Pasanen, M. (2008). Mobile banking innovators and early adopters: How they differ from other online users? *Journal of Financial Services Marketing*, *13*(2), 86–94. DOI: 10.1057/palgrave.fsm.4760077

Law, B. (2024). *Can You Use AI for Legal Research?* Bloomberg Law.

Law, B. B. (2024). *Key Considerations in AI-Related Contracts*. Byte Back Law.

Lazo, M., & Ebardo, R. (2023). Artificial intelligence adoption in the banking industry: Current state and future prospect. *Journal of Innovation Management*, *11*(3), 54–74. DOI: 10.24840/2183-0606_011.003_0003

Le Trung, H. (2020). Deep Reinforcement Learning for Stock Portfolio Optimization. *International Journal of Modeling and Optimization*, *10*(5), 139–144. DOI: 10.7763/IJMO.2020.V10.761

Lee, I., & Shin, Y. J. (2018). Fintech: Ecosystem, business models, investment decisions, and challenges. *Business Horizons*, *61*(1), 35–46. DOI: 10.1016/j.bushor.2017.09.003

Lee, J., Serafin, A. M., & Courteau, C. (2023). Corporate disclosure, ESG and green fintech in the energy industry. *Journal of World Energy Law and Business*, *16*(6), 473–491. DOI: 10.1093/jwelb/jwad018

Leikas, J., Johri, A., Latvanen, M., Wessberg, N., & Hahto, A. (2022). Governing ethical AI transformation: A case study of AuroraAI. *Frontiers in Artificial Intelligence*, *5*, 836557. DOI: 10.3389/frai.2022.836557 PMID: 35224480

Leo, M., Sharma, S., & Maddulety, K. (2019). Machine learning in banking risk management: A literature review. *Risks*, *7*(1), 29. DOI: 10.3390/risks7010029

Liao, X. (2024). Machine Learning Algorithm Applications in Empirical Finance: A Review of the Empirical Literature. *3rd International Conference on Economic Development and Business Culture (ICEDBC 2023)*, 311–316. https://doi.org/DOI: 10.2991/978-94-6463-246-0_38

Li, B., & Xu, Z. (2021). Insights into financial technology (FinTech): A bibliometric and visual study. *Financial Innovation*, *7*(1), 69. Advance online publication. DOI: 10.1186/s40854-021-00285-7 PMID: 35024290

Lim, T. (2024). Environmental, social, and governance (ESG) and artificial intelligence in finance: State-of-the-art and research takeaways. In Artificial Intelligence Review (Vol. 57, Issue 4). Springer Netherlands. https://doi.org/DOI: 10.1007/s10462-024-10708-3

Lima, M. A., Carvalho, P. C., Fernández-Ramírez, L. M., & Braga, A. P. (2020). Improving solar forecasting using Deep Learning and Portfolio Theory integration. *Energy*, *195*, 117016. DOI: 10.1016/j.energy.2020.117016

Lin, C. C., Tseng, C. H., & Ho, S. L. (2023). Applying Random Forest Algorithm and Mean-Variance Model in Portfolio Optimization in the China Stock Market. Eurasia Conference on IOT, Communication and Engineering, ECICE 2023, 361–364. https://doi.org/DOI: 10.1109/ECICE59523.2023.10382968

Link, G. D. S. (n.d.). *Credit risk management process: Best practices & techniques*. Retrieved October 27, 2024, from https://www.gdslink.com/credit-risk-management-process-best-practices-techniques/

Li, P. (2020). Research on the application and security of artificial intelligence in financial industry. *IOP Conference Series: Materials Science and Engineering*. https://doi.org/DOI: 10.1088/1757-899X/750/1/012102

Liu, X., Yang, Y., Jiang, Y., Fu, Y., Zhong, R. Y., Li, M., & Huang, G. Q. (2023). Data-driven ESG assessment for blockchain services: A comparative study in textiles and apparel industry. *Resources, Conservation and Recycling*, *190*, 106837. DOI: 10.1016/j.resconrec.2022.106837

LLP, S. A. (2024). Artificial Intelligence in Financial Markets: Systemic Risk and Market Abuse Concerns. *Butterworths Journal of International Banking and Financial Law*.

Lo, A. W. (2021). The Financial System Red in Tooth and Claw: 75 Years of Co-Evolving Markets and Technology. *Financial Analysts Journal*, *77*(3), 5–33. DOI: 10.1080/0015198X.2021.1929030

Lommers, K., El Harzli, O., & Kim, J. (2021). Confronting Machine Learning with Financial Research. *The Journal of Financial Data Science*, *3*(3), 67–96. DOI: 10.3905/jfds.2021.1.068

Loos, B., Sauer, A., & Wiederkehr, C. (2020). Enhanced portfolio diversification and reduced home bias through robo-advisory platforms. *Journal of Financial Economics*, *14*(4), 225–242.

Lorentzon, J. I., Fotoh, L. E., & Mugwira, T. (2024). Remote auditing and its impacts on auditors' work and work-life balance: Auditors' perceptions and implications. *Accounting Research Journal*, *37*(1), 1–18. DOI: 10.1108/ARJ-06-2023-0158

Loukeris, N., & Eleftheriadis, D. (2015). Asset allocation strategies with bankruptcy detection for enhanced investment decision-making. *European Financial Management Journal*, *21*(2), 310–329. DOI: 10.1111/eufm.2015.00233

Ludkovski, M. (2023). Statistical Machine Learning for Quantitative Finance. *Annual Review of Statistics and Its Application*, *15*(19), 271–295. DOI: 10.1146/annurev-statistics-032921-042409

Lumen. (2024). *Secure Your Future: The Benefits of Ethical AI Governance*. Monroe, Louisiana, USA: Lumen Technologies, Inc.

Macchiavello, E., & Siri, M. (2022). Sustainable finance and Fintech: Can technology contribute to achieving environmental goals? A preliminary assessment of 'Green Fintech' and 'Sustainable digital finance'. *European Company and Financial Law Review*, *19*(1), 128–174. DOI: 10.1515/ecfr-2022-0005

Machireddy, J. R., Rachakatla, S. K., & Ravichandran, P. (2021). AI-Driven Business Analytics for Financial Forecasting: Integrating Data Warehousing with Predictive Models. *Journal of Machine Learning in Pharmaceutical Research, 1*(2), 1–24.

Macpherson, M., Gasperini, A., & Bosco, M. (2021). Artificial intelligence and FinTech technologies for ESG data and analysis. SSRN *Electronic Journal.* DOI: 10.2139/ssrn.3790774

Mäenpää, K., Kale, S. H., Kuusela, H., & Mesiranta, N. (2008). Consumer perceptions of Internet banking in Finland: The moderating role of familiarity. *Journal of Retailing and Consumer Services, 15*(4), 266–276. DOI: 10.1016/j.jretconser.2007.05.007

Maia, S., de Benedicto, G., do Prado, J., Robb, D., Bispo, O., & de Brito, M. (2019). Mapping the literature on credit unions: A bibliometric investigation grounded in Scopus and Web of Science. *Scientometrics, 120*(3), 929–960. DOI: 10.1007/s11192-019-03165-1

Majumder, T. (2023). The Evaluating Impact of Artificial Intelligence on Risk Management and Fraud Detection in the Commercial Bank in Bangladesh. *International Journal of Applied and Natural Sciences, 1*(1), 67–76. DOI: 10.61424/ijans.v1i1.75

Malladhi, A. (2023). Artificial Intelligence and Machine Learning in Forensic Accounting. *SSRG International Journal of Computer Science and Engineering*, 6-20.

Manoharan, G., & Rajoli, S. B. (2024). Leveraging Technology for Enhancing Performance Appraisal. In Employee Performance Management for Improved Workplace Motivation (pp. 289-310). IGI Global. DOI: 10.4018/979-8-3693-4387-6.ch012

Manoharan, G., Ashtikkar, S. P., & Nivedha, M. (2024). Artificial Intelligence in Decision-Making: Reinventing Business Strategies. In Generative AI for Transformational Management (pp. 25-50). IGI Global.

Manoharan, G., Jyothi, B. S., Bhat, R., Acharjee, P. B., Sharma, A., & Rawal, P. (2023, December). Utilizing Machine Learning for Advanced Natural Language Processing and Sentiment Analysis in Social Media Platforms. In International Conference on Mechanical and Energy Technologies (pp. 111-125). Singapore: Springer Nature Singapore.

Manoharan, G., Nithya, G., Rajchandar, K., Razak, A., Gupta, S., Durai, S., & Ashtikar, S. P. (2024). AI in Finance and Banking: The Act of Gyration. In Revolutionizing Customer-Centric Banking Through ICT (pp. 1-28). IGI Global.

Manoharan, G., Ali, S. D. N. H., Sathe, D. M., Karthik, A., Nagpal, A., & Sidana, A. "Fraud Detection in E-commerce Transactions: A Machine Learning Perspective," *2024 International Conference on Advances in Computing, Communication and Applied Informatics (ACCAI)*, Chennai, India, 2024, pp. 1-5, DOI: 10.1109/ACCAI61061.2024.10601813

Manoharan, G., Ashtikar, S. P., & Kumar, S. (2024). Extenuating Digital Transformation: Revolutionizing Hotel Operations Through AI Technology. In Talukder, M., Kumar, S., & Tyagi, P. (Eds.), *Hotel and Travel Management in the AI Era* (pp. 257–274). IGI Global., DOI: 10.4018/979-8-3693-7898-4.ch012

Manoharan, G., Mishra, A. B., Adusumilli, S. B. K., Chavva, M., Damancharla, H., & Sahaya Lenin, D. "Supervised Learning for Personalized Marketing Strategies," *2024 International Conference on Advances in Computing, Communication and Applied Informatics (ACCAI)*, Chennai, India, 2024, pp. 1-6, DOI: 10.1109/ACCAI61061.2024.10602307

Manoharan, G., Nithya, G., Razak, A., Durai, S., Sharma, S., & Ashtikar, S. P. (2024). Enhancing Financial Literacy: Strategies, Challenges, and Global Initiatives. In Singh, D., Bansal, R., Gupta, S., & Ansari, Y. (Eds.), *Emerging Perspectives on Financial Well-Being* (pp. 111–128). IGI Global., DOI: 10.4018/979-8-3693-1750-1.ch006

Manoharan, G., Nithya, G., Razak, A., Sharma, S., & Ashtikkar, S. P. (2024). Challenges and Opportunities in Green Finance: Overcoming Barriers and Scaling up Sustainable Investments. In Misra, S., Jadeja, R., & Mittal, M. (Eds.), *Practical Approaches to Agile Project Management* (pp. 398–413). IGI Global., DOI: 10.4018/979-8-3693-3318-1.ch022

Maple, C. S. (2023). *The AI Revolution: Opportunities and Challenges for the Finance Sector.* Ithaca, New York: arXiv preprint arXiv:2308.16538.

Maple, C., Szpruch, L., Epiphaniou, G., Staykova, K., Singh, S., Penwarden, W., Wen, Y., Wang, Z., Hariharan, J., & Avramovic, P. (2023). The AI Revolution: Opportunities and Challenges for the Finance Sector. http://arxiv.org/abs/2308.16538

Maree, C., & Omlin, C. W. (2021). Understanding Spending Behavior : Recurrent Neural Network Explanation and Interpretation. https://doi.org//arxiv.2109.11871DOI: 10.48550

Maree, C., Modal, J. E., & Omlin, C. W. (2020). Towards Responsible AI for Financial Transactions. *2020 IEEE Symposium Series on Computational Intelligence (SSCI)*. https://doi.org/DOI: 10.1109/SSCI47803.2020.9308456

Markowitz, H. (1952). Portfolio Selection. *The Journal of Finance*, *7*(1), 77–91.

Marr, B. (2020). *The Amazing Ways How Mastercard Uses Artificial Intelligence to Stop Fraud and Reduce False Declines*. Bernard Marr & Co.

Marr, B. (2024). How Mastercard Uses AI Strategically: A Case Study. *Forbes*.

Marsal, A. (2024). *Balancing Act: Managing AI Governance Risks in Financial Services*. Alvarez & Marsal Holdings, LLC.

Martinelli, A., Mina, A., & Windrum, P. (2021). Digital innovation and the evolution of market structures. *Research Policy, 50*(9), 104321. DOI: 10.1016/j.respol.2021.104321

Martinez, C. (2021). *3 Case Studies Where AI Has Been Successfully Implemented in the Finance Industry*. Medium.

Maseke, B. F. (2024). The transformative power of artificial intelligence in banking client service. *South Asian Journal of Social Studies and Economics, 21*(3), 93–105. DOI: 10.9734/sajsse/2024/v21i3787

Mashrur, A., Luo, W., Zaidi, N. A., & Robles-Kelly, A. (2020). Machine learning for financial risk management: A survey. *IEEE Access : Practical Innovations, Open Solutions, 8*, 203203–203223. DOI: 10.1109/ACCESS.2020.3036322

Masrek, M. N., Susantari, T., Mutia, F., Yuwinanto, H. P., & Atmi, R. T. (2024). Enabling Education Everywhere: How artificial intelligence empowers ubiquitous and lifelong learning. *Environment-Behaviour Proceedings Journal, 9*(SI18), 57–63. DOI: 10.21834/e-bpj.v9iSI18.5462

Mastercard. (2024). Fraud Detection Using AI: Inside the Algorithm. *Mastercard Newsroom*.

Mastercard. (2024). Mastercard Accelerates Card Fraud Detection with Generative AI Technology. *Mastercard Newsroom*.

Mastercard. (2024). Mastercard Expands First-of-its-Kind AI Technology to Help Banks Protect More Consumers from Scams in Real-Time. *Press Release*.

Mathur, P. (2018). Machine learning applications using python: Cases studies from healthcare, retail, and finance. *Apress Media, LLC*. Advance online publication. DOI: 10.1007/978-1-4842-3787-8

Mazars, F. (2025). *AI Governance – From Concept to Compliance*. Forvis Mazars.

Mazraeh, N., Daneshvar, A., zaj, M., & Roodposhti, F. (2022). Stock Portfolio Optimization Using a Combined Approach of Multi Objective Grey Wolf Optimizer and Machine Learning Preselection Methods. Computational Intelligence and Neuroscience- Hindawi.

Melnyk, V. (2024). Transforming the nature of trust between banks and young clients: From traditional to digital banking. *Qualitative Research in Financial Markets, 16*(4), 618–635. DOI: 10.1108/QRFM-08-2022-0129

Mende, M., Scott, M. L., Ubal, V. O., Hassler, C. M., Harmeling, C. M., & Palmatier, R. W. (2024). Personalized communication as a platform for service inclusion? Initial insights into interpersonal and AI-based personalization for stigmatized consumers. *Journal of Service Research, 27*(1), 28–48. DOI: 10.1177/10946705231188676

Méndez-Suárez, M., García-Fernández, F., & Gallardo, F. (2019). Artificial Intelligence Modelling Framework for Financial Automated Advising in the Copper Market. *Journal of Open Innovation, 5*(81), 81. DOI: 10.3390/joitmc5040081

Menkveld, A. J. (2013). Does high-frequency trading cause market volatility? Evidence from trader withdrawal scenarios. *Financial Markets and Portfolio Management, 27*(4), 321–348.

Mhlanga, D. (2021). Financial Inclusion in Emerging Economies : The Application of Machine Learning and Artificial Intelligence in Credit Risk Assessment. *International Journal of Financial Studies, 9*(39), 39. DOI: 10.3390/ijfs9030039

Milojević, N., & Redzepagic, S. (2021). Prospects of Artificial Intelligence and Machine Learning Application in Banking Risk Management. *Journal of Central Banking Theory and Practice, 10*(3), 41–57. DOI: 10.2478/jcbtp-2021-0023

MindBridge. (2024). *Operational Risk Management: AI Tools and Best Practices for Finance and Audit.* MindBridge Blog.

Mironowicz, P., Mandarino, A., Yilmaz, A., & Ankenbrand, T. (2024). Applications of quantum machine learning for quantitative finance. arXiv preprint arXiv:2405.10119.

Mohammadi, S., & Nazemi, A. (2020). On portfolio management with value at risk and uncertain returns via an artificial neural network scheme. *Cognitive Systems Research, 59*, 247–263. DOI: 10.1016/j.cogsys.2019.09.024

Mohan, R., Boopathi, M., Ranjan, P., Najana, M., Chaudhary, P. K., & Chotrani, A. K. (2024). Ai in fraud detection: Evaluating the efficacy of artificial intelligence in preventing financial misconduct. *Journal of Electrical Systems, 20*(3s), 1332–1338. DOI: 10.52783/jes.1508

Moharrak, M., & Mogaji, E. (2024). Generative AI in banking: Empirical insights on integration, challenges and opportunities in a regulated industry. *International Journal of Bank Marketing*.

Mökander, J., Axente, M., & Floridi, L. (2022). Ethics-based auditing in the European AI regulation: Designing conformity assessments for trustworthy AI. *AI and Ethics*, *2*(3), 247–259. DOI: 10.1007/s43681-021-00050-4

Mökander, J., & Floridi, L. (2021). Ethics-based auditing to develop trustworthy AI. *Minds and Machines*, *31*(2), 323–327. DOI: 10.1007/s11023-021-09557-8

Mökander, J., & Floridi, L. (2022). The European Union's AI regulation and its impact on auditing: Guidelines for high-risk AI systems. *Journal of Responsible AI*, *2*(3), 234–248.

Mökander, J., Schuett, J., Kirk, H. R., & Floridi, L. (2023). Auditing large language models: A three-layered approach. *AI and Ethics*, •••, 1–31.

Monteiro, A., Cepêda, C., Da Silva, A. C. F., & Vale, J. (2023). The relationship between ai adoption intensity and internal control system and accounting information quality. *Systems*, *11*(11), 536. DOI: 10.3390/systems11110536

Morley, J., Elhalal, A., Garcia, F., Kinsey, L., Mökander, J., & Floridi, L. (2021). Ethics as a service: A pragmatic operationalisation of AI ethics. *Minds and Machines*, *31*(2), 239–256. DOI: 10.1007/s11023-021-09563-w PMID: 34720418

Mor, S., Aneja, R., Madan, S., & Gupta, S. (2022). Artificial intelligence and loan default: The case of commercial banks in India. *Strategic Change*, *31*(6), 571–580. DOI: 10.1002/jsc.2529

Motwani, B., Haryani, S., Manoharan, G., & Razak, A. (2024). Impact of Workforce Emotional Intelligence on Patient Satisfaction: A Sentiment Analysis Approach Using Supervised Machine Algorithms. In Rajapakshe, W. (Ed.), *Employee Performance Management for Improved Workplace Motivation* (pp. 263–288). IGI Global., DOI: 10.4018/979-8-3693-4387-6.ch011

Mullankandy, S. (2024). Transforming Data into Compliance : Harnessing AI / ML to Enhance Regulatory Reporting Processes Introduction : Objectives : Method : Journal of Artificial Intelligence General Science (JAIGS), 24(1). https://ojs .boulibrary.com/index.php/JAIGS%0ATransforming

Mulyandini, V. C. (2023). The Relationship between Emotional Intelligence and Audit Judgment: A Study on Internal Auditors in Indonesian Financial Institutions. Asian Journal of Economics. *Business and Accounting*, *23*(9), 34–38.

Muterera, J. (2024). THE AUDITOR SELF-EFFICACY SCALE: MEASURING CONFIDENCE IN TECHNICAL SKILLS, TECHNOLOGICAL ADAPTATION, AND INTERPERSONAL COMMUNICATION. *Finance & Accounting Research Journal*, *6*(3), 331–346. DOI: 10.51594/farj.v6i3.873

Mutran, V. M., Ribeiro, C. O., Nascimento, C. A., & Rêgo, E. E. (2018). Bioenergy investments in sugarcane mills: An approach combining portfolio theory with neural networks. *Computer-Aided Chemical Engineering*, *44*, 967–972. DOI: 10.1016/B978-0-444-64241-7.50156-7

Nadiah, A. H., Hajar, A. S., & Zarinah, A. R. (2017). The influence of core competency skills of IRBM tax auditors towards their performance. *Revue des Sciences Fondamentales et Appliquées*, *9*(5S), 958–988. DOI: 10.4314/jfas.v9i5s.68

Naqvi, A. (2023). *Artificial Intelligence for Audit, Forensic Accounting, and Valuation: A Strategic Perspective*. Routledge.

Nassiry, D. (2019). The role of Fintech in unlocking green finance. *Handbook of Green Finance*, 315-336. DOI: 10.1007/978-981-13-0227-5_27

Natarajan, S., Salgotra, P., Krishna, M. H., Revathi, V., Sobti, R., & Adhav, S. (2024). Risk Management in Financial Institutions with Applied Machine Learning. International Conference on Communication, Computer Sciences and Engineering, IC3SE 2024, 1514–1519. https://doi.org/DOI: 10.1109/IC3SE62002.2024.10593631

Nazemi, A., & Fabozzi, F. J. (n.d.). Interpretable Machine Learning for Creditor Recovery Rates. 1–32.

Nazemi, A., Heidenreich, K., & Fabozzi, F. J. (2018). Improving corporate bond recovery rate prediction using multi-factor support vector regressions. *European Journal of Operational Research*, *271*(2), 664–675. DOI: 10.1016/j.ejor.2018.05.024

Nesvetailova, A. (2014). Innovations, fragility and complexity: Understanding the power of finance. In Government and Opposition (Vol. 49, Issue 3, pp. 542–568). Cambridge University Press. https://doi.org/DOI: 10.1017/gov.2014.12

News, B. (2015). *Goldman Gets Serious About High-Speed Trading*. Bloomberg.

News, P. (2024). *AI's Impact on Compliance in Finance*. PyQuant News.

Ngai, E. W., Hu, Y., Wong, Y. H., Chen, Y., & Sun, X. (2011). The application of data mining techniques in financial fraud detection: A classification framework and an academic review. *Decision Support Systems*, *50*(3), 559–569. DOI: 10.1016/j.dss.2010.08.006

Nguyen, D. K., Sermpinis, G., & Stasinakis, C. (2023). Big data, artificial intelligence and machine learning: A transformative symbiosis in favour of financial technology. *European Financial Management*, *29*(2), 517–548. DOI: 10.1111/eufm.12365

Nguyen, T. P. L., Chew, L. W., Muthaiyah, S., Teh, B. H., & Ong, T. S. (2023). Factors influencing acceptance of Robo-Advisors for wealth management in Malaysia. *Cogent Engineering*, *10*(1), 2188992. DOI: 10.1080/23311916.2023.2188992

Nithya, G., Manoharan, G., & Ashtikar, S. P. (2024). India's Fintech and AI-Related Regulation Framework. In The Adoption of Fintech (pp. 51-72). Productivity Press.

Northey, G., Hunter, V., Mulcahy, R., Choong, K., & Mehmet, M. (2022). Man vs machine: How artificial intelligence in banking influences consumer belief in financial advice. *International Journal of Bank Marketing*, *40*(6), 1182–1199. DOI: 10.1108/IJBM-09-2021-0439

Nurlaela, E., Mappanyukki, R., & Surjandari, D. A. (2021). The effect of the internal audit roles and auditor professionalism on fraud prevention. *Studies in Media and Communication*, *9*(2), 24–35. DOI: 10.11114/smc.v9i2.5324

Odeyemi, O., Awonuga, K. F., Mhlongo, N. Z., Ndubuisi, N. L., Olatoye, F. O., & Daraojimb, A. I. (2024). The role of AI in transforming auditing practices: A global perspective review. *World Journal of Advanced Research and Reviews*, *21*(2), 359–370. DOI: 10.30574/wjarr.2024.21.2.0460

Okeleke, P. A., Ajiga, D., Folorunsho, S. O., & Ezeigweneme, C. (2024). Predictive analytics for market trends using AI: A study in consumer behavior. *International Journal of Engineering Research Updates*, *7*(1), 36–49. DOI: 10.53430/ijeru.2024.7.1.0032

Okwiri, M. I. O., & Muathe, S. M. (2024). Competitiveness of Tier three Commercial Banks in Kenya: The Role of Strategic Leadership Practices. *International Journal of Management Research and Emerging Sciences*, *14*(1).

Oladeinde, M., Okeleke, E. C., Adaramodu, O. R., Fakeyede, O. G., & Farayola, O. A. (2023). Communicating IT audit findings: Strategies for effective stakeholder engagement. *Computer Science & IT Research Journal*, *4*(2), 126–139. DOI: 10.51594/csitrj.v4i2.612

Oladoyinbo, T. O., Olabanji, S. O., Olaniyi, O. O., Adebiyi, O. O., Okunleye, O. J., & Ismaila Alao, A. (2024). Exploring the challenges of artificial intelligence in data integrity and its influence on social dynamics. *Asian Journal of Advanced Research and Reports*, *18*(2), 1–23. DOI: 10.9734/ajarr/2024/v18i2601

Olan, F., Arakpogun, E. O., Jayawickrama, U., Suklan, J., & Liu, S. (2022). Sustainable supply chain finance and supply networks: The role of artificial intelligence. *IEEE Transactions on Engineering Management.*

Omarini, A. E. (2018). Banks and Fintechs: How to develop a digital open banking approach for the bank's future. *International Business Research, 11*(9), 23. DOI: 10.5539/ibr.v11n9p23

Omoteso, K. (2012). The application of artificial intelligence in auditing: Looking back to the future. *Expert Systems with Applications, 39*(9), 8490–8495. DOI: 10.1016/j.eswa.2012.01.098

OneStream. (2024). *10 Ways Companies Are Using AI in the Finance Services Industry*. OneStream Software LLC.

Onwubuariri, E. R., Adelakun, B. O., Olaiya, O. P., & Ziorklui, J. E. K. (2024). AI-Driven risk assessment: Revolutionizing audit planning and execution. *Finance & Accounting Research Journal, 6*(6), 1069–1090. DOI: 10.51594/farj.v6i6.1236

Osterrieder, J. (2023). Machine Learning for Asset Management:Revolutionizing Financial Analysis and Decision-Making with Data Science Techniques. SSRN Electronic Journal. https://doi.org/DOI: 10.2139/ssrn.4638186

Owolabi, O. S., Uche, P. C., Adeniken, N. T., Efijemue, O., Attakorah, S., Emi-johnson, O. G., & Hinneh, E. (2024). Comparative Analysis of Machine Learning Models for Customer Churn Prediction in the U. S. Banking and Financial Services : Economic Impact and Industry-Specific Insights. *Journal of Data Analysis and Information Processing, 12*(3), 388–418. DOI: 10.4236/jdaip.2024.123021

Owolabi, O. S., Uche, P. C., Adeniken, N. T., Ihejirika, C., Islam, R. B., & Chhetri, B. J. T. (2024). Ethical implications of artificial intelligence (AI) adoption in financial decision-making. *Computer and Information Science, 17*(1), 1–49. DOI: 10.5539/cis.v17n1p49

Oyeniyi, L. D., Ugochukwu, C. E., & Mhlongo, N. Z. (2024). Implementing AI in banking customer service: A review of current trends and future applications. *International Journal of Science and Research Archive, 11*(2), 1492–1509. DOI: 10.30574/ijsra.2024.11.2.0639

Ozbayoglu, A. M., Gudelek, M. U., & Sezer, O. B. (2020). Deep learning for financial applications: A survey. *Applied Soft Computing, 93*, 106384. DOI: 10.1016/j.asoc.2020.106384

Padmaavathy, P. A., Manoharan, G., Billa, P., Purushottamashtikar, S., Selvaraj, F., & Razak, A. (2024, June). Retail customers' utilization of bank kiosk among selected private sector banks in coimbatore. In AIP Conference Proceedings (Vol. 2971, No. 1). AIP Publishing.

Pai, N., & Ilango, V. (2020). Neural Network Model for Efficient portfolio Management and Time Series Forecasting. IEEE, *4th International Conference on Intelligent Computing and Control Systems (ICICCS)*, Madurai, India, 150-155. DOI: 10.1109/ICICCS48265.2020.9121049

Pandl, K., Thiebes, S., Schmidt-Kraepelin, M., & Sunyaev, A. (2020). On the Convergence of Artificial Intelligence and Distributed Ledger Technology: A Scoping Review and Future Research Agenda. *IEEE Access : Practical Innovations, Open Solutions*, *8*, 57075–57095. DOI: 10.1109/ACCESS.2020.2981447

Paramesha, M., Rane, N., & Rane, J. (2024). Artificial intelligence, machine learning, deep learning, and blockchain in financial and banking services: A comprehensive review. [PUMRJ]. *SSRN*, *01*(02), 68–83. DOI: 10.2139/ssrn.4855893

Park, J. Y., Ryu, J. P., & Shin, H. J. (2016). Robo advisors for portfolio management. *Advanced Science and Technology Letters*, *141*(1), 104–108. DOI: 10.14257/astl.2016.141.21

Patil, D. (2024). Artificial Intelligence in Financial Risk Assessment and Fraud Detection: Opportunities and Ethical Concerns. *International Journal of Financial Studies*, 78-95.

Paul, M. (2024). Artificial Intelligence in Financial Services. *The Cambridge Handbook of Responsible Artificial Intelligence*, 1-20.

Pendergast, M. (2024). AI's transformative effects on finance: Decision-making, risk management, and efficiency. *Financial Innovation and Technology Journal*, *18*(1), 44–58.

Perumalsamy, J., Althati, C., & Shanmugam, L. (2022). Advanced AI and Machine Learning Techniques for Predictive Analytics in Annuity Products: Enhancing Risk Assessment and Pricing Accuracy. *Journal of Artificial Intelligence Research*, *2*(2), 51–82.

Petukhina, A., Trimborn, S., Härdle, W. K., & Elendner, H. (2021). Cryptocurrency trading dynamics and the role of AI and human expertise. *Journal of Banking & Finance*, *122*, 106224. DOI: 10.1016/j.jbankfin.2020.106224

Philippon, T. (2016). The FinTech opportunity. DOI: 10.3386/w22476

Phoon, K. F., & Koh, C. C. F. (2018). Robo-advisors and wealth management. *Journal of Alternative Investments*, *20*(3), 79–94. DOI: 10.3905/jai.2018.20.3.079

Pichl, L., & Kaizoji, T. (2017). Volatility and sentiment analysis in cryptocurrency markets: A HAR model application. *Finance Research Letters*, *22*, 116–121. DOI: 10.1016/j.frl.2016.10.009

Pistoia, M., Ahmad, S. F., Ajagekar, A., Buts, A., Chakrabarti, S., Herman, D., Hu, S., Jena, A., Minssen, P., Niroula, P., Rattew, A., Sun, Y., & Yalovetzky, R. (2021). Quantum Machine Learning for Finance. https://doi.org/DOI: 10.1109/ICCAD51958.2021.9643469

Prado, J., Alcântara, V., Carvalho, F., Vieira, K., Machado, L., & Tonelli, D. (2016). Multivariate analysis of credit risk and bankruptcy research data: A bibliometric study involving different knowledge fields (1968---2014). *Scientometrics*, *106*(3), 1007–1029. DOI: 10.1007/s11192-015-1829-6

Pristiyono, P., Juliana, J., & Prayoga, Y. (2022). Measuring customer trust through digital transformation of banking as a competitive advantage. *Jurnal Ekonomi Bisnis Dan Kewirausahaan*, *11*(2), 214. DOI: 10.26418/jebik.v11i2.51986

Purwanto, E., Deviny, J., & Mutahar, A. M. (2020). The mediating role of trust in the relationship between corporate image, security, word of mouth and loyalty in M-banking using among the millennial generation in Indonesia. *Management & Marketing*, *15*(2), 255–274. DOI: 10.2478/mmcks-2020-0016

PwC India. (n.d.). *Integrating ESG in the payments ecosystem*. Retrieved October 27, 2024, from https://www.pwc.in/industries/financial-services/fintech/payments/integrating-esg-in-the-payments-ecosystem.htm

Quinn, B. (2022). Teaching Open Science Analytics in the Age of Financial Technology. *QMS Research Paper, 1*.

Radial. (2023). Reducing False Positives in eCommerce Fraud Detection. *Radial Insights*.

Rahmani, A. M., Rezazadeh, B., Haghparast, M., Chang, W. C., & Ting, S. G. (2023). Applications of Artificial Intelligence in the Economy, Including Applications in Stock Trading, Market Analysis, and Risk Management. *IEEE Access : Practical Innovations, Open Solutions*, *11*(July), 80769–80793. DOI: 10.1109/ACCESS.2023.3300036

Rahman, M., Ming, T. H., Baigh, T. A., & Sarker, M. (2023). Adoption of artificial intelligence in banking services: An empirical analysis. *International Journal of Emerging Markets*, *18*(10), 4270–4300. DOI: 10.1108/IJOEM-06-2020-0724

Rai, H. P., Padyana, U., & Patil, G. (2023). Real-time decision making in wealth management: The role of AI and predictive analytics. *ESP JETA*, *3*(2), 110–119.

Raj, M., & Seamans, R. (2019). AI, labor, productivity, and the need for firm-level data. In Agrawal, A., Gans, J., & Goldfarb, A. (Eds.), *The economics of artificial intelligence: An agenda* (pp. 553–565). University of Chicago Press. DOI: 10.7208/chicago/9780226613475.003.0022

Rane, N., Choudhary, S., & Rane, J. (2023). Education 4.0 and 5.0: Integrating Artificial Intelligence (AI) for Personalized and Adaptive Learning. SSRN Electronic Journal, 1(1), 29–43. https://doi.org/DOI: 10.2139/ssrn.4638365

Rane, N. L., Choudhary, S. P., & Rane, J. (2024). Artificial Intelligence-driven corporate finance: Enhancing efficiency and decision-making through machine learning, natural language processing, and robotic process automation in corporate governance and sustainability. *Studies in Economics and Business Relations*, *5*(2), 1–22. DOI: 10.48185/sebr.v5i2.1050

Ranković, M., Gurgu, E., Martins, O., & Vukasović, M. (2023). Artificial intelligence and the evolution of finance: Opportunities, challenges and ethical considerations. *EdTech Journal*, *3*(1), 20–23. DOI: 10.18485/edtech.2023.3.1.2

Rather, A., Sastry, V., & Agarwal, A. (2017). Stock market prediction and Portfolio selection models: A survey. *OPSEARCH*, *54*(3), 558–579. DOI: 10.1007/s12597-016-0289-y

Ratzan, J., & Rahman, N. (2023). Measuring responsible artificial intelligence (RAI) in banking : A valid and reliable instrument. *AI and Ethics*, *0123456789*. Advance online publication. DOI: 10.1007/s43681-023-00321-5

Rawashdeh, A. (2024). A deep learning-based SEM-ANN analysis of the impact of AI-based audit services on client trust. *Journal of Applied Accounting Research*, *25*(3), 594–622. DOI: 10.1108/JAAR-10-2022-0273

Reher, M., & Sokolinski, S. (2024). Robo advisors and access to wealth management. *Journal of Financial Economics*, *155*, 103829. DOI: 10.1016/j.jfineco.2024.103829

Remolina, N. &.-M. (2023). *Artificial Intelligence in Finance: Challenges, Opportunities, and Regulatory Developments.* San Francisco, CA: AI Startups Publications.

ResearchGate. (2024). *The Impact of Predictive Analytics on Financial Risk Management in Businesses*. ResearchGate.

Reuters, T. (2023). *Sources of Legal Research: Primary, Secondary and the Role of AI*. Thomson Reuters Legal.

Ridho Kismawadi, E., Irfan, M., & Shah, S. M. A. R. (2023). Revolutionizing islamic finance: Artificial intelligence's role in the future of industry. In *The Impact of AI Innovation on Financial Sectors in the Era of Industry 5.0* (pp. 184–207). DOI: 10.4018/979-8-3693-0082-4.ch011

Ridzuan, N. N., Masri, M., Anshari, M., Fitriyani, N. L., & Syafrudin, M. (2024). AI in the financial sector: The line between innovation, regulation and ethical responsibility. *Information (Basel)*, *15*(8), 432. DOI: 10.3390/info15080432

Rieschel, E. (2024). Detecting Spoofing in Financial Markets: An Unsupervised Anomaly Detection Approach. *(Master's Thesis)*, 60.

Rikhardsson, P., Kristinn, T., Bergthorsson, G., & Batt, C. (2022). Artificial intelligence and auditing in small-and medium-sized firms: Expectations and applications. *AI Magazine*, *43*(3), 323–336. DOI: 10.1002/aaai.12066

Romānova, I., & Kudinska, M. (2016). Banking and Fintech: A Challenge or Opportunity? In *Contemporary studies in economic and financial analysis* (pp. 21–35). DOI: 10.1108/S1569-375920160000098002

Rosati, P., Gogolin, F., & Lynn, T. (2022). Cyber-security incidents and audit quality. *European Accounting Review*, *31*(3), 701–728. DOI: 10.1080/09638180.2020.1856162

Rosman, C. (2018). Mad about erica: Why a million people use Bank of America's chatbot. *American Banker*, *183*, 114.

Roy, J. K., & Vasa, L. (2024). Machine Learning and Artificial Intelligence Method for FinTech Credit Scoring and Risk Management: A Systematic Literature Review. [IJBAN]. *International Journal of Business Analytics*, *11*(1), 1–23. DOI: 10.4018/IJBAN.347504

Rühr, A., & Böhme, R. (2020). Robo-advisor configuration: An investigation of user preferences and the performance-control dilemma. ResearchGate. https://www.researchgate.net/publication/341386490_Robo-Advisor_Configuration_An_Investigation_of_User_Preferences_and_the_Performance-Control_Dilemma

Rusydiana, A. S., & Kanz, R. A. D. (2023). Scientometric Analysis on Digital Banking Innovation Model. *Applied Marketing and Sustainability*, *1*(1).

Ryu, H. S. (2018). What makes users willing or hesitant to use Fintech?: The moderating effect of user type. *Industrial Management & Data Systems*, *118*(3), 541–569. DOI: 10.1108/IMDS-07-2017-0325

Sabău Popa, C., Ioan, D., & Moga, M. (2021). AI classifiers for financial performance prediction. *Economic Computation and Economic Cybernetics Studies and Research*, *55*(3), 195–212.

Sabharwal, R., Miah, S. J., Wamba, S. F., & Cook, P. (2024). Extending application of explainable artificial intelligence for managers in financial organizations. *Annals of Operations Research*. Advance online publication. DOI: 10.1007/s10479-024-05825-9

Sabillon, R. (2018). A practical model to perform comprehensive cybersecurity audits. *Enfoque UTE : Revista Científica*, *9*(1), 127–137. DOI: 10.29019/enfoqueute.v9n1.214

Sachs, G. (2024). *Gen AI: Too Much Spend, Too Little Benefit?* Goldman Sachs Research.

SafetyCulture. (2025). *AI in Regulatory Reporting: Is It Worth It?* SafetyCulture.

Saini, A. (2024). The Impact of Business Analytics in the Finance Industry. SSRN Electronic Journal. https://doi.org/DOI: 10.2139/ssrn.4843086

Samo, Y.-L., & Vervuurt, A. (2016). Stochastic Portfolio Theory: A Machine Learning Perspective. arXiv:1605.02654 [q-fin.PM].

Sander, L. (2021). Human decision-making in the era of robo-advisors: Balancing prediction and discretion. *Journal of Behavioral Finance*, *8*(4), 456–470.

Sangeetha, M., Gupta, R., Reddy, K. S., Nanda, C. S. K., Mannar, B. R., Manoharan, G., & Liudmyla, I. (2024). Detailed Investigation of Digital Transformational Strategies to Enhance Business Productivity. In Recent Advances in Management and Engineering (pp. 45-51). CRC Press. DOI: 10.1201/9781003532026-8

Saraiva, L. (2024). Moral Agency and Responsibility in AI Systems. *International Journal of Philosophy*, *3*(1), 25–36. DOI: 10.47941/ijp.1867

Sarin, S., Singh, S. K., Kumar, S., Goyal, S., Gupta, B. B., Alhalabi, W., & Arya, V. (2024). Unleashing the Power of Multi-Agent Reinforcement Learning for Algorithmic Trading in the Digital Financial Frontier and Enterprise Information Systems. *Computers, Materials & Continua*, *80*(2), 3123–3138. DOI: 10.32604/cmc.2024.051599

Sari, W. K. (2024). A Qualitative Study on the Use of Data Analytics in Auditing. *Golden Ratio of Auditing Research*, *4*(1), 33–42. DOI: 10.52970/grar.v4i1.387

Sarker, I. H., Janicke, H., Amine, M., & Abuadbba, A. (2024). Internet of Things Multi-aspect rule-based AI : Methods, taxonomy, challenges and directions towards automation, intelligence and transparent cybersecurity modeling for critical infrastructures. Internet of Things, 25(September 2023), 101110. https://doi.org/DOI: 10.1016/j.iot.2024.101110

Sarker, I. H. (2021). Machine Learning : Algorithms, Real - World Applications and Research Directions. *SN Computer Science*, *2*(3), 1–21. DOI: 10.1007/s42979-021-00592-x PMID: 33778771

Sassen, S. (2000). Is High-Finance an Extractive Sector? *Indiana Journal of Global Legal Studies*, *25*(2), 583–593. DOI: 10.2979/indjglolegstu.25.2.0583

Savi, R., Shen, J., Tsaig, Y., & Dufour, T. (2024). AI-driven advancements in investment strategy: Market themes, text analysis, and decision-making tools. *Journal of Financial Technology and Analytics*, *8*(2), 45–67.

Scanner, S. (2024). *Artificial Intelligence and Anti-Money Laundering*. Sanction Scanner Blog.

Science, S. D. (2023). *J.P. Morgan - COiN - a Case Study of AI in Finance*. Superior Data Science.

Selvaraj, F. J., Sheeja, R., Manoharan, G., Razak, A., Kukreja, J., & Ashtikar, S. P. (2024, June). Evaluation of Customer Loyalty and Customer Relationship Management in Mobile Communication Lesson from New Normal. In 2024 3rd International Conference on Computational Modelling, Simulation and Optimization (ICCMSO) (pp. 216-221). IEEE. DOI: 10.1109/ICCMSO61761.2024.00052

Sen, R., & Das, S. (2023). Supervised Learning. In Computational Finance with R (pp. 1–351). Springer Nature Singapore. https://doi.org/DOI: 10.1007/978-981-19-2008-0_20

Senjith, A., Manoharan, G., Razak, A., Rao, C. B., Kukreja, J., & Ashtikar, S. P. (2024, June). Social Media Marketing: Does it Create Impact on Women Entrepreneurs. In 2024 3rd International Conference on Computational Modelling, Simulation and Optimization (ICCMSO) (pp. 222-227). IEEE.

Service, C. R. (2024). *Artificial Intelligence and Machine Learning in Financial Services*. Congressional Research Service.

Service, E. P. (2020). *The Ethics of Artificial Intelligence: Issues and Initiatives*. European Union.

Settlements, B. f. (2024). *Intelligent Financial System: How AI is Transforming Finance*. Bank for International Settlements.

Setyahadi, R. R., & Narsa, I. M.SETYAHADI. (2020). Corporate Governance and Sustainability in Indonesia. *The Journal of Asian Finance, Economics and Business*, *7*(12), 885–894. DOI: 10.13106/jafeb.2020.vol7.no12.885

Setyaningrum, D., Mita, A. F., & Rosdini, D. (2022). Internal auditor competency gap: Perception of students, academics and practitioners. Jurnal Reviu Akuntansi dan Keuangan, 12(3), 696-710.

Sha, X. (2024). Research on Financial Fraud Algorithm Based on Federated Learning and Big Data Technology. *arXiv*, 5.

Shakdwipee, P., Agarwal, K., Kunwar, H., & Singh, S. (2023). Artificial Intelligence in Finance and Accounting: Opportunities and Challenges. In Tuba, M., Akashe, S., & Joshi, A. (Eds.), *ICT Systems and Sustainability* (Vol. 765, pp. 165–177). Springer Nature Singapore Pte Ltd., DOI: 10.1007/978-981-99-5652-4_17

Shanmuganathan, M. (2020). Behavioural finance in an era of artificial intelligence: Longitudinal case study of robo-advisors in investment decisions. *Journal of Behavioral and Experimental Finance*, *27*, 27. DOI: 10.1016/j.jbef.2020.100297

Sharbek, N. (2022). How Traditional Financial Institutions have adapted to Artificial Intelligence, Machine Learning and FinTech? *Proceedings of the International Conference on Business Excellence*, 16(1), 837–848. DOI: 10.2478/picbe-2022-0078

Sharma, P., & Manhas, S. (2023). The future of finance: Revolutionizing the industry with artificial intelligence. Leveraging AI and Emotional Intelligence in Contemporary Business Organizations, 187–210. https://doi.org/DOI: 10.4018/979-8-3693-1902-4.ch011

Sheth, J. N., Jain, V., Roy, G., & Chakraborty, A. (2022). AI-driven banking services: The next frontier for a personalised experience in the emerging market. *International Journal of Bank Marketing*, *40*(6), 1248–1271. DOI: 10.1108/IJBM-09-2021-0449

Shivram, V. (2024). Auditing with AI: A theoretical framework for applying machine learning across the internal audit lifecycle. *EDPACS*, *69*(1), 22–40. DOI: 10.1080/07366981.2024.2312025

Shiyyab, F. S., Alzoubi, A. B., Obidat, Q. M., & Alshurafat, H. (2023). The impact of artificial intelligence disclosure on financial performance. *International Journal of Financial Studies*, *11*(3), 115. DOI: 10.3390/ijfs11030115

Shneiderman, B. (2020). Bridging the gap between ethics and practice: Guidelines for creating reliable, safe, and trustworthy AI systems. *Communications of the ACM*, *63*(3), 54–63. DOI: 10.1145/3359629

Shukla, A. F. (2024). Artificial Intelligence in Financial Auditing: Innovating Traditional Practices for Enhanced Accuracy. *Journal of Informatics Education and Research*, 55-78.

Siek, M., & Sutanto, A. (2019). *Impact Analysis of Fintech on Banking Industry*. DOI: 10.1109/ICIMTech.2019.8843778

Simhadri, N., & Polireddi, A. (2024). Measurement : Sensors An effective role of artificial intelligence and machine learning in banking sector. Measurement: Sensors, 33(November 2023), 101135. https://doi.org/DOI: 10.1016/j.measen.2024.101135

Singh, B. P., & Joshi, A. (2024). Ethical Considerations in AI Development. In The Ethical Frontier of AI and Data Analysis (pp. 156-179). IGI Global. DOI: 10.4018/979-8-3693-2964-1.ch010

Singh, C. (2024). Artificial intelligence and deep learning: Considerations for financial institutions for compliance with the regulatory burden in the United Kingdom. *Journal of Financial Crime*, *31*(2), 259–266. DOI: 10.1108/JFC-01-2023-0011

Singh, G., Garg, V., & Tiwari, P. (2020). *Application of Artificial Intelligence on Behavioral Finance*. Springer. DOI: 10.1007/978-3-030-34152-7_26

Singh, I., & Kaur, N. (2017). Wealth management through robo advisory. *International Journal of Research-Granthaalayah*, *5*(6), 33–43. DOI: 10.29121/granthaalayah.v5.i6.2017.1991

Singh, J., Brady, M., Arnold, T., & Brown, T. (2017). The emergent field of organizational frontlines. *Journal of Service Research*, *20*(1), 3–11. DOI: 10.1177/1094670516681513

Sinha, S., & Lee, Y. M. (2024). Challenges with developing and deploying AI models and applications in industrial systems. *Discover Artificial Intelligence*, *4*(55), 55. Advance online publication. DOI: 10.1007/s44163-024-00151-2

Sironi, P. (2016). *FinTech innovation: from robo-advisors to goal based investing and gamification*. John Wiley & Sons. DOI: 10.1002/9781119227205

Sivakumar, P., Pillai, A. D., Manoharan, G., Rajesh, G. A., Razak, A., & Ashtikar, S. P. (2024, June). Blockchain technology moving beyond cryptocurrencies in finance sector. In AIP Conference Proceedings (Vol. 2971, No. 1). AIP Publishing. DOI: 10.1063/5.0195724

Skandali, D., Magoutas, A., & Tsourvakas, G. (2023). Artificial Intelligent Applications in Enabled Banking Services: The Next Frontier of Customer Engagement in the Era of ChatGPT. *Theoretical Economics Letters*, *13*(5), 1203–1223. DOI: 10.4236/tel.2023.135066

Smarsh. (2023). Managing AI to Ensure Compliance with Data Privacy Laws. *Smarsh.*

Smith, G. (2023). *The AI Delusion*. Oxford University Press.

Smith, J. (2024). AI in the Financial Sector: The Line between Innovation, Regulation, and Compliance. *Information (Basel)*, •••, 432.

Solana-González, P., Vanti, A. A., García Lorenzo, M. M., & Bello Pérez, R. E. (2021). Data mining to assess organizational transparency across technology processes: An approach from it governance and knowledge management. *Sustainability (Basel)*, *13*(18), 10130. Advance online publication. DOI: 10.3390/su131810130

Soleymani, S. A. (2020). Financial Portfolio Optimization with Deep Learning and Blockchain. *Procedia Computer Science*, •••, 1361–1366.

Solutions, M. (2024). *AI Governance for Financial Services*. ModelOp Solutions, Inc.

Song, D. (2022). Application of Machine Learning in Finance. In B. J. Jansen, H. Liang, & J. Ye (Eds.), International Conference on Cognitive based Information Processing and Applications (CIPA 2021) (Vol. 85, pp. 543–549). Springer Nature. https://doi.org/DOI: 10.1007/978-981-16-5854-9_69

Song, F., & Thakor, A. V. (2010). Financial system architecture and the co-evolution of banks and capital markets. *Economic Journal (London)*, *120*(547), 1021–1055. DOI: 10.1111/j.1468-0297.2009.02345.x

Son, H. (2017). *JPMorgan Software Does in Seconds What Took Lawyers 360,000 Hours*. Bloomberg.

SpringerLink. (2024). The Role of Artificial Intelligence in the Supply Chain Finance Innovation Process. *Operations Research.*

Staff, F. (2017). *An AI Completed 360,000 Hours of Finance Work in Just Seconds.* Futurism.

State Bank of India. (n.d.). *Fintech innovation & incubation program.* Retrieved October 27, 2024, from https://www.sbi.co.in/web/business/information/fintech-innovation-incubation-program

Statista Robo-Advisors. (n.d.). Retrieved May 7, 2023, from https://www.statista.com/outlook/dmo/fintech/digital-investment/robo-advisors/worldwide

Stiglitz, J. E. (2014). Tapping the brakes: Are less active markets safer and better for the economy?.

Strielkowski, W., Zenchenko, S., Tarasova, A., & Radyukova, Y. (2022). Management of Smart and Sustainable Cities in the Post-COVID-19 Era: Lessons and Implications. *Sustainability (Basel)*, *14*(12), 7267. Advance online publication. DOI: 10.3390/su14127267

Sudarshan, K. C. (2023). Emotional Intelligence and Work-Life Balance of Female Staff in Commercial Banks in Kathmandu District. *Quest Journal of Management and Social Sciences*, *5*(2), 206–218.

Sullivan, C. C. (2019). *Machine Learning Saves JPMorgan Chase 360,000 Hours of Legal Work*. FindLaw.

SumatoSoft. (2023). *Predictive Analytics in Finance: Challenges, Benefits, Use Cases*. SumatoSoft Blog.

Suryono, R. R., Budi, I., & Purwandari, B. (2020). Challenges and trends of financial technology (Fintech): A systematic literature review. *Information (Basel)*, *11*(12), 590. DOI: 10.3390/info11120590

Tabbassum, A., Chintale, P., Praveen, G., & Najana, M. (2024). The Impact of AI on Future Employment Patterns. International Journal of Global Innovations and Solutions (IJGIS).

Taleeb & Khadum. (2024). The role of environmental social and governance (ESG) practices in enhancing financial performance in companies with a focus on the banking sector: A literature review. *International Development Planning Review*, *23*(01), 1129–1252.

Tanaka, H. Y. (2024). A New Era of Financial Services: How AI Enhances Investment Efficiency. *International Journal of Intelligent Systems in Accounting Finance & Management*, •••, 45–67.

Tang, W., & Wang, Y. (2004). Intelligent method for dynamic portfolio selection with probability criterion. IEEE International Conference on Systems, Man and Cybernetics (IEEE Cat. No.04CH37583).The Hague, Netherlands, 4, 3323-3327.

Tao, M., Wei, Z., & Wang, H. (2021). Cost-effective portfolio management across risk models: Robo-advisor efficiencies. *International Journal of Portfolio Management*, *22*(3), 312–328.

Taylor, S., & Todd, P. A. (1995). Understanding information technology usage: A test of competing models. *Information Systems Research*, *6*(2), 144–176. DOI: 10.1287/isre.6.2.144

Teoh, C. S., & Mahmood, A. K. (2018). Cybersecurity workforce development for digital economy. *The Educational Review, USA*, *2*(1), 136–146. DOI: 10.26855/er.2018.01.003

Thakor, A. V. (2012). Incentives to innovate and financial crises. *Journal of Financial Economics*, *103*(1), 130–148. DOI: 10.1016/j.jfineco.2011.03.026

Thangavel, K., & Varalakshmi, P. (2020). Secure cloud data storage with ternary hash tree framework: Enhancing user trust through audit verification. *Journal of Information Security and Applications*, *53*, 102498. DOI: 10.1016/j.jisa.2020.102498

The Institute of Internal Auditors. (2022). *International Standards for the Professional Practice of Internal Auditing (Standards)*. The Institute of Internal Auditors.

Thiruma Valavan, A. (2023). AI Ethics and Bias: Exploratory study on the ethical considerations and potential biases in ai and data-driven decision-making in banking, with a focus on fairness, transparency, and accountability. *World Journal of Advanced Research and Reviews*, *20*(2), 197–206. DOI: 10.30574/wjarr.2023.20.2.2245

Thottoli, M. M. (2024). Leveraging information communication technology (ICT) and artificial intelligence (AI) to enhance auditing practices. *Accounting Research Journal*, *37*(2), 134–150. DOI: 10.1108/ARJ-09-2023-0269

Tillu, R., Muthusubramanian, M., & Periyasamy, V. (2023). From Data to Compliance : The Role of AI / ML in Optimizing Regulatory Reporting Processes RBC Capital Markets, USA Discover Financial Services, USA Hexaware Technologies, USA. *Journal of Knowledge Learning and Science Technology*, *2*(3). Advance online publication. DOI: 10.60087/jklst.vol2.n3.p391

Times, F. (2024, September 15). Algorithmic Analyst Aversion. *Financial Times*.

îrcovnicu, G. I., & Ha egan, C. D. (2023). Integration of artificial intelligence in the risk management process: An analysis of opportunities and challenges. *Journal of Financial Studies*, *8*(15), 198–214. DOI: 10.55654/JFS.2023.8.15.13

Torvekar, N., & Game, P. S. (2019). Predictive analysis of credit score for credit card defaulters. *International Journal of Recent Technology and Engineering*, *7*(5), 283–286. https://www.scopus.com/inward/record.uri?eid=2-s2.0-85063812699&partnerID=40&md5=df9cca7c0ea49806b491ae7721bec355

Treasury, U. D. (2024). *Artificial Intelligence in Financial Services*. U.S. Department of the Treasury.

Tripathi, V. (2019). On present use of machine learning based automation in finance. 11th International Joint Conference on Knowledge Discovery, Knowledge Engineering and Knowledge Management, 3(k), 412–418. https://doi.org/DOI: 10.5220/0008480504120418

Tsaih, R.-H., Lin, H.-W. W., & Ke, W. (2014). An Abductive-Reasoning Guide for Finance Practitioners. *Computational Economics*, *43*(4), 411–431. DOI: 10.1007/s10614-013-9390-y

Tsang, E. P. (2023). *AI for Finance*. CRC Press. DOI: 10.1201/9781003348474

Tulcanaza-Prieto, A. B., Cortez-Ordoñez, A., & Lee, C. W. (2023). Influence of customer perception factors on AI-enabled customer experience in the Ecuadorian banking environment. *Sustainability (Basel)*, *15*(16), 12441. DOI: 10.3390/su151612441

Ülgen, F. (2014). Schumpeterian economic development and financial innovations: A conflicting evolution. *Journal of Institutional Economics*, *10*(2), 257–277. DOI: 10.1017/S1744137414000022

Van Doorn, J., Mende, M., Noble, S. M., Hulland, J., Ostrom, A. L., Grewal, D., & Petersen, J. A. (2017). Domo arigato Mr. Roboto: Emergence of automated social presence in organizational frontlines and customers' service experiences. *Journal of Service Research*, *20*(1), 43–58. DOI: 10.1177/1094670516679272

Vasarhelyi, M. A. (2025). *Artificial Intelligence in Accounting and Auditing*. Markus Wiener Publishers.

Venkatesh, V., & Davis, F. D. (2000). A theoretical extension of the technology acceptance model: Four longitudinal field studies. *Management Science*, *46*(2), 186–204. DOI: 10.1287/mnsc.46.2.186.11926

Villegas-Ch, W., Govea, J., & Revelo-Tapia, S. (2023). Improving Student Retention in Institutions of Higher Education through Machine Learning: A Sustainable Approach. *Sustainability (Basel)*, *15*(19), 14512. Advance online publication. DOI: 10.3390/su151914512

Vorecol. (2024). The Rise of AI-Powered Investment Tools: Transforming Portfolio Management. *Vorecol Blog*.

Vy, N. N. T.VY. (2023). Ai implementation in odr: A game-changer or a trouble-maker of data protection. *Vietnamese Journal of Legal Sciences*, *08*(01), 1–24. DOI: 10.2478/vjls-2023-0001

Wang, R., Yu, C., & Wang, J. (2019). Construction of Supply Chain Financial Risk Management Mode Based on Internet of Things. *IEEE Access : Practical Innovations, Open Solutions*, *7*, 110323–110332. DOI: 10.1109/ACCESS.2019.2932475

Wang, Y., Li, X., & Wei, Q. (2020). Enhancing procurement audit compliance with AI-based frameworks: Automation and efficiency in auditing practices. *Journal of Financial Regulation and Compliance*, *28*(1), 67–78. DOI: 10.1108/JFRC-01-2019-0010

Wanke, P., Azad, M. A. K., & Barros, C. P. (2016). Efficiency in Malaysian Islamic banks: A comparative analysis. *International Journal of Islamic and Middle Eastern Finance and Management*, *9*(4), 545–564. DOI: 10.1108/IMEFM-01-2015-0006

Wassie, F. A., & Lakatos, L. P. (2024). Artificial intelligence and the future of the internal audit function. *Humanities & Social Sciences Communications*, *11*(1), 1–13. DOI: 10.1057/s41599-024-02905-w

WatersTechnology. (2024). *BlackRock Developing AI Copilots for Aladdin*. WatersTechnology.

Weller, B. M. (2018). Does algorithmic trading reduce information acquisition? *Review of Financial Studies*, *31*(6), 2184–2226. DOI: 10.1093/rfs/hhx137

Wijayati, D. T., Rahman, Z., Rahman, M. F. W., Arifah, I. D. C., & Kautsar, A. (2022). A study of artificial intelligence on employee performance and work engagement: The moderating role of change leadership. *International Journal of Manpower*, *43*(2), 486–512. DOI: 10.1108/IJM-07-2021-0423

William & Mary. (2024). *The transformative impact of AI and machine learning on finance: Algorithmic trading, risk management, and personalized services*. William & Mary Financial Studies.

Wilson, H. J., Daugherty, P., & Bianzino, N. (2017). The jobs that artificial intelligence will create. *MIT Sloan Management Review*, *58*(4), 14–16.

Xin, D., Wu, E. Y., Lee, D. J.-L., Salehi, N., & Parameswaran, A. (2021). Whither AutoML? Understanding the Role of Automation in Machine Learning Workflows. *CHI Conference on Human Factors in Computing Systems (CHI '21)*. https://doi.org/DOI: 10.1145/3411764.3445306

Yablonsky, S. A. (2020). AI-Driven Digital PlatformInnovation. *Technology Innovation Management Review*, *10*(10), 4–15. DOI: 10.22215/timreview/1392

Yadav, Y. (2015). How algorithmic trading undermines efficiency in capital markets. *Vanderbilt Law Review*, *68*, 1607.

Yang, L., & Zhu, H. (2020). Back-running: Seeking and hiding fundamental information in order flows. *Review of Financial Studies*, *33*(4), 1484–1533. DOI: 10.1093/rfs/hhz070

Yang, Q., Wang, Y., & Ren, Y. (2019). Research on financial risk management model of internet supply chain based on data science. *Cognitive Systems Research*, *56*, 50–55. DOI: 10.1016/j.cogsys.2019.02.001

Yang, S. A., & Birge, J. R. (2018). Trade credit, risk sharing, and inventory financing portfolios. *Management Science*, *64*(8), 3667–3689. DOI: 10.1287/mnsc.2017.2799

Yin, L., Wang, H., & Li, S. (2020). Social media sentiment analysis for stock market prediction: A case study with Twitter data. *Journal of Financial Markets*, *50*, 100536. DOI: 10.1016/j.finmar.2020.100536

Yi, S., Goh, Y. N., Tan, G. W. H., & Loh, X. M. (2023). Impact of robo-advisors on millennials' financial behaviour: An extended TPB approach. *Asian Academy of Management Journal*, *28*(1), 41–66. DOI: 10.21315/aamj2023.28.1.2

Yi, Z., Cao, X., Chen, Z., & Li, S. (2023). Artificial Intelligence in Accounting and Finance: Challenges and Opportunities. *IEEE Access : Practical Innovations, Open Solutions*, *11*(November), 129100–129123. DOI: 10.1109/ACCESS.2023.3333389

Yoon, H., Koo, B., & Shin, Y. (2021). Early auditing systems in AI: Risk management and continuous monitoring. *The Journal of Auditory Research*, *36*(3), 234–249. DOI: 10.1002/jar.2159

Yoon, K., Hoogduin, L., & Zhang, L. (2021). Real-time auditing of data-driven processes: A layered structure for continuous auditing. *Journal of Accounting and Public Policy*, *40*(2), 106812. DOI: 10.1016/j.jaccpubpol.2021.106812

Young, J. E., Hawkins, R., Sharlin, E., & Igarashi, T. (2009). Toward acceptable domestic robots: Applying insights from social psychology. *International Journal of Social Robotics*, *1*(1), 95–108. DOI: 10.1007/s12369-008-0006-y

Yusuf, R. A. J. I., Esther, I. O., Isaiah, O. O., & Scotty, N. O. Forensic Audit Technology and Audit Report Quality of Selected Audit Firms in Nigeria.

Zakaria, N., Sulaiman, A., Min, F. S., Feizollah, A., Zakaria, N., Sulaiman, A., Min, F. S., & Feizollah, A. (2023). Machine learning In the financial industry : A bibliometric approach to evidencing applications MEDIA & COMMUNICATION STUDIES | REVIEW ARTICLE Machine learning In the financial industry : A bibliometric approach to evidencing applications. *Cogent Social Sciences*, *9*(2), 2276609. Advance online publication. DOI: 10.1080/23311886.2023.2276609

Zhang, X., & Liu, J. (2022). Incentive Mechanism and Value-Added in PPP Projects Considering Financial Institutions' Early Intervention. *Journal of Construction Engineering and Management*, *148*(4), 04022001. Advance online publication. DOI: 10.1061/(ASCE)CO.1943-7862.0002248

Zhao, F., & Zhao, Z. (2023). Research on Voluntary Internal Audit of Irish Business. *Theoretical Economics Letters*, *13*(5), 1266–1280. DOI: 10.4236/tel.2023.135070

Zhao, J., Li, X., Yu, C., Chen, S., & Lee, C. (2022). Riding the FinTech innovation wave: FinTech, patents and bank performance. *Journal of International Money and Finance*, *122*, 102552. DOI: 10.1016/j.jimonfin.2021.102552

Zhao, X., Zhang, H., & Wu, L. (2018). AI-based prediction models for portfolio selection and risk assessment. *Journal of Asset Management*, *19*(5), 356–372. DOI: 10.1057/s41260-018-0085-2

Zheng, L., Wang, C., Chen, X., Song, Y., Meng, Z., & Zhang, R. (2023). Evolutionary machine learning builds smart education big data platform: Data-driven higher education. *Applied Soft Computing*, *136*, 110114. DOI: 10.1016/j.asoc.2023.110114

Zheng, X., Gildea, E., Chai, S., Zhang, T., & Wang, S. (2024). Data Science in Finance: Challenges and Opportunities. *AI*, *5*(1), 55–71. DOI: 10.3390/ai5010004

Zheng, X., Zhu, M., Li, Q., Chen, C., & Tan, Y. (2019). FinBrain: When finance meets AI 2.0. *Frontiers of Information Technology & Electronic Engineering*, *20*(7), 914–924. DOI: 10.1631/FITEE.1700822

Zheng, Z. X. (2017). An Overview of Blockchain Technology: Architecture, Consensus, and Future Trends. *IEEE International Congress on Big Data*, 557-564. DOI: 10.1109/BigDataCongress.2017.85

Zhong, X., & Enke, D. (2017). Forecasting daily stock market return using dimensionality reduction. *Expert Systems with Applications*, *67*, 126–139. DOI: 10.1016/j.eswa.2016.09.027

Zhou, X., Tang, X., & Zhang, R. (2020). Impact of green finance on economic development and environmental quality: A study based on provincial panel data from China. *Environmental Science and Pollution Research International*, *27*(16), 19915–19932. DOI: 10.1007/s11356-020-08383-2 PMID: 32232752

Zhuk, A. (2025). Beyond the blockchain hype: Addressing legal and regulatory challenges. *SN Social Sciences*, *5*(2), 1–37.

About The Contributors

Fadi Ghosn is an accomplished scholar and educator in finance and economics, currently serving as a full-time Assistant Professor of Finance at the Lebanese International University. Dr. Ghosn holds a PhD in Business Administration, providing a comprehensive understanding of financial theory and research methodologies, which they bring into the classroom., using a student-centered approach that applies financial theory to real-world scenarios. In addition to teaching, Dr. Ghosn is actively involved in research, coordination, and administrative duties. His research focuses on banking, sustainable finance, and global economic challenges. As CEO and co-founder of Success Gate International, a consultancy firm, he brings valuable industry experience into the classroom, effectively bridging academia and practice. Their expertise is regularly sought by prestigious media outlets to discuss domestic and international trends in financial markets.

Ghina Awad is a researcher specialising in artificial intelligence across various business fields, including human resources and auditing. She has multiple publications in high-ranked journals. Additionally, she is an adjunct professor teaching in France, Germany, and Lebanon, and a reviewer for two ABS journals.

Karim Darwich is a researcher at ICN Business School in Nancy, France, specializing in the intersection of artificial intelligence and financial services. His research explores the transformative potential of AI technologies within the banking and finance sectors, with a particular focus on how machine learning, predictive analytics, and intelligent automation can be leveraged to improve financial decision-making, optimize risk management practices, and increase operational efficiency. Karim's work contributes to both academic scholarship and practical insights for industry stakeholders navigating the rapidly evolving landscape of financial technology. He is particularly interested in ethical AI implementation, algorithmic transparency, and the impact of AI on regulatory compliance and customer experience in financial institutions. Karim's academic contributions reflect his expertise in AI applications in finance, internal audit, and economic sustainability, which positions him as a promising figure in the field.

***

Saifullahi Adam Bayero is pursuing his final year MBA program at SR University and he is a research enthusiast.

Dhanya K A is presently serving as Assistant Professor at School of Business Management, Christ University, Bangalore. She holds PhD in Commerce from University of Calicut, M Phil from Bharathiar University, M. Com from Calicut University and MBA from Madras University. She has also qualified UGC-NET and JRF in commerce in 2004. To her credit she has 15 publications in different national and international journals and 12 paper presentations in national and international conferences. She has been awarded with Minor Research Project sponsored by the UGC New Delhi in 2014. She has co -authored 2 books and edited 3 books. She has been Resource person in more than 10 seminars and conferences. She has a teaching experience of more than 16 years and has held various academic and administrative positions. She served as Head of the Department of Commerce and Management Studies, Amal College of Advanced studies, Nilambur Kerala during 2010- 2024. She has undertaken a social project in 2019 for revamping tribals in Nilambur Taluk. Due to her contributions in academia and society she has been awarded 'Vanitha Rathna Puraskar' by Jan Shikshan Sansthan Malappuram.

Rui Manuel Teixeira Santos Dias. Postdoctoral degree in Finance at the State University of Feira de Santana (BR), Department of Exact Sciences. Doctor of Finance at the University of Évora—Institute of Research and Advanced Training (PT). Diploma of Advanced Studies in Doctoral Studies (DEA), at the University of Extremadura (ES), in the scientific area of Financial Economics. He served as Chief Financial Officer in various companies for 26 years.

Mohammad Irfan is presently working as an Associate Professor at School of Business and Management, Christ University, Bengaluru, India. Dr. Irfan has done his Ph.D. from the Central University of Haryana. He is MBA (Finance), M.Com (Account and Law), and MA (Economics). He has qualified UGC-JRF/SRF/NET in Management and Commerce. Dr. Irfan certified NSEs (NCFM) and BSEs certification. He has experience of more than sixteen years in the area of SAPM, Artificial Intelligence, Machine Learning, Blockchain, Cryptocurrency, Financial Engineering, Fintech, Green Finance, and Alternative Finance. He has to his credit more than 67+ Scopus Indexed articles, includes The Journal of Economic

Cooperation and Development (Q2), International Journal of Business Excellence (IJBEX), International Journal of Economics and Management (IJEM), Montenegrin Journal of Economics (Q2), Cogent Business & Management (Taylor & Francis) (Q2), Indian Journal of Finance (IJF) and Journal of Islamic Monetary Economics and Finance (JIMF). His citations reached 527+ along with 12 H-index. Dr. Irfan has published 9 books in Springer, IGI Global Publication (Scopus indexed).

Rohit Kaushik is an Assistant Professor at Jagannath International Management School and did PhD from Banasthali Vidyapith, Jaipur. Dr. Rohit Kaushik has 10 years of teaching experience with research publications with reputed publishers like Springer, IGI Global. Reseach areas involves Behavioral Finance.

Early Ridho Kismawadi, S.E.I, MA is a lecturer at the Department of Islamic Banking, Faculty of Islamic Economics and Business IAIN Langsa, Aceh, Indonesia, he has been a lecturer since 2013, he has completed a doctoral program in 2018 majoring in Sharia economics at the State Islamic University of North Sumatra. He was appointed head of the Islamic economics Law study program (2023) Islamic banking study program (2020) and Islamic financial management study program (2019) at Langsa State Islamic Institute (IAIN Langsa), Aceh, Indonesia. His research interests include financial economics, applied econometrics, Islamic economics, banking, and finance. He has published articles in national and international journals. In addition, he is also a reviewer of several reputable international journals such as Finance Research Letters, Financial Innovation, Cogent Business &; Management, Journal of Islamic Accounting and Business Research. He has also presented his papers at various local and international seminars. Dr. Early Ridho Kismawadi, S.E.I, MA, can be contacted at kismawadi@iainlangsa.ac.id.

Sanjeev Kumar is an accomplished expert in Food and Beverage. He currently holds the positions of Professor in Lovely Professional University, Punjab, India. With over a decade of experience in the field, food Service Industry, his research focuses on Alcoholic beverages, Event management and Sustainable Management Practices, Metaverse, AI Machine Learning and Artificial Intelligence. He has published more than 60 research papers, articles and chapters in Scopus Indexed, UGC Approved and peer reviewed Journals and books. Dr. Sanjeev Kumar participated and acted as resource person in various National and International conferences, seminars, session chair, research workshops and industry talks and his work has been widely cited.

Shikha Malhotra is PhD in Finance and FRM (GARP) certified. She has a 10 years of working experience with State Bank of India in various domains. She is also CFA Level 2 passed. She has worked in EdTech startup as a mentor for various esteemed exams. She has various publications (ABDC-B and C). Currently, she is working as an Assistant Professor in Christ University, Bangalore

GeethaManoharan is currently working in Telangana as an assistant professor at SR University. She is the university-level PhD program coordinator and has also been given the additional responsibility of In Charge Director of Publications and Patents under the Research Division at SR University.

Priyakrushna Mohanty (PK) is an Assistant Professor at the Department of Business and Management, Christ University, Bengaluru. Holding a Ph.D. in Tourism Studies from Pondicherry University, where he was a UGC Senior Research Fellow, Dr. Mohanty is a recipient of the prestigious Travel Corporation (India) Gold Medal for his Master's in Tourism Studies. His academic qualifications extend to an M.Com. in Finance and PG Diplomas in Rural Development, Research Methodology, and Teaching Skills. With prior industry experience at Indian Railway Catering and Tourism Corporation Ltd., he brings a practical perspective to his role. A prolific researcher, Dr. Mohanty has authored over forty publications and co-edited five books with renowned publishers such as Routledge, Emerald, Springer Nature, and CABI. His research interests encompass Research Methodology, Tourism Sustainability, Livelihood, Events Tourism, e-Tourism, and Gender issues in Tourism Development.

Partap Singh Professor, MMIM, Maharishi Markandeshware University (MMU), Mullana Haryana, India. (ORCHID ID: 0000-0002-4653-7984) Partap Singh is committed to teaching and research in Finance and Investment domain since last 18 years+. His qualification is PhD (Commerce), M. Com (Finance& Accounting), and MBA(Finance). He has rich work experience in the field of Teaching, administration and research as well. He held various responsibilities like Editor, Co-editor, and Editorial Board member, Associate Editor in number of national and international journals. He has regularly been receiving offers for writing books from the top publishing houses of India and received many letters of thanks& compliments for giving valuable suggestions and commendable views concerning improvement of many leading Publications/Books. He has written and published 5 books namely Financial Management, Risk Management, working capital Management, Management Accounting and Analysis of Financial Statements. Further, he has published more than 60 papers and book chapters in good reputed journals and he has also contributed numerous research papers in national and international conferences or seminars. He has good participation in MDPs. FDPs and STCs as well as Life Membership of reputed academic bodies. His future interest area of research is Financial Market, Financial Derivatives, Technological innovations in Finance& Investment, Artificial Intelligence and Its Impact on Finance and Investment." Dr Partap Singh is currently working as Professor, Maharishi Markandeshwar Institute of Management, Maharishi Markandeshwar (Deemed to be University) University, Mullana, Haryana, India."

Index

A

B

C

D

L

P

R

S

W

www.ingramcontent.com/pod-product-compliance
Lightning Source LLC
LaVergne TN
LVHW061549290926
849162LV00004B/949
9798337301297